QUALITY MIDDLE SCHOOL LEADERSHIP

QUALITY MIDDLE SCHOOL LEADERSHIP

Eleven Central Skill Areas

L. David Weller, Jr.
University of Georgia

TECHNOMIC
PUBLISHING CO., INC.

LANCASTER · BASEL

Quality Middle School Leadership

aTECHNOMIC publication

Technomic Publishing Company, Inc.
851 New Holland Avenue, Box 3535
Lancaster, Pennsylvania 17604 U.S.A.

Printed in the United States of America
10 9 8 7 6 5 4 3 2 1

Main entry under title:
  Quality Middle School Leadership: Eleven Central Skill Areas

A Technomic Publishing Company book
Bibliography: p.
Includes index p. 455

Library of Congress Catalog Card No. 98-86722
ISBN No. 1-56676-681-8

To my wife, Sylvia, whose support
and love made it all come together

CONTENTS

This volume, *Quality Middle School Leadership: Eleven Central Skill Areas,* is designed to assist middle school principals in their efforts to reform middle school education through practical application of the effective schools research and the quality management principles of W. Edwards Deming with the goal of meeting the daily challenges of the role of leaders. The context of the volume was conceived out of the twin senses of need and urgency, both from my students and colleagues, who called for a work that was practical in scope, research-based in nature, and yet addressed the contemporary demands for school reform and quality outcomes.

The contents for this volume originated from my work with middle school principals as a consultant in assisting them to reform and restructure their schools through the quality management principles of W. Edwards Deming and my research on high-achieving middle school principals. My interest focused on three questions: (1) What are the essential skills needed for effective middle school leadership? (2) What are the essential components of quality-producing middle schools? (3) What should a book contain to provide maximum assistance to new middle school principals in becoming effective leaders while implementing the most essential components of the middle school concept? The book, therefore, is designed to prepare those aspiring to become effective and quality-oriented middle school principals as well as to assist the practitioners who continuously seek to improve middle school education.

The contents within the text have been arranged to provide the reader with theory and research first and then provide specific examples for how this research can be applied in actual practice. All too often, theory and research findings are merely presented in a "this is what works in this situation; now you go try it and good luck" format. The research in that kind of setting is often sterile, is sometimes complicated, and is sometimes viewed with suspicion by the practitioner. Research presented in such a manner often makes practical applications difficult to visualize and, therefore, become a reality in practice. This sometimes causes one to question the reason for the inclusion of such information.

Consequently, the attempt to fuse theory, research, and practice is to go beyond the customary standard. It is hoped that this work will provide real meaning to the knowledge and skills presented within this text. It is only when theory and research can be internalized and viewed as being beneficial to the practitioner that theory and research reap their intended rewards. Research for the sake of research does little to foster educational improvement. It is hoped, therefore, that this work will make a unique contribution to the literature on middle school leadership and will serve as a reference to enhance the abilities of aspiring and current leaders in middle school education as they seek to become more effective in their challenging role of reformer and innovator.

ACKNOWLEDGEMENTS

This book has been the combined efforts of the author and the highly experienced and talented editors and publishers at Technomic Publishing Company, Inc. Their valuable suggestions and cooperative assistance were essential ingredients in capturing and presenting the full intent of this work.

Special recognition goes to Frances White for her valuable assistance in manuscript preparation and review of the work's style and conformity to standards. Her skills, her dedication, and her sense of professionalism are deeply appreciated. Special appreciation also goes to Donna Bell and Linda Edwards for their valuable assistance in manuscript preparation.

The author is also deeply appreciative of the assistance and professional courtesy extended by the exemplary middle school principals interviewed for the case study segments of this book. Their candor and willingness to share freely with the author their personal philosophies and experiences, their guiding principles, and what does and does not work in "the real world" of middle school leadership are deeply appreciated. Unfortunately, time, resources, and book space required that the author be selective in presenting examples of effective middle school leadership within each chapter. It is hoped, however, that the illustrations selected truly capture the spirit and context of their related experiences. Principals from schools receiving national and/or state awards for Schools of Excellence are Joan Akin, Wesley Clampitt, George Dougherty, Walker Davis, and Wayne Watts.

INTRODUCTION

Over the last three decades, the middle school movement has gathered increasing momentum, with some 15,000 schools to its credit; however, some of these schools are in name only and have adopted the middle school name for various reasons, be they political, social, or economic. Some middle schools have embraced the essential components of the "true" middle school concept as defined by the literature while some have approached the infusion of the middle school concept with caution and are introducing the middle school concept in a fragmented fashion. Others carefully pick and choose the components of the middle school that best appeal to their needs or educational philosophy. And some adopt the middle school name but still adhere to the educational philosophy and instructional practices associated with the old junior high school.

With the growing number of middle schools and the increased desire on the part of middle school principals to adopt the criteria of a true middle school, there comes the problem of identifying the essential skill and knowledge areas needed to become an effective middle school principal. What are the essential leadership characteristics deemed necessary to make a middle school leader effective and provide quality-oriented results? The literature is replete with research-based studies on leadership style and characteristics (over 3,500) and there are over 300 definitions of "leader." For the practitioner, however, this provides little direction or substantive value. Often, this plethora of research leads to confusion among aspiring and seasoned leaders and has two debilitating results: (1) the research is inconclusive, provides little direction, and, therefore, has little or no value to them personally, and (2) any definition of leadership and any style of leadership one chooses to adopt is as good as any. Unfortunately, this posture becomes counterproductive in a decade where educational reform and restructuring are the prevailing concepts and where documented evidence exists that shows that certain leadership characteristics in middle schools provide superior results, while other leader behaviors provide educational outcomes that are deemed less than satisfactory. Therefore, two central questions arise. What are the characteristics and skills of effective middle school leaders? What are the essential middle school components that are necessary to provide preadolescent students the kind of education needed to help them develop intellectually, emotionally, socially, and physically? To this end, the current volume addresses itself.

Without question, no school can be called a middle school where its principal, assistant principals, and all instructional personnel lack a clear knowledge and understanding of the goals and objectives of the middle school concept. Such a knowledge and understanding is important in an era where individualized instruction and an emphasis on meeting individual needs of students are deemed essential to later school success and for becoming productive, responsible citizens in a growing global economy. Chapter 1 discusses this and points out that the middle school serves a distinct and unique purpose in educating preadolescents, ages 10 through 14, who are rapidly developing physically, intellectually, socially, and emotionally in one or more areas at the same time. Growth during the middle school years represents a turning point in the life of each preadolescent, and middle schools become a dispenser of knowledge and skills, a socializing institution, and a source of emotional stability during these turbulent years of development. Lacking a knowledge and understanding of preadolescents' unique needs and failing to provide the necessary programs and atmosphere essential to helping them make a healthy and well-adjusted transition from elementary school (childhood) to high school (adolescence) is to revert to the education provided by the junior high school, to ignore the research on the transescent, and to become a middle school in name only.

Chapter 2 focuses on leadership effectiveness for the middle school. Leaders make a difference in schools, and schools make a difference in their students. Effective leaders possess a common philosophy and practice certain leadership characteristics that set them apart from the mediocre. Core leadership skills and competencies of exemplary middle school principals are presented, as well as how they infuse the elements of effective schools research and the quality management principles of W. Edwards Deming. Case studies illustrating the principal's effectiveness follow this chapter, as they do each of the remaining chapters. It is clear that the type of leadership exhibited by principals in high performing middle schools is the most important variable in promoting school reform and effectiveness and in providing the necessary leadership to implement and sustain the essential components of the true middle school.

The first essential component of an effective and quality-producing middle school is discussed in Chapter 3 under Leadership for the Exploratory Curriculum. Exploratory courses are essential to the true middle school concept since they allow students the opportunity to explore the intellectual, emotional, social, and physical dimensions of their talents and interests. Less structured than the traditional academic core courses, exploratory courses provide essential learning experiences that supplement and complement the core and enrichment offerings of the curriculum.

Chapter 4 focuses on the importance of interdisciplinary teacher teams in promoting the true middle school concept. Their role and responsibilities in curriculum development and their importance in providing continuity within the instructional delivery system are discussed. Salient characteristics of high-performing teams are presented, as well as the essential components necessary for the middle school principal to build and sustain effective interdisciplinary teacher teams.

Interdisciplinary curriculum is discussed in Chapter 5 which presents the core curriculum areas and the development of thematic units within the core as an effective instructional approach for imparting essential knowledge and skills while providing continuity across curricular areas. Curriculum content must be designed with the characteristics of the preadolescent in mind if the middle school is to accomplish its mission. The role of the principal in the development of a responsive curriculum to meet the needs and interests of the transescent is vital for an effective curriculum.

Chapter 6 examines the role and importance of intramural athletics to the middle school concept and to the social, emotional, and intellectual development of the transescent. The principal must ensure that intramurals are well planned and that they focus on the physical concerns and needs of the preadolescent. The importance of a strong physical education program is discussed, as is the prevailing philosophy that students should have access to activities and resources necessary for developing basic skills and a positive attitude toward good personal health habits and lifelong physical activity.

The principal's role in developing advisor/advisee programs as part of a comprehensive school guidance program is presented in Chapter 7. Although this program is not designed to replace professional counseling, it is essential in providing preadolescents with regular, supportive council from a concerned adult concerning each student's academic progress, personal concerns, and adjustment to school. Helping students enjoy success and develop strong and healthy self-concepts is central to the middle school concept and to any advisor/advisee program.

Chapter 8 addresses the need and importance of providing programs designed to specifically meet the needs of at-risk students and those needing remedial assistance. The principal must support the development of responsive programs and understand the varying factors that contribute to students deemed to be at-risk and in need of remedial help. How to provide instructional programs specifically designed to assist these students is presented, as well as ways to identify these special needs students.

Scheduling for instruction can be achieved in a variety of ways and is the single most important variable in promoting quality education and infusing components of a true middle school. Whether the schedule is block, flexible-modular, flexible-block, or a variation of these approaches, the schedule is the vehicle that serves to bridge the gap between the self-contained elementary school classroom, with teachers structuring instructional time slots, and the rigid, departmental approach of the high school, which forces the instructional program into 50- or 55-minute time slots. The importance of providing flexible time blocks for teacher planning and instruction is discussed, as is the need for the principal to involve teachers in the selection of a scheduling process. Since there is no one "right" way to design a schedule, the staff and the school's curriculum will be the main determinants of the scheduling configuration used in each middle school.

Chapter 9, Leadership for Home and Community Involvement, stresses that schools do not exist in and of themselves and that middle school principals need to provide ways to use the community as a learning laboratory and as an extension of the school's learning environment. The importance of promoting social responsibility among students, the intrinsic rewards of community involvement, and the duties of citizenship are only part of the middle school's community involvement programs that meet transescents' needs. Home involvement, through parent partnerships and programs, is central to meeting the goals of middle school education. Parent aide, volunteer, and involvement programs provide an area of school-home support necessary to assist preadolescents through their difficult growth periods. The parent's role in school governance and programs designed to help parents of at-risk students in their home is also presented.

The importance of grouping students heterogeneously for instruction is presented in Chapter 11. A variety of grouping practices and ways to group students heterogeneously for instruction are explored. The existence of and reasons for homogeneous grouping are also discussed in the context of the role of interdisciplinary teacher teams and flexible scheduling configurations as ways to promote heterogeneous grouping in the middle school.

Finally, Chapter 12 presents the more common quality management tools and action research methods effective middle school principals use to promote quality learning and teaching. These instructional improvement tools and methods are central to providing effective learning outcomes through the quality principle of continuous improvement, and they are based on the scientific method of inquiry. Decisions made by quality-oriented principals and teachers are based on fact and experimentation, rather than intuition and experience, which can often yield hit-or-miss outcomes. Teams of teachers in quality schools apply the quality tools to their daily work and have their students use these tools to solve instructional and real-life problems. With the goal of continuous improvement, quality-oriented middle schools have their educational mission already established and work cooperatively to achieve this constancy of purpose.

Throughout the text, references are made to sources that will prove useful to the practitioner and inquiring student. In some chapters, brief examples are provided to illustrate certain concepts but are not fully explored because of time and book space limitations. In these instances, references are provided for further explanation of theory, research, and practical applications.

Case studies come from middle school principals whose schools have been designated as state and/or national Schools of Excellence and have won other awards for excellence as well. These studies provide examples of how practitioners lead their schools into the domains of quality and effectiveness. Their candid opinions, given freely, are presented to help the reader understand that theory and research can play a vital role in shaping and sustaining schools of excellence.

CHAPTER 1

The Middle School:
A Conceptual Framework

The middle school is built around the educational concept that the pre-adolescent learner needs a special learning environment which is developmentally responsive to the unique needs of ten-to-fourteen-year-olds as they develop into adolescence at different cognitive, emotional, social, and physical growth rates. This concept is supported by research on learning and the intellectual development of ten-to-fourteen-year-olds. If principals are to promote quality middle school education, they must have a firm understanding of the rationale for the middle school and a knowledge of the true middle school's philosophy, organizational structure, and instructional practices. In this context, their knowledge of the research on human development regarding the physical, intellectual, social, and emotional development of ten-to-fourteen-year-olds can be effectively applied to achieve the goals and objectives of middle school education.

RATIONALE FOR THE MIDDLE SCHOOL

The rationale for the middle school is research-based. It comes from the research on the human development phases of ten-to-fourteen-year-olds as they "bridge the gap" between elementary school and high school and from research on the learning and intellectual development of these transescents as they progress through the preadolescent or emerging adolescent years. During these developmental years, ten-to-fourteen-year-olds experience a series of dramatic changes in their physical, social, emotional, and intellectual life as a result of maturation. More than at any other time, students at this age are easily influenced, distracted, and confused about life in general. They seek to explore new experiences, finding life a very complex affair

1

and questioning their identities and their roles in the real world. Their most common characteristic is their differences as they develop through these crucial and unfamiliar changes at varying times and rates.

Transitional learners, preadolescents, transescents, early adolescents, in-between-agers, and pubescents are names given to ten-to-fourteen-year-olds who comprise the middle school learner. Because their growth rates occur at different times, chronological age is not correlated to changes which occur in their physical, intellectual, and emotional development. To adequately meet the uncommon needs of these uncommon learners, specially prepared principals and teachers must work together in providing a child-centered curriculum which can be maximized through an organizational structure and educational philosophy designed to meet the needs of the emerging adolescent. It is primarily for this reason that the middle school came into existence.

EMERGENCE OF THE MIDDLE SCHOOL

The middle school has its roots in the junior high school movement. The traditional junior high school, established more than eighty years ago, had a different philosophy than that of the current middle school and was a product of its time. Several reasons are given for the emergence of the junior high school. The turn of the century witnessed an increased demand for secondary education and better preparation in basic skills needed for the high school, which was basically college preparatory in nature (Frederick, 1968). Developments in technology began to reduce the need for child labor and resulted in larger numbers of students staying in school. This, in turn, called for the reorganization of grade structure to accommodate increased enrollment (Klingele, 1979). Some educators called for a school program which would better prepare students for the transition from elementary school to high school while others were concerned that the benefits of vocational training found in high schools would be denied to those who dropped out after completing elementary school (Howard and Stoumbis, 1970). However, a more compelling reason for the development of the junior high school was the growing research in psychology, sociology, and physiology. A general awareness developed that the preadolescent age group had unique needs and that special programs were needed to accommodate these needs. The work of G. Stanley Hall (1904) at the turn of the century was particularly influential on the junior high school movement in that his research noted rapid changes in physical development, erratic behavior, emotional turbulence, the assertion of independence, and high levels of anxiety in ten-to-fourteen-year-olds. Other research at this time focused on the development of the intellect and noted that distinct changes took place in this age group as they moved from childhood to adolescence (Alexander, Williams, Compton, Hines and Prescott, 1968).

Unfortunately, much of the existing human development research was not applied to the early junior high school program. It was not until the late 1960s that this research had a discernable impact. At this time experimental schools introduced nongraded configurations through flexible scheduling which emphasized individualized instruction. During the formative stages of the junior high school, educators paid little attention to these physical and organic studies and deemed this age group to have few special problems which educators themselves could not handle. Any "personal" problems students incurred could be adequately addressed by counselors (Alexander et al., 1968, pp. 24–25).

THE JUNIOR HIGH SCHOOL

The impetus for establishing a junior high school was well-meaning and, for the most part, many of the conceptualized goals and objectives of the early junior high school were fulfilled. By 1960, the junior high school movement reached its peak with over 5,000 such schools in existence. However, as the popularity of this movement increased, the junior high school became more like the high school, and, in some cases, a social and educational copy. One indication of this is the very name, "junior" high school. The junior high school was to prepare students for high school work. Another indication is the organizational structure of the junior high school. Teachers were based in academic departments rather than organized by interdisciplinary groups. Students were promoted or retained on subject performance with a subject-centered curriculum, electives were specialized areas of study which would better prepare students for high school courses, and ability grouping patterns were inflexible with I.Q. scores the predominant means for determining grouping assignments. Interscholastic athletics, modeled after high school programs, dominated at the expense of intramurals, and lack of knowledge of preadolescent needs was evident (George, Stevenson, Thomas, and Beane, 1992).

Growing dissatisfaction with these conditions as well as calls for social reform further pointed out the inadequacy of the junior high school. By the early 1960s, critics of the educational process were touting reform in education at all levels, and those specifically interested in adolescent education focused on an emerging educational program, the middle school.

RESEARCH FOR THE EMERGING MIDDLE SCHOOL

Alexander, Grantes, Noyce, Patterson, and Robertson were early leaders in calling for a new school, a school "in the middle" to specifically address the unique needs of preadolescent learners as they progress through varying stages of physical and organic development (Alexander and Williams, 1965). The educational program these reformers envisioned consisted of an organizational structure which would house grades 6–8, not grades 7–9 as was typical of the junior high school. It would also be an educational program planned for preadolescents which built on the childhood-oriented program of the elementary school, yet prepared the middle grades learner for the adolescent-oriented demands of the high school. Within this new organizational structure, reformers envisioned flexible and block scheduling practices, ungraded class groupings, teachers who applied the research of physical and organic development, and guidance services which addressed the needs of the "whole" child (Grantes, Noyce, Patterson, and Robertson, 1961).

Physical Development

The work of Donald Eichhorn (1966) on the physiological development of ten-to-fourteen-year-olds also had a significant impact on the emerging middle school concept. His work on the unique characteristics of this age group led to the term "transescence" which connotes the difference in human development cycles and patterns of these students as they make the transition from childhood to adolescence. Transescence is characterized by stages of development which begin prior to the onset of puberty and continue through the early stages of adolescence. Because puberty occurs at different times with different students, no one specific age can be pinpointed as the time this distinct change in body chemistry takes place. However, prior to and during transescence, there are changes in the physical, social, emotional and intellectual makeup of the student, with stability in these changes not fully occurring until puberty is reached. For this reason, Eichhorn advocated an educational program designed around the unique physiological changes of the transescent (Romano and Georgiady, 1994).

Other research focused on generic growth patterns which all individuals follow. However, this pattern varies greatly from one individual to another. While some develop at an "average" pace, others vary because of heredity and environmental variables such as diet, exercise, and health care (Alexander et al., 1968). During preadolescence, youth experience physical change which is greater than at any other time except during infancy. Transescents are deeply aware of these changes and their effects on their daily activities. These changes coincide with the onset of puberty or pubescence, the two-year time period prior to puberty—the time at which youth are capable of reproduction. Although this gradual maturation process takes place over a

3½- to 5-year time span and provides some general patterns of growth and development for this age group, the individual differences are a cause of stress among the preadolescent. With pubescence beginning in girls as early as age 8½ and in boys at or before age 10, and with pubescence taking as long as age 11½ for girls and as long as age 15½ for boys, grades 5–8 are the grade configurations in which all of these pubescents will be in some stage of transition (Tanner, 1966).

Physical changes in students are noticed earlier in some than in others. For example, some 5th grade girls are physiologically 15 year olds or 9th graders, while some 5th grade boys are physiologically 7 year olds or 2nd graders. Conversely, some 8th grade boys are physiologically 17 year olds or 12th graders while others are only 10 year olds or 5th graders physiologically. For 8th grade girls, some are physiologically 19 year olds or college freshmen while some girls are only 12 years old physiologically. This data notes a range of 8 to 9 years in which physical maturation takes place. Such diverse differences in physical development decrease after grade 8 and continue to do so during the high school years (Alexander et al., 1968).

Many physical changes are related to height and weight rather than to age. Weight increases during preadolescence as a result of growth in body fat, muscles, and bone size. Until age 14, girls tend to weigh more than boys, with girls' weight being largely fat content while boys' weight is more muscle. Height, a major concern among boys, comes in spurts with boys beginning their growth around age 12½ with a growth rate of about 4 inches a year. However, muscular development and bone growth are often disproportionate. Girls begin their growth around age 10½ and grow about 3½ inches a year. Until age 14, girls are usually taller than boys (Tanner 1966, 1971). These physical developments become topics of discussion and, in some cases, concern among adolescents.

Growth of pubic and body hair begins earlier for girls than boys. For girls, growth begins between ages 10 and 12 and for boys between 11 and 13. The onset of menstruation is about age 13 and usually takes place after the growth spurt. Testicular development in boys usually occurs around age 11 and begins about 6 months after breasts in girls begin to develop (Faust, 1977).

Physical development characteristics trigger adolescents' preoccupation with personal appearance. They have a desire to be the "same" as their peers but their differences are all too obvious. During this age, skin problems surface, eyeglasses appear, orthodontic attention is needed, height and weight increase, and bones grow faster than muscles. Being different from the peer group causes inner turmoil but such turmoil is often hidden from teachers and other adults. Frustration, excessive energy, periods of lethargy, stooped posture, the need to constantly move and squirm, awkwardness, inquisitiveness, and challenge of authority are other characteristics of the ten-to-fourteen-year-old age group as they attempt to adapt to their bodily changes (Alexander et al., 1968).

The rate of physical growth also impacts social and psychological development. Tanner (1962) reports that youth in the transitional years, grades 5 through 8, encounter problems of personal and social adjustment as the physical stability of childhood is replaced by rapid body changes. Most notably, these social and psychological adjustments center around appearance and the importance our society places on looks and image (Alexander et al., 1968). For preadolescents, a positive image of their own physical characteristics generally means a positive image of the self and good social relations with peers and adults (Brooks-Gun and Warren, 1988).

Transescents spend much time talking about their bodies and making comparisons of body development among their peers. Boys are preoccupied with height, weight, and strength while girls focus on appearance and social relationships. Brooks-Gun and Warren (1988) note that breast development in girls is associated with healthy social adjustment, good peer relations, and a positive self-concept. Boys who mature early are more positive about their physical changes and their self-image, but tend to be more prone to deviant behavior (Duncan, Ritter, Dornbusch, Gross, and Carlsmith, 1985). Early maturing girls, like early maturing boys, tend to date more and have a wider circle of friends, but girls seem to have more conflicts with their parents than do early maturing boys (Susman, Nottlemann, Inoff-Germain, Dorn, Culter, Loriaux, and Chrousos, 1985).

Health concerns, poor diet, lack of proper exercise, and eating disorders impact physical growth and occupy the thoughts of the preadolescent. At this age, faddish diets and peer group opinion about facial and body appearance are taken seriously. Deviation from the norm in these areas can cause alteration in diet which can cause excess weight or contribute to acne. Both obesity and acne during this time period can have a negative impact on the transescent's social relations, psychological development and sexual identity. The use of tobacco, alcohol, and drugs may begin during the middle school years which will also impact the physical development of these transescents. Peer pressure is a main cause for their use, and many of these transescents lack the necessary information to make informed choices about the use of these detrimental products.

Intellectual Development

Research in the area of intellectual development increased significantly during the 1960s with the clinical work of Jean Piaget and his Geneva group (Apple, 1977). Piaget's findings (Inhelder and Piaget, 1958) on cognitive development provided further impetus for the middle school movement with research supporting the idea of intellectual growth as a progression taking place during sequential periods or stages. According to Piaget, three periods of cognitive development are present in all human beings. Development in each of these three periods is situation-specific with full maturation dependent upon environment, biological maturation, and personal experiences. Two of the three stages of development are present in the ten-to-fourteen-year-old learner and have direct implications for the learning environment and the middle school (Muth and Alverman, 1992).

The cognitive development of the transescent coincides with the physical, emotional, and social development of this age group. Cognitive development concerns itself with changes in mental processes and draws on the field of cognitive psychology for explanation. Cognitive psychology holds that the learning process involves more than a simple response to a stimulus. Cognitive psychologists maintain that such things as memory, attention, perception, and decision making greatly impact the learning phenomena and that for learning to take place there must be meaningful interaction between the learner and that which is to be learned.

As transescents strive for greater independence from adults, they begin to make decisions independent of adult influence. Transescents also begin to make generalizations from observations and data and to develop reasoning power as they look for relationships beyond traditional fact-based cause-and-effect happenings. Their desire to be creative in finding solutions to problems begins to mature. They begin to plan their own activities and make preparations for a future which is less dependent on parental support. At this stage, the transescent becomes more perceptive, as well as suspicious, about adult behavior, and they begin to ask questions and challenge reasons and facts adults use to make decisions. These behaviors are a result of the intellectual maturation process transescents are experiencing.

Theories and definitions of learning and intellectual development abound with no one definition or learning theory being satisfactory to all educators. However, a generic definition is that learning is the changing or modifying of behavior. This definition can be applied to both the cognitive and affective domains of learning and has direct implications for the middle school learner. Middle school educators are as concerned with the development of the intellectual and cognitive skills as they are with the affective—the development of values, attitudes, behaviors, and social and citizenship responsibilities. Central to changing or modifying behavior is the idea of experiencing, interacting with the environment, learning by doing, and making meaningful connection between the stimulus and the response. Learning, then, becomes an acting-reacting activity with the reaction or response being "desired," "meaningful," "required," or "creative" depending upon the lesson to be learned or the context of the situation. This definition is most applicable to the goals of a quality middle school.

Theories on cognitive or intellectual development are many, but the theory of Jean Piaget and his associates has particular application to the middle school learner (Alexander et al., 1968). Piaget, a developmental psychologist, made major contributions to theories about intellectual development processes through clinical studies and research. According to Piaget, cognitive structures are not inherited, but are generated by the manner in which we interact with our environment *and* our mode of functioning which remains primarily unchanged as we progress through life. Cognitive development then is a progression through cognitive stages that are sequential and unchangeable in their progression. However, as it is with physical development, not all people reach the same level of intellectual development. Limiting factors include environment, type and quality of experiences, emotions, and physical development. Movement from one cognitive stage to another does not take place at the same time nor at the same chronological age in all people (Inhelder and Piaget, 1958).

Piaget (Inhelder and Piaget, 1958) believed that intellectual development progresses through four stages: the sensorimotor stage, the preoperational stage, the concrete operations stage, and the formal operations stage. Learning experiences, social life, and physical development greatly impact the movement from one stage to the next. Piaget theorizes that while the four stages are distinct, they overlap as the transition from one state to another occurs. A salient feature of this developmental theory is that a student can perform functions associated with the formal operations stage in one subject area and not in another. The last two of the four stages (concrete operations and formal operations) have direct implications for middle school educators and will be discussed more fully than the others in the following pages. Most transescents are either at one of these two stages of development or are in a transition from one stage to the other.

The four stages are as follows:

(1) The sensorimotor stage occurs from birth to approximately age 2 years. In this stage, interaction with the environment dominates the cognitive development process with trial and error being the primary learning vehicle.

(2) The preoperational stage, which lasts from age 2 to about age 7 or 8 years, evidences intuitive thinking and egocentricity. This stage is a transitional period between the sensorimotor stage and the stage of concrete operations. At this stage, the child's reality is that which is seen or perceived with no extrapolation to reality outside the tangible.

(3) The concrete operations stage includes youth from ages 7 or 8 to ages 11

or 12 years and evidences the rise of independent thinking and the use of concrete mental operations based on ordering, classifying, and higher order mathematical reasoning. The use of concrete data for learning and reasoning is no longer an absolute necessity.

(4) The formal operations stage begins from ages 11 or 12 to ages 13 or 14. This stage signifies movement into abstract thinking and the tying together of all previous operations connected with the concrete operations stage. During the formal operations stage, hypothesis testing and experimentation become possible as the student grows in the ability to manipulate concrete data and, at the same time, begins to explore the possibilities of applying the concrete to the abstract (Kindred, Wolotkiewicz, Michelson, and Coplein, 1981).

The concrete and formal operations stages of Piaget (Inhelder and Piaget, 1958) have particular application to Howard Gardner's (1993) multiple intelligence theory which was first advanced in 1983. Gardner, in this more recent research, maintains there are seven intelligences or human abilities which each person possesses. Each individual can develop each intelligence to an adequate level of competency and the seven intelligences work together in complex ways. Gardner emphasizes the diversity of ways individuals can demonstrate their talents both within and between these intelligences.

To Gardner, growth and competency in the seven intelligences is attained through the use of those intelligences. Lack of use or exposure to activities and experiences which foster the development of these abilities thwarts maturation, the ability to apply these intelligences to their full potential. Each individual has "proclivities" toward certain of these intelligences which usually begin prior to school age. However, just because there is a proclivity toward one or more of these intelligences at school entry does not mean that these abilities will remain dominant since others can and should be developed and may very well become dominant by school exit. Armstrong (1994) finds Gardner's multiple intelligence theory highly applicable to teaching and learning.

According to Gardner (1993), these seven intelligences are as follows:

(1) Linguistic intelligence is the capacity to use words effectively, both oral and written.

(2) Logical-mathematical intelligence is the ability to use numbers effectively and reason logically through abstractions such as patterns, relationships, and functions of cause and effect.

(3) Spatial intelligence is the ability to visualize images, use colors, shapes, space and lines to graphically represent visual or spatial ideas.

(4) Bodily-kinesthetic intelligence is the ability to use the body to express ideas and feelings and to use one's hands to create or to facilitate learning.

(5) Musical intelligence is the ability to transform, discriminate, and express ideas in musical form.

(6) Interpersonal intelligence is the ability to perceive differences in moods, motivations, and feelings of others and respond effectively to cues displayed by others.

(7) Intrapersonal intelligence is the ability to know one's self, one's strengths and weaknesses, one's motivations and intentions, and one's temperament and goals.

The concrete operations stage of Piaget's theory (Inhelder and Piaget, 1958) encompasses the ability to perform mental manipulations such as classifying data, and identifying relationships such as spatial and cause and effect. The transescent learner not only has the capacity to develop these functions, but is chronologically ready to engage in these activities. These concrete operations are taught in subjects such as social studies, language arts, science, and mathematics. At this stage, most students cannot engage in abstractions or higher order logical reasoning exercises without first having concrete examples.

The application of the multiple intelligence theory to the concrete operations stage of the transescent, ages 7 or 8 to 11 or 12, has many implications. Students in the concrete operations stage who learn best from manipulative and spatial activities are prone to use their bodily-kinesthetic and spatial intelligences for learning. Some students may have a proclivity toward linguistic intelligence but not all are prone to both verbal and visual stimuli. Reading problems, for example, can promote learning in some while verbal problems appeal more to others. Logical-mathematical intelligence grows with the use of puzzles, word and computer games, and strategy games such as chess and checkers. The interpersonal intelligence can be developed by providing time and activities to socialize, participate in clubs, and engage in courses which offer high peer interaction. Interpersonal intelligence can be fostered through activities which promote independence, self-discovery, goal setting, and the exploration of values and feelings. Armstrong (1994) points out that students need concrete experiences and the opportunity to explore their varied interests if their latent abilities are to mature and their current abilities are to continue to develop.

Transescents enter the formal operations stage between ages 11 or 12, a stage which continues throughout adult life. Abstract reasoning, hypothesis testing and experimentation, and higher order logical thinking are characteristics of formal operational thought. The use of concrete data and experiences to promote learning in several of the intelligences are no longer essential in the formal operations stage, and transescents now begin to develop more of their intrapersonal intelligence by analyzing feeling and thinking processes and forming an appreciation for the values and views of others.

Gardner's multiple intelligences theory (1993) also has applications for the formal operations stage. No longer needing to depend on concrete sources to promote learning, students should be provided more challenging exercises to promote linguistic intelligence and logical-mathematical intelligence through the writing of short stories or poetry and the development of their own computer programs or strategy games. To promote spatial intelligence, students can make films (video movies), draw maps, paint pictures, sculpt, and draft plans for a house or building. Bodily-kinesthetic intelligence activities can include using the body to express feeling or tell a story through a dance or a play, or to construct a tool chest or small storage shed. Interpersonal and intrapersonal intelligences can be promoted through group activities, debates, open ended diaries for self-expression and self-analysis or time to work alone and independently create new ideas and practice introspection (Armstrong, 1994).

Recently, left and right brain research has provided new insights into the basic functions of the brain's two hemispheres. This research relates that the brain processes information in two different ways and that one or the other side of the brain tends to be dominant in each one of us (Springer and Deutsch, 1985).

Left brain's processes are analytical, linear, and step-by-step. This hemisphere controls the function of logical thought, linear, numerical and geometric thought, and is analytical in scope in that it organizes new information into pre-existing knowledge or thought patterns and categories. Oral and written language are examples of the left brain function.

Right brain functions tend to be more integrating and simultaneous, and more specialized in creativity, intuition, spatial and visual abilities, fantasy, symbols, and aesthetic processes. The right brain can create leaps in knowledge by discerning larger patterns and can invent ideas that do not fit into pre-existing reference points or experiences. The scientist, the musician, and the painter who create new and previously unseen or unheard of things tend to be right brain dominant.

Other research on cognitive development which pertains to transescents is the work of Toepfer (1979) who reported that brain growth and body growth occur simultaneously and that the most rapid growth periods for the brain also occur between ages 10 to 12 and 14 to 16. During these two growth periods, transescents have an average mental age growth of 38 months with a minimal growth period (7 mental age months) from age 12 to 14. Findings by Epstein (1990) support the idea of brain growth coinciding with body growth and note that reasoning differences are apparent at each of the four levels of Piaget's cognitive development stages. This growth in mental age in transescents should be of greater concern to educators than chronological age since it is important that each student be challenged according to individual rate of growth.

Social and Emotional Development

Other research, focusing on personal development, also influenced the need for a new and different school for the ten-to-fourteen-year-old. During the ten-to-fourteen-year age span, bodily changes and variations in intellectual development impact the social behavior of the transescent. Emotional behavior is turbulent and there is a desire to be an individual. Behavior moods and patterns vary frequently and include amiability, aggressiveness, worry, belligerence, and argumentativeness (Gesell, Ily, and Ames, 1956).

Transescents also experience turbulence in developing their self-concepts, relating with peers and family, and defining their sex roles. Early research in these areas also had great influence on the emerging middle school movement. Self-concept, although a life-long process, changes dramatically during the middle school years. Early childhood security rests with family and home, but as maturation progresses, the "me" becomes more evident with less dependence on family. There is a developing awareness of "me" as an entity separate from the rest of the world. The transescent has left the world of childhood but is not yet mature enough for the world of adulthood. Leaving the security and dependency of the family, the transescent seeks to define values through peers and other adults (Weller, Brown, Short, Holmes, DeWeese, and Love, 1987).

Peers, peer groups, and the school significantly impact the transescent since they provide support, friendship, security, and access to social activities. Self-concept becomes a function of how transescents view their own personal worth and performance in relationship to the feedback they receive and the esteem in which they are held by others whom they value. At this age, the need to conform is strong, likeness with others is highly valued, and yet sensitivity to differences and a need for independence is paramount (Gordon, 1962).

Sex role differences at this time become acute. Close friends are often of the same sex and the transescent learns what it means to be male or female. As with self-concept, sex role identification is highly influenced by peers, adults, and the school environment. In the elementary grades, children of both sexes freely interact, and close friends are of both sexes. During the preadolescent years, certain behaviors associated with males and females are reinforced as they learn to think, act, and feel like a member of their own sex group. Boys are expected to be aggressive, active, and interested in sports and "man-like" play. Girls, on the other hand, are expected to be "ladylike," reserved, and quiet. These behaviors are strongly expected and reinforced by peers and the peer group and are also encouraged by parents and the school. Boys feel it is important to dissociate themselves from anything construed as being feminine and from female control, and the need to model themselves after a strong male emerges. Girls become *less* comfortable with their expected behavior and become more assertive and aggressive. Some develop interests in sports and other "masculine" activities. Consequently, the appropriate behavior associated with sex identification is a challenge which preoccupies the transescent (Gordon, 1962).

The connection between transescent social development and cognitive development has been made by Vygotsky (1978) and Kohlberg (1969). Cognitive development takes place when students interact with others who can provide support for learning. Group work facilitates cognitive development through interaction and the enhancement of self-concept which comes through peer recognition of the transescent's achievements and abilities. The level at which a student can be successful at a given task in a given subject depends on the level of social development (Vygotsky, 1978). Kohlberg notes that social development takes place in stages and that role-playing facilitates the ability to understand different points of view as well as to define more clearly the student's own point of view. Social relations in the classroom play an important part in the social growth patterns of transescents. Elkind (1967) found that egocentrism, the act of considering one's own point of view and disregarding the views of others, decreases as the transescent progresses through the cognitive stages of Piaget's developmental theory.

The early middle school reformers called for a middle school which would contain the necessary organizational structure, scheduling configurations, and educational programs necessary to more adequately address the unique needs of the human development cycles of the transescent than did the junior high school. A school to "bridge the gap" between childhood and adolescence was needed which had a different educational philosophy and organization which would lead the preadolescent through these turbulent years. Such a school needed to be student-centered, not subject-centered and college-or-vocational oriented as is found in high schools; nor was it to be a series of self-contained classrooms, imparting general knowledge or providing the security of one teacher which is the case in elementary schools. Commitment to these ideas was the basis for the new middle school.

GROWTH OF THE MIDDLE SCHOOL

In slightly more than three decades the middle school concept has gained wide popularity. Beginning in the early 1960s with a few hundred schools, the middle school, grades 5 or 6–8, grew to about 1,100 in 44 states by 1968 (Alexander et al., 1968). By the end of the 1970s, there were more than 4,000 middle schools (Brooks and Edwards, 1978). From 1970 to 1990, middle schools increased by over 200 percent, while the junior high school decreased by over 50 percent. It is predicted that many more junior high schools will disappear by the turn of the century (Alexander and McErwin, 1989).

Unfortunately, in the early years of the middle school movement, many schools adopted the name "middle school" without incorporating many of the basic tenets of the middle school philosophy or the organizational structure envisioned by early middle school reformers. In many instances, there seems to be a regression to the subject-centered and college- or vocational-oriented curriculum, with instruction coming from teachers housed in academic departments and with a social structure and athletic program which emulates the high school. Reasons abound as to why some middle schools fail to implement the tenets of a true middle school. Generally, the reasons are as follows:

(1) The natural tensions that exist when applying the theoretical to the practical and the economic and political underpinnings associated with change.

(2) The "bandwagon effect" which is characteristic in education. The adoption of the name "middle school" is vague and gives the appearance of innovation and educational reform while the philosophy and organizational structure remain junior high school in nature.

(3) Inadequately prepared teachers and administrators with insufficient knowledge to meet the needs of youth who go through the varying physical and organic developments of this age group.

(4) The racial desegregation of public schools. This caused some school districts to change grade configuration by moving the ninth grade to the high school, closing their junior high schools, and creating new middle schools with grades five or six through eight which allowed for busing to the more desegregated middle schools. Here, again, "middle school" became a change in name without the application of the tenets of the middle school concept.

(5) Declining student enrollments and obsolete school buildings. These problems cause the gap between the implementation of an ideal middle school and one which functions in name only. A reduction in the number

of high school students and an increase in the number of elementary school students caused many school districts to place grades five and/or six in newly created middle schools and move grade nine to the high school as mentioned above. This decreased the chances of closing high schools which would have led to a reduction in force of both teachers and administrators and provided more classroom space. Dated buildings, old high schools or junior high schools, were made into middle schools, but they lacked the necessary space and structural requirements to accommodate the middle school concept which calls for easy access to the instructional materials center, rooms varying in size for large and small groups for independent study and exploration activities, space for special types of instruction or laboratories, and wings or clusters that facilitate decentralization into schools-within-schools (George et al., 1992).

It seems evident that the only valid reasons for adopting the name of "middle school" to designate an educational program lies in the following: First, the philosophy and organization of a middle school must reflect the philosophy and incorporate the tenets of a true middle school, and, second, its instructional program must specifically meet the unique needs of the transescent learner. To merely adopt the middle school name, without meeting these essential components of the true middle school, will be cosmetic at best, and the desired educational results for ten-to-fourteen-year-olds will not be fully realized.

THE TRUE MIDDLE SCHOOL

The true middle school can be characterized as one which fully accommodates the ten-to-fourteen-year-olds whose chronological age is dominated by problems of coping with change—changing interests, changing social and emotional behavior, and changing bodies. A true middle school draws its strengths from the nature of transescents and their awakening need to interact with peers, the non-family adult world, and the school and society in general. Its uniqueness comes not only from courses, groupings, and schedules, but also from the attitudes, perceptions, and sensitivity of the principals and teachers who educate these preadolescents (Weller et al., 1987).

The true middle school is also a combination of philosophical, organizational, and instructional practices which support the research on the human development of the transescent learner. Understanding the physical, intellectual, social, and emotional development of these ten-to-fourteen-year-olds as well as having a sound knowledge of the physical changes they undergo during this transitional period are essential to the successful achievement of the goals of middle school education. Child-centeredness and humaneness are important characteristics of middle school principals, as are teachers who complement the unique organizational pattern and curriculum of the middle school. The fact that students in this age range constitute a distinct grouping—physically, socially, and intellectually—calls for an educational program which is student-centered, not subject-centered. Consequently, the true middle school focuses on the esoteric needs and human development patterns of this age group and provides educational programs and practices to make the transition from childhood to adolescence educationally successful and personally rewarding.

Grade configuration has played a part in defining a true middle school but is of secondary importance to the philosophy behind the educational program. The middle school configuration usually consists of grades 5 or 6–8 as opposed to the traditional junior high school of grades 7–9. The rationale for grades 5 or 6–8 lies in the research on the uniqueness of the transescent learner. Students in grade 9 are more similar in their intellectual, physical, and emotional characteristics to grade 10 students than to grade 8 students and desire the more adolescent treatment afforded them in the high school. Physical growth research finds pubescence to occur around age 10½ for girls. Sexual development begins at around age 12½ for girls and age 14½ for boys (Tanner, 1971). Girls can enter the puberty period as early as age 8 (5th grade) or as late as age 11, with boys entering the transition stage by age 10 (6th grade) or as late as age 15. Consequently, the grades during which most students are in the transition period are grades 5–8 (Weller et al., 1987). However, the most popular grade configuration for the middle school is the 6–8 arrangement based on the idea that 10 year olds in grade 5 are, in general, too immature both physically and socially to be included in this group (MacIver, 1990).

National research surveys indicate that the number of middle schools adopting the true middle school philosophy is increasing. One study reports that from 1968 to 1988, the number of middle schools implementing the interdisciplinary team concept increased by more than 20 percent, with nearly 400 middle schools having advisor-advisee programs. The attention given to the exploratory program has increased with a much wider offering of courses and activities. Principals in many of these schools have a clear rationale for the middle school and report that it is anchored in the belief that the transescent has unique needs and characteristics which must be addressed. In the past, the rationale for middle school implementation had focused more on administrative, political, and economic reasons. The study notes that programs central to the middle school concept are expanding faster than the actual number of middle schools but cautions that these reporting schools still have gaps between desired and actual practice (Alexander and McErwin, 1989).

According to Cawelti (1988), another national survey by the Association of Supervision and Curriculum Development (ASCD), conducted in 1988, yielded similar results to the Alexander and McErwin (1989) study. Findings included the wide use of interdisciplinary teaching teams, the use of block scheduling, exploratory activities, and the teacher-as-advisor program. These progressive middle schools stress the importance of staff development and provide comprehensive staff development programs to better prepare teachers in all aspects of the middle school philosophy and, in particular, emphasize the importance of applying various teaching and learning strategies to meet the specific needs of their students. The grade configuration 6–8 is most prevalent and seems to be the organizational structure most likely to accommodate the major middle school characteristics deemed essential to meet the unique needs of the transescent (Cawelti, 1988).

In 1989, the Carnegie Council on Adolescent Development published findings from the Task Force on Education of Young Adolescents. In *Turning Points*, the council reported its recommendations for preparing students for the 21st century with many of the recommendations coinciding with the research of Alexander and McErwin (1989) and ASCD as cited in Cawelti (1988). The council reinforced the need for and value of the middle school concept for the middle grades age group of students and rejected an educational program which was high school–oriented for the middle grades learner. The report noted the mishmash of programs in middle grade schools and cautioned that middle grade schools are the most powerful force we have to help youth during the turbulent years of growth. However, the report also noted that some schools are ignoring the needs of these learners through their organizational structures and curriculum and are exacerbating the problems associated with this age group. As a result, learning decreases, alienation sets in, and the rates of absenteeism and dropout increase. For the 21st century, the report cautions, poorly or minimally educated students will hinder our workforce through decreased job opportunities and learning power which will have a negative impact on our nation as we strive to compete in a global economy. Moreover, the danger of further increasing the division between the affluent, educated population and the poor, ill-educated grows if these students do not receive the educational programs and experiences necessary to help them through the difficult middle grade years.

The recommendations of the Carnegie report are as follows:

(1) Establish small learning communities within the school to foster close, stable relationships with adults and peers to enhance personal and intel-

lectual development. Central to this recommendation is the interdisciplinary teacher team concept and the advisor-advisee program.

(2) Maintain a core academic program which promotes critical thinking, learning how to learn, citizenship and ethical behavior, and responsibility for personal health and social order.

(3) Provide for successful experiences for all students through the elimination of tracking and ability grouping and use cooperative learning and flexible scheduling to ensure adequate instructional time and resources for teachers.

(4) Empower teachers to make decisions about the instructional program through governance committees to help principals in designing and coordinating experiences for middle age learners and give teachers the necessary autonomy to foster an intellectual and emotional environment which meets the specific needs of this age learner.

(5) Employ teachers who are expert at teaching transescents and who have been certified in middle grades education.

(6) Improve academic performance through programs which promote health and fitness. Counselors and a health coordinator as well as programs designed to address the importance of health care complement the goals of quality middle grades education.

(7) Give families meaningful roles in the education of their children through shared school governance and support of the goals of middle school education in the home.

(8) Reconnect the school with the community through service projects and activities which foster a partnership between school and community, make use of existing community resources as part of the middle school curriculum, and provide students social and citizenship responsibilities (Carnegie Council on Adolescent Development, 1989).

In 1990 a national study was conducted by researchers at the Middle Grades Program at the Johns Hopkins University Center for Research on Elementary and Middle Schools (CREMS). Middle school principals who responded to the study's survey reported that middle grade students were being provided core courses but little was being done to create learning opportunities responsive to the needs of the transescent. On the other hand, an increasing number of these principals were planning to implement more exploratory courses into the curriculum, adopt the interdisciplinary teaching team concept, and move away from the subject-centered approach to teaching and learning. Responding principals primarily used flexible scheduling with a six-period day which structures course periods. They favored the use of cooperative learning and were developing programs to increase parental involvement in home-school activities. However, it was obvious that the lack of other scheduling methods, such as block-flexible scheduling, was limiting the organizational structure and curricular offerings of these schools (Maeroff, 1990).

The CREMS study (1990) also revealed that grade span, grades 5 or 6–8, was linked to identification of a school as a middle school, but noted that the curriculum and type of activities provided within the grade span were more important than the grade configurations themselves. Programs such as school-transition programs, advisor-advisee programs, and interdisciplinary teaching teams were reported as having high impact, and those principals not having such programs were moving toward their implementation (MacIver, 1990).

The findings of these four national studies, conducted within the same time frame, complement each other and support the fact that middle school education is rapidly growing and that many of the tenets called for by the early middle school reformers are maturing. Nationally, the middle school has now become a recognized, legitimate, and distinct educational program (George et al., 1992).

THE MIDDLE SCHOOL PHILOSOPHY

At the center of the middle school philosophy lies the belief that students in the ten-to-fourteen-age group (grades 5 or 6–8) are remarkably different from those who are educated in either the elementary or high school grades. As a transitional school, the middle school needs the freedom to operate independently from the philosophies and expectations of the two institutions which it bridges. To do this effectively, the middle school must develop an educational program which is child-centered and which has a direct focus on the unique needs of *learners* as they progress from childhood to adolescence (Weller et al., 1987).

Being child-centered, not subject-centered, is the essential characteristic which should dictate the educational program and permeate all grade levels and activities. Opportunities should be designed which specifically address and promote the various developmental stages occurring within students ten-to-fourteen-years of age. To address these needs, organized learning experiences within the total curriculum are necessary to allow students to grow and develop according to their own unique capacities and abilities. Because each student is in the process of becoming a more mature individual, there should be high concern for the identity, self-concept, and personal needs of each student. Students in this age group are highly independent and seek to explore and create at their own pace; therefore, principals and teachers should accommodate the needs of these students through programs, schedules, and activities that allow for individual differences, provide flexibility in the learning environment, and move the transescent from childhood dependence to young adult independence. Programs and activities which adequately address the middle school philosophy must provide for social and emotional development which corresponds to the physical development of this age group, activities which promote physical and mental health and foster a positive self-concept, and an instructional program which ensures academic achievement and personal success (Wiles and Bondi, 1993).

CHARACTERISTICS OF THE MIDDLE SCHOOL

The common characteristics of a true middle school are devised from several studies and represent the core of the modern middle school. These characteristics reflect the needs and uniqueness of the middle school learner, can provide an increased understanding of the middle school philosophy and can be used as program goals and evaluation criteria for middle school principals and teachers.

(1) *Child-centered, self-paced programs:* because the transescent growth stage is marked by individual differences, programs designed to allow students to develop at their own pace and to improve continuously are essential. The instructional program and learning activities should be designed around this concept of continuous improvement which allows all students to enjoy success as they progress through sequential learning experiences at their own rates. Tracking and chronological grouping patterns work against the concept of continuous improvement.

(2) *Core academic program for all students:* the academic core includes English/language arts and its subcomponents of literature, grammar, spelling, reading, and writing; mathematics; social studies; and science. In these last three core courses, critical thinking, problem solving, and experimentation are central learning experiences. The CREMS (1990) report called for programs and activities which promote social responsibility, good citizenship, personal health care, and ethical behavior in addition to the academic core.

(3) *Variable class scheduling configurations:* scheduling configurations such as flexible scheduling, flexible-modular scheduling, and block scheduling can be used to promote the overall effectiveness of the middle school. In the middle school, the program determines the scheduling configuration. That is, the scheduling practice selected is determined by the priorities of the educational program

which are based on the unique needs of the preadolescent and the goals of the curriculum. This differs from the elementary grades in which the self-contained concept prevails and where teachers decide, for the most part, how time will be utilized and for what purposes. It also differs from the high school's tightly structured schedule utilizing the departmentalized approach in which the principal assigns both teachers and students to a locked-in schedule.

(4) *Exploratory and enrichment programs:* a wide range of courses are offered as electives and focus on special topics designed to meet the variety of interests transescents have about the world and themselves. Courses and programs of this nature provide students the opportunity to consider options and make informed choices, assist them in developing their creative talents and satisfying their curiosity, and allow them to explore their interests in a wide variety of areas which are not necessarily academically-oriented.

(5) *Interdisciplinary teaching teams and planning:* "a keystone for effective education in the middle grades" is the interdisciplinary teaching team (MacIver, 1990, p. 460). Small groups of teachers represent each of the content areas, and members of these teams teach the same group of students. The members of these teacher teams are located in the same area of the school to increase interaction and facilitate team planning. Teachers on these teams are allocated blocks of time together to plan their instructional activities so they can better assist students in making connections from one subject to another. Students benefit from the cohesion and relevance of this type of instruction and from the teaching strength of teacher teams which is maximized through the interdisciplinary approach.

(6) *Independent study:* used as a means to individualize instruction, independent study is a learning technique which focuses on individualized instruction through specially prepared materials. Independent study allows students to choose and pursue areas of personal interest free of many of the traditional classroom restraints. Independent study is highly motivational since the learner pursues the topic out of curiosity and for its intrinsic value. Homework and regular class projects are not considered independent study since student self-motivation and curiosity are often lacking in these activities.

(7) *Guidance and the advisor-advisee program:* teachers and counselors share the responsibility for middle school guidance services. The guidance program is designed to meet the basic needs of the middle school student with services generally focused on physical and character development, emotional development, and career guidance. Guidance

programs are individualized and both teachers and counselors have a sound knowledge of the developmental stages of the transescent. Counselors, teachers, and principals make decisions about the specifics of the guidance services provided with counselors being responsible for coordinating the overall program. Because of the nature of the transescent learner, individualized and personal help is needed during these years with the teacher assuming a new role—that of personal advisor to a specific group of students. Meeting daily in a group or individual setting, teachers provide their students with the security and comfort of knowing that at least one adult personally cares about them and will provide understanding and guidance as they relate their problems and concerns. When difficulties arise that fall outside the expertise of the teacher-as-advisor, students are referred to counselors or other professionals for more specialized help.

(8) *Intramural programs and physical activities:* intramural programs allow all students to participate, regardless of their abilities and talents, if they desire to do so. These programs are unlike the highly competitive programs found in interscholastic competition. Such competitive programs may be physically damaging to the middle school student due to the rapid and uneven growth spurts which occur during this age span. Such programs also cause undue pressure to excel for both the students and the adults. Intramurals provide equal opportunities for boy/girl participation in sports which is not characteristic of the traditional high school program. In intramural programs, fun, skill development, recreational interests, and good sportsmanship are emphasized over competition and winning.

Other physical activities appropriate for this age group are equally important and should be planned and conducted by physical education teachers. Activities should help students understand their physical development and use of their bodies, good personal hygiene habits, and sports as life-long recreation.

(9) *Social development:* middle school students are in the process of maturing between childhood and adolescence and are identifying appropriate behavior patterns for relating and interacting with adults, peers, and the opposite sex. This is generally referred to as socialization. They watch and imitate the behavior of others while at the same time they seek autonomy, support, and friendship. They have a desire to be popular and to conform, but at the same time they seek independence from parents. Their interests in social activities increase, and learning their proper roles in the context of social interaction is important at this state of their development for successful social and psychological experiences.

(10) *Auxiliary programs and activities:* auxiliary programs and services in middle schools serve to complement and strengthen the primary tenets of a true middle school education.

   a. The involvement of parents and community members in the school: effective home-school programs in which parents work closely with the principal and teachers in providing support and assistance in fulfilling the goals of middle school education should be developed. Parents can assist the school by providing regularly scheduled time at home to complete homework and other school assignments, serving as tutors and advisors for their children in the home atmosphere, and working together with school personnel to help students with special problems. Parents can also assist the school by serving on advisory committees, supporting the school's Parent Teacher Organization, and serving as classroom volunteers and resource personnel.

   The community in which the middle school resides is a rich learning laboratory for instruction in the core curriculum and in values, citizenship, and social responsibility. Community members provide a wealth of knowledge and experience which can be tapped through exploratory courses or mini-courses and guest lectures. Community members can also serve as resource people for student projects and independent study.

   The role of the middle school principal in taking the initiative in parent-community programs cannot be emphasized too highly. The principal's attitude toward the importance of parent and community involvement dictates the degree to which these programs are initiated and pursued. Principals are the public relations agents for their schools and the quality of the school is often judged by the personality of the principal. By maximizing community and parental involvement in the school, the principal promotes good public relations with these external publics and strengthens the learning environment for the transescent (Farmer, Gould Herring, Linn, and Theobald, 1995).

   b. Strengthening basic skills: helping students at the middle school level in basic skill remediation is an important part of the overall instructional program. Students lacking basic skills in one or more areas need special support and work with teachers and tutors to increase their skill development. Those who cannot compete academically are prone to develop poor self-concepts and may become dropouts in later years. Using peer groups to help with remediation should be approached with caution for when these remedial students fail to measure up to the expectations of their peers, they retreat into their own world of isolation and become less receptive to teachers and the activities offered by the school. As a result, self-image suffers, willingness to become actively engaged diminishes, and academic performance declines.

SUMMARY

A true middle school is a combination of philosophical, organizational, and instructional practices supported by research on human development for the ten-to-fourteen-year-olds. Child-centeredness and humaneness are important characteristics of middle school principals and teachers. Such characteristics complement the unique organizational pattern and curriculum of the middle school which is designed to help students achieve quality outcomes and experience successful learning experiences as they develop physically, intellectually, emotionally, and socially.

The rationale for the middle school, based on human development research, is to better prepare transescents to bridge the gap between childhood and full adolescence as they enter a period of time characterized by confusion, frustration, distraction, and emotional turmoil. In their search for independence and adult responsibility, transescents need the security, guidance, understanding, and love of caring adults who understand their human development needs.

During these impressionable years, transescents need strong role models and an educational program specifically designed to facilitate healthy development during these turbulent years of cognitive, emotional, social, and physical growth.

Quality-producing middle schools have principals and teachers who are well-educated in the unique needs and human development patterns of the emerging adolescent. Principals employ teachers who know their subject matter and who are thoroughly trained in the middle school concept. Instructional and auxiliary programs and scheduling practices exist which allow for individual student differences, self-paced learning, and flexibility in the learning environment. Exploratory and mini-courses, teacher teams, and nongradedness, in which students progress according to their own growth rates and not chronological age, provide for child-centered learning and personalized instruction.

Principals design the middle school program around four distinct yet overlapping areas of human development: physical, emotional, intellectual, and social. Each of these four areas has pertinent research which middle school principals can infuse into their middle school program to promote the goals and objectives of a quality-oriented, true middle school.

REFERENCES

Alexander, W. M. and C. K. McErwin. 1989. *Earmark of Schools in the Middle: A Research Report.* Bone, NC: Appalachian State University.

Alexander, W. M. and E. L. Williams. 1965. "Schools in the Middle Years," *Educational Leadership*, 23(3):217–223.

Alexander, W. M., E. L. Williams, M. Compton, V. A. Hines, and D. Prescott. 1968. *The Emergent Middle School.* New York: Holt, Rinehart and Winston, Inc.

Apple, M. H. 1977. "The Application of Piagetian Learning Theory to the Science Curriculum," in *Topics in Cognitive Development*, Vol. 1. M. H. Apple and L. S. Goldberg, eds. The Jean Piaget Society. New York: Plenum Press.

Armstrong, T. 1994. *Multiple Intelligences in the Classroom.* Alexandria, VA: Association for Supervision and Curriculum Development.

Brooks, K. and F. Edwards. 1978. *The Middle School in Transition: A Research Report on the Middle School Movement.* Lexington, KY: College of Education, University of Kentucky.

Brooks-Gun, J. and M. P. Warren. 1988. "The Physical Significance of Secondary Sexual Characteristics in Nine-to-Eleven-Year-Old-Girls," *Child Development*, 59:1061–1069.

Carnegie Council on Adolescent Development. 1989. *Turning Points: Preparing American Youth for the 21st Century.* New York: Carnegie Corporation of New York.

Cawelti, G. 1988, November. "Middle Schools a Better Match with Early Adolescent Needs, ASCD Survey Finds," *ASCD Curriculum Update*, Alexandria, VA: Association for Supervison and Curriculum Development.

Center for Research on Elementary and Middle Schools. 1990. "Implementation and Effects of Middle Grades Practices," *CREMS Report.* Baltimore, MD: Johns Hopkins University Center for Research on Elementary and Middle Schools.

Duncan, P. D., P. L. Ritter, S. M. Dornbusch, R. T. Gross, and J. M. Carlsmith. 1985. "The Effects of Pubertal Timing on Body Image, Social Behavior, and Deviance," *Journal of Youth and Adolescence*, 14:117–235.

Eichhorn, D.H. 1966. *The Middle School.* New York: The Center for Applied Research in Education.

Elkind, D. 1967. "Egocentrism in Adolescence," *Child Development*, 38:1025–1034.

Epstein, J. L. 1990. "What Matters in the Middle Grades—Grade Span or Practices?" *Phi Delta Kappan,* 71(6):438–444.

Farmer, R. F., M. W. Gould, R. L. Herring, F. J. Linn, and M. A. Theobald. 1995. *The Middle School Principal.* Thousand Oaks, CA: Corwin Press, Inc.

Faust, M. S. 1977. "Somatic Development of Adolescent Girls," *Monographs of the Society for Research in Child Development*, 42 (1, Serial No. 169).

Frederick, R. 1968. "Evaluation of Early Adolescent Education," in *The Middle School*, Thomas E. Curtis, ed. Albany, NY: State University of New York at Albany, New York Center of Curriculum and Research Services, pp. 17–23.

Gardner, H. 1993. *Multiple Intelligences: The Theory in Practice.* New York: Harper Collins Publishers, Inc.

George, P. S., C. Stevenson, J. Thomas, and J. Beane. 1992. *The Middle School and Be-*

yond. Alexandria, VA: Association for Supervision and Curriculum Development, pp. 1–14.

Gesell, A., F. L. Ily, and L. B. Ames. 1956. *Youth: The Years from Ten to Sixteen*. New York: Harper & Row.

Gordon, I. J. 1962. *Human Development: From Birth through Adolescence*. New York: Harper & Row.

Grantes, J., C. Noyce, F. Patterson, and J. Robertson. 1961. *The Junior High School We Need*. Washington, DC: Association for Supervision and Curriculum Development, p. 19.

Hall, G. S. 1904. *Adolescence*. New York: Appleton-Century-Crofts.

Howard, A. W. and G. C. Stoumbis. 1970. *The Junior High and Middle School: Issues and Practices*. Scranton, PA: Intex Educational Publishers.

Inhelder, B. and J. Piaget. 1958. *The Growth of Logical Thinking from Childhood to Adolescence*. Translated by Anne Parsons and Stanley Milgram, New York: Basic Books, Inc.

Kindred, L. W., R. J. Wolotkiewicz, J. M. Michelson, and L. E. Coplein. 1981. *The Middle School Curriculum: A Practitioner's Handbook*. Second edition. Boston: Allyn & Bacon.

Klingele, W. E. 1979. *Teaching in Middle Schools*. Boston, MA: Allyn & Bacon, Inc.

Kohlberg, L. 1969. "Stage and Sequence: The Cognitive-Developmental Approach to Socialization," in *Handbook of Socialization Theory and Research*, D. A. Gaslin, ed. Chicago: Rand McNally, pp. 347–380.

MacIver, D. 1990. "Meeting the Needs of Young Adolescents: Advisory Groups, Interdisciplinary Teaching Teams, and School Transition Programs," *Phi Delta Kappan*, 71(6):458–464.

Maeroff, G. I. 1990. "Getting to Know a Good Middle School: Shoreham-Wading River," *Phi Delta Kappan*, 71:505–516.

Muth, K. D. and D. E. Alverman. 1992. *Teaching and Learning in the Middle Grades*. New York: Harper and Row.

Romano, L. G. and N. P. Georgiady. 1994. *Building an Effective Middle School*. Madison, WI: WCB Brown & Benchmark.

Springer, S. and G. Deutsch. 1985. *Left Brain, Right Brain*. New York: W.H. Freeman.

Susman, E. J., E. D. Nottlemann, G. E. Inoff-Germain, L. D. Dorn, G. B. Culter, D. L. Loriaux, and G. P. Chrousos. 1985. "The Relation of Relative Hormonal Levels and Physical Development and Social-Emotional Behavior in Young Adolescents," *Journal of Youth and Adolescents*, 14:245–264.

Tanner, J. M. 1962. *Growth of Adolescence*. Oxford, England: Basil Blackwell & Mott, Ltd.

Tanner, J. M. 1966. "Galtonian Eugenics and the Study of Growth: The Relation of Body Size, Intelligence Test Score, and the Social Circumstances in Children and Adults," *Eugene Review*, 58:122–135.

Tanner, J. M. 1971. "Sequence, Tempo, and Individual Variation in the Growth and Development of Boys and Girls Aged Twelve to Sixteen," *Daedalus*, 100:907–930.

Toepfer, C. 1979. "Brain Growth Periodization—A New Dogma for Education," *Middle School Journal*, 10(3):18–22.

Vygotsky, L. S. 1978. *Mind in Society: The Development of High Mental Processes*. Cambridge, MA: Harvard University Press.

Weller, L. D., C. L. Brown, M. L. Short, C. T. Holmes, L. S. DeWeese, and W. G. Love. 1987. *The Middle School*, Monograph in Education No. 2, Bureau of Educational Services, College of Education, University of Georgia, Athens, GA.

Wiles, J. and J. Bondi. 1993. *The Essential Middle School*. Second edition. New York: Macmillian Publishing Company.

CHAPTER 2

Leadership for Effective Middle Schools

Effective schools are schools which make a difference and, quite obviously, some schools are more effective than others. Effective schools have certain research-based core characteristics which make them quality producing schools of excellence. The mere infusion of these characteristics of effective schools alone, however, will not provide effective schools results. Effective schools have a governance structure which is initiated and sustained by leaders who possess certain skills and competencies which allow them to forge together those independent characteristics of effective schooling into a structured systematic delivery process. The essence which promotes and sustains effective school outcomes lies in the commonality of these essential leadership skills and competencies.

Specifically, this chapter will examine the following questions:

- What are the essential characteristics of effective schools research?
- What is "leadership"?
- What are the key leadership skills and competencies of effective principals?
- What does the effective schools research say about the principal's role and leadership qualities in terms of being an instructional leader, building vision, developing a positive school climate, utilizing research, assessing student progress, and promoting positive home/school relations?

THE EFFECTIVE SCHOOLS MOVEMENT

One of the most intriguing aspects of research on effective schools is the lack of a clear and accepted definition of school effectiveness. The combined literature on effective schools seems to agree that effective schools are schools which make a *difference*, with some schools being more effective than others (Purkey and Smith, 1983). Effective schools have certain research-based characteristics which make them schools of quality or schools of excellence (Ogden and Germinario, 1994). Schools of quality are those schools which embrace the quality management philosophy of W. Edwards Deming (1986, 1993) and practice his fourteen points of Total Quality Management (TQM). TQM is a new way of thinking and working, a new management philosophy about people and how to achieve organizational and personal effectiveness. Quality schools have strong, energetic principals who are committed to the quality philosophy and principles of vision building, constancy of purpose, team work, systems thinking, and continuous improvement.

Schools of excellence are more difficult to define since they are not based on any one specific philosophy or set of guiding principles as are quality schools. Sergiovanni (1984) finds schools of excellence "hang together" through a sense of purpose, a common cause, a spirit of working together, and "with accomplishments easily recognized" (p. 4). They are more than schools with high morale, high achievement test scores, or high numbers of students attending college. Sergiovanni notes, "Excellence is all of these and more" (p. 4). Excellence, defined by Lightfoot (1983), is "goodness" which is not a static or absolute quality that can be reduced to one measure of success. *Goodness* or *effectiveness* is a complicated concept which refers to the various parts of schooling which make a whole. These parts include people, relationships, structures, goals, ideology, and the curricula.

These philosophical definitions of excellence were supplemented by research findings which attempted to identify specific variables which produced excellent schools, schools which promoted results which could be measured objectively, such as student achievement on standardized measures. This line of study initiated the effective schools research which focused on processes of schooling, unlike previous research which focused on the quantities of resources available to schools and individual student characteristics.

Other researchers believed that success on standardized tests was not strictly related to basic skills mastery, nor was test performance an accurate reflection of the overall mission of education. Rather effective schools should be assessed regarding their ability to meet the social, emotional, and physical, as well as the academic, needs of students. Moreover, these researchers held that standardized test scores reflected socioeconomic background, intelligence, and school effectiveness (Serow and Jackson, 1983). Interest in the social and emotional development of students began to take on greater importance as educators and parents reexamined their value to the overall mission of education and their implications for impacting student test performance. As a result, defining effective schools based on student performance of mathematics and reading skills in just a few grades alone began to be seen as an inadequate measure of assessing school effectiveness. A more accurate definition of effectiveness began to include affective variables such as student attitudes, self-esteem and social responsibility, and higher order thinking skills (Cuban, 1984). The concept of a school as a social system in which a myriad of processes takes place and contributes to student cognitive and affective achievement throughout their years of schooling triggered a wider range of research-investigated variables over a longer time frame. Instead of brief "snapshots" of student performance, investigation of the total process of schooling began which included assessment of student variables at entrance and at exit of the schooling experience (Houlihan, 1983).

This line of research yielded several important findings: First, there are several variables or factors that make a school effective; second, some schools are more effective than other schools; and third, there is no one list of characteristics or factors which are found in every effective school. Effectiveness results from a combination of many policies, behaviors, and attitudes within the school itself.

In summary, while there is no universally accepted definition of what constitutes an effective school there has emerged from the research literature of the 1970s and 1980s a common core of practices or characteristics which are believed to have a significant impact on how much students learn. The sum of this continuing research-based literature is collectively known as "effective schools research." The core characteristics presented below are those most often cited in the research literature. According to Hoy and Miskel (1991), these characteristics have been numbered at as few as three and as many as ten, but those listed below seem to have a broad base of general acceptance:

- strong leadership from the principal who emphasizes instruction
- safe and orderly environment which emphasizes academic achievement
- high expectations for student and teacher success
- academic emphasis through collective vision, planning, and goal setting
- emphasis on basic skills and quality instruction
- continuous monitoring of student progress
- positive and active home-school relations

IN SEARCH OF THE CONCEPT OF LEADERSHIP

A strict and universally accepted definition of leadership has yet to be embraced by the literature despite the more than 3,000 empirical studies conducted on the nature and characteristics of leadership (Lunenburg and Ornstein, 1991). Farmer, Gould, Herring, Linn and Theobald, (1995) note, for example, that leadership "is a much observed phenomenon, but little understood" (p. 12), and Yukl (1989) states that "the field of leadership is in a state of ferment with many continuing controversies about conceptual and methodological issues" (p. xii). Confusion and controversy over a clear and concise definition of leadership arise from the nature of the tasks the leader performs and the skills required to be an effective leader. This gives rise to the following questions. Is leadership an art or is it a science? The *art* of leadership requires the practice of excellent human relations and interpersonal communications skills—being people-oriented, showing empathy, and understanding the personal and psychological aspects of human nature. The *science* of leadership is research-based. Successful leaders are students of the research literature, they keep current by reading professional journals and attending conferences and seminars, and they then actively apply relevant findings to their work situations. Leaders who excel practice both the art and the science of leadership.

Compounding the search for a generic definition of leadership is the innate fascination people have with the concept of leadership itself and the personal definitions they attribute to those in leadership positions. Also, the phenomenon of and fascination with leadership can in no small measure be attributed to the mysteries and legends surrounding leaders and the historical events which triggered their ascension to positions of power. Both benevolent and malevolent leaders have existed and the events surrounding their rise to leadership have been the source of the search for common denominators for their success. Their rise to positions of power and influence, the special abilities applied to attain these leadership positions, and the circumstances which surrounded their elevation to power provide each of us with a personal "leadership index" for studying and assessing the outcomes of their behavior. These personal judgments, either good or bad, right or wrong, are often based on our own experiences with leaders and the personal behaviors these leaders display.

Researchers themselves investigate leadership variables based on their own perceptions of the leadership phenomenon and they have provided more than 350 definitions of leadership (Bennis and Nanus, 1985). This empirical investigation has not yet yielded the exact nature of the leadership concept which still remains elusive and somewhat mystical. In fact, any individual definition of leadership would coincide with much that has already been written and would be just as valid and reliable as any other.

There are many basic constructs of a leadership definition. Those in leadership roles have been described as having certain traits and behaviors, role relationships, positions of authority, influence, manipulative abilities, and power. Common terms found in leadership definitions include influencing, guiding and directing, structuring, using power and authority, persuading, delegating, and facilitating. These terms imply a leader-follower relationship whether it be one follower or many. Leaders, therefore, do not exist in isolation and can be found in both formal and informal settings. The former implies leadership by virtue of legitimate authority and positional power over others while the latter implies having influence over others or leading by consent to attain mutual goals.

For purposes of this book, leadership will be presented as behaviors exhibited in the formal and informal context. Principals have positional power and legitimate authority by virtue of their representing the state constitutional power and authority vested in their school boards of education. Their informal power, which cannot be truly separated from their formal power, resides in their ability to influence, guide, persuade, and serve their subordinates. Leaders who rely on the authority and power of their position never don the role of an informal leader in the strictest of terms. Leadership, therefore, becomes the choice to emphasize one form of leadership behavior over another. Effective leaders seem less likely to call on their positional power to achieve the goals and objectives of the school and more likely to use influence, persuasion, and guidance to achieve their ends. Effective leadership can then be defined as the willful and successful choice of exerting behaviors of power and authority or influence and persuasion to accomplish the goals of the organization with the least amount of subordinate resistance.

Leaders vs. Managers

Debate over the leader-manager paradox has existed for some time. Is a leader a leader, a manager, or both? The actuality is that a leader must not only lead the organization but manage the organization as well. Managers are functionaries and focus on microconcepts of the organization such as enforcing policy and structuring the work environment for better productivity; they concern themselves with attending to the daily functions of employees and making sure rules and regulations are adhered to as prescribed by the organization. They pay attention to detail; they are organized; they address daily problems and enforce policy; and they reward, praise, and marshall resources for people to do their work. However, good leaders also conceptualize; take a macrocosmic view of the organization; develop operational strategy; provide organization, purpose, and direction; and control the activities of others within the organization to achieve its goals (Levitt, 1976). Leaders are proactive: they spend their time shaping ideas; changing attitudes; creating high expectations; and changing attitudes; creating high expectations; and changing how people think about themselves, the organization, and their work (Zaleznik, 1977).

Effective leaders are those who truly make a difference in the organization's effectiveness. They are results-oriented, they plan for change, and they develop a vision of what the organization should and could be. Effective leaders have an image of the future and concern themselves with the adequacy of the goals and resources to make that image a reality. They are people-oriented and evoke in individuals the desire to achieve their vision with zeal, commitment, and a new attitude toward the purpose of their work (Hoy and Miskel, 1991). Effective leaders fully utilize the talents of their people through teams which have the power to make decisions and solve problems that impact their daily work situations. Through teamwork, subordinates share in the governance of the organization and take responsibility for their actions and accomplishments. Effective leaders spend time motivating and influencing others to commit to and support their vision and aspirations. They have high expectations for themselves and their people, and they take charge by providing direction, being creative, and instilling a new culture which is characterized by shared values, symbols, and philosophy (Mintzburg, 1989).

Cultural transformation in an organization represents a social rather than a technical change which takes time, effort, and commitment. Cultural change means instilling a work ethic and new set of values in order to inspire subordinates to achieve effectiveness in their daily work efforts (Deal, 1985). Etzioni (1988) believes that effective leaders practice *value-added leadership*, placing greater emphasis on what people believe and how they feel (their values and commitment) and then providing motivators and meeting those needs. Value-added leadership creates a moral order which bonds the leader and followers in a work environment which allows for job satisfaction and responsibility, personal fulfillment, and a mutual commitment to a common set of values and philosophy.

Finally, the effective leader uses power as part of the leadership role. Power for effective leaders lies not so much in positional authority as it does in the ability to persuade others to commit to and then work diligently toward achieving a commonly agreed upon end. This perspective of the power-influence part of leadership is best captured by the definitions of leadership of two former presidents, Dwight D. Eisenhower and Harry S. Truman.

> He gets men to go along with him because they want to do it for him and they believe in him [Eisenhower].
>
> [He is a] man who has the ability to get other people to do what they don't want to do and like it [Truman]. (Brussell, 1988, p. 317)

And yet with all the attempts to accurately define leadership, to come up with a commonly accepted set of behavior and characteristics, the phenomenon still remains elusive. Perhaps Bennis (1989) said it best, when talking about the complexity and mystique of leadership, when he likened leadership to a thing of beauty: "You know it when you see it, yet it is difficult to define" (p. 17).

LEADERSHIP SKILLS AND COMPETENCIES
OF EFFECTIVE PRINCIPALS

Effective schools are those in which principals and teachers "operate from a belief system concerning the nature and purpose of the school" (Ogden and Germinario, 1994, p. 7) and are bonded together by the belief that student achievement can best be attained through a common mission, common goals, and shared governance. Effective schools are also those which are in a constant state of dissatisfaction. They are dissatisfied with their outcomes and seek new and better ways to improve the process of schooling. Effective schools have the intrinsic motivation to provide the best instructional program possible so students can maximize their full potential (Ogden and Germinario, 1994).

What makes this possible? The answer repeatedly focuses on the leadership provided by the principal of the school. The principal is the most important factor in the transformation of a non-effective school into an effective school. Leaders of effective schools have an attitude that change for the better is possible regardless of the existing circumstances. Principals of effective schools have a vitality which motivates them to seek improvement, move forward, and strive for excellence. Good leaders are dissatisfied with being average or with the status quo and have higher goals for themselves and for others (Gardner, 1990). Ogden and Germinario (1994) state:

> Leadership is the most important role of the principal. In case after case, it has been demonstrated that it was the principal who has made the most significant difference in the transformation of the school from a loose collection of individual classrooms to an effective connected school with a shared mission and successful student outcomes. (p. 9)

Studies from the early 1970s and into the 1990s consistently reveal that effective schools have principals who are instructional leaders. But what does "instructional leadership" really mean? The number of characteristics associated with instructional leaders are almost as many as those associated with effective schools. Like effective schools characteristics, a core of leadership variables has emerged from the literature which seems to have replaced the attempt to define effective leadership singularly. Lunenburg and

Ornstein (1996) relate that the overriding characteristic of effective school principals is their high visibility and heavy involvement in every phase of the school's program. Through such active involvement, the principal has a sustaining impact on the school's instructional program.

The Northwest Regional Education Laboratory (1990) identified several characteristics of an effective instructional leader:

- Emphasizes academics with learning being the most important reason for students being in school
- models the belief that all students can learn and that schools make a difference between success and failure
- models the school's mission and has high expectations that all students can and will learn the curriculum content and master the basic skills
- keeps teachers focused on the mission of the school and supplies the necessary time, resources, and technical assistance necessary to promote effective classroom teaching and learning
- maintains a safe and orderly environment (climate) which is conducive to learning and teaching
- is actively involved in all phases of the school's instructional program
- consistently evaluates the effectiveness of the curriculum and student progress in achieving the goals and objectives of the instructional program
- maintains a good home-school relations program which involves parents in student learning and fosters support for the mission of the school involves teachers in making decisions about the curriculum and school governance policies
- consumes and applies new research to improve instruction and plans with teachers for the implementation of new programs and strategies
- rewards and praises student and teacher success and informs both parents and the community of these achievements

The common core characteristics of effective school leadership, therefore, which emerge from the literature are presented below:

- instructional leadership
- school-wide vision
- school climate
- application of research
- knowledge of research on effective schools and teaching and learning methods as they affect student progress

- parent and teacher support and involvement programs

Each of these core areas of effective leadership is explored in detail in the remainder of this chapter.

Leadership and the Instructional Program

Effective principals lead by inspiration, not manipulation. They are assertive leaders and have a clear vision of what they want the school to become. They are conceptualizers, planners, and risk-takers. They inspire others to achieve their goal-oriented vision and they see the connections between decisions and outcomes. They take the responsibility for making the vision a reality. They know effective schools do not become effective on their own. Effective leaders are human engineers—they motivate their staff by knowing and practicing "people skills" through the use of excellent communication skills. Principals in these schools exercise "controlled direction" over their school, the curriculum, and the instructional program. In effective schools, principals are more assertive in their beliefs and convictions than those principals in ineffective schools, and they employ participatory management practices with teachers, allowing them the freedom and flexibility to make independent decisions regarding the teaching-learning phenomenon (Chubb and Moe, 1990).

Assertive leadership is based on courage, resolution, and consistency. Effective principals have high standards and expectations for success, the courage to implement their convictions, and the resolution to stand firm over time on their beliefs. Lunenburg and Ornstein (1996) note the importance of assertiveness and of strong conviction when they state that "a powerful and long-term commitment is required to bring about substantial, widespread, and enduring gains in the performance of students" (p. 348). Assertiveness also means making tough unpopular decisions, setting instructional priorities, and keeping teachers focused on the school's vision. Assertive leaders are risk-takers. They take calculated risks based on research findings or proven successful practices and refrain from making changes based on intuition or experience alone.

Effective principals know that lasting change comes from within the organization and not through external mandates. They know that teacher participation provides a strong sense of ownership and commitment and that teacher participation in decision making provides the intrinsic motivation needed to sustain the dedication necessary to achieve school effectiveness. Assertive leaders also motivate their staffs by rewarding and praising their teachers' efforts and progress as they move toward achieving the goals of effective schooling. These principals encourage and support risk-taking on the part of teachers and teacher teams with the goal of always improving past performance as they strive to realize the school's vision.

Shared decision making, collaboration, and consensus building are practices principals employ to promote effective instructional leadership (Sagar, 1992). Through teacher teams, principals solidify the energies and creativity of teachers to work toward instructional improvement in the curriculum and the classroom. Collegial decision making in the areas of curriculum and classroom instruction strengthens teachers' commitment to the goals of school effectiveness and enhances the overall instructional program. Principals, through teacher teams, ensure that knowledge and requisite skills are incorporated into programs that have meaning for students and are matched to the instructional goals of the school with appropriate learning materials and delivery systems. This provides continuity across grade levels and ensures content coverage, basic skills development, and the use of appropriate student assessment techniques.

Principals themselves are actively involved in curricular decisions in the following ways:

- scheduling daily blocks of time for teacher teams to plan instructional activities together and to monitor student progress
- providing adequate fiscal and technical resources for teachers to achieve their instructional goals
- freeing teachers from unnecessary assignments and responsibilities to allow them to focus on their most important task—being effective classroom teachers
- constantly keeping teachers focused on the school's vision and communicating the high standards and expectations held for student and teacher success

Having a sound knowledge and understanding of effective school practices is essential to effective instructional leadership. Understanding child growth and development patterns and teaching and learning theories are essential in helping teachers become effective in classroom performance. Principals serve teachers in these areas as mentors, coaches, and resource persons. Principals also facilitate instructional improvement by promptly providing teachers with assistance, either internal or external, which falls outside their area of expertise.

Planning and providing staff-development programs that are personally meaningful to teachers are also part of effective school leadership. The effective principal has teachers choose topics which they deem important and then schedules these programs in a timely manner in order to facilitate effective instruction. All too often, ineffective principals choose topics important to themselves and the scheduled presentations are met with a passive audience.

Providing mentoring and peer coaching programs for new and veteran teachers also promotes school effectiveness (DuFour and Eaker, 1992). Mentoring programs help new teachers understand the school's culture and vision. Peer coaching helps teachers acquire new knowledge and skills or refine existing skills through peers of their choice. This non-threatening approach to instructional improvement promotes collegiality among teachers and makes principal evaluations less threatening.

Good management skills support instructional leadership skills. Good leaders are highly organized; are able to handle routine tasks with efficiency and speed; and make effective use of personnel, facilities, and resources through careful planning and budgeting procedures. Effective principals are good managers of their own time and jealously guard the instructional time of their teachers. They practice "management by walking around," trouble-shoot, and anticipate and attend to problems which may distract teachers from instructional tasks. Principals also serve as buffers between teachers and external distractions which may interfere with time spent on instruction.

Part of school management is the enforcement of district policy. However, relaxing certain rules and regulations which may impede effective instruction is an important management consideration. Using aides or volunteers to free teachers from lunchroom and bus duties is another example of service leadership. Teachers need time to reflect on their accomplishments and problems during the school day and any additional free time can be used for instructional planning. Strother (1983) describes an effective manager as one who watches for opportunities to ward off frustration before it prevents aimlessness among the staff. Good principal-managers turn confusion and chaos into order and purpose.

PRINCIPAL AS MASTER TEACHER

Total involvement by effective school principals means both knowing and modeling effective classroom teaching strategies. As effective instructional leaders, principals have a thorough knowledge of the teaching-learning process and assist teachers in becoming more effective in their instructional activities (Ogden and Germinario, 1994). Their ability to work closely with teachers to improve their classroom instructional skills is crucial to creating effective schools (Klopf, Scheldon, and Brennan, 1982).

Principals in effective schools visit classrooms regularly and spend time with their teachers modeling instructional strategies and assisting them with other classroom problems. Klopf et al. (1982) found that involved principals conduct more classroom observations, discuss problems more frequently with their teachers, and are more willing to provide external sources of help for professional development. These external sources include providing teachers with research-related readings, allowing teachers to attend professional conferences and workshops, and arranging time during the school day for teachers to observe other teachers. Peer coaching networks and interest seminars are also initiated by principals. Peer networks allow teachers to work with other teachers, exchanging ideas about the teaching-learning process and observing one another's teaching. Interest seminars, conducted during the planning block, address topics of teacher interest and are led by peers, the principal, or outside consultants. These informal give-and-take seminars address current teacher concerns and provide immediate and practical assistance to teachers. The principal is an active participant in each of these enrichment activities and facilitates teacher development by providing substitute teachers and other necessary fiscal resources.

Principals in effective schools model good teaching strategies in the classrooms. These principals serve as role models by demonstrating effective teaching as well as other behaviors conducive to effective instruction. Their presence in classrooms allows them to talk to teachers about their work and special problems and to model the school climate variables of effective schooling. Purkey and Smith (1983) relate that effective principals must have many competencies in the area of instruction, but that the principal cannot be expected to be competent in all instructional strategies. For this reason, principals call on other teachers to provide additional assistance.

TEACHING-LEARNING STRATEGIES

Much research has been conducted on effective teaching-learning strategies. Two excellent resources on this topic are the works of Paul D. Eggan and Donald P. Kauchak (1988) *Strategies for Teachers: Teaching Content and Thinking Skills* and Donald P. Kauchak and Paul D. Eggan (1989) *Learning and Teaching*. Other sources essential to planning for and facilitating effective classroom instruction are Bloom, Engelhard, Furst, Hill, and Krathwohl (1956) *Taxonomy of Educational Objectives: Handbook I: The Cognitive Domain*; Krathwohl, Bloom, and Masia (1964) *Taxonomy of Educational Objectives: Handbook II: Affective Domain*; and Harrow's (1972) *A Taxonomy of the Psychomotor Domain: A Guide for Developing Behavioral Objectives*. These taxonomies present the levels of the hierarchy of learning as learning in these domains moves from the basic or the simple to the complex or abstract.

Howard Gardner's work on multiple intelligences has gained wide recognition and credibility. Gardner's book (1993), *Frames of Mind: The Theory of Multiple Intelligences*, presents the theory of seven intelligences existing beyond the confines of the I.Q. score. Some view Gardner's theory as a philosophy of education or as a meta-model for education with practical, applicable techniques and strategies.

The differentiation of knowledge types and teaching and learning strategies has direct implications for the middle school learner. Middle school students are by nature active and students who are actively involved are more successful than those who are passively involved. The transescent is ready to learn concepts, generalizations, and abstractions. Their cognitive development, discussed in Chapter 1, is at the operational stage and teaching and learning strategies must address this level of development if students are to learn what they are capable of learning.

TEACHER-DIRECTED STRATEGIES

Teaching strategies are activities performed by the teacher during the teaching-learning process. Content can be characterized as either *declarative* knowledge (knowledge about something) or *procedural* knowledge (knowledge about how to do something). Declarative knowledge encompasses facts, concepts, and generalizations. Procedural knowledge is the learning of skills. These knowledge areas are not independent of each other and often interact.

Teaching strategies are based on which of the two knowledge areas is to be taught. Teaching strategies or teacher-directed strategies are those which teachers direct to instruct students and they are useful in teaching facts and basic skills which lead to comprehension, application, and evaluation. These strategies require little active involvement on the part of the student and, as such, have major advantages and disadvantages. These strategies include the following:

(1) *Lecture*—formal lectures where teachers require little or no student participation and informal lectures requiring student questions and comments. Informal lectures are most effective when questions are also asked by teachers to promote the higher cognitive development of students through comprehension, analysis, synthesis, and evaluation.

(2) *Explicit teaching*—also called direct instruction where teachers control the pace and timing of the lesson to test student understanding as the lesson progresses. Explicit teaching allows for student participation. Learning is conducted in small steps and students have class time to work on the content or skills being taught.

(3) *Demonstration*—the use of models or experiments to provide the learner with both auditory and visual learning experiences.

(4) *Recitation*—a type of questioning process (of which there are many) which requires individual student interaction with the teacher. Probing questions form the basis of this interaction and it is used to test the student's knowledge of facts, theories, and laws. It is also used to probe or explore student understanding and generate creative thinking.

(5) *Drill and practice*—used to develop speed and accuracy through repetition. Teachers drill students for information while students respond (practice).

(6) *Discovery learning*—often referred to as problem-solving learning. Discovery learning is designed to show students *how* to learn rather than *what* to learn. Discovery learning can be teacher-supervised through the use of structured activities and materials, or it can be guided, in which case the teacher allows for great flexibility in the discovery activities.

(7) *Brainstorming*—used in quality schools as an effective problem-solving technique and in effective schools to stimulate creative thinking. Teachers interact with students by posing problems and asking probing questions. Students generate ideas and possible solutions. Asking students to formulate ways to evaluate solution outcomes calls for the application of the higher cognitive skills presented by Bloom et al. (1956).

LEARNER-DIRECTED STRATEGIES

Learner-directed strategies are designed to involve students in the learning process and to take the initiative for self-learning. Learners use these strategies to understand the more complex concepts and abstract ideas presented through the teacher-directed learning strategies. These strategies may include the following:

(1) *Problem solving* is an independent or group strategy which allows the student to work on problems posed either by the teacher or the student. Problem-solving activities call for the use of comprehension, analysis, synthesis, application, and evaluation.

(2) *Independent study* is self-directed learning. It allows students an opportunity to identify problems of interest and seek solutions on their own. Teachers act as resource persons and support the students' independent investigations by providing avenues for research and personal encouragement.

(3) *Debates and small group discussion panels* are self-directed learning

strategies wherein the teacher allows students to choose areas of investigation and interact with other students without teacher input. Teachers serve as resource persons and students are free to organize their facts and arguments as they debate the merits of issues or attempt to find solutions to problems.

(4) *Role playing* is also student-directed and can be highly effective. Students act the part or assume the role of another which may require them to assume a different perspective, set of emotions, and values. Often research is needed to play the role if the setting is historical in nature. Role playing also allows students to express their feelings, practice interpersonal skills, and relieve frustration.

Teachers in effective schools integrate the use of both teacher-directed and student-directed learning strategies in their classrooms. The key to their effectiveness lies in the appropriate selection of these strategies for the intended instructional outcomes.

MULTIPLE INTELLIGENCES THEORY

The use of a variety of teaching and learning strategies is central to the implementation of the multiple intelligences theory. Gardner (1993) identified seven "intelligences" found in individuals. People usually develop some of these intelligences to a high level while the other intelligences are either modestly developed or under-developed. Each of these intelligences can be developed to a reasonably high level of performance given the appropriate encouragement, enrichment, and instruction. The seven intelligences work together in complex ways to perform individual functions of social and work life, and there are many ways to demonstrate intelligence characteristics within each of the seven intelligences. Gardner's work seriously challenges the commonly held belief that intelligence, or human potential, can be determined by a single I.Q. score.

Multiple intelligence theory has direct implications for student learning style theories and teaching strategies theories. Learning styles of students are what Gardner (1993) calls "proclivities" or inclinations in specific intelligences and are exhibited at a very early age. By the time they enter school, most students have developed their preferred way of learning (the use of their preferred intelligences). The role of the teacher becomes that of a diagnostician who identifies the student's preferred learning style and then provides instructional activities which best accommodate that style of learning. Gardner cautions that all students can learn through each of the intelligences and care must be taken to nurture those which are not preferred or viewed as dominant.

This theory opens the door to innovative approaches to teaching. Since students have different proclivities, no one set of teaching strategies will be best for all students. Armstrong (1994), in his book *Multiple Intelligences in the Classroom*, presents thirty-five teaching strategies for the seven intelligences which are general in scope and can be applied to any grade level. Following are a few of the examples, by intelligence category, as presented by Armstrong:

(1) Linguistic intelligence: storytelling, brainstorming, and writing journals

(2) Logical-mathematical intelligence: Socratic questioning, calculations and quantifications, and scientific thinking

(3) Spatial intelligence: picture metaphors, idea sketching, and graphic symbols

(4) Bodily-kinesthetic intelligence: hands-on thinking, body maps, and classroom theater

(5) Musical intelligence: rhythms, songs and raps, musical concepts, and discographies

(6) Interpersonal intelligence: people sculptures, cooperative groups, and simulations

(7) Intrapersonal intelligence: goal-setting sessions, choice time, and one-minute reflection periods (Armstrong, 1994, pp. 68–85)

Classroom arrangements and the degree of teacher interaction will differ depending on the teaching-learning strategies employed. Gardner (1993) cautions that not all students will respond in like manner to each of the teaching strategies. This calls for creativity on the part of the teacher to organize the instructional activities to both match and stimulate whole-group instruction. Armstrong (1994) notes that for some students small group and independent work may best facilitate the teaching of certain facts, concepts, and skills while others are engaged in teacher-led activities. Gardner (1993) states that "any concept worth teaching . . . can be approached in at least five different ways" (p. 203) and he designates these varied approaches as "entry points" (p. 203) to the topic. Students will find some entry points into a topic easier than others and, upon entry, will prefer certain paths for pursuing the topic over other paths. Gardner notes:

> Awareness of these entry points can help the teacher introduce new materials in ways in which they can be easily grasped by a range of students; then, as students explore other entry points, they have the chance to develop those multiple perspectives that are the best antidote to stereotypical thinking. (p. 203)

LEADERSHIP AND VISION

Vision, like leadership, means many things to many people with no singularly agreed upon definition. Vision has been defined as lofty goals, a dream, an ideal, shared values, a philosophy, and an inspirational concept. Vision is all of these things and more. The importance of vision is stressed in quality-producing organizations, quality schools, and effective schools (Weller, Hartley, and Brown, 1994). A vision statement expresses purpose and has two major components: it provides purpose and overall direction, and it embodies a philosophical framework for the school. It presents a clear picture of what the leader wants the school to become and an image in which all can share and all can use as a daily criteria for assessing their work.

In effective schools, the importance of goals, norms, and shared values are stressed and translated into a vision for excellence. Principals, as instructional leaders, have a personal vision of their school and their role in making that vision a reality. Without assertive leaders, the dream or ideal, no matter how well-expressed or well-intended, may never materialize. Visionary principals know what they want and then clearly communicate their vision to others. This is especially important in the reform movement of the 1990s. At this time various segments of the public are calling on schools to be all things to all people and to satisfy their many diverse needs and expectations. However, when goals are diverse and conflicting, little if anything is done well.

Vision building starts with the principal who relates the dream of what the school can become through a vision statement. Presented in clear and concise terms and communicated to all, it embodies the high expectations needed to promote teacher and student success. Vision statements are futuristically oriented and serve as an inspiration or guiding force which motivates people to keep going, stay on track, and focus on what is important. Vision helps add meaning to work outcomes and daily efforts. When people see meaning in their work, they strive to grow both personally and professionally (Weller et al., 1994).

Schools that are effective and are quality-oriented have vision statements which focus on curricular and instructional goals, and these goals become the framework for everything the school does. Vision statements have key words which serve as the overarching goals and values for the school and which provide the springboard for joint vision building.

Building a Shared Vision

How does one create a shared vision? The vision statement first presented by the principal acts as an index for achieving excellence and as a point of departure for discussion among teachers, parents, students, and community members. Since the purpose of schooling means many things to many people, teacher responses to the question of the purpose of education will differ from those of students, parents, and members of the community. This disparity is natural since these groups have their own needs, goals, and values. Common ground must be found so groups can work together from a broad yet mutually acceptable definition of what education should be. Therefore, vision-building at the school level should be accomplished by a committee of parents, teachers, students, and community representatives. Teachers, however, must be involved since these are the key people who will make the vision a reality. A teacher representative on the vision-building committee should serve as liaison for teachers.

Core values and beliefs are the foundation on which vision is built. For example, trust, honesty, respect for learning, and the pursuit of excellence are time-honored values which are mutually accepted by both school and society. Core values must be real and not espoused values since the latter will lead to criticism and cynicism when the hypocrisy is revealed, as it will eventually be. Core values are intrinsic beliefs and motivators that are essential to an attainable vision. Four or five core values, agreed upon by group consensus, serve as the nucleus of the purpose or mission statement for the school.

Purpose or mission is the second step in developing vision and is derived from the core values and beliefs. The purpose statement is future-oriented and inspirational, and it conveys the basic human needs to be fulfilled by the school (Drucker, 1974). Broad in scope, the purpose statement allows for dreaming and paints an attainable picture of the future. The question "What do we aspire to be in the future?" provides the guidepost for the purpose statement. An example of a mission statement is: "The school will provide students with the knowledge and skills necessary to be responsible and productive citizens and will foster in students respect for learning, pride in work, and human dignity."

Goals make up the third component of vision and state specifically what the school is to accomplish. Goals clearly focus on the future, guide the school toward its vision, and are specific, action-oriented statements. Goals must be realistic, attainable, and few in number. Too many goals can lead to fragmentation of effort, confusion as to which goals are most important, and a feeling of being overpowered with achievement demands. Five or fewer goal statements are ideal and provide the basis for long-range planning and act as indices to measure the school's progress.

An example of a vision-building model follows. It has been modified from the original Weller et al. (1994) model. To develop a shared school vision, a principal should perform the following steps:

- Step 1: group selection. The principal selects representatives from teachers, parents, community members, staff, and students to develop a school vision, and teaches the vision-building process. Teacher representatives should represent the consensus of teachers.
- Step 2: vision-building orientation. The principal defines vision, its purpose, and its importance to the group and provides a working index for discussion. The vision should reflect the values, purpose, and goals of the school. The principal provides definitions and examples of values, mission, and goals, and these items are discussed among group members. When a clear understanding of these three components of vision exists, group work begins on Step 3, identifying core values.
- Step 3: identifying core values. Core values are those commonly held by family, peers, and society. They are time-honored and mutually accepted by the school and its constituents, and they are the moral fabric of our culture. The principal leads the group to consensus on the core values. An example of core values for achieving school excellence is as follows:
  (1) Having and showing dignity and respect for all people
  (2) Working to one's fullest capabilities and having pride in one's work
  (3) Having the right to a quality education in a safe and orderly environment
- Step 4: writing the mission statement. The mission statement provides an image of the future and accurately reflects the core values of the school. Written in a single sentence, the mission statement provides future direction for the school and answers the question: "What do we aspire to be in the future?" Again, the principal leads the group to consensus. An example of a mission statement is as follows. "Students will have the knowledge and skills necessary to be productive and responsible citizens, will be able to learn in a safe and orderly environment, will take pride in their work, and will be taught by teachers who challenge students to their fullest capabilities while fostering the idea of dignity and respect for all people."
- Step 5: writing goals. Goals state specifically what the school intends to accomplish, are long-range in nature, and will measure what the school hopes to accomplish. Action-oriented, goals serve as the basis for strategic planning and reflect the ideals of schooling. Consensus among group members is a must. Examples of goal statements are as

follows. Goal 1. To provide quality learning through effective schooling processes. Goal 2. To provide a safe and orderly environment. Goal 3. To instill in students respect for all people.
- Step 6: identifying the vision. The vision statement reflects the school's core values, purpose, and goals. It is attainable but futuristic in scope and communicates the heart and mind of the school's teachers, parents, staff, community, and students as it challenges and unites them in an effort to achieve excellence. Again, common agreement is needed among group members since the vision statement is one which will be used to unify and guide the school's staff as they perform their daily responsibilities. An example of a vision statement might be: "Our job, our dedication, and our future is to pursue excellence in education."

Having a vision without commitment is useless. Principals achieve vision through others and they must motivate others to embrace and engage in the school's vision. Constantly modeling the school's vision with enthusiasm sends a clear message to others that the principal supports the vision of the school and is dedicated to its attainment.

Risk of failure is minimized because the vision is developed jointly by the school's constituents. This joint ownership in developing the school's vision provides a level of enthusiasm and commitment among others while modeling the vision serves as a daily reminder of its importance and acceptance. Modeling the school's vision is a leadership behavior which evokes emotion, promotes action, and sustains attention.

LEADERSHIP AND SCHOOL CLIMATE

School climate is made up of identified patterns of perceived or actual behavior in the effective school and it is usually measured by quantitative techniques to isolate and confirm critical behavior patterns. These multivariate analyzed behavior patterns are significant in bringing about school outcomes (Hoy and Miskel, 1991). School culture differs from school climate in that the culture is the sum of strongly held and widely shared basic assumptions and common values found and practiced in the school. Culture is more a symbolic social system which is often abstract and open to interpretation. Culture is investigated through qualitative research methods associated with sociology and anthropology. These research methods provide broad descriptions of the symbols used to convey meaning to the school (Ouchi and Wilkins, 1985).

In effective schools there is an "organizational vitality" that is evidenced through the senses—seeing, hearing, and feeling (Ogden and Germinario, 1994). Effective schools are like a quality product: you know it when you see it, when you use it, or when you buy it. Observable interactions among students, parents, teachers, and principals in classrooms, offices, and halls radiate a common sense of purpose and excitement and a feeling that significant and meaningful learning is taking place whether it be in the cognitive, affective, or psychomotor domains. In effective schools, principals consider the development of a positive school climate as one of their most important tasks since climate has a profound effect on the school, the academic quality of its programs, and the effectiveness of the learning-teaching phenomenon.

In effective schools, the principal is the instructional leader of the school's instructional team and believes the purpose of the school is student learning. As such, the principal sets the example by modeling these behaviors and continuously striving to make improvements in the instructional program to increase its effectiveness. Johnson (1985) notes that in effective middle schools, climate is related to the "driving vision" of the principal which places emphasis on achieving excellence in the four basic areas of school climate: physical, academic, organizational, and socio-emotional. In each of these areas, a high level of caring, responsiveness, and pride is exhibited by the principal and there is a willingness to adapt school practices and programs to the individual differences of students as presented below.

(1) Physical climate
   a. Schools are well-kept and well-lit; grounds are well-manicured and free of litter.
   b. Schools are safe, orderly, and clean; there are no damaged walls, doors, or bathrooms; and halls and classrooms are free of graffiti and trash.
   c. Teachers have good working conditions and well-equipped classrooms.
(2) Academic climate
   a. Teachers and students talk about academics and academics form the basis for leisure activities.
   b. Expectations for success are high for both teachers and students, but they are also reasonable.
   c. Academic achievements are rewarded and widely recognized and achievement is highly prized and respected.
(3) Organizational climate
   a. Schools have few rules. The rules they do have are reasonable, clear, and widely communicated.
   b. Teachers have a large part in decision making concerning school policy, instruction, and curriculum.

   c. Students participate in school-wide decision-making activities and have an influence in policy-making decisions, and the student council serves the school in both an advisory and service capacity.

(4) Socio-economic climate
   a. The school is a welcoming and comfortable place.
   b. There is an aura of respect and trust that permeates the school.
   c. The school feels safe to be in.
   d. The school is a fun place where student needs are met without a sense of irritation.

Academic achievement, faculty morale, and student behavior are directly related to school climate. Shared decision making, collaborative policy making, and a mutual commitment to the goal of making the school effective are clearly evident. According to Bossett, Dwyer, Rowen, and Lee (1982), a warm and supportive environment and relationship among adults and students lead to gains in traditional achievement measures. This environment is fostered by the type of leadership displayed by the principal.

School climate has been compared to an individual's personality. Like personality, the climate of the school projects the sum of the individual and produces an atmosphere which is clearly recognizable. Squires, Huitt, and Segars (1984) found that in effective schools, "climate consists of three weather conditions: an emphasis on academics, an orderly environment, and expectations for success" (p. 66). Effective schools have an ongoing interaction between these variables and teachers, students, principals, and parents.

An emphasis on academics is exhibited by principals, teachers, and students. Students are expected to master their subjects, complete their homework, be prepared for class, complete all project assignments, and obey classroom rules. Teachers are expected to plan ahead for instruction, assign homework, expect students to succeed at their work, spend classroom time on teaching academics, and reward and praise student achievement. Principals support the school's academic focus by doing the following:

(1) Spending most of their time and energy on instructional activities, not administrative work
(2) Modeling daily the vision and climate of the school, and promoting a safe and orderly environment
(3) Providing time, through scheduling, for teachers to plan together for instruction and conferring with teachers about their instructional programs
(4) Observing classrooms regularly, checking on teacher assignments, and rewarding and praising teacher and student accomplishments (Squires et al., 1984)

Connected with the emphasis on academics is an emphasis on basic skills and time on task. Basic skills usually refers to those skills which are tested on standardized achievement instruments—mathematics, reading, science, and social studies. Some interpret basic skill emphasis as working independently with students who fall below acceptable levels of achievement in mathematics and reading. The importance of students having a sound foundation in basic skills is, without question, a primary responsibility of the schools. In effective schools, principals find creative and fun ways to help teachers teach basic skills by employing reading specialists, supplementary teachers, and teacher aides to provide individual and group instruction to students needing basic skills work (Ascik, 1984).

Time on task correlates with student achievement and, in some studies, engaged time has the strongest relationship of any variable to gains in student achievement (Squires et al., 1984). To ensure more time on task, principals restrict classroom interruptions by visitors and P.A. system announcements, have fewer "pull out students," and schedule study breaks instead of recess. Busy work is not instruction. Instruction promotes a high rate of success—90 percent or better—and is tied to learning goals and objectives and clear student performance expectations; in addition, student evaluation instruments are clearly aligned with instructional goals (Spady and Max, 1984).

An orderly environment comes about through a focus on the daily conduct of students and teachers in the school as they adhere to the rules and expectations set forth by the school's culture and climate. Students perceive that discipline and school rules are fair and uniformly applied and that classrooms are safe and orderly places to learn. Students have respect for the school's property and that of others and have positions of responsibility concerning school governance. Teachers start and end lessons on time and control classroom activities. Teachers handle their own discipline problems, administer punishments fairly, enforce the rules equally, and consult with students about their behavior. To provide the framework within which these things occur, principals do the following:

(1) Develop school rules and regulations with teachers and students

(2) Communicate school rules and expectations of teacher and student conduct

(3) Support teachers in the application of school rules and assist teachers through inservice programs or personal coaching in handling their own discipline problems

(4) Deliver punishment which is fair and firm and avoids humiliating students and modeling violence

Expectations for success in effective schools are expressed constantly and in such a way that teachers and students know what is expected of them and that these standards can be attained. These standards increase student motivation and positive self-concept and are correlated with student achievement (Squires et al., 1984). Students believe that teachers help them master their academic work and that hard work is more important than luck in being successful. Students believe that they can achieve and that outside forces will not hamper their success. Teachers believe that their own efforts govern their success and that their own work will bring rewards and recognition. Teachers expect students to succeed and to have high expectations for their own success.

Principals reinforce expectations for success by supporting and modeling the elements associated with an emphasis on academics and an orderly environment. Principals promote expectations for success in the following ways:

(1) Rewarding and praising teachers and students based on their achievements, not on bias or favoritism
(2) Inculcating the idea that working hard provides rewards and making sure that individual effort is praised and recognized
(3) Expecting success from teachers and students (Squires et al., 1984)

The importance of the principal in promoting a positive school climate and culture in effective schools cannot be over-emphasized. Although learning primarily takes place in classrooms, the environment of the classroom is nested within the larger environment of the school which is set by the political-administrative structure advanced by the principal (Mackenzie, 1983). School effectiveness then comes down to those behaviors exhibited in individual classrooms by individual teachers. Teachers themselves must be leaders of their own classrooms and model the behavior of the principal. But without a change in the environment and support for this change from the principal, environmental change in classrooms will not occur. Efficacy and efficiency, therefore, depend on the attitudes, values, and behaviors of the principal. Actively modeling beliefs and values becomes the key to environmental change.

Changes in the environment can be accomplished through a variety of activities. Some of the more common ways are changing school policies, sharing school governance with teachers, setting up teacher-principal strategic planning, providing staff development programs, and making funds available for professional conferences and workshops. The principal must ask "What can I do best to facilitate change in behavior?" and then take the appropriate steps for intervention.

Discipline, part of the school climate in effective schools, is uniformly and quickly administered by teachers and principals and, in effective schools, "has sounded the death knoll of the permissive era in education" (Ascik, 1984, p. 16). Discipline policies are clearly defined, posted, and enforced. Effective instruction cannot take place in classrooms where the environment is disorderly and void of seriousness of purpose. The lack of excessive punishment in effective schools, particularly physical punishment, is evident. Such punishment can lead to low student and teacher morale.

An effective schools study by George and Oldaker (1985) found that when teachers and principals collaborated on policy making, there was a significant reduction in disciplinary problems (80 percent); a significant increase in student emotional health, creativity, and confidence in self-directed learning (80 percent); and a significant increase in positive student self-concept and social development (90 percent). With a decrease in discipline problems, vandalism also decreases and school attendance for teachers and students increases. Schools that are safe and orderly are places where people enjoy being. In such schools, there is a respect for property and the rights of others.

Principals play the most significant role in providing a safe, orderly, and productive learning environment. The key is to allow teachers, students, and parents input in policy-making decisions about the discipline code, the punishments for infractions, and behavioral expectations. It is the responsibility and duty of parents and teachers to support these decisions. The principal has the responsibility of ensuring that the school's code of conduct is distributed and understood by parents and that parental support is provided. Through school and home support, students learn the value of common courtesy, respect for the rights and property of others, and the responsibilities of civil accountability (Hartzell and Petrie, 1992).

LEADERSHIP AND RESEARCH

According to English (1992), "The English word *research* is derived from the French word *researcher*, which means 'to investigate thoroughly' " (p. 338). However, the definition of research is frequently interpreted to mean library research which consists of reading books and articles, gathering references, and presenting the sum of the investigation in some written or documented form. Research of this nature often suffices for college courses but misses the full intent and purpose of research.

Research, according to Charles (1988), is the careful, systematic, patient investigation given to an idea or phenomenon in order to answer a question or seek an explanation about the phenomenon. Different reasoning procedures in research exist: inductive reasoning where the researcher moves from isolated facts or observations to generate theories; and deductive reasoning where the researcher moves from propositions or theories to examine a phenomenon. Hypotheses (propositions) require action on the part of the investigator. Developing the research design or plan to test the hypotheses requires careful, systematic, and patient investigation. Often, control and experimental groups are used to test a hypothesis with the new idea or treatment assigned to the experimental group. Methods to analyze the effects of the treatment are then chosen in accordance with the hypothesis and the research design. Research methods are many but primarily include historical, descriptive, and statistical methods. Findings of the experiment or inquiry are then written and exist for application, debate, or as a source for replication or ideas for new research. This is applied research which is conducted to solve problems or contribute to a body of knowledge.

Most principals and teachers have neither the time, inclination, nor expertise to conduct research. Research findings that have the most significance for them are those which are of a practical nature and easy to apply. Consequently, most practitioners are consumers of research rather than conductors of research. Active consumers of research are found among effective school principals and teachers and it is this active consumption and application of research which largely contributes to making their schools effective.

There are several ways effective principals keep current about research and apply its findings. Active participation in professional organizations provides research-oriented journals with practical suggestions for school improvement. Attendance at professional conferences, seminars, and workshops provides research information and dialogue with other principals about what works and what does not and why.

Principals realize the importance of effective school research both for its ideology and common sense. Effective school research is theory-based and practical, with direct relationship to the daily experiences of educators (Mackenzie, 1983). Squires et al. (1984) note that the value of effective school research lies in its optimism for practitioners and the special promise it holds for transforming ordinary classrooms into those with purpose. Most importantly, the effective schools research actually improves schools if its tenets are embraced and applied.

School improvement implies change and in effective schools principals are the primary change agents. In effective schools, principals take the lead and acknowledge the value of research and move to implement programs that have practical appeal and provide positive results. Hall, Rutherford, Hord, and Hulling (1984) call these principals initiators. Initiators rely on their leadership ability to influence and guide their staff in school improvement. Changing the school's environment is the responsibility of the principal and requires good communication skills and a strong, personal conviction that the effective school criteria is sound. With this commitment principals actively support their staff and participate in the transformation process.

Disagreement exists regarding which strategy to use in transforming schools into effective schools. Brookover, Beamer, Efthim, Hathaway, Lezotte, Miller, Passalacqua, and Tarnatsky (1982) cite research that when everyone is involved in making the decision to change, the only consensus to emerge will be not to change. They suggest that the principal commit to change and then involve the staff in deciding how changes will occur. Essential to this change strategy is a high degree of patience on the part of the principal and the willingness to provide the necessary time and resources. Unless sustained commitment from the principal is evidenced by the staff, teachers will lose enthusiasm and the transformation process is likely to fail. As in those schools implementing the quality philosophy, effective school variables usually take three or more years to yield effective results. There are no quick fixes.

LEADERSHIP AND THE ASSESSMENT OF STUDENT PROGRESS

Effective schools have adopted the quality philosophy of continuous improvement. These schools are never satisfied with their teachers' performance or the performance of their students. To allow for more quality classroom time, principals provide adequate instructional planning time for teachers to plan individually and in teams. This planning time centers around the top priority of monitoring student progress. For example, time is spent on assessing information about student needs; preparing tests and other evaluation instruments to accurately assess student learning; reading research about effective teaching practices and student evaluation techniques; and assessing student achievement through careful examination of homework, projects, reports, and test data (Lezotte and Jacoby, 1992).

Effective schools have a process for how they define mastery learning as well as what knowledge and skills are most essential for students. Methods are then identified or developed to assess mastery. English (1990) relates that in effective school districts, the written, taught, and tested curriculum are aligned. When student evaluation measures accurately reflect what is taught and teachers actually teach what they intended to teach, an accurate measure of mastery can then result.

Classroom assessment in effective middle schools also tests and sets standards for skill demonstration which may not be paper-and-pencil tests. These schools test in a more comprehensive fashion by using assessment measures which test for problem solving, analysis and synthesis, skill performance, and application and evaluation. Assessment is accomplished through both formal and informal assessment techniques.

Formal Assessments

Formal assessment of student performance is usually accomplished through standardized tests of achievement designed to assess mastery of basic skills and to compare student progress both among and within schools. These tests provide the most uniform, valid, and reliable measures of student progress in the basic skills of reading comprehension and mathematics computation. Squires et al. (1984) note that if schools are not successful in teaching basic skills, they are probably not considered successful by parents, the school board, or the community. Moreover, "achievement on standardized tests generally predicts achievement for succeeding years, and gains or deficits in standardized tests tend to have a cumulative effect when viewed across a number of years" (Squires et al., 1984, p. 7). Mastery of the basic skills is essential to future success in school. If students lack a firm foundation in the basics, they lack the essential tools to do more complex and demanding work. The lack of these essential skills often causes frustration within the student due to poor academic performance and may contribute to dysfunctional behavior and lead to school dropout.

The emphasis placed on standardized test results has given rise to a debate on how much help teachers should provide students in getting ready to take these formal assessments of achievement. Some argue that short of teaching the test (telling students the actual questions on the test) teachers should provide students with the competitive edge to do their best by using the same examples in their classroom instruction as are found in questions on the test. For example, if pie charts, histograms, and the like are used to test understanding of percents and fractions, teachers should use these graphs in their own classroom instruction. Some effective schools teach their students test-taking skills. It seems only natural that any competitive edge educators can provide their students, short of actually teaching test questions, is acceptable (Weller and Weller, 1997).

Informal Assessments

Informal assessment measures of student progress, constructed by teachers, should accurately reflect what is taught in the classroom and should be continuous, valid, reliable, and comprehensive measures of achievement. Content assessment takes place before, during, and after instruction. This ensures continuous monitoring of student progress. It is essential that content being tested coincides with the student's prior learning and mastery of skill and knowledge areas. Since students cannot be expected to master material without the prerequisite knowledge or skills, pre- and post-tests should be administered to determine what students know prior to any type of instruction. Pre- and post-testing supplements other information on student readiness such as prior grades, standardized test results, and cumulative portfolios. Pre- and post-testing is a strong diagnostic tool to help teachers individualize and group for instruction.

Content which is assessed must be taught by the teacher and reflect the goals and objectives of the curriculum. Content which is assessed but not taught yields lower gains in student achievement and reveals virtually nothing about student progress or learning. Following are some typical informal assessment techniques.

Teacher-made tests are the most common informal assessment technique, and these tests should be valid and reliable. Valid means the test is an accurate assessment of what is taught or what it purports to measure. Reliable means that a test yields consistent, noncontradictory results. In other words, it is a consistent and accurate measure of that which it is supposed to measure. Consequently, assessing reliability is a more straightforward concept than validity since it addresses the accuracy of measurement rather than the appropriateness of measurement. In assessing reliability, computation can be used. In assessing validity, judgment is the assessment criteria. When tests have been assessed for validity and reliability, teachers are on safer ground when they report student progress in quantifiable terms.

There are five different types of test validity with each type having its own method of assessing the validity for its specific purpose or use. These are content validity, criterion-related validity, concurrent validity, predictive validity, and construct validity. For classroom tests, teachers need be most concerned about content validity. For a full discussion of all five types of test validity, see Borg and Gall (1989).

Content validity should be of primary concern to classroom teachers because it is the most important property of any measuring instrument. Content validity is the degree to which test items represent the content to be tested. Content validity is not to be confused with "face validity" which is subjective judgment as to what the test "appears" to measure. Rather, content validity is acquired through questions which are truly representative of the classroom content being tested and appear on the test in a complete and balanced way.

The degree to which test content is valid is not expressed in a correlation coefficient as are other types of test validity, but is assessed "by an objective comparison of the test items with curriculum content" (Borg and Gall, 1989, p. 176). For classroom teachers, developing content validity is an easy process and should be done every time teaching objectives and instructional content change. Teachers can develop content validity by doing the following:

(1) Follow a logical, systematic appraisal system to ensure there is a direct relationship between the content covered and content tested. There must be a balance between test items on the test and covered content.

(2) When writing test questions, correlate each question to the objective of the content covered in the classroom. This includes both textbook and all supplementary material content used for instruction. Reference each test item with page number, paragraph, and sentence of content material on a separate worksheet.

(3) Submit the test to a "panel of judges," peer teachers who are well-acquainted with the content. Here, two or more teachers or school administrators may serve as judges. Judges assess each test item and indicate whether the items measure predetermined criteria, objectives, and/or content.

(4) Revise test items based on judges' recommendations and resubmit for a second appraisal of content validity. The goal is to get greater than 90 percent agreement between test questions and content.

This same procedure can be used for essay questions. In essay questions, the domain being assessed (cognitive or affective) needs to be specified as well as the specific objectives within each domain's hierarchy. The question(s) must then be accompanied by content covered in the classroom which is referenced to the test question(s) and the objectives found in the hierarchy being assessed. A sample exemplary answer to the question(s) should accompany the material presented to the panel of judges. Revision in essay questions should be made in accordance with the judges' recommendations and a second review process should then follow.

Reliability is the extent to which a test or measurement is accurate and consistent over time. To be highly reliable, the test must consistently measure whatever it purports to measure, over time. Because no measurement instrument is perfect, there is variability or error associated with all tests. However, the smaller the error, the greater the reliability of the test.

Error in measurement comes from a variety of factors but is usually attributed to the test itself, human conditions, or the surroundings in the testing site. The goal in developing tests with high reliability is to minimize the influences of error that make test results ambiguous or unreliable. McMillan and Schumacher (1984) identify some of the most common error sources as being ambiguity in test wording, confusing directions, inadequate number of items to measure an attribute, noise or interruptions when test-taking takes place, and human conditions such as student health, motivation, fatigue, anxiety, and attitude. High reliability on a test is not, however, sufficient in itself for a good classroom test. As Hopkins and Antes (1990) point out, a test may be highly reliable, it may do what it is doing with high reliability, but still have low validity—not doing what it *should be* doing.

An important consideration exists when teachers plan to build high reliability into their classroom tests. They must make sure the test is domain-referenced. That is, they must stratify test items from carefully specified content area to be tested. For example, students "will be able to add two-digit numbers with regrouping" instead of students "will be able to demonstrate achievement in arithmetic." Writing problems to test problem-solving skills instead of fact skills in basic addition requires a different domain application. Consequently, careful delineation of the domains within subject areas should be done prior to writing test items and these should serve as guides for test development.

The reliability coefficients vary for tests between zero and ± 1.00 with 1.00 or -1.00 indicating perfect reliability. Because error contributes to variance in reliability coefficients, the closer reliability scores are to 1.00, the more the test is free of error variance, such as test wording and other human factors cited above. Coefficients of .80 or greater generally indicate acceptable test reliability; that is, student test results will probably be influenced more by student knowledge than by error variability.

There are several ways to compute test reliability for classroom use. These include split-half reliability, a method for rational equivalence, alternate-form reliability, and test-retest reliability. Each takes into account different sources of error. Borg (1987) notes that higher reliability coefficients can be found in single test administrations rather than in test-retest or split-half testing situations which are more prone to the inclusion of human error factors. The single administration of a test can easily assess reliability for classroom teachers and will yield a dependable estimate of the test's reliability.

Teachers wanting to assess reliability can follow the procedure listed below:

- Step 1. Taking the test items developed through the test validity process, develop at least a 30 item test (the longer the test, the more likely it is to have an acceptable degree of reliability—a coefficient of .80 or better).
- Step 2. Arrange test scores (X_i's), by student names, in a column.
- Step 3. Compute the average test score (M) for all students taking the test by dividing the total number of all student raw scores by the number of students taking the test (this is the same process used to get the arithmetic mean).
- Step 4. Compute the standard deviation of the student scores:

$$s^2 = \frac{\Sigma(X_i - M)^2}{N}$$

where s^2 is the variance, $\Sigma(X_i - M)^2$ is the sum (Σ) of the squared deviation scores, $(X_i - M)$ is the deviation score, and N is the total number of scores.

- Step 5. After computing and squaring the standard deviation, all information exists to compute the KR-21 or Kuder-Richardson Formula 21 to assess test reliability. The KR-21 formula is:

$$KR\text{-}21 = \frac{(K)(s^2) - M(K - M)}{s^2(K - 1)}$$

In the example presented in Figure 2.1, after computing the mean, standard deviation, variance, and total, the KR-21 formula is applied to get a test reliability coefficient with 15 students and a total of 40 test questions.

Variable	Mean	Standard Deviation	Variance	Sum
Scores	25.07	5.35	28.64	376.00
Square	655.07	259.46	6719.50	9826.00

Substituting the above computation into the KR-21 formula, the reliability coefficient (r) for the test is obtained.

That is:

$$KR\text{-}21 = \frac{(K)(s^2) - M(K - M)}{s^2(K - 1)}$$

$$= \frac{40(28.64) - 25.07(40 - 25.07)}{28.64(40 - 1)}$$

$$= \frac{1445.6 - 25.07(14.93)}{1116.96}$$

$$= \frac{771.3049}{1116.96}$$

$$r = .6905$$

The .6905 is the reliability coefficient of the classroom test and this is too low for acceptable reliability. The teacher should analyze the test items for students' misinterpretation of test item wording and the accuracy of content coverage. If necessary, more test items should be added and the revised test should be rechecked for reliability.

	Student	Test Score (X_i)	Test Score Squared
1.	Jill	$26 = X_1$	676
2.	Tom	$29 = X_2$	841
3.	Sally	28 etc.	784
4.	Pete	20	400
5.	Sam	21	441
6.	Jack	33	1089
7.	Maud	15	225
8.	Judy	19	361
9.	Eva	26	676
10.	Ted	28	784
11.	Joe	29	841
12.	Linda	18	324
13.	Donna	24	576
14.	Bill	28	784
15.	Harry	32	1024
	TOTAL	376	9826

FIGURE 2.1. Test scores of 15 students on a test of mathematical problem solving [Kuder-Richardson (KR-21) formula].

Assessing reliability for essay questions focuses on the preparation of the questions and their scoring. The major difference between objective and essay tests is the response form. Essays are usually written in ways most appealing or appropriate to the test question writer (teacher). It is argued that essay tests lend themselves more to the appraisal of higher-level cognitive processes than objective tests. Therefore, teachers often use essay tests to assess reasoning, judgment, conceptualization, originality and creativity, abstract thinking, arguments, and inference. However, in attempting to assess these higher order skills, higher scorer reliability is lacking which defines the essence of the objective test—consistency in scoring test responses. There are several precautions a teacher can take to make the scoring of essay tests more consistent from one student to another student and minimize sources of human error which promote test unreliability. Teachers need to be cognizant of the following error sources while grading essays.

(1) *The "halo effect"*—this is an error in judgment of the scorer of the qual-

ity of the answer made by the student due to the over-all quality of the paper. Should the student write well or impress the scorer on an answer to a question during the first part of the test, later test questions may be favorably evaluated even though they lack quality. Ideally, the teacher should read the responses of all students to a single question, grade the question, and then move on to subsequent questions.

(2) *Influence of extraneous factors*—judgment is influenced by beauty of handwriting, correct grammar, and spelling, or the overall organization of the response. Ideally, the scorer should make a list of the essential factors (content, facts, etc.) that should be found in the "ideal" essay answer. Some suggest the "ideal" answer be written by the scorer for each essay question and then used as the grading key. The "ideal" answer should be broken down into its essential components and a specific number of points should be assigned to each component. Students should know in advance what the component parts are and the scoring weight assigned to each component.

(3) *Name recognition*—judgments are sometimes made before reading the answers to test questions based on student names. This can be overcome to a degree by using codes devised by students in place of names on the test, and the code sheet should be withheld from the scorer until grades are assigned. This does not work in small classes where handwriting is easily identified or when students take make-up tests due to absences.

(4) *No scoring key*—when no scoring key is made, and several essays have to be graded, the scorer is subject to a reliance on intuition about the quality of the responses from one test to another. This is especially true between the first and last essays read by the scorer when memory becomes a factor in test scoring. That is, the first paper may be excellent, receive a grade of 98, but the last essay read may be even better but receive a grade of 90. Scoring keys keep scorers from grading from intuition or grading from memory lapses.

Enhancing the reliability of essay tests can be accomplished during the development phase of test construction. Teachers can do the following to ensure greater test reliability:

(1) Allow adequate time for constructing the test. Do not write tests carelessly or in haste. This leads to a poor sampling of content coverage and ambiguity in test questions.

(2) Write the essay question in accordance with the procedures used to ensure test validity as discussed earlier. That is, make sure content to be tested is covered in class, provide clear and adequate directions, use understandable terms which have been defined in class, and specify ex-

actly how the student is to answer each essay question. Do not direct the student to merely "discuss" the topic.

(3) Asking several short answer questions is often preferable to asking a few questions demanding long answers. Several short-answer questions can more adequately cover the content being tested than one or two questions designed to assess the overall content covered in class.

(4) Teacher should carefully reread each question to ensure that questions do not focus on recall and fact-based data. These knowledge areas are best assessed through objective-type tests.

(5) Although time consuming, a panel of judges (peers) should be used to evaluate the results of the tests. Judges should have a copy of the scoring key and point distribution for each question. Two or more judges should be used with their evaluations being given equal weight to that of the teacher. Each evaluation should be carefully assessed, the questions rewritten, based on the merit of assessments, and resubmitted to the judges for a final critique.

Homework is another informal assessment technique. In effective schools homework is not busy work but purposeful work having two major goals. First, homework is used to monitor student understanding of class content and, second, it extends academic time on task which correlates strongly to student achievement. Homework is most effective when it reinforces or allows for practice of classroom learning, challenges students to go beyond that which is covered in the classroom (without causing frustration), and is used to provide immediate feedback to students about their progress (Squires et al., 1984). Brophy and Good (1986) found that while the amount of homework will vary in effective schools, there is a positive correlation between the number of hours spent on homework per week and student achievement.

Homework which is graded, commented on, and returned quickly increases student achievement (Elawar and Corno, 1985). Teacher comments not only serve to reinforce student learning but reflect the teacher's awareness of students' progress toward mastery. Incomplete or incorrect homework should be reassigned and rechecked. Teachers should have a homework checklist which correlates with skill and/or knowledge area(s) being assessed and they should use this as an additional record of student mastery and progress.

Observation, either direct or indirect, is another informal method which can be used to assess student mastery and progress. Teachers observe students constantly in their classrooms and these observations, conducted correctly, can provide important information about student learning. Guerin and Maier (1983) relate that direct observation procedures are effective when conducted systematically and when student responses are recorded on an observation checklist. Indirect observations call for teacher memory and are more subjective in nature since student assessments are made expost facto and usually without explicit criteria relating to specific instructional objectives being assessed. Indirect observations become more valid when periodic logs are kept on each student's progress and consulted prior to each grading period.

Portfolio assessment is a collection of student work and is of two kinds: teacher-collected and student-collected. In teacher-collected portfolios, the collection of student work provides the teacher with an overview of the development of each student's abilities. Student-collected portfolios contain work students select themselves and reflect their best efforts in accordance with the criteria set by the student and/or teacher. Portfolio assessments have particular value to the middle school learner. Portfolios are more developmentally responsive to the goals of the middle school and promote higher cognitive levels of thinking while actively engaging students in making decisions about what reflects their best work effort and why (Maeroff, 1991).

In summary, classroom evaluation methods designed to monitor middle school student progress, whether formal or informal, take into account several carefully considered procedures. The use of a variety of student assessment methods provides a more realistic and concise picture of student development and achievement. Classroom assessments must be continuous, valid, reliable, and comprehensive and tests should be designed for specific purposes. For transescents, comprehensive and frequent evaluation is essential since students develop at different rates and times physically, socially, emotionally, and intellectually.

LEADERSHIP AND PARENTAL INVOLVEMENT PROGRAMS

Effective school principals take the initiative in developing parental involvement programs and fostering a school culture where parents feel welcome and are viewed as important members of the school's instructional team. Parent involvement in school activities not only promotes student achievement, but it also fosters a more positive attitude toward school on the part of the student (Jones, 1991).

Good home-school relations come about as a result of hard work on the part of the principal and teachers. Opportunities must be provided for parents to be actively involved in the school and make positive and meaningful contributions to their children's education. Principals have the primary responsibility for implementing such programs and ensuring that teachers support and foster parent involvement. Epstein (1987, 1988) elaborates on meaningful ways principals can involve parents. First, use parents as re-sources and aides in the schools; second, involve parents in school govern-ance, advisory, and planning committees; third, have an active PTA program; and fourth, have a comprehensive parent-school communication network which informs parents about the school's goals and objectives and their children's achievements. Parent programs are more likely to succeed when they are based on high expectations for parent involvement and when they accommodate the specific needs of families.

Middle schools responsive to the unique needs of the early adolescent learner implement involvement programs which provide parents with the particular skills necessary to be effective educational partners. Johnson (1990) describes these schools as "family friendly" and identifies three ar-eas of focus for effective principals: (1) they are aware of the family back-grounds of their students, (2) they provide special programs and services needed to help parents help their children, and (3) they provide a variety of avenues for parent participation in school activities.

ORGANIZATION OF HOME-SCHOOL PROGRAMS

Effective schools have parent involvement programs which are compre-hensive in scope and designed to meet the specific needs of parents and stu-dents. A 1993 study by the National Committee for Citizens in Education (NCCE) found that parent programs which address the needs and interests of parents are more likely to have high participation and to make a critical difference in the school's efforts to raise student achievement regardless of their socioeconomic status. The NCCE report also found that active paren-tal involvement through a variety of activities improved student attitudes toward school, reduced the number of discipline problems, and contributed to the overall success of the school.

Parent surveys are the starting point for building an effective home-school program. Principals lay the foundation for a strong parent involvement pro-gram by assessing the needs and interests of parents. Coupled with student records and teacher input, this information provides data on the educational background of parents, language skill levels, ethnic and cultural back-grounds, and family structure. Because of the changing and varied make-up of the family unit, a variety of programs is needed for meaningful impact. Traditional programs such as PTA and Open House are no longer sufficient.

From the survey information, programs for parents are developed which target their particular needs. Such programs might include the following:

(1) *Parenting skills development programs* provide information on the

growth and development characteristics of the transescent and on how to deal effectively with these children as they develop socially, physically, emotionally, and intellectually. Discipline procedures and conflict resolution skills are pertinent topics for middle school parents.

(2) *Parents-as-learning-partners programs* provide parents with information on how to assist the school in reinforcing its goals and objectives at home, the importance of providing structured time to complete homework and other assignments, and the importance of parents being actively engaged with their children as they complete school work.

(3) *Nutrition, health, and child safety programs* provide information to parents about these essential areas as they specifically relate to this age group. Topics such as balanced diet, personal hygiene, and drug and alcohol use are of particular interest to middle school parents.

(4) *General learning programs* provide information and lists of books, journals, and videos for parents to explore various topics of their own interests and responsibilities as they relate to parenting. Some schools conduct regularly scheduled discussion groups on topics suggested by parents; others have year-long video-viewing seminars where parents attend sessions of their choice and discuss the video's content with a teacher or expert.

(5) *Parent involvement programs* provide information on the various kinds of activities available to parents and the roles and responsibilities parents have as participants in these activities. These activities may include school governance and advisory councils, volunteer programs, clubs, and enrichment groups.

Effective middle school programs focus on basic family obligations. They have counselors and health professionals develop specific programs to help parents provide healthy lifestyles for their children and to help them learn about adolescent development. Without a thorough understanding of the developmental characteristics of the transescent, parents cannot be effective partners in their children's education (Epstein, 1987).

Through these programs, schools solicit active support from parents. Since many parents work and daily involvement is out of the question, principals look for creative ways to involve parents in school activities. Such activities can take place once a month or once a year, on weekends or evenings, or during school break. Some ways principals can involve parents are as field trip chaperones, library and classroom aides, tutors, story readers, guest speakers, clerical assistants, and volunteers.

In successful volunteer programs principals extend personal invitations to potential volunteers, match volunteers to their interest areas, and give recognition to those volunteering. Principals offer recognition through

awards ceremonies, certificates of appreciation, announcements of participation in local newspapers, and pictures of parent volunteers displayed in
the school's reception area. These programs have orientation programs conducted by the principal which acquaint the parent with their assigned duties
and responsibilities, the philosophy and policies of the school, and the people with whom they will work.

Teachers who have not worked with aides or volunteers before will need
to be briefed on the effective use of their parent volunteers. Teachers and
their volunteers need to plan together so parent interests and skills can be
maximized. Parents who feel their efforts are meaningful and appreciated
will have sustained commitment to their work and will be a source of good
public relations for the school.

School governance and advisory councils are vehicles which allow parents to make policy decisions at the school level. The principal should use
two major criteria for the selection of parents for school governance committees. First, parents must be competent and willing to make meaningful
contributions to the school's effort. Second, parent representation should
reflect a cross section of the student population. With principals selecting
committee members and serving as members of parent committees, certain
pitfalls can be avoided which may lead to dysfunctional work. Principals
make clear the mission and goals of the committee and provide direction
when members seek to use their membership as a platform for their own political agendas. Next, principals work with those parents who lack the necessary background to understand specific educational problems. And
finally, principals provide the ongoing support and encouragement necessary to sustain enthusiasm, commitment, and goal attainment.

Parent involvement in policy decisions has maximum benefit when parent representatives understand their roles as committee members. Their major function is to assist principals and teachers in identifying problems and
proposing solutions that are specific to the school, not the school system.
Areas for parent involvement in school governance include strategic planning for long- and short-term goals, establishing budgetary priorities, planning for curriculum change, and improving school-community relations.

Parental involvement in advisory committees has several other advantages:

(1) Parents bring a broad range of experience and expertise to the committee which provides for different perspectives and solutions to problems.
(2) Parents can relate concerns and problems about the school from community members of which school personnel may be unaware.
(3) Parents are often a part of a larger community network and can relate the
positive aspects and achievements of the school and garner greater support and acceptance of the school efforts in the community.

(4) Parent representatives can relate to the concerns of other parents and provide the school's perspective from a parental point of view.

(5) Parents often have access to the business community which can open doors for greater student participation in community programs and provide additional resources for the school's instructional programs.

OTHER WAYS TO INVOLVE PARENTS

Some parents choose not to be actively involved in school activities. Active parental involvement is important and desirable, but as Davies (1991) points out, the real goal of any home-school program is to attain parent support for the school's educational mission. Support comes from home involvement and an understanding of what the school is trying to accomplish and that parent support is essential in maximizing these educational benefits for their children. Information to parents aimed at garnering such support can be communicated in a variety of ways:

(1) *Newsletters* are often the major source of information parents receive about the school. They should be frequently published (at least monthly), contain concise and easy to read information, and encourage parents to respond to its contents. Information often found in newsletters concerns the school's curriculum and instructional programs, study and discussion groups, services provided by the school, the school's mission, student and teacher accomplishments, parent involvement programs, calendar of school events, programs needing parent involvement, school achievement and ranking data, and a principal's message section which is serious in tone and highly informative about current trends and happenings in education. In school systems with large non-English speaking families, steps should be taken to accommodate various language preferences.

(2) *Letters to parents* which are personal in nature and come from the principal and teacher improve communication and foster greater support for the school. Letters should both praise the child and solicit parental support in specific areas needing reinforcement. Form letters to parents should be used sparingly and then should be personally signed on top quality paper with quality print. All written publications present an image of the school and poorly written or printed material conveys the wrong message.

(3) *Telephone calls,* like letters, should be positive in tone and express praise for student achievement or conduct before soliciting parental assistance. Telephone calls require tact and good judgment, and profes-

sional and courteous behavior are a must. Care should be taken to avoid conflict over the telephone through a negative tone of voice or negative remarks about the student. Praise and assistance are called for over the telephone, but more serious matters concerning students are best reserved for conferences at school.

(4) *Home meetings with parents* are highly effective ways to communicate with parents, especially those who are not willing to participate in school activities such as PTO, Open House, or Parent-Teacher Conferences. The principal and some of the teachers of the students schedule short, highly informative meetings with parents in their homes. Information is shared about the school, events and activities for parental involvement, and the progress of the student.

PROMOTING MIDDLE SCHOOL LEADERSHIP: CASE STUDIES

West Jackson County Middle School in Jefferson, Georgia embraces the quality principles of Deming (1986) and the student-oriented philosophy of the true middle school. The principal, Walker Davis, is past president of the Georgia Middle School Association and was one of four original grant recipients to start middle school education in Georgia. Known as a middle school innovator throughout Georgia, Davis believes in *Kaizen* (Japanese for unending improvement) and in *gambare* (Japanese for persistence) as driving quality forces to provide excellence in the school's program.

Modeling, to Davis, is a key to leadership success. "If the principal doesn't model his expectations, how can he expect improvement?" He goes on to say that modeling ensures constancy of purpose, builds trust and commitment among teachers, and sustains the school's climate. "Getting teachers to buy into your beliefs is an internal process which comes from their own success and self-satisfaction," he states. Davis notes that good practical-applications inservice programs are essential to providing teachers the skills and knowledge they need to get any program started.

According to Davis, trust, from the interpersonal perspective, is another key variable to successful leadership and is crucial in developing a healthy school climate. Trust is a relationship, not an attitude, which requires full participation and takes time to develop. Davis points to the school's shared governance model as an example of implementing the trust factor. At West Jackson County Middle School (WJCMS) governance is shared through a five-layered group approach to problem solving and decision making. Grade level teachers, grades 6 through 8, make up one team; the academic block or interdisciplinary teacher teams form another group; special programs and exploratory teachers comprise the third group; and the principal, assistant principal, school counselor, and media specialist make up a fourth team. The school counselor and media specialist "float" with membership status in each of the other groups since their functions cut across instructional categories. The fifth group is the school-wide leadership team consisting of a representative from each subgroup. This team is chaired by the principal and includes the school counselor and media specialist. The importance of applying technology to improve instruction and adhering to the student-centered philosophy of the middle school makes participation of the media specialist and counselor on all teams a must.

Trust was first developed among the 43 teachers at WJMCS through the following steps:

- having teachers develop the quality-oriented vision and mission statements of the school with minimal input from the principal and assistant principal
- allowing teachers to develop yearly instructional goals and action plans to achieve these vision-related goals
- allowing teachers to make decisions on how goals were to be achieved and the resources and time needed to achieve them

Administrators serve as facilitators of the school's goals. Figure 2.2 presents the goals and action plans for WJCMS for the 1996–1997 academic year.

Davis points out that informing teachers up front about negotiable and non-negotiable items in their school governance role does much to foster trust between him and his staff. The only non-negotiable items are practices or programs which violate federal, state, or local school board policy. At the local level, if board policy or superintendent mandate conflicts with WJCMS goals, efforts are made on his behalf to work within the framework of existing practices. "If policy is made for the good of the students, it can be unmade for that same purpose," Davis states. Davis believes that keeping his word is absolutely crucial to the trust factor: "I don't *ever* go back on my word, or there would be hell to pay. They [teachers] would either run me off or they would leave themselves. That's a no-win situation."

Good communication and conflict management skills are essential leadership skills which also foster good school climate. Davis notes the importance of open and honest communication between teachers and teachers and between teachers and principal in building trust and reducing conflict. Effective communication for Davis is measured by how well the goals of the school are being implemented, the quality of classroom instruction, and the daily behaviors of teachers as they interact with their students. Davis does a lot of "management by walking around" at which time he reinforces the student-centered quality philosophy of the school through brief talks with

A.   Instructional Goals

    1.   Reduce the end-of-year retention rate for students in grades six through eight.

    2.   Involve more parents and community members in the education of students grades six through eight.

    3.   Improve overall reading scores and reading comprehension subtest scores in grades six through eight.

    4.   Improve active student participation in all areas of the curriculum to improve student attendance rates.

B.   Action Plans

    1.   Establish the "Save Our Student Program" for those students in danger of repeating a grade level or having academic problems.

    2.   Establish a monthly parent and community member breakfast program with students, teachers and administrators.

    3.   Establish a more comprehensive parent and community school and classroom volunteer program.

    4.   Establish more school-business partnerships with local and area businesses.

    5.   Establish the "Book Smart Program" for students in grades six through eight.

    6.   Establish a "participation points system" for students in grades six through eight.

    7.   Establish an "attendance lottery" for students in grades six through eight.

FIGURE 2.2. West Jackson County Middle School's instructional goals and action plans (1996–1997).

teachers and staff personnel. Davis finds that repetition, repeating the vision and mission of the school in different ways at different times, is the most important factor in maintaining the quality-oriented, student-centered climate. "Either they [teachers and staff] get tired of my persistence and leave, or they catch the climate and talk-the-talk back to me," he says.

Developing good interpersonal skills, adopting a win-win philosophy, and seeking areas for compromise with teachers and staff are essential in reducing personal conflict and achieving constancy of purpose. Teachers and administrators need training in conflict resolution skills which can help get at what Davis calls "the real issue, the bottom line of the problem." Davis notes that if principals cannot or are unwilling to make or take time and expend the effort to get to the root of teacher conflict or frustration and then pursue measures to eliminate these roadblocks to professional and personal development, morale problems arise that not only spread but detract from classroom performance. Davis says that such situations "eat away at the school climate and ultimately impact students negatively." To Davis, the goals and policies of the school should serve teacher needs as well as student needs.

Knowing how and when to delegate responsibility is another key leadership skill according to Davis. To delegate effectively, the principal must first know the strengths and limitations of the teachers, and, second, the principal must match the teachers' responsibilities to their strengths and motivational levels. Davis prefers oral communication over written correspondence. A persuasive speaker, he communicates orally and delegates written communication to the assistant principal. Teams of teachers are given maximal latitude in making decisions on the best use of instructional time within the block schedule. Davis relates that in the first year of block scheduling, teachers were always checking with him about decreasing or increasing instructional time for core courses or changing the sequence in which they were taught. His philosophy is that the teacher is the educational expert, and the schedule and its time modules are merely tools to facilitate instruction. His practice of directing all questions about instructional management to teacher teams is standard practice and he believes that his intervention at this point would show lack of trust in the teachers and the governance structure. Davis does review lesson plans weekly to point out potential policy problems and offer suggestions for dealing with these problems.

Another example of team decision making and responsibility at WJCMS was the teachers' decision to eliminate bells signaling the start and finish of classes. Effective schools research (Lezotte, 1991) found that such interruptions thwart student learning and concentration. According to Davis, the decision was made to pilot test the elimination of bells for one year. After only nine weeks, the teachers called for the permanent elimination of bells, and classes now change with synchronized classroom clocks for exploratory courses and the advisor/advisee program.

Knowledge of school management is yet another key leadership skill. "In the real world," Davis states, "you had better be a good manager—good at attending to the nuts and bolts of school administration—or the lofty ideals of principal as leader will be short-lived. You can't lead if you don't have leadership position." Lunenburg and Ornstein (1996) endorse this practical approach to leadership by noting the importance of principals having knowledge of scheduling practices, budget and finance processes, school law, and personnel policies. Paperwork from the superintendent's office, reports from state and federal agencies, and annual budget preparation and teacher evaluations are a few of the managerial tasks that must be performed accurately and on time. One of the quickest ways to get into trouble with the superintendent, Davis notes, is "to start dropping the ball on the paper-work." In any bureaucracy, the performance of one layer depends on the performance of another. "If you want to lead," says Davis, "you first pay attention to management tasks and *then* pay attention to your leadership responsibilities."

Creekland Middle School in Lawrenceville, Georgia is a Georgia Middle School of Excellence and winner of the International Inviting School Award. Led by Joan Akin, a principal with a dynamic personality who has an abounding enthusiasm for her job and is deeply dedicated to the philosophy of the true middle school, Creekland Middle School (CMS) typifies the description of high performing schools found in effective schools research. Akin believes that "the principal sets the tone for the school and then provides the drive necessary for promoting quality instruction." Tone translates into school climate, the aura which permeates both the interior and exterior of the school, and creating a positive school climate is Akin's top priority. "When students are in a pleasant, warm, and friendly environment, when they feel safe and secure, when school goals are clearly communicated [to them], and when they are taught by caring teachers, students know what's important." This kind of atmosphere, she says, promotes pride, a sense of belonging, and mutual respect among students and teachers.

Creekland Middle School's exterior is plush with well-manicured grounds and the school is surrounded by a plethora of seasonal planting which sets the external tone of the school. Waterfalls greet visitors in the main foyer and relax them in the library. Pictures of students adorn the walls of highly polished, spacious hallways. Classrooms and office areas are richly carpeted, have color-complemented furnishings, and have plants throughout the interior which radiate with ambiance. The interior "feeling" comes from warm and caring interactions between and among teachers, staff, and students which can best be characterized as polite, friendly, and professional.

But just how is this internal climate developed? Akin says there is "no magic formula to creating atmosphere, just simple, common sense." Agreeing with Walker Davis, principal at West Jackson Middle School, Akin says that trust is a crucial factor in health climates. Trust-building, both principals maintain, takes time and effort, and has to begin with genuine caring and respect for each individual as a unique human being. Akin adds that to build trust, "your word has to be your bond, and your actions have to be consistent and predictable. You must model what you expect from others."

Akin's personal philosophy that "no problem or concern is too small" for her attention also fosters a positive school climate. "Each concern of every person in my school is my concern because it affects their daily lives as people and professionals." Her door is always open to students, teachers, and staff; and she listens, provides advice, and offers help. In both formal and informal conversations with teachers, staff, and students, Akin makes the vision and mission of the school topics of conversation with her enthusiastic attitude clearly punctuating the importance she places on these goals. "Quality and excellence in education are our goals, but I tell my teachers that first of all, all decisions must be for the good of the student, not for themselves or the parents." Staff members, clerical, food-service, and custodial, are important in contributing to school climate. Akin and her assistant principals meet regularly with support personnel to discuss their concerns and needs and to remind them of the important roles they play in meeting the school's vision.

"Creating a sense of family," Akin says, "does a lot for school climate." Each fall, a retreat is scheduled in a recreational area where administrators, teachers, and staff personnel get together for a weekend "to just have fun." Playing softball, board games, and having cookouts, says Akin, builds friendship and trust. While no formal agenda exists, participants often "dream a little" and seeds are planted for innovation and change. But what happens, she says, is that "the interaction really promotes a sense of community, a common but important reason why all of us are at Creekland Middle School."

Empowering teachers, another way of demonstrating trust, is central to the CMS governance structure. One of the largest middle schools in the nation, CMS is the largest in Georgia with over 2,300 students (Steep, 1996). Creekland is organized into grade level communities with five communities housing grades six, seven, and eight. Each community is located in a separate wing, has its own assistant principal, and practices interdisciplinary team teaching. Each team schedules its own instructional time for their students for teaching mathematics, language arts, social studies, science, and reading, and for work with other support personnel in the school. Each community has its own counselor who is a member of teacher teams and coordinates the advisor/advisee program. Exploratory teachers are adjunct team members at the time students are taking those courses. Each group of students has a homeroom, their own lockers within the room and, with the exception of physical education and some exploratory courses, instruction is carried out within the community wing. There are five assistant principals and each of them has an instructional area of expertise (the four core subjects plus physical education and health) and they "float" among grade level teams to provide assistance in these instructional areas.

While interdisciplinary teacher teams are the foundation for instructional decision making and problem solving, the School-Wide Leadership Team

STATEMENT OF PHILOSOPHY
(Vision and Mission)

The Creekland Middle School faculty and staff believe that all children have the right to develop to their fullest potential. We further believe that education is a vehicle by which individuals may advance; therefore, we are committed to providing all students with the best possible educational opportunities, thereby contributing to their success as individuals and future citizens.

We believe that students should be guided through a curriculum in which careful attention has been given to the growth characteristics of pre- and early adolescents. In keeping with these ideals, flexibility in student learning activities must be provided and a variety of teaching methods and strategies employed. Students should be encouraged to explore and develop their interests in a wide range of activities through courses dealing with academic, cultural, and motor skills. We further believe that learning is a lifelong endeavor, and thus, should be approached as a process, rather than as an end in itself.

STATEMENT OF GOALS

1.	To provide a positive environment conducive to intellectual, social, emotional, and psychomotor development of the middle school child.

2.	To help students acquire knowledge, skills, values, attitudes, and behavior that equip them for effective participation in democratic society.

3.	To promote student success by providing for individual differences through application of various teaching styles, methods, and new strategies based on accepted learning theories.

4.	To significantly build upon basic principles of education in all areas of the curriculum, thereby helping students become independent, self-directed learners.

5.	To create an atmosphere of cooperation between student, teacher, and parent and use such a relationship to foster a relaxed, positive, and achievement oriented attitude toward school.

6.	To aid students in the understanding of the nature and nurture of the human body.

7.	To encourage students to look ahead to the possibilities of career choice and to offer assistance in moving toward these choices.

8.	To examine frequently our objectives and goals for the purpose of revision in the light of changes within the community.

FIGURE 2.3. Creekland Middle School's statement of philosophy and goals.

concerns itself with overall school governance. Two teachers representing each of the five communities, the principal, and the five assistant principals make up this team which develops action plans and policy. All proposals for action are returned to the entire faculty for discussion and approval before final action is taken. Vision and mission statements and school goals were developed with full faculty and staff participation and are quality-oriented and student-centered (Figure 2.3). Academic excellence through teamwork captures the school's vision while providing a caring, supportive, and nurturing environment for individual student success and healthy maturation summarizes the school's mission.

The school's Advisory Committee is comprised of seven parents, seven teachers, the principal, and the five assistant principals. Assistant principals select parent representives while teacher representives are selected by the principal—one from each community and two exploratory teachers. The Advisory Committee addresses all problems and concerns of the school and the school's community and makes recommendations to the School-Wide Leadership Team on curricular matters such as sex education, homogeneous and heterogeneous grouping practices, and exploratory course offerings. Akin adds that while the committee's recommendations are only recommendations, they are "very carefully considered."

Akin believes strongly in a broad-based approach to parent and student input and has two other layers of governance, less formal but vital to the school's organization. The Parent-Teacher Association's (PTA) president meets frequently with the principal to discuss concerns and program activities for the school. Parent participation is community-centered with each community functioning as a school-within-a-school. Parent participation is primarily at the grade-level community structure with each community having its own programs and committees coordinated by an elected parent. These parents meet regularly with the school-wide PTA president to coordinate overall parent-school involvement. Students have their own government structure through the school-wide student council with elected representatives from grades six through eight. Here, learning about governance through doing is just as important as the recommendations they make concerning school policy and curriculum. Akin points out, however, that with all team decisions, "I'm totally honest with them on this point, that the buck stops here. After all, I'm the one ultimately responsible for the quality of the educational program and accountable to the superintendent and school board."

Besides creating trust and a positive climate, Akin sees other leadership skills as important for successful principals. Communication is high on Akin's list of core competencies and she means more than good written and oral skills. To her, the ability to "read people," to "communicate effectively with the various school publics—teachers, parents, students, staff, and community members—is a survival skill." When "you can talk their talk" and "understand their priorities" you can then "strike the right chord that allows for real communication." Communication also means constantly keeping the vision, mission, and school goals in front of both internal and external publics. At faculty meetings, through PTA programs, and in the school newsletter, the goals of CMS are communicated. The monthly newsletter includes a "Principally Speaking" column which focuses on the vision and mission of the school, PTA news, features on selected core curriculum areas and exploratory courses, and a counselor's column which provides tips on parenting the preadolescent.

Flexibility is another core leadership skill. Flexibility means "open mindedness," the ability to accept the ideas of others and realize that the principal does not have all the answers. Akin likes "multiple input because it broadens my perspective and knowledge base." Here, she says, "I have to be receptive, respect their opinion, and really listen to the meaning of the message." Sometimes she finds her perspective to be too narrow and solicits free thinking and the "what ifs."

Honesty and a sound knowledge of the school budget procedures are also key leadership skills. Trust is built on honesty and is the main ingredient for gaining and sustaining the respect of others—"Your word is your bond!" Like Walker Davis, Joan Akin notes the importance of being a successful school manager. "Paying attention to the paperwork first, frees you to be the instructional leader you need to be." Fiscal management skill based on a real knowledge of how the school budget works, what you can and can't do with your dollar allocations, is the most important of all managerial skills.

Risk taking and credibility are also necessary leadership competencies. Akin says that a strong instructional background, a knowledge of good teaching practices, and a willingness to model these skills from time to time adds credibility to the principal's suggestions to teachers. "Those years of experience in the classroom really pay dividends when helping teachers with improving their instructional techniques," she states. Risk taking is taking "calculated risks and not taking risks for risk's sake." Calculated risks, she says, are grounded in some knowledge base or data, have been discussed at length with multiple inputs, and have damage control capabilities. That is, "we are reasonably sure of success and the new and different will not harm the students in any way."

The current scheduling procedures illustrate her trust in the teacher team structure and her calculated risk philosophy. Akin would prefer block scheduling throughout the school with all interdisciplinary teacher teams, but teachers were leery of its merits and preferred the traditional period schedule with bells signaling period or class change. After much discussion and research about block/scheduling, Akin allowed teacher teams within the five communities to choose their own form of scheduling with the one restriction that all teams *must* have four and one-half hours of uninterrupted academic instruction (lunch being the only exception). The result is a slow but steady movement toward block scheduling and away from the traditional fifty-minute period day. Many advocates of the traditional period-bell day are now ignoring the bells and consolidating periods into time blocks because of the flexibility and instructional continuity provided by block scheduling. In this case, teachers are pleased with their autonomy and freedom to make instructional decisions and the principal has maintained the trust and respect of the teachers while achieving her goal of moving all instructional teacher teams toward block scheduling.

Finally, the ability to instill in teachers the "importance of keeping current with the latest research and trends in middle school education and to try new things and explore possibilities [to improve instruction]" is an important part of effective school leadership. Akin believes in Deming's (1993) quality principle of "educate and re-educate to provide quality instruction" and sets aside monies each year for professional conferences and staff development seminars. All teachers are encouraged to attend professional meetings of their choice and to submit a list of topics for staff development. When topics come from teachers, she reports, teachers are more inclined to take the seminars seriously because they represent areas of personal interest or need. Parent fund raisers and PTA activities provide additional funds for staff improvement as well as instructional materials. As the educational leader in the school, Akin conducts staff development seminars herself, as well as bringing in outside consultants and central office personnel.

But that's not all. After careful reflection on her list of core competencies and skills for effective leaders, she says with careful deliberation: "The bottom line is you have to have a genuine love for kids and a real dedication to the profession."

Edwards Middle School, in Conyers, Georgia, has been named a National School of Excellence and a National Blue Ribbon School, and is a six-time winner of the Georgia School of Excellence award. Its principal, Dr. Wayne Watts, is quality-oriented and practices many of the findings of the effective schools research.

To Watts, the most salient leadership skill is "good human interaction skills which are being able to read your people and empathize with their concerns." Reading people is knowing the "perspectives from which the various publics come with whom you interact daily." Teachers, students, parents, and community members all have different sets of problems, needs, and expectations. Watts says, "Empathy is to truly understand what they mean in their message, not just listening to their words. In short, you have to try to put yourself in their position, internalize their perspective." To Watts, each group has its own "language," its own "trigger words" that, when used, really connect. "This is being able to talk their talk effectively." The acid test for effective communication Watts notes, is: "Does the talk translate into desired behavior?"

Watts believes that the work of Hersey and Blanchard (1992) is also highly applicable to successful leadership in the middle school. Watts finds the tenets of situational leadership of high value to practicing administrators and these tenets reinforce his basic belief that "you must know what makes people 'tick' before you can provide the right kind of assistance to maximize their potential." Some need total freedom, some need direction, some need to be coached, while some need reassurance and ongoing support. "Knowing the right kind of assistance to provide teachers is a real motivator, a way to help them self-actualize."

Watts says that another skill of effective leadership is "intestinal forti-tude," being able to say "no" to requests that are worthy, have merit, or have personal benefit. The principal must place the good of the student before those of other individuals and "enforce school policy and regulations that seem unfair or unjust to some people. This is where people skills really come into play." He adds that making unpopular decisions which reside within the prerogative of the principalship "tests one's mettle, but you have to make decisions which are student-centered." Sometimes, he says, "your decisions come from a private knowledge-base that is confidential, and this information simply cannot be disclosed." These decisions call for a high de-gree of teacher trust: "You need to be open and honest with the faculty about why you are making these decisions. They need to know the constraints within which these decisions are made."

Like Davis and Akin, Watts believes trust is a central leadership skill. Trust is built over time, through consistent behavior which then translates into predictable behavior. "When you pledge your word as your bond, your reputation is at stake and if you have to break your word you better be able to explain the circumstances to their [teachers'] satisfaction." Watts adds that honesty is an "everyday thing, not just big-issue-involvement. It's the daily follow-up you promise teachers, the ordering of supplies, the 'I'll get back to you's,' and so on." Honesty is also letting teachers know up front what is-sues are negotiable and which are non-negotiable when it comes to school governance. "I let my teachers know the issues over which we have control and the issues which reside within other jurisdictions." This candor allevi-ates much frustration, saves teacher time and effort, and keeps them from working on "done deals." However, Watts says, "If my staff feels strongly about an issue that [they believe] impacts negatively on our school, and it lies within the non-negotiable category, I'm always willing to explore the possibility of compromise. And they know that."

Watts says that having a child-centered philosophy is vital to effective middle school leadership: "I can't imagine a principal being really success-ful who does not enjoy working with middle school students—you really have to love this crazy age group." Here, the Deming (1986) quality princi-ples begin to surface in his leadership philosophy. To Watts, parents are the customers and students are the clients. Parent needs and expectations are fused with those of teachers and the goals of the school, and the curriculum and professional expertise of the teacher is the service provided to the stu-dent. "Customer expectations have to be met, but the professional care and decisions on how best to serve our students reside with the teachers." School goals, the driving force behind the instructional program, provide con-stancy of purpose, while the school's vision targets continuous improve-ment for teachers, students, administrators, and staff members. Watts notes that the particular value of Deming's principles is as a "leadership template" to guide the school toward quality performance and outcomes. In particular, the area of school climate depends greatly on fusing the quality principles with effective schools research.

Climate, to Watts, translates into building a "sense of community, a common force which is driven by a set of core values which are held by all." Many of these values, he maintains, are associated with the concept of the true middle school and effective schools research. For example, teachers at Edwards Middle School believe in order and discipline and having high expectations for students in a safe, positive, cheerful atmosphere in which learning can take place. But teachers also believe that students need rewards, love, respect, and a chance to be successful in school. "These values cement the staff together and provide the force which allows our curriculum to make a positive impact on student learning." Watts likens himself to a conductor of an orchestra when discussing his role in building school climate: "As a conductor of professionals [teachers], my job is to make sure they can maximize their individual talents and skills, provide the assistance to sustain harmony, and allow each to solo while being fully supported by the entire orchestra." Support means providing the necessary time, resources, and personal encouragement to do their job the way they know best. Occasionally, Watts says, "I have to do a bit of fine-tuning" which means pointing out to teachers areas needing improvement. But improvement is a team effort at Edwards Middle School when teacher support networks and interdisciplinary teams supplement the workshops and conferences made available for teacher assistance. "We are all in this together—the helping hand concept, and teachers both know and appreciate this."

Shared governance is also important in promoting effective leadership at the middle school level. At Edwards Middle School, school governance is based on a teacher-developed school charter which specifies school governance procedures. The School Improvement Council (SIC) is designed to address curriculum and instructional problems and consists of an elected teacher representative from each interdisciplinary team at each grade level (6 through 8). Exploratory team teachers are also represented with one teacher from the exploratory core, one from the physical education (health) field and the school counselor. The principal is a voting member of the council which is chaired by a teacher.

Parent and student representation comes through their respective committees. Parents have input through the PTO and the Local School Advisory Council (LSAC). Each parent group is advisory in nature with no policy-making function; however, their recommendations impact significantly on the decisions made by SIC. The LSAC is open to all parents and meets four times a year to discuss issues and concerns relative to Edwards Middle

School. Subcommittees are formed to address specific interest areas and recommendations are presented to the principal.

Students have input through the student council with each homeroom in each grade level electing its own representative. Advisory in nature, the student council also performs service activities in the school and community. Currently, the council is drafting a Student Statement of Responsibilities and Rights for ratification. When completed, this statement will serve as a code of conduct and offer guiding principles for all students.

Modeling one's beliefs, "acting out what one truly believes in and then making these beliefs topics of continuous conversation is important for good leadership," says Watts. Principals set and sustain the tone of the school by their daily behavior and they keep it alive through their daily conversations with teachers, parents, and students. "For example," Watts says, "I start off the year with a State of the School Address in which I give my candid assessment of last year's performance and where we are on achieving the goals of the school" (see Appendix for a copy of Watts's 1996–97 report). The speech both praises successes and admonishes staff members to do better, to improve continuously, and to remain student focused.

Watts' State of the School Address is an excellent example of leadership in action. In it, one sees the skillful practice of leadership as both an art and a science. Finely honed communication skills combined with an understanding of the psychological aspects of human nature allow Watts to deliver a powerful message to his staff concerning the future direction of the school. The deft handling of the complex issue of a teacher's role and responsibilities within the larger framework of a school's purpose ensures that his staff is not only challenged to set higher goals but motivated to achieve them. This State of the School Address leaves no doubt that there is a leader at work at Edwards Middle School.

REFERENCES

Armstrong, T. 1994. *Multiple Intelligences in the Classroom.* Alexandria, VA: Association for Supervision and Curriculum Development.

Ascik, T. R. 1984. "Looking at Some Research on What Makes an Effective School," in *A Blueprint for Educational Reform.* C. Marshner, ed. Chicago, IL: Regnery Gateway, pp. 141–165.

Bennis, W. 1989. *On Becoming a Leader.* Reading, MA: Addison-Wesley.

Bennis, W. and B. Nanus. 1985. *Leaders: The Strategies for Taking Charge.* New York: Harper & Row.

Bloom, B. S., M. T. Engelhard, E. J. Furst, W. H. Hill, and D. R. Krathwohl. 1956. *Taxonomy of Educational Objectives: Handbook I: The Cognitive Domain.* New York: David McKay.

Borg, W. R. 1987. *Applying Educational Research: A Practical Guide for Teachers.* Second edition. White Plains, NY: Longman.

Borg, W. R. and M. D. Gall. 1989. *Educational Research: An Introduction.* Fifth edition. White Plains, NY: Longman.

Bossett, S. T., D. C. Dwyer, B. Rowen, and G. V. Lee. 1982. "The Instructional Management Role of the Principal," *Educational Administration Quarterly*, 18:34–64.

Brookover, W., L. Beamer, H. Efthim, D. Hathaway, L. Lezotte, S. Miller, J. Passalacqua, and L. Tarnatsky. 1982. *Creating Effective Schools: An In-Service Program for Enhancing School Learning and Climate and Achievement.* Holmes Beach, FL: Learning Publications.

Brophy, J. E. and T. E. Good. 1986. "Teacher Behavior and Student Achievement," in *Handbook of Research on Teaching.* Third edition. M. C. Wittrock, ed. New York: Macmillan.

Brussell, E. E., ed. 1988. *Dictionary of Quotable Definitions.* Englewood Cliffs: NJ: Prentice-Hall.

Charles, C. M. 1988. *Introduction to Educational Research.* White Plains, NY: Longman, Inc.

Chubb, J. E. and T. M. Moe. 1990. *Politics, Markets, and America's Schools.* Washington, DC: The Brookings Institute.

Cuban, L. 1984. "Transforming the Frog into a Prince: Effective Schools Research, Policy, and Practices at the District Level," *Harvard Educational Review*, 54:129–151.

Davies, D. 1991. "Schools Reaching Out: Family, School, and Community Partnerships for Student Success," *Phi Delta Kappan*, 72(5):376–382.

Deal, T. E. 1985. "The Symbolism of Effective Schools," *Elementary School Journal*, 85:601–620.

Deming, W. E. 1986. *Out of the Crisis.* Cambridge, MA: MIT University Press.

Deming, W. E. 1993. *The New Economics for Industry, Government, Education.* Cambridge, MA: MIT Center for Advanced Engineering Study.

Drucker, P. F. 1974. *Management: Tasks, Practices, Responsibilities.* New York: Harper and Row.

DuFour, R. and R. Eaker. 1992. *Creating the New American School: A Principal's Guide to School Improvement.* Bloomington, IN: National Educational Service.

Eggan, P. D. and D. P. Kauchak. 1988. *Strategies for Teachers.* Second edition. Englewood Cliffs, NJ: Prentice Hall.

Elawar, M. C. and L. Corno. 1985. "A Factorial Experiment in Teachers' Written Feedback on Student Homework: Changing Teacher Behavior a Little Rather than a Lot," *Journal of Educational Psychology*, 58:438–481.

English, F. W. 1990. *Curriculum Auditing.* Lancaster, PA: Technomic Publishing Co., Inc.

English, F. W. 1992. *Educational Administration: The Human Science.* New York: Harper Collins Publishers, Inc.

Epstein, J. L. 1987. "What Principals Should Know About Parental Involvement," *Principal*, 66:(3)6–9.

Epstein, J. L. 1988. "How Do We Improve Programs for Parent Involvement?" *Educational Horizons*, (66):58–59.

Etzioni, A. 1988. *The Moral Dimension: Toward a New Theory of Economics.* New York, The Free Press.

Farmer, R. F., M. W. Gould, R. L. Herring, F. L. Linn, and M. A. Theobald. 1995. *The Middle School Principal.* Thousand Oaks, CA: Corwin Press, Inc.

Gardner, H. 1993. *Frames of Mind: The Theory of Multiple Intelligences.* Tenth-Anniversary Edition. New York: Basic Books.

Gardner, J. 1990. *On Leadership.* New York: The Free Press.

George, P. S. and L. Oldaker. 1985. *Evidence for the Middle School.* Columbus, OH: National Middle School Association.

Guerin, G. R. and A. S. Maier. 1983. *Informal Assessment in Education.* Palo Alto, CA: Mayfield.

Hall, G., W. L. Rutherford, S. M. Hord, and L. L. Hulling. 1984. "Effects of Three Principal Styles on School Improvement," *Educational Leadership*, 41(5):22–29.

Harrow, A. J. 1972. *A Taxonomy of the Psychomotor Domain: A Guide for Developing Behavior Objectives.* New York: David McKay.

Hartzell, G. N. and T. A. Petrie. 1992. "The Principal and Discipline: Working with School Structures, Teachers, and Students," *The Clearing House*, 65(60):376–380.

Hersey, P. and K. Blanchard. 1992. *Management of Organizational Behavior.* Sixth edition. Englewood Cliffs, NJ: Prentice-Hall.

Hopkins, C. D. and R. L. Antes. 1990. *Educational Research: A Structure for Inquiry.* Third edition. Itasca, IL: F.E. Peacock Publishers, Inc.

Houlihan, G. T. 1983. "Using the Right Variables in Measuring School Effectiveness," *NASSP Bulletin*, 67(465):9–15.

Hoy, W. K. and C. G. Miskel. 1991. *Educational Administration: Theory, Research, Practice.* Fourth edition. New York: McGraw-Hill, Inc.

Johnson, J. H. 1985. "Four Climates of Effective Middle Level Schools." *NASSP Schools in the Middle: A Report on Trends and Practices.* Reston, VA: National Association of Secondary School Principals.

Johnson, J. H. 1990. *The New American Family and the School.* Columbus, OH: National Middle School Association.

Jones, L. T. 1991. *Strategies for Involving Parents in Their Children's Education*, Fastback, No. 315, Bloomington, IN: Phi Delta Kappa Education Foundation.

Kauchak, D. P. and P. D. Eggan. 1989. *Learning and Teaching.* Boston, MA: Allyn & Bacon.

Klopf, G. J., E. Scheldon, and K. Brennan. 1982. "The Essentials of Effectiveness: A Job Description for Principals," *Principal*, 61:35–38.

Krathwohl. D. R., B. S. Bloom, and B. B. Masia. 1964. *Taxomony of Educational Objectives: The Classification of Educational Goals. Handbook II: Affective Domain.* New York: David McKay Company, Inc.

Levitt, T. Summer, 1976. "Management and the Post Industrial Society," *The Public Interest.*

Lezotte, L. W. 1991. *Correlates of Effective Schools: The First and Second Generation.* Okemos, MI: Effective Schools Products, Ltd.

Lezotte, L. W. and B. C. Jacoby. 1992. *Sustainable School Reform: The District Contest for School Improvement.* Okemos, MI: Effective Schools.

Lightfoot, S. L. 1983. *The Good High School: Portraits of Character and Culture.* New York: Basic Books.

Lunenburg, F. C. and A. C. Ornstein. 1991. *Educational Administration: Concepts and Practices.* Belmont, CA: Wadsworth Publishing Company.

Lunenburg, F. C. and A. C. Ornstein. 1996. *Educational Administration: Concepts and Practices*. Second edition. Belmont, CA: Wadsworth Publishing Company.

Mackenzie, D. E. 1983. "Research for School Improvement: An Appraisal of Some Recent Trends," *Educational Researcher*, 12(4):5–16.

Maeroff, G. I. 1991. "Assessing Alternative Assessments," *Phi Delta Kappan*, 73(4):272–281.

McMillan, J. H. and S. Schumacher. 1984. *Research in Education: A Conceptual Introduction*. Boston, MA: Little, Brown, and Company.

Mintzburg, H. 1989. *Mintzburg on Management*. New York: The Free Press.

National Committee for Citizens in Education. 1993. *Taking Stock*. Washington, DC.

Northwest Regional Education Laboratory. 1990. *Effective School Practices: A Research Synthesis 1990 Update*. Northwest Regional Education Laboratory School Improvement Project.

Ogden, E. H. and V. Germinario. 1994. *The Nation's Best Schools: Blueprints for Excellence (Volume I: Elementary and Middle Schools)*. Lancaster, PA: Technomic Publishing Co. Inc.

Ouchi, W. G. and A. L. Wilkins. 1985. "Organizational Culture," *Annual Review of Sociology*, 11:457–483.

Purkey, S. C. and M. S. Smith. 1983. "Effective Schools: A Review," *Elementary School Journal*, 83:427–452.

Sagar, R. D. 1992. "Three Principals Who Made a Difference," *Educational Leadership*, 49(5):13–18.

Sergiovanni, T. J. 1984. "Leadership and Excellence in Schooling," *Educational Leadership*, 41(5):4, 6–13.

Serow, R. C. and H. L. Jackson. 1983. "Using Standardized Test Data to Measure School Effectiveness," *NASSP Bulletin*, 67(465):20–25.

Spady, W. G. and G. Max. 1984. *Excellence in Our Schools: Making It Happen*. Arlington, VA: American Association of School Administrators and San Francisco: Far West Laboratory for Educational Research and Development.

Squires, D.A., W. G. Huitt, and J. K. Segars. 1984. *Effective Schools and Classrooms: A Research-Based Perspective*. Alexandria, VA: Association for Supervision and Curriculum Development.

Steep, D. R. 1996. "A Class Fact," *Atlanta Journal-Constitution, Section C (Local News)*. Friday, November 1, 1996, p. C1.

Strother, D. B. 1983. "The Many Roles of the Effective Principal," *Phi Delta Kappan*, 65(4):291–294.

Weller, L. D. and S. J. Weller. 1997. Quality Learning Organizations and Continuous Improvement. National Association of Secondary School Principals Bulletin.

Weller, L. D., S. H. Hartley, and C. L. Brown. 1994. "Principals and TQM: Developing Vision," *The Clearing House*, 67(5):298–301.

Yukl, G. A. 1989. *Leadership in Organizations*. Englewood Cliffs, NJ: Prentice Hall.

Zaleznik, A. 1977. "Managers and Leaders: Are They Different?" *Harvard Business Review*, 55(3) 67–68.

CHAPTER 3

Leadership for the Exploratory Curriculum

This chapter will explore the significance of exploration in the middle school curriculum and the importance of leadership in promoting quality exploratory programs. The middle school curriculum is typically organized around three basic components: the core or basic curriculum, the exploratory curriculum, and the enrichment or special interest curriculum. Core courses are those considered to be essential for all students and in part are determined by the state and local school system. In contrast, the exploratory program offers regularly scheduled classes in a variety of areas as part of the regular schedule with students free to choose these courses based on their own interests. Exploratory courses are less structured than core curriculum courses, but provide essential learning experiences, skills, and competencies which supplement and complement those courses. Elective courses and activity programs are optional opportunities for enrichment and frequently build on exploratory or core-course experiences. Elective courses complement exploratory courses in that these are high-interest areas for students who have discovered success and special talents in exploratory courses and wish to pursue their interests further.

To develop successful relevant experiences for students, principals and teachers must understand the unique needs and characteristics of the transescent, determine the focus of their program, identify suitable experiences and activities, and determine the organizational structure to support the program focus and make exploration a school-wide reality. Essential to the success of the exploratory program is the principal's leadership ability to unite teachers so they have a focus of purpose which establishes the program as a viable, ongoing part of the school's curriculum. This communicates a clear vision and meaningful connection to the middle school philosophy, especially for those who advocate academics only. A clearly defined purpose also makes exploratory experiences easier to integrate across the curriculum which moves away from the concept of exploratory as a set of separate courses.

Examples of successful programs and curricular offerings will be presented in this chapter, as well as a list of the more commonly offered exploratory and elective courses. The most common pitfalls and barriers to the successful implementation of an exploratory program will also be presented. Through case studies, actual experiences of middle school principals who have implemented exploratory programs will be explored.

This chapter looks at the following questions:

- What are the historical underpinnings for the exploratory curriculum?
- How does the school's vision impact the exploratory curriculum?
- Why does the transescent need a developmental middle school curriculum?
- What curricular practices are currently in place in middle schools?
- What is the core curriculum?
- How does the exploratory curriculum build on the core curriculum?
- What is the difference between exploratory and elective courses?
- What is the leadership role of the principal in developing and sustaining an exploratory curriculum?
- What process should be used in determining the focus of the exploratory curriculum?
- What should be offered in the exploratory curriculum?
- What are the data gathering procedures to be used in building an exploratory curriculum?
- When and how should exploratory courses be offered? Who will teach the courses and how will they be scheduled?

THE MIDDLE SCHOOL CURRICULUM

Historical Underpinnings of the Exploratory Curriculum

The historical underpinnings of the exploratory curriculum in the middle school came from the rise of the junior high school movement. Central to the idea of having a distinct middle level of schooling were the ideas that transescents have individual differences and abilities at this age level and that their socioeconomic, physical, and intellectual uniqueness calls for different kinds of experiences and programs not found in traditional schooling. This uniqueness triggered the introduction of activities and courses in the junior high school which allowed students to explore and discover new areas of interest and develop new skills and talents. Through exploration and discovery, it was thought that students would take a more active interest in learning and could learn to make informed choices to better prepare them for entering the high school's academic, vocational, or general track (Melton, 1984).

The exploratory curriculum, an essential part of the middle school concept, provides for relevant, less structured learning experiences while electives provide students selected enrichment. The exploratory curriculum is best viewed as a process, rather than a list of courses, which allows students to explore their individual interests and talents and to excel in these interest areas. The exploratory curriculum in different middle schools varies in scope and size but has common, essential elements. It is designed to assist students in making informed choices and learning more about their special interests in a variety of areas as they develop socially, emotionally, physically, and intellectually. Exploratory courses are offered regularly and are part of the student's daily schedule, and they both complement and supplement the components of the core curriculum and elective course offerings. Exploratory courses may run three, six, or nine weeks in length or may be taught on a semester or yearly basis. This is accomplished through a variety of scheduling methods. Courses are taught by teachers, administrators, staff personnel and community members, depending on their expertise and interests.

The philosophy behind the exploratory curriculum allows middle school educators to apply the tenet of Herbert Spencer first posed in 1894 when he said that meaningful and relevant curriculum design should be guided by asking the question: "What knowledge is of the most worth?" (Spencer, 1894, p. 1). Exploratory experiences which are student-centered, relevant, enjoyable, and interesting and which allow students to connect school learning with their daily lives is knowledge of the most worth.

Exploratory courses, sometimes known as minicourses, are the heart of the middle school's emphasis on providing the essential exploratory experiences called for by Alexander, Williams, Compton, Hines, and Prescott (1968) who noted that a true middle school provides experiences for students to make choices, be responsible for their own learning, and excel in their interest areas and learning experiences as they develop intellectually, socio-emotionally, and physically. Theorists such as George and Lawrence (1982), Arnold (1985), Vars (1987), and Beane (1990) have reinforced Alexander et al. (1968) by calling for more and varied exploratory offerings within the middle school curriculum which are developmentally responsive to the needs of the preadolescent which impact their daily lives. Unfortunately, what is called for and envisioned as part of the "true" middle school has not come to fruition. Becker (1990) reports national survey data which shows only 39% of America's middle schools offering minicourses or electives. Thirty percent of these students had the exploratory experiences or minicourses during the seventh and eighth grades. It seems that the exploratory part of the curriculum, although central to the middle school concept, is sorely lacking in existence.

The Vision of Middle School Curriculum vs. Reality

The curriculum represents the sum total of experiences, both structured and nonstructured, to which students are exposed. This broad definition of curriculum, while accurate, lacks specific direction for middle school educators and has led to a vacuum in the middle school curriculum (George and Alexander, 1993). Beane (1990) notes this lack of direction over the past three decades and attributes it to the various national, state, and local constraints and demands placed on middle school curriculum developers. Weller and Hartley (1994) note the changing and popular educational themes of the times and the resulting demands placed on school administrators over the last three decades. For example, the 1970s emphasized "accountability" with educators responding to national, state, and local demands to show cost-effective programs yielding demonstrated student learning. The 1980s era called for school "excellence" with a cry of "back to basics" and an emphasis on a totally academic curriculum. Much of this momentum came from national-level commission reports such as *A Nation at Risk* (1983) issued by the National Commission on Excellence in Education and *Action for Excellence* (1983) released by the Task Force on Education for Economic Growth. The 1990s emphasizes school reform and restructuring as its improvement theme with an emphasis on reorganizing the school's organizational infrastructure, its teaching practices, and its instructional delivery system. *America 2000* (U.S. Department of Education, 1991) has been the primary mover of this school reform movement.

Local school boards embraced many of these themes and recommendations, and state legislatures passed specific acts which focused on establishing more rigor within the curriculum and higher academic standards for promotion and graduation. The result was an emphasis on academics, basic skills, and standardized tests of academic achievement to demonstrate student learning. Such pressure leaves little time or inclination to focus attention on curricular areas falling outside the area of academics. As a result, the middle school curriculum lacks uniqueness and reflects a patchwork of courses and activities that may or may not be related (Beane, 1990).

The need for curriculum relevance is reinforced by the CREMS (1990) study which found that American middle schools varied according to size of school, student/teacher ratio, and type of community. The report stated: "The curriculum offered basic or core subjects and one or two other subjects, paying little attention to creating learning opportunities that are more responsive to the characteristics of young adolescents. There is a general conservative emphasis on basic skills" (pp. 3–4). Middle schools, therefore, are primarily academically oriented, emphasizing subject-based learning and lacking an integrated and exploratory curriculum. Despite the middle school's mission of providing preadolescents with relevant life experiences and interest and talent exploration, old rather than new programs abound which are modeled after the high school's subject-oriented practices (George and Alexander, 1993).

The Need for a Developmental Middle School Curriculum

A developmental curriculum for middle school learners is described by Glatthorn (1987) as a curricular construct which fits the needs of the emerging adolescent. The developmental approach to curriculum building is process-oriented and views the learner as one who is continuously developing mental capabilities, skills, and talents but at different rates and times than other learners. Learning is a creative, interactive process which is best promoted when content areas interact with other learning activities. Knowledge, to the developmentalist, is acquired through experiences which provide personal meaning through interaction with the environment. Personal meaning and environmental interaction provide the necessary basis for creative thinking and the transfer of training necessary to make connections between content and personal learning experiences. Becker (1990) relates that the quality of the learning activity depends on the type of interaction activities transescents engage in with adults and peers. A real impact on learning, from a developmental approach to middle school curriculum, comes from exploratory courses which are appropriately designed to meet the varying intellectual, social-emotional, and physical maturation levels of the preadolescent.

Current Middle School Curricular Practices

Curriculum is what is taught and instruction is the method used to teach that curriculum. Goodlad (1977) found five conceptual levels of school curriculum:

(1) The ideal curriculum offered by theorists as desirable
(2) The formal curriculum prescribed by state and local laws or regulations
(3) The perceived curriculum which teachers attend to as they meet the needs of their students
(4) The operational curriculum which is what really happens in the classroom

(5) The experiential curriculum which students perceive as being offered and to which they can relate

Each of these conceptual levels of the curriculum is important to middle school education when they are addressed within the context of the needs—intellectual, social-emotional, and physical—of the transescent learner. Glatthorn (1987) states that middle schools have a core or basic curriculum that is made up of the recommended (ideal), the written (formal), the supported (perceived) and the taught and tested (operational) curriculum, but that many schools lack an experience-based (experiential) curriculum which is central to the true middle school concept.

The Core Curriculum in Middle Schools

The core or basic curriculum of the middle school is comprised of concepts and skills considered essential for all students and is made up of courses in mathematics, language arts/reading, science, and social studies. The concepts and skills largely consist of the ideal, formal, and perceived curriculum with emphasis on the formal or externally mandated requirements. These courses have scope and sequence—scope deals with how much of a topic or subject is included in a program, and sequence deals with the order in which concepts and skills are taught within and between grade levels. This standard approach to curriculum development provides little, if any, evidence of being developmentally responsive to the middle school learner's needs or interests (Lounsbury and Clark, 1990).

Some middle schools are taking a more developmentally responsive approach to curriculum building by introducing interdisciplinary thematic units. These thematic units allow students to make connections among content areas through common instructional themes. The most common efforts are being placed on reading and writing across the curriculum. However, much of the core curriculum does not relate to the real life issues of the pre-adolescent nor does it appeal to the particular interests of this age learner (George and Alexander, 1993). Berryman (1993) notes that many classrooms are passive places which foster passive learning and leave no room for student interaction with the environment or with each other. Teacher talks, textbook readings, and worksheets dominate in passive classrooms. Berryman relates that the emphasis on passive learning reduces time and opportunities for exploration and discovery, allows little opportunity for students to make choices and to be responsible for their own decisions, and fosters problems with motivation and discipline.

Passive learning classrooms, dominated by teacher-focused learning, emphasize direct instruction, which most frequently comprises lecture, drill, and practice. This type of instruction was used in 98 percent of the schools studied by Cawelti (1988). Inquiry teaching was used in only 41 percent of the schools, cooperative learning was used in only 40 percent of the schools, and independent study was found in only 30 percent of the schools. Epstein and MacIver (1990) concluded that middle schools have not fully implemented active and exploratory learning in their curriculum and that the goal of making education relevant and providing real life experiences is, for the most part, still a vision.

Active learning, engaging students in the learning process both mentally and physically, coincides with the philosophy of the true middle school. To create an active learning classroom, teachers must provide students with various learning opportunities that make instruction relevant, motivating, challenging, and personally meaningful and rewarding. Active learning strategies include cooperative learning activities, team projects, peer tutoring, computer assisted instruction, and independent study.

EXPLORATORY CURRICULUM

Philosophical Underpinnings of the Exploratory Curriculum

Exploration is a means of providing students the opportunity to actively explore the intellectual, social, emotional, and physical dimensions of the changes they are undergoing and to excel and demonstrate competence in a number of areas. Exploratory courses are nongraded, allowing for student and interaction across grade levels, and they differ from elective courses and activity programs which are optional opportunities for enrichment and are frequently built on the exploratory or core-course experiences. Elective courses are designed to complement exploratory courses in that they are high interest areas for students who have discovered success and special talents in exploratory courses and wish to pursue their interests further. Electives are usually offered throughout the year and during the part of the school day known as the activity period.

Unlike the role they play in implementing a mandated core curriculum, the role administrators play in determining the nature of exploratory experiences is a major one. The principal's role is twofold: to develop an organizational schedule to support the program's focus and make exploration a school-wide reality, and to unite teachers in a common purpose to make exploratory activities meaningful, enjoyable, and an ongoing part of the curriculum. A clearly defined purpose makes exploratory experiences easier to integrate across the curriculum and keeps them from being discrete courses separate from the core curriculum.

Leadership for the Exploratory Curriculum

Strong leadership is needed in building an exploratory middle school program. The principal must be both leader and manager simultaneously and be quality-oriented in the approach to curriculum development. Purpose or mission precludes the effective application of leadership and managerial skills in attaining a quality-oriented program. Without a clearly defined purpose or objective, the leadership variable of influencing others to follow through mutual consent cannot be practiced. The coordinator and facilitator role of the manager cannot be accomplished without an end goal. The authority aspect of management can, of course, demand or dictate direction, but such behavior will lead to "form without substance" (Farmer, Gould, Herring, Linn, and Theobald, 1995, p. 12).

In quality-oriented leadership, vision is the moving force which provides the synergy to effect and sustain change. Vision, much like mission in the effective schools research literature, is the glue or shared values which hold the school together to promote high achieving outcomes. Vision as defined by Weller, Hartley, and Brown (1994), is the overarching concept and the compelling force of the organization and it expresses the purpose and philosophy of the organization. These authors also note that although vision originates from the leader, the vision statement will be mutually developed by representatives of the various groups who make up the organization. This mutual development, which forges a common image and understanding of what is to be achieved, becomes central to the development of the exploratory curriculum. In middle schools where supportive leadership and shared vision exist, teachers have "the willingness and ability to adapt all school practices to the individual differences in intellectual, biological, and social maturation of their students" (Lipsitz, 1984, p. 174).

Middle school principals set the tone and direction for their schools. Contemporary leadership research focuses on leadership as displayed behaviors or behavior patterns, rather than personal characteristics, which influence subordinate satisfaction and performance. Shared governance, engaging teachers in decision making, problem solving, and planning, has long-term positive effects on morale, dedication to school goals, and continuous school improvement (Hoy and Miskel, 1996).

Effective middle school principals are proactive; they initiate change, challenge their staff, and excite emotions. They are aware that their actions are contagious and recognize direct relationships between their actions and outcomes. Effective leaders recognize that leadership is a transitional process and that their power to lead comes from the willingness of others to follow and provide support. Central to this leadership variable is belief in oneself and in subordinates' abilities to bring about change in the organization.

The principal as manager, the other major function of effective school leadership, pays attention to administrative detail, coordinates internal and external activities, and facilitates the daily operations of the school's total program by providing the necessary time, resources, and support teachers need to accomplish their tasks. According to Zaleznik (1977), managers concentrate their energies on how things get done while leaders concern themselves with what these things mean to people. The manager executes positional authority and focuses on the responsibilities of the job while the leader influences, stimulates commitment, and excites and challenges. Farmer et al. (1995) relates the importance of both the leadership and management dimensions for middle school principals when noting that principals are catalysts who provide an environment which promotes continuous improvement within the school based on the guiding principles and philosophy of the middle school concept. The management functions of planning, organizing, staffing, distributing, and accounting are necessary to keep the middle school operating smoothly and effectively. In terms of the exploratory curriculum, the principal as manager will organize the school's instructional program into a master schedule which facilitates the school's curriculum and employ teachers committed to the middle school philosophy and the unique needs of the transescent learner.

George and Alexander (1993) maintain that "spirited" leadership, vision, and teacher empowerment (making curriculum and instructional decisions) are the essential qualities needed for middle schools to redesign themselves into schools which practice the full middle school concept. They relate that these essentials are specifically needed in curriculum development to address the mismatch which currently exists between the organizational structure and the curriculum in middle schools, and they see these elements as the necessary vehicle to transform middle schools into schools which prepare students for young adulthood. George and Anderson (1989) note that in those middle schools where teachers have a clear vision of what the curriculum should be, a knowledge and appreciation for the needs and characteristics of transescents, and a clear concept of themselves as a part of the leadership team, there are quality middle school programs.

The Exploratory Curriculum Broadly Defined

Exploratory courses provide opportunities for students to explore their interests and talents and to develop a positive self-image through personally successful and rewarding experiences. As such, exploratory activities should be offered across the middle school curriculum and be arranged around a required sequence of courses and electives or enrichment courses (Lounsbury, 1990). To Lounsbury, the middle school is an exploratory school and exploration should be at the heart of all curricular experiences. George and Alexander (1993) stress that the value of exploration courses also resides in having these courses form links across the curriculum in order for students to see the interconnectedness of their learning experiences.

Exploratory activities and student creativity are interconnected. The area of creativity is central to exploratory courses because the exploratory curriculum provides avenues for students to pursue areas of special interest where they are exposed to new and different stimuli and knowledge. The application of Gardner's (1983) theory of multiple intelligences and the nature of the middle school learner, discussed in preceding chapters, coincide naturally with the philosophy behind the implementation of exploratory experiences. The growing curiosity and interests of transescents develop rapidly as they emerge from childhood and move into an expanding world which provides unique opportunities and ways to learn about special interest areas. Experiences which lend themselves to the development of students' creative talents as they apply these talents to basic skills and core content form the basis of student achievement (Gowan, Khatena, and Torrance, 1981). The philosophy of learning behind the multiple intelligences theory provides educators the opportunity to be creative in learning settings and to tap the different talents of students. Armstrong (1994) argues that since each person possesses all seven intelligences which function together in unique ways, teachers have their own creative learning laboratory where they can make their classroom activities appeal to the broad array of learning styles.

COMMON EXPLORATORY COURSES

Exploratory courses should be a required sequence of courses for students during their middle school years. Some of the most frequent and required exploratory courses are industrial arts, physical education, home economics, art, music, foreign language, chorus, industrial arts, and computer technology. These courses should be restructured to allow students to explore, indepth, their skills, interests and talents and to make practical application of knowledge, skills, and information learned in other subjects. George and Lawrence (1982) call these the unified arts. In addition to the unified arts area, there are three other areas in which exploratory courses are offered: academic inquiry, independent learning, and expanding the disciplines (George and Lawrence, 1982).

Elective or enrichment courses provide optional learning opportunities for students and allow them to make choices and be responsible for their own learning decisions. Enrichment activities should build on core content and exploratory courses. Electives are highly specialized courses or activities within a subject or broad-field content area. For example, in the art curriculum, specialized courses might be oil and watercolor painting, ceramics, weaving, and sculpting.

Unified Arts

As discussed above, these are the most common courses offered to students and are either semester- or year-long. Exploratory in nature, these courses should place less emphasis on competition and have content related to the core academics which occurs through interdisciplinary team teaching and planning.

Academic Inquiry

Academic inquiry courses are related to the core academic courses in science, mathematics, social studies, and language arts, but they are different in scope. Taught by academic area teachers, these courses are designed to allow students to study specific topics or areas found within the larger academic core areas. These mini-courses provide students the opportunity to explore indepth topics of their interest.

Students should be able to choose from a range of course offerings which provides relevant, real-life experiences or applications and which is exploratory in design. Captivating student interest is a major objective of mini-courses and grading is flexible so students can learn without fear of failure (George and Lawrence, 1982). Mini-courses in some middle schools go outside the core curriculum and are taught by either teachers or community volunteers. Engel and Weller (1975) point out that mini-courses such as these are effective in promoting both student learning and community involvement in the schools by having parents, retired teachers, and community members teach short, two- or three-week courses in their areas of expertise. Students themselves may suggest topics for exploration, and enrollment is open to all students.

Independent Learning

Independent learning is part of the regular, organized curriculum and allows students the opportunity to learn independently outside their regular classes. Ideally, this learning offers students a variety of topics with guidance from teachers. Students may choose their own topics based on interest, and exploration time may be a week, a month, or longer (George and Lawrence, 1982). Independent study offers an excellent opportunity to teach research skills with the community and media center used as learning laboratories. Students may present the results of their independent study in oral or written form, which helps them develop responsibility and self-discipline. Open to all students, this type of indepth investigation often creates a deeper interest in subjects not yet present in the learner and frequently motivates students to learn more about subject areas tangential to their topics of exploration (Engel and Weller, 1975).

Expanding the Disciplines

In this area of exploratory courses, teachers use the concept of exploration as a teaching goal to illustrate how their subject area relates to other disciplines. Social studies teachers, for example, will encourage students to explore areas such as sociology, economics, and political science, while science teachers may introduce the areas of ecology, astronomy, and geology for further exploration (George and Lawrence, 1982).

Exploratory courses vary in number and content from school to school and depend primarily upon available fiscal and material resources and qualified personnel to teach the courses. In some states, like Georgia, certain courses are mandated by the state department of education. Courses can last from two weeks to one year depending upon state requirements and school scheduling practices. Figure 3.1 presents a sample list of exploratory courses taught in middle schools.

Building an Exploratory Curriculum

Developing an exploratory curriculum takes time, organization, and teamwork. Principals, teachers, parents, students, and community members work together to build a meaningful exploratory curriculum which addresses the needs of the transescent. Messick and Reynolds (1992) relate the importance of applying research techniques and teamwork to the school vision when building an exploratory curriculum. George and Alexander (1993) discuss the importance of middle school teachers and principals going through a self-analysis of their current curricular offerings and then relating these findings to the purpose of their instructional mission by asking key questions. Central to building an exploratory curriculum are the interests and expertise of the faculty who are primarily responsible for its deliverance.

APPLYING RESEARCH TECHNIQUES

Data gathering is an essential element in building quality educational programs. Gathering data from those closest to the problem is a way to get

Social Studies

Historical Research
Civil War Battles
War Tactics and Strategy
Culture Appreciation
Colonial America
Government Structures
Crime and Punishment
Values and Citizenship

Current Events
Prejudices
Conflict Management
Art of Negotiation
Chess
Medieval History
Poverty and Wealth
Geography
Power and Politics
Gangs and Society

Language Arts

Creative Writing
Drama
Short Story
Great Books
Mythology
Newspaper Writing

Mass Media
Public Speaking
The Play
Poetry

Science

Astronomy
Oceanography
Scientific Research
UFOs
Solar System

Ecology
Birds, Bugs, and Fish
Einstein's Mystery
Space Travel
Reptiles
Rivers, Streams, and Forests

Mathematics

Probability
Populations and Samples
History of Mathematics
Bridge Building
Cathedral Construction
Mathematics for the Home

Mathematics for Consumers
Charts and Graphs
Launching Missiles
Basic Statistics
The Metric System

FIGURE 3.1. Examples of exploratory courses.

Career Education and Technology/Computer

Computers	Home Economics	Agriculture
Keyboarding	Industrial Arts	Television
Programming	Metal Work	Plumbing
Radio Communications	Masonry	World of Work
Lasers	Career Education	Drafting
Space Flight	Journalism	Engineering
Weather	Bachelor Cooking	Auto Repair
Aerodynamics	Sewing and Needlepoint	Home Repair
Gardening		

Fine Arts/Foreign Language

Art	Foreign Language Appreciation
Music	Latin
Art Appreciation	French
Music Appreciation	Spanish
Pottery	Japanese
Dance	
Watercolor	
Cartoon Drawing	
Music History	
Art History	
Band	
Chorus	
Jazz Band	
Composing Music	
Sketching	

Health/Physical Education

Health	Physical Education
Diet and Nutrition	Football and Baseball Rules
Healthy Eating	Tennis
Child Care	Badminton
Personal Grooming	Life Sports
	Soccer
	Game Fishing
	First Aid
	Aerobics

FIGURE 3.1 (continued). Examples of exploratory courses.

accurate, first-hand information about what is right and what is wrong with the system (Deming, 1993). Surveys, interviews, discussions, and check-lists are research techniques which can be applied to assess the value and relevancy of the existing exploratory curriculum. A series of questions, developed by the principal and teachers, serves as the basis for the data collection procedures. Students, parents, and community members should also be assessed as to the relevancy and value of these activities. Only after the current exploratory program is assessed can a new series of exploratory activities be developed to meet the needs of the learner and respond to the goals of middle school education.

GUIDING QUESTIONS FOR RESEARCH DATA

Questions on the exploratory survey instruments should be guided by the school's vision and the middle school philosophy behind the exploratory curriculum. Principals and teachers take the initiative in developing these questions through a series of self-assessment sessions where brainstorming is used as the primary vehicle to foster reflective thinking. The questions should be exploratory in nature and allow for creative responses. Some examples of such questions are: Does this experience foster the vision of the school? Is this course developmentally appropriate for the preadolescent student in our current society? The emphasis on making experiences relevant to real-life situations is an important concern since many changes have taken place since existing exploratory courses were developed. Roles and career opportunities for males and females have changed; greater emphasis is being placed on personal health and nutrition; technology is advancing at rapid rates; new knowledge is expanding, especially in the sciences; and fine arts area is becoming more popular. Other questions which can be used to guide the assessment of the current exploratory program can be grouped into two broad areas as follows:

(1) Questions to assess the current program offerings:
   - What is the content of the current exploratory experiences and is it relevant to the school's purpose and the needs of the learner?
   - Do the goals of the current activities reflect today's social, intellectual and environmental changes?
   - Is the current offering of exploratory courses wide enough to appeal to student and teacher interest?
   - Is the exploratory curriculum permeating the entire curriculum?
(2) Questions to identify future exploratory courses:
   - What are the particular strengths and interests of each teacher? Principals can also teach mini-courses and assessing their interests and strengths is also helpful.

- What are the interests and needs of the students? Both students and parents should be asked to express their needs and interests.
- What experiences will be offered? Who will teach the courses? Will parents and community members be involved in teaching exploratory experiences? Will team teaching of the courses exist between teachers and other staff members?
- When and how often will courses be offered? Which courses are appropriate for week-long and semester-long mini-courses?
- Will the resources of the community be used as a learning laboratory? How will the resources of the community be used in the exploratory curriculum?

Scheduling Exploratory Courses

Once the exploratory curriculum is developed by school administrators, teachers, parents, and students, and consensus is reached on the number and kinds of experiences to be offered, as well as who teaches what and when, the principal schedules the exploratory activities. A variety of scheduling patterns can be used and will be discussed more fully in Chapter 9; however, as a general guideline, scheduling is based on the number of teachers, students, and activities to be offered. One scheduling example is the activities block. Using the traditional six- or seven-period day, this program offers one-, two-, or three-week mini-courses or a semester-long course at a specific time slot each day. This time block can also be used for in-class, whole school activities such as special events or guest speakers. The block schedule replaces the typical fifty-minute scheduling unit with larger time blocks. These blocks provide more daily time for students to get involved in their activities, and they also provide teachers more time to plan and coordinate exploratory experiences.

THE EXPLORATORY CURRICULUM: CASE STUDIES

The success of any exploratory curriculum in the middle school depends upon two essential factors: first, the principal's leadership ability to convince teachers of the important role and purpose the exploratory program plays in the overall developmental process of the transescent; and second, the available resources, both fiscal and material, for exploratory course offerings. There is a bridge between the academic block or core courses and exploratory courses which allows students to explore their own aptitudes, interests, and special talents as they develop intellectually, socially, emotionally, and physically.

Principal Joan Akin of Creekland Middle School (CMS), which has won both the Georgia School of Excellence Award and the International Inviting School Award, has a strong, comprehensive exploratory curriculum which, in her words, is "designed to allow every student to investigate a wide range of experiences which help identify aptitudes and interests which will challenge them and guide them in future education and career choices." The real value of the exploratory program lies in students' being exposed to new learning experiences which broaden their interests and personally excite them. "Realistically," Akin says, "for some students, the exploratory program will be the only time in their lives when they are exposed to some of these [learning] experiences."

Building a strong and enriching exploratory curriculum takes personal commitment from the principal and time and support from the core academic teachers, parents, and the community. Akin states, "Without a principal who honestly believes in the exploratory philosophy, is willing to build the program beyond state [Georgia] minimums, and champions its benefits, the exploratory program will be mediocre at best." Principal Walker Davis at West Jackson Middle School (WJMS) relates that "strong leadership for exploratory programs not only ensures their success but sustains their existence."

According to Davis, who was one of four original grant recipients to start middle school education in Georgia and who is past president of the Georgia Middle School Association, a comprehensive exploratory program is a function of economics and is limited by available funds necessary to hire staff and purchase equipment. Davis would like to offer more foreign language courses but lacks the funds to hire new teachers. Akin at CMS plans to expand the intramural program, part of the exploratory program, but lacks funds for equipment and qualified personnel. Both Davis and Akin are real-world principals who have political savvy and, therefore, pay close attention to parent and community surveys in providing exploratory course offerings. To a degree, the high school curriculum also dictates exploratory course offerings since interest in high school subjects has to be stimulated in the middle school.

Availability of qualified teachers is a major factor in what is offered in the exploratory curriculum. When courses have high student and/or parent interest, principals have a few options at their disposal. First, hire teachers qualified to teach the subject (if funds permit) or second, find interested teachers, currently employed, to take add-on certification courses. "A smart principal will find monies somewhere to help teachers add on courses over the summer. Of course, this all goes back to how much support the principal wants to put behind the course and if there is teacher interest in an add-on," Davis says. "Practically speaking," he continues, "once a course can be offered, there is always the question of money to buy necessary materials and [classroom] space to teach the course." Demand for exploratory courses is one thing, while the availability of qualified personnel, principal support, adequate finances, and space are other factors which must to be considered.

In some states, like Georgia, state requirements set minimum standards for exploratory programs for middle schools. In Georgia, each middle school student is required to take at least one course from each of four exploratory areas: formal learning, personal learning, vocational education, and technological education. These four broad areas allow middle schools wide latitude in their exploratory course offerings which frequently reflect local community needs and the priorities of the middle school staff. In rural Jackson County, Davis' exploratory curriculum primarily reflects the agricultural location of WJMS and the curriculum of the high school. Davis states that "while the textbook goal of the exploratory program is good and sound, and I believe in its basic premise, the reality of the situation is [you offer] what parents want, what the community wants, and what the kids will need for high school and work."

WJMS offers a variety of courses in the agricultural-technological (Ag-Tech) exploratory area which includes world of work, career exploration, consumer economics, technology for business and for agriculture, and computers. Courses differ in time frame with some being six weeks and some nine weeks in length. In the Ag-Tech area, there is also a sixteen-course block in which students can enroll for an entire year. Each of these exploratory courses are ten to twelve days long with many of the courses having a practical application component through partnerships with local businesses and agriculture cooperatives. These partnerships sponsor youth service projects and field trips and serve as a resource for the school's speaker program. Other exploratory courses at WJMS include art, foreign language, careers, computers, word processing, general music, industrial arts, and band and chorus (both are year-long courses). The curriculum and course offerings differ at each grade level with all students rotating through the exploratory schedule based on student preference of courses and principal assignment. Each course is forty-five minutes in length with students heterogeneously grouped in all three grade levels for both exploratory and core academic courses. Often, student preference is a secondary consideration to principal assignment which is based on state requirements.

At WJMS, band and chorus drive the exploratory schedule, Davis explains. Band and chorus are electives which students can choose, they are year-long courses, they meet for forty-five minutes every day, and they fulfill the requirements for the fine arts or formal learning area of the exploratory curriculum. Based on which of these two electives a student selects, the principal assigns these students to other exploratory courses which will not conflict with their band or chorus time and yet will fulfill minimum state requirements of one exploratory course in each of the four areas of exploration when enrolled in grades six through eight. Physical education is a required exploratory course and students must have sixty contact hours in this course per year. Health, also a required course, must be provided for each student for thirty hours a year. Both courses fulfill the requirement in the personal learning area of exploration.

Effective exploratory courses, according to Davis and Akin, depend on two essentials: teachers need adequate planning time, and the exploratory curriculum must correlate with the core curriculum. In Georgia, state requirements provide for a minimum of eighty-five minutes per day for individual and/or team planning. At WJMS, exploratory teachers have a forty-five minute block of planning time each day, an extended lunch period, and thirty minutes at the end of the school day. Exploratory teachers jointly plan with core academic teachers the thematic units of each grade-level curriculum. This ensures instructional continuity across all three grade levels. Davis points out that an important leadership role of the principal "is to *require* joint planning between exploratory and academic block teachers so students can easily make the connections between exploration content and content taught in the academics." Without strong leadership, Davis believes that many exploratory teachers would choose not to deliver their course content through thematic units but would choose a more traditional approach.

Minicourses and other electives are in the planning stage at WJMS. The implementation of these courses will depend on fiscal resources and both teacher interest and time in their already demanding schedules. This, Davis says, is a "real world situation which somehow doesn't come out in graduate classes that focus on the 'you ought to' aspects." Two areas in which electives are planned are theater and dance, but their implementation will depend not just on teacher interest but the amount of assistance teachers can get from community volunteers. Mini-courses, also known as enrichment or special-interest courses, are also planned to allow students to explore more deeply certain subtopics or areas found within the exploratory course offerings or electives. According to Davis, like elective courses, teacher expertise, interest, and time will dictate "if and what kind of mini-courses will be offered. I have to then worry about available space, resources, and my block schedule."

Davis provides a concluding example (see Figure 3.2) of how joint planning between exploratory and core academic teachers and thematic instruction actually work. The example is a four to five week topic entitled "People and Their Earth."

The exploratory curriculum at CMS complements the core academic block with joint planning through a thematic curriculum developed by exploratory and core academic teachers. Exploratory teachers work closely with interdisciplinary teacher teams in each of the five communities which house approximately 450 sixth, seventh, and eighth grade students. Each student attends two exploratory classes each day and rotates through a variety of courses each year. As in the core academic block, students in exploratory courses are heterogeneously grouped for instruction and must meet the

Theme of Study: People and Their Earth

Social Studies focuses on human development, exploration, human behavior, governmental and societal structures, and the importance of history.

Language Arts focuses on social studies themes with written and oral reports, position papers, literature and folk tales, and poetry, legends, and myths.

Science focuses on tools for scientific investigation, the ecology, weather, astronomy, natural resources, limited space, and interdependency of conservation.

Mathematics focuses on reading problems and basic computation relative to man's survival, charts and graphs relative to population, GNP, and food and water supply, and using mathematics for consumers and conservation.

Exploratory curriculum would be correlated to the theme topic.

A day or more in a cross section of the thematic unit presented above could be as follows:

Social Studies:

1.   Exploration - economic and political reasons for seeking new territory. Developing a constitution for government in the new level.

Language Arts:

1.   Exploration - stories, myths, legends, folk tales about exploration, space, oceans, and land travel. Writing a poem or story about exploration.

Science:

1.   Exploration - charts, maps, and astronomy relative to the importance of exploration. Figuring nautical miles, navigating an ocean voyage with tolls available at the time of exploration and how to get drinking water from seawater.

Mathematics:

1.   Exploration - determining the amount of food and water needed for a voyage, length of a voyage estimated on sea and air currents.

FIGURE 3.2. Example of thematic unit involving exploratory and core academic teachers at WJMS.

<u>Exploratory courses:</u>

<u>Health</u>

1. Exploration - What nutritious foods would be needed on a voyage and what personal health-care items would be needed.

<u>Physical Education</u>

1. Exploration - the amount of exercise needed and kinds of exercise voyagers could have. Games played during the exploration period and recreational activities available.

<u>Music</u>

1. Exploration - the type of instruments played during the exploration period, types of dances danced, and the kinds of music written and played which reflected the culture of the explorers.

FIGURE 3.2 (continued). Example of thematic unit involving exploratory and core academic teachers at WJMS.

Georgia state requirements for instruction. The requirement is two exploratory courses in three areas and one course in all four areas during their three-year middle school experience. Students may choose a year-long elective each year from the school's state award-winning music classes—band, orchestra, and chorus—or from the foreign language component. Exploratory courses include art, general music, computer science, foreign language, journalism, family and consumer services, technology education, and career connections.

Activities such as organizations and clubs are planned and are open to all students. More than twenty different activities are available for student choice in the areas of school leadership, community service, publishing, personal enrichment, and academic exploration. In addition, a comprehensive after school intramural program is offered during fall and spring quarters in the school's two large gymnasiums. Winter quarter, eighth grade cheerleading and basketball teams compete against other county middle school teams.

Technology is a major part of the school's exploratory and academic core curriculum. Each community has a computer in each administrator's and counselor's office and in each classroom. Each community also has a computer laboratory that is connected into the media center via a schoolwide network with connections to the County Wide Area Network and Internet. Students can access personal data files and the media center's on-line card catalog, reference software on CDs, and use instructional software. The network supports an electronic grade book and attendance system, and e-mail.

Four computer laboratories are for academic classes while the other is the Computer Science Exploratory Laboratory for computer exploration classes. Here, programming, presentation, telecommunications, history of technology, word processing, database, keyboarding, spreadsheet, and graphics are taught. A subset of the exploratory computer laboratory is a state-of-the art IBM lab for explorations in technology. A broad spectrum of modules are taught which include animation, robotics, radio communications, aerodynamics, weather, space flight, pneumatics and mechanics, hydroponics, and lasers.

In addition, a mobile laboratory, housing two word processing labs, an instructional lab, graphic calculators, and closed circuit television aid students in creating their own work and conducting research. Technology plays a major role in teaching and learning at CMS.

At CMS, students can request exploratory course assignment but, for the most part, they are randomly assigned in a regular rotation for the nine-week exploratory courses. Health is required for nine weeks while physical education is required for eighteen weeks. "Realistically," says Akin, "I would like to allow students more choice in their exploratory selections, but with state requirements, the 2,300 plus students, and [the number of] course offerings, I have to make random assignments."

Like Walker Davis at West Jackson Middle School, Akin relates that the exploratory program is only as good and as comprehensive as the financial backing it receives. "Hiring teachers and buying instructional materials rest on an economic foundation." Akin is quick to add that teacher expertise and interest in teaching an exploratory course are also major factors in having a strong exploratory program. She tells of her active search for several years to find a Latin teacher certified in grades six through eight. In this particular instance, the demand for Latin in the exploratory curriculum was present and came from three sources: her own personal belief in the value and importance of the language, parent requests, and student interest. While she had a budgeted line item for a Latin teacher (in this case money was not the problem), until this year she could not find a qualified teacher to meet the demand.

However, adequate finances and teacher interest and expertise are not in themselves sufficient for a strong exploratory program in the middle school. "Principals," she states, "must personally believe in the value of the exploratory program and be committed to the goals and objectives of exploratory experiences or the program will not be totally successful." Moreover, principals have to show leadership by convincing some of the core academic teachers that exploratory courses are valuable and "complement the academic program." This is not always an easy task, she says, and can only be accomplished over time through the principal's own determination, by working with these teachers and personally demonstrating how exploratory and academic courses interrelate, and by reminding teachers of the goals of middle school education.

Within the exploratory program at CMS are developmental courses for at-risk students and classes for the gifted and talented students. Developmental courses concentrate on basic skills in reading and mathematics with computer assisted instruction playing a major role. Gifted and talented students are identi-fied through standardized tests, teacher recommendations, and past perform-ance data and these students receive instruction for one academic subject (their strongest identified subject) daily from certified gifted and talented teachers.

Akin maintains that any exploratory program, to be ultimately success-ful, must provide students the opportunities to succeed in diverse areas, must allow for different experiences to spark student interest in new and un-explored activities, and must foster the idea that learning is fun and person-ally rewarding. She believes that "students should be exposed to everything, if only for a brief time. You never know what sparks interest. Remember," she adds, "exploration is not for making career decisions or choices, but for personal satisfaction and enjoyment."

REFERENCES

Alexander, W. M., E. L. Williams, M. Compton, V. A. Hines, and D. Prescott. 1968. *The Emergent Middle School.* New York: Holt, Rinehart, and Winston, Inc.

Armstrong, T. 1994. *Multiple Intelligences in the Classroom.* Alexandria, VA: Associa-tion for Supervision and Curriculum Development.

Arnold, J. 1985. "A Responsible Curriculum for Early Adolescence," *Middle School Journal* 16(3):14–18.

Beane, J. A. 1990. *A Middle School Curriculum: From Rhetoric to Reality.* Columbus, OH: National Middle School Association.

Becker, H. J. 1990. "Curriculum and Instruction in the Middle-Grade Schools," *Phi Delta Kappan,* 71:450–457.

Berryman, S. E. 1993. "Learning for the Workplace," in *Review of Research in Educa-tion, Vol. 19. L.* Darling-Hammond, ed. Washington, D.C.: American Educational Research Association, pp. 343–401.

Cawelti, G. 1988, November. "Middle Schools, a Better Match with Early Adolescent Needs, ASCD Survey Finds," *ASCD Curriculum Update.* Alexandria, VA: Asso-ciation for Supervision and Curriculum Development.

Center for Research on Elementary and Middle Schools. 1990. "Implementation and Ef-fects of Middle Grades Practices," *CREMS Report.* Baltimore, MD: Johns Hopkins University Center for Research on Elementary and Middle Schools.

Deming, W. E. 1993. *The New Economics for Industry, Government, Education.* Cam-bridge, MA: MIT Center for Advanced Engineering Study.

Engel, R. and L. D. Weller. 1975. "Mini-courses: Maxi Morale," *The High School Jour-nal,* 56(3):142–149.

Epstein, J. L. and D. J. MacIver. 1990. "National Practices and Trends in the Middle Grades," *Middle School Journal,* 22(2):35–39.

Farmer, R. F., M. W. Gould, R. L. Herring, F. J. Linn, and M. A. Theobald. 1995. *The Middle School Principal.* Thousand Oaks, CA: Corwin Press, Inc.

Gardner, H. 1983. *Frames of Mind: The Theory of Multiple Intelligences.* Tenth Anniversary Edition. New York: Basic Books.

George, P. S. and W. A. Alexander. 1993. *The Exemplary Middle School.* Second edition. Fort Worth, TX: Harcourt Brace Jovanovich College Publishers.

George, P. S. and W. G. Anderson. 1989. "Maintaining the Middle School: A National Survey," *National Association of Secondary School Principals Bulletin 73*, pp. 67–74.

George, P. and G. Lawrence. 1982. *Handbook for Middle School Teaching.* Glenview, IL: Scott, Foresman.

Glatthorn, A. A. 1987. *Curriculum Leadership.* Glenview, IL: Scott, Foresman and Company.

Goodlad, J. I. 1977. "What Goes on in Our Schools?" *Educational Researcher* 6:3–6.

Gowan, J. C., J. Khatena, and E. P. Torrance. 1981. *Creativity: Its Educational Implications.* Second edition. Dubuque, IA: Kendall/Hunt Publishing Company.

Hoy, W. K. and C. Miskel. 1996. *Educational Administration: Theory, Research, Practice.* Fifth edition. New York: McGraw-Hill, Inc.

Lipsitz, J. 1984. *Successful Schools for Young Adolescents.* New Brunswick, NJ: Transaction Books.

Lounsbury, J. H. 1990. "Middle Level Schools—Once Around the Elephant," in *Schools in the Middle: A Report on Trends and Practices.* Reston, VA: National Association of Secondary School Principals.

Lounsbury, J. H. and D. C. Clark. 1990. *Inside Grade Eight: From Apathy to Excitement.* Reston, VA: National Association of Secondary School Administrators.

Melton, G. E. 1984. "The Junior High School: Success and Failures," in *Perspectives: Middle School Education, 1964–1984.* J. H. Lounsbury, ed. Columbus, OH: National Middle School Association, pp. 5–13.

Messick, R. G. and K. E. Reynolds. 1992. *Middle Level Curriculum in Action.* White Plains, NY: Longman.

National Commission on Excellence in Education. 1983. *A Nation at Risk.* Washington, D.C.: United States Government Printing Office.

Spencer, H. 1894. *Education: Intellectual, Moral, and Physical.* New York: D. Appleton and Company.

Task Force on Education for Economic Growth. 1983. *Action for Excellence.* Denver, CO: Education Commission of the States.

U.S. Department of Education. 1991. *America 2000: An Educational Strategy.* Washington, DC: Author.

Vars, G. F. 1987. *Interdisciplinary Teaching in the Middle Grades.* Columbus, OH: National Middle School Association.

Weller, L. D. and S. H. Hartley. 1994. "Total Quality Management and School Restructuring: Georgia's Approach to Educational Reform," *Quality Assurance in Education, 2*(2):22–25.

Weller, L. D., S. H. Hartley, and C. L. Brown. 1994. "Principals and TQM: Developing Vision," *The Clearing House, 67*(5):298–301.

Zaleznik, A. 1977. "Managers and Leaders: Are They Different?" *Harvard Business Review, 55*(5):67–78.

CHAPTER 4

Teams, Team Building, Team Planning, and Team Teaching: The Role of the Middle School Principal

Effective middle school principals know that teams and teamwork are a major factor in achieving high performance in both educational and business organizations. Research abounds regarding the significant impact made by teams in promoting quality schools and corporations. However, the best schools and businesses take care to develop a collaborative philosophy in which the configuration of teams and their roles and responsibilities are carefully thought out and well-defined. Teaming for teaming's sake, without purpose or mission, leads to frustration and failure.

High achieving teams are often distinguished by the following characteristics: a clear vision with high achieving goals; a results-driven structure; competent team members; a unified commitment; a collaborative climate with high expectations for the team and self; adequate resources, time, and recognition; and dedicated principal support and leadership. These eight criteria of effective teams provide essential guidelines for the middle school principal in evaluating and renewing teamwork in middle schools. These criteria serve as the foundation for high team performance in middle schools.

Specifically, this chapter will address the following questions:

- What is the role and what are the responsibilities of the principal in building quality teams?
- What are the essential components of effective teams and what skills and knowledge are needed to make teachers effective team members?
- Why is team-building important?
- What are effective ways to prepare teachers for teamwork and team teaching?
- What are the major considerations principals face in building an effective teacher team?

109

- What are the major advantages and disadvantages of teams?
- What are the instruments principals can use to develop teacher profiles for building effective teacher teams?
- What are the major considerations principals face when both implementing and scheduling team planning activities?
- What kind of space, resources, and scheduling configurations are needed to allow teachers to maximize their planning efforts?
- What are ways principals can show support and leadership for teacher teams?
- What are the most common problems and issues teachers must address during team planning and why are they important?
- What are the major disadvantages of failure to provide time for teachers to plan?
- What is team teaching?
- What are the benefits of team teaching for teachers, students, and the instructional program?
- What is "turn teaching" and why is it less effective than team teaching?

This chapter will include examples of schedules designed to accommodate team teaching, instruments used to assess teacher personalities and their ability to work effectively in teams, team planning guides, effective team meeting guides, and team teaching planning guides in the core and exploratory curriculum areas. Pitfalls to avoid will also be presented when discussing each of the following topics: teams, team building, team planning, and team teaching. Case studies of building quality, high-performing interdisciplinary teams will also be presented.

TEAMS

The idea that professionals should pull together, work cooperatively, and place individual interests second to those of the profession or organization has long been espoused by leaders in business, education, and the public service areas. Working together as a team to achieve common goals, to plan cooperatively, and to share responsibility for meeting the desired ends of the profession are worthy concepts and values which receive universal support, but they are, in fact, not commonly implemented. The attitude of "rugged individualism," the competition among individuals to succeed and achieve personal recognition and to protect one's own turf and self-interests, prevails, with teamwork being both a worthy goal and a difficult concept to achieve. When competition among individuals overpowers cooperation, alienation and frustration occur and blame is placed on management or colleagues for failures impacting the work life of the individual (Weller, 1995). In quality-oriented middle schools, teamwork is emphasized and shared governance structures exist which foster cooperation and collaboration, and reduce alienation.

Teams and School Restructuring and Reform

Within the last decade the call for teamwork in the public and private sectors has increased significantly. The quality movement in business, often referred to as Total Quality Management (TQM), sparked the introduction of empowered teams and made clear the advantages of teamwork through the success of cooperative endeavors to increase product performance and profit margins by producing quality products. Traditional bureaucratic administrative hierarchies and rigid directive management of the employee were replaced by teams of workers empowered to solve problems and make decisions. Deming (1986) realized the value and power in cooperative enterprise and maintained that if organizations tapped the power of their human resources by giving employees the freedom to be creative and the responsibility to solve problems confronting them in their workplace, quality products and service would result.

In education, public criticism over the public schools' failure to produce quality education and to compete favorably on international tests of achievement with students from foreign countries contributed to a call for school reform and restructuring. Weller and Hartley (1994) note that the Deming principles (1986) of empowered teams and collaboration are being used widely in schools practicing the TQM principles and site-based management paradigms for school reform and restructuring. Schmoker and Wilson (1993), in presenting case studies of successful TQM schools, relate positive gains in student achievement, student self-esteem, and teacher morale and self-esteem. Central to these gains are the Deming principles of creating vision, striving for continuous improvement, and empowering subordinates to solve problems and make decisions.

Teams in TQM schools play a vital role in school governance procedures and, in some site-based management schools, teams of teachers, parents, administrators, and community members have the primary responsibility of running the school. Restructuring schools around teams of teachers responsible for making decisions about school governance and student learning are the same principles found in the middle school movement (Maeroff, 1993). The research literature on effective schools and effective school principals points out that teacher teams and shared governance structures are major factors in achieving high performance from students and teachers alike (Purkey and Smith, 1983). Principals in these schools provide a large measure of autonomy to their teachers by allowing them to work cooperatively, to teach what they want to teach how they want to teach it, and to solve problems impacting classroom instruction (DuFour and Eaker, 1992). The research on teacher motivation finds that empowered teacher teams who can influence the curriculum and share in the governance of the school exhibit increased morale and performance and a greater sense of professionalism. DuFour and Eaker state: "Recent research on effective organizations, effective leaders and effective schools calls for a new definition of the principalship" (p. 47) and they envision this definition as encompassing four major roles:

(1) Empowerer of teachers
(2) Promoter and protector of values
(3) Leader of instruction
(4) Manager of climate

While teams and team teaching were not an essential concept in the original middle school movement, teams and team teaching arrangements began to emerge in middle schools as an organizational pattern in the form of interdisciplinary teams and single-subject teams. The restructuring paradigms for the 1990s have included the use of teams as a central element in reform education. Whitaker and Moses (1990), in discussing school restructuring, state that a need exists in education "to include multiple interactions rather than one way directives, leadership by knowledge rather than authority, and inquiring behavior rather than mandated behavior" (p. 4). Wiles and Bondi (1993) discuss the positive aspects of the middle school movement and note that teacher teams formed around intact groups of students better promote learning and help students assume more responsibility for their learning experiences. Successful teams in middle schools, they state, are those which are dedicated to the ideals of the middle school concept, are student-focused, and place the unique needs of the transescent above all other considerations.

Effective middle school principals, however, do not form teams just for the sake of teaming. They do so with a clearly defined purpose or mission. Configurations of teams and their roles and responsibilities are carefully thought out and well-defined. Planning such as this decreases the likelihood of failure and reduces frustration among teacher team members.

Characteristics of Effective Teams

Garner (1988) relates that a group of people gathered together to achieve a goal or perform a task is not a team. The name "team" affixed to a group does not ensure cooperation, dedication, or accomplishment. There are, however, certain distinguishing characteristics of high achieving teams. According to Larson and LaFasto (1989), who researched effective teams in business, education, and service sector agencies over a three-year period, effective teams have eight consistent characteristics. These are as follows:

(1) Clear goals and objectives, with the goals of the team taking priority over individual goals: teams with goals have a definite purpose, a sense of urgency, and a belief that their tasks can make a difference.

(2) A structure driven by desired results: teams require different types of structure based on the results expected from the team. Larson and LaFasto found problem resolution teams must promote trust among team members, be open in sharing ideas and feelings, and be able and willing to gather data and discuss results objectively; creative teams must promote autonomy and be free of common constraints that hinder brainstorming, creative ideas, innovative programs, and a "new" way to approach problems; tactical teams must promote planning and emphasize order and clarity regarding what, when, how, why, and by whom a task will be done.

(3) Competent team members: competent teams are comprised of members with both technical and personal skills. Each type of skill complements the other to accomplish the team's task. Central to team skills are conflict resolution and interpersonal skills which are necessary if the task is to be accomplished with the desired outcome and within the required time frame. These skills can and should be taught to all team members through planned staff development activities prior to the implementation of teams in a shared governance structure (Weller, 1995).

(4) Unified commitment: team members must be personally committed to the task at hand and to their team members. The individual and the team are one and have a shared sense of responsibility.

(5) Collaborative climate: clear roles and responsibilities and open communication among team members are essential to task achievement. There is trust among members and careful consideration is given to the comments and ideas of all team members. Each team member feels valued for individual contributions and expertise and is encouraged to participate and lead when appropriate.

(6) Standards of excellence: high standards are set which will measure the success or failure of the team, individuals within the team, and the team's project. Larson and LaFasto (1989) present four criteria to judge these standards of excellence: (1) personal evaluation of one's own performance and that of the team and the project; (2) team evaluation as a whole of the teamwork and project success; (3) the success or failure of the project; and (4) outside evaluation sources.

(7) External support and recognition: teams need administrative support,

time, and resources to do their job effectively. They also need recognition and rewards for their work. Weller (1995) notes that teams work in a way which supports the values and philosophy of the organization. When administrative support and recognition is a given, teams are productive and tasks are taken seriously. When support and recognition is lacking, teamwork becomes counterproductive.

(8) Principled leadership: leadership is essential for teamwork success. Larson and LaFasto (1989) identified three elements of successful leaders: (1) they establish a vision, (2) they promote change, and (3) they unleash talent. Leadership of this nature requires leaders to share power by delegating to teams the responsibility to solve problems, make decisions, and implement their solutions.

Larson and LaFasto (1989) state that these eight characteristics can serve as a template for the evaluation of team performance and can be used to pinpoint areas of weakness in team performance. Since each characteristic supports or reinforces the others, identifying weak links and taking measures to correct them become essential.

Team Development and Group Decision Making

Many team-development and group decision-making models explain the various stages groups go through to reach a decision, with each model defining these stages differently. Tuckman (1965) relates that each group is different and, therefore, must go about the decision-making process differently. A decision is defined as the outcome of group interaction which reflects a choice made by the team from two or more alternatives. A decision, usually reached by consensus, implies agreement and commitment, but does not necessarily mean unanimous consent (Fisher, 1980). The phenomenon of consensus without a unanimous decision depends not on individual agreement with the decision but the extent of group *loyalty* shared by team members to support the group decision and the socio-emotional behaviors displayed within the decision-making process itself (Zaleznick and Moment, 1964). Principals must know and understand the process of group decision making, how groups make decisions and achieve consensus, and how members exert influence on one another during the different stages of the decision-making process if they are to provide training and assistance to teachers before implementing shared governance in schools.

Two four-phase models of group development and decision making are presented below as examples of this process. In addition to the two models presented here, principals may wish to examine the Interaction Process

Analysis (IPA) model by Bales and Strodtbeck (1951) and The Special
Model of Decision Making by Scheidel and Crowell (1964).

THE FOUR-PHASE MODEL OF GROUP DEVELOPMENT

The four-phase models of Dunphy (Fisher, 1980, p. 138) and Tuckman
(1965) purport that a group accomplishes the most productive work in the
latter stages of the group decision-making process. Both models view group
productivity as a result of first establishing a stable social structure in order
to become task-oriented. These models explain how groups move through
four phases to reach productivity. Each model describes each of the four
phases or stages differently but they have common characteristics. The first
stage is that of orientation or testing wherein group members get to know
each other, assume roles, test alliances, and become task-oriented. The second stage denotes conflict or infighting which occurs as the members set
procedures, clarify the task, and establish values. The third stage witnesses
group cohesion and the beginning of task accomplishment through purpose
and expectations. The fourth stage, task completion, is where members
reach consensus and complete the task.

The first four-phase model described by Dunphy (Fisher, 1980, p. 138) is
presented in terms of socio-emotional dimensions. These are as follows:

- Stage 1: dependency is where group members look to a leader for
  direction.
- Stage 2: fight-flight is where group members resist the direction of
  the leader to whom they turned for guidance and develop their own
  direction.
- Stage 3: pairing is where group members begin to display group
  cohesiveness and establish a sense of mission and commitment to a
  common goal.
- Stage 4: work is where group members begin in earnest to work
  together to achieve their agreed-upon goal.

The four-phase model of group decision making developed by Tuckman
(1965) emphasizes the social structure and personal interaction of group
membership. The four stages occur in the following order:

- Stage 1: forming. The group identifies the group task or goal and
  gets to know one another as group members. Trust among members
  is low.
- Stage 2: storming. Group members test each other's wills,
  identifying where they stand as the task is being identified and work
  assignments are being delineated. Emotional responses to personal

challenges occur at this stage and infighting over purpose and leadership takes place.

- Stage 3: norming. The group achieves unity or a shared sense of purpose within the membership, becoming a cohesive group. There is free and open expression of ideas without fear of personal attack concerning individual opinion or views.
- Stage 4: performing. The group reaches consensus on a solution to the task with this goal being the focal point of the group.

The idea that teams and teamwork can promote quality outcomes is sound and is part of those various elements found in both the effective schools movement and in TQM schools. However, to use self-managed, empowered teams effectively, the principal must give these teams the power, the support, and the time necessary to achieve their tasks.

TEAM BUILDING

If team planning and team teaching are to promote an effective instructional delivery system, the process of team building then becomes a critical issue. When building a team, the principal must consider a number of factors since each team is comprised of teachers with different personalities, different strengths and weaknesses, and different teaching styles and abilities. Careful selection of teachers for teamwork is important because the team process is ongoing throughout the middle school program, and effective and efficient teams must operate on mutual trust and in a spirit of cooperation and collaboration. Team members must be flexible and cooperative since they must often make short-notice changes and attend frequent meetings. Members must be amenable to compromise and open to innovative ideas. Team members, therefore, must be objective and professional, and they must examine ideas—not personalities.

Central to the team building process is the idea of teacher empowerment. Empowered teacher teams share in school governance and provide the vehicle for teacher leadership in the schools. Empowered or self-managed teams are the link between the hierarchy of the school and the customer—students, and principals in effective middle schools build teams around this concept (Spady and Marshall, 1991). Empowerment, however, can be a hollow concept if the principal does not take into consideration the factor of human nature. One of the most fundamental concepts of team building is that teams are comprised of individuals, with each person having individual idiosyncrasies, human frailties, and personal values. When individuals are placed in team situations, the dominant behavior continues to be that of individualism as opposed to group or team thinking. The idea of being a team player is second to the inbred notion of self-reliance and individualism taught by parents, teachers, and others who have a dominant effect on maturation (Weller, 1995). The principal must acknowledge this given of human nature and set in place a process to overcome it. Establishing a clear vision and a positive school climate is the first step.

Team Environment

The environment or climate found in schools directly impacts the overall instructional program within the school. Effective middle schools have a shared vision which includes the values, norms, and traditions of the school which are perpetuated by both principal and staff. The environmental characteristics of the school set the tone for the daily work activities found within the school whether these activities be teamwork, team planning, team teaching, or individual classroom instruction. Hoy and Miskel (1996) note that school climate is influenced by the personalities of the participants, mostly its leadership, and results in the collective behavior set forth within the school. The perceptions of the general work environment and the internal characteristics that distinguish one school from another influence the behavior of its membership. School climate is to the school as personality is to the individual.

Central to effective school climate are a safe and orderly school for teachers to work and students to learn; high expectations for students and teachers to succeed; strong instructional leadership emphasizing academics and continuous improvement for the professional development of teachers; a clear vision that unifies all school members; and community and parental support for the school. Lezotte (1991) notes that while no single factor accounts for a successful school environment, all of these characteristics are found in successful schools.

Team Member Components

Teams, made up of individual teachers, reflect the climate of the school in which they exist and the perceptions of that climate held by themselves and others. Personalities of teachers, differing teaching styles of teachers, and teachers' ability to function cooperatively as group members are important considerations for the school environment and team building. Skills in conflict resolution and interpersonal communications are necessary for team effectiveness. Balancing stronger teachers with weaker teachers is an important consideration. Some teachers, however, are simply not "team players" and will need specific counseling with the principal.

Working together effectively is the essential element in productive teamwork. The team leader, appointed by the principal or elected by team members on a rotating basis, is the most important role in the team because of the coordinating and administrative responsibilities of the team leader and the leadership tasks that the leader must perform (Wiles and Bondi, 1993). Coordinating and conducting team meetings takes time. A knowledge of what constitutes an effective meeting and how to manage time considerations are important. Setting agendas and team meeting times and coordinating parent conferences are major functions needing consideration prior to team meetings. Carrying out administrative responsibilities such as preparing reports, ordering and distributing supplies, disseminating information, delegating responsibility, recommending changes in the curriculum, and evaluating both team and team member performance are important duties requiring attention to detail. Leadership calls for "team thinking" and "team acting." Being fair to all, providing an atmosphere where all can express their opinions and ideas openly and freely, being committed to the vision of the school and to success, and providing a supportive environment are quality leadership behaviors for team leaders. Three other behaviors contributing to leadership effectiveness are loyalty, keeping promises and being reliable; creativity, encouraging team members to think beyond the traditional paradigms and to explore new ways to solve problems; and maturity, being truthful and realistic.

Assessing each team member's strengths and weaknesses is essential for good team balance. Essential traits for effective middle school team members are a belief in and knowledge of the middle school philosophy and concept; knowledge of the special needs, traits, and characteristics of the transescent learner; flexibility and tolerance; and enthusiasm about work and working collaboratively (Wiles and Bondi, 1993). Other desirable traits in high performing team members include a capacity to work both as a team member and independently, function under stressful or personally compromising situations, remain focused and dedicated to the task and the team concept, remain tolerant of others with conflicting views, and be enthusiastic and willing to learn and grow personally and professionally (Wilkinson and Smith, 1995).

Individual Needs of Team Members

Teams are comprised of individuals with different needs and personalities. Matching needs and personalities in teams can promote greater group harmony, cooperation, and collaboration and lead to greater team productivity. Like an organization, teams are open social systems which have the following characteristics:

(1) Social systems are goal-oriented, comprised of interdependent parts and activities which contribute to the whole organization.

(2) Social systems are comprised of people who have different needs, roles, and goals.

(3) Social systems are normative in that all people within them behave in the way their roles are perceived by themselves, by others, and by the organizational hierarchy.

(4) Social systems provide sanctions for individual behavior through rewards and punishments.

(5) Social systems are relative and conceptual and the concept applies to any size or type of social organization. This system can be a family, a group, or a large organization (Getzels and Guba, 1957).

Individuals in a team (a social system) have personalities, needs, and roles. Individuals, through their behavior, shape the roles they occupy according to their needs and perceptions of the roles they are in, which, in turn, are tempered by the expectations of the individuals in those roles. In the Getzels and Guba (1957) model, personality is defined as behavior, but also as an internal motivational system which sees a goal as attractive or repugnant. The personality is changing, self-regulating, and interacting with the system. It is dynamic in scope since no two people are motivated by the same needs or expectations. Needs of the individual vary and affect the goals of the individual and the way the individual perceives the team. There have been many theories offered on individual needs. The most useful and well known is Maslow's needs hierarchy theory (1970). Basically, Maslow asserts that human needs are on five levels and range from the most common or physiological needs such as food, shelter, and water to the highest order of self-actualization which is maximal self-development.

The needs theory of Maslow (1970) has five levels which progress in hierarchy with the higher level needs becoming activated as lower level needs are satisfied. As each level is satisfied, new needs emerge and satisfaction is sought until the next highest need level is attained. It goes without saying that very few individuals reach the stage of self-actualization because needs at the lower levels have not been met. Motivation of the individual, therefore, lies in satisfying the needs of the individual at the place on the hierarchy where the needs disposition lies. The need levels of Maslow are as presented below from lowest to highest:

- Level 1: physiological—food, water, shelter
- Level 2: safety and security—protection, stability, freedom from fear
- Level 3: belonging, love, social acceptance—good working relationships, peer acceptance, friendship

- Level 4: esteem—respect from peers, value as a person, status, self-esteem
- Level 5: self-actualization—achievement of full potential

The work needs of the individual and the degree to which these needs are satisfied impact the individual's work behavior. The demands of the work role and the needs of the individual have a direct relationship. When the needs of the individual are not met in the workplace or fulfilled by the individual's perception of the work role, motivation toward attaining the team's goals or those of the organization is low and work effort can be counterproductive. Since teams operate inside the environment of the organization, both organizational and team needs must be satisfied if the individual is to be highly motivated. Personality conflicts, which result from lack of individual need fulfillment from the organization or team, cause internal stress in both the individual and the work environment. This stress leads to behavior which is not compatible with role or organizational norms or expectations.

Personality Types of Team Members

Personality can be defined "as an individual's distinctive and relatively stable pattern of behavior, motives, and thoughts" (Wade and Travis, 1990, p. 417). Carl Jung (1971), the Swiss psychologist, believed that the predisposition toward personality preference is inborn, but that personality type development is a lifelong process. For Jung, people are motivated by future goals and the desire to fulfill their aspirations. Jung's work resulted in his theory of personality type which purports that "seeming chance variation in human behavior is not due to chance; it is in fact the logical result of a few basic, observable preferences" (Myers and McCaulley, 1985, p. 11).

According to Jung's theory (1971), all conscious mental activity can be characterized within the four functions of sensing, intuition, thinking, and feeling. Sensing and intuition are two kinds of perception, and thinking and feeling are two kinds of judgment. Each individual has a preferred method of perceiving, how that person takes in information, and a preferred method of judging, how that person makes decisions based on that information. Extroversion and introversion, according to Jung, are complementary attitudes toward life and each individual is predisposed toward one or the other. Extroversion is an attitude that is outer-world oriented, with attention focused on people and objects in the environment. Introversion is an attitude that is inner-world oriented, with attention focused on concepts and ideas.

Jungian personality theory (1971) also maintains that personality development is life-long and during midlife people tend to become generalists where all four functions are developed and used. Optimal development is when each of the four functions can be used for situations and tasks for which they are best suited. Two additional functions, judgment and perception, were added to Jung's four functions by Myers and Briggs (Myers, 1980) and are measured on the Myers Briggs Type Indicator (MBTI) along with Jung's introversion and extroversion attitudes and the sensing, intuitive, thinking, and feeling functions. Judgment and perception relate to decision making and focus on flexibility.

APPLICATION OF PERSONALITY TYPE THEORY

The MBTI can be used to measure Jungian personality type. The MBTI measures preference scores on four dichotomous indices and a self-reporting form is available for practical use. The indices are extroversion-introversion, sensing-intuition, thinking-feeling, and judgment-perception. For principals and team leaders, information about personality type can be helpful for selecting employees and team members for team balance and team task assignments. Myers and McCaulley (1985) also suggest other ways the MBTI can be used in educational settings:

(1) To help teachers, administrators, and parents work together in constructive ways
(2) To develop different teaching and communication methods to meet the needs of different type personalities
(3) To help individuals understand their strengths and weaknesses based on their personality preferences
(4) To guide individuals in their choice of school, majors, professions, occupations, and work settings

For educational leadership, Morris (1985) explained the necessity of "congruency" (p. 22) between the personality of an individual and the requirements of effective leadership. Effective leadership research reports that certain leadership behaviors are more effective than others and that certain procedures and characteristics are essential for effectiveness, but, according to Morris, these "leadership behaviors lie outside the natural predisposition" (p. 22) of some leaders. Knowledge of individuals' "predispositions" toward certain leadership behaviors can provide important insight into what may be the outcomes if these individuals are placed in leadership positions. For principals, this information about personality type can be used for teacher employment and team member selection to facilitate work tasks. Matching personality types decreases the chances of role-personality conflict which often occurs in group situations. Personality types have implications for teachers and students in the classroom as well.

Individual Learning Styles

Individual learning styles have been identified by Goloy (1982), Dunn (1991), and McCarthy (1991). Goloy applies the work of Jung (1971) to learning styles and focuses on the mental functions of sensing, intuition, thinking, and feeling. Each individual has certain psychological preferences and each function is developed differently. Skills and interests as well as behavior patterns are developed early and dominate our interactions. Research supports that teachers and students have one of sixteen personality types as identified by the MBTI and that each type has a preferred learning style. For teachers, their preferred learning styles determine their preferred teaching styles while students' preferred learning styles influence their knowledge and skill acquisition.

Learning style preference has also been tied to left and right brain research. The two hemispheres of the brain work together but develop differently for certain functions. Left brain processing is more analytical, linear, and step-by-step (verbal, rational, logical). Right brain processing is oriented to the visual, spatial, imaginative, symbolic, and aesthetic. McCarthy (1991) found that learning styles are connected to brain hemispheres and that learning activities which focus on these processes promote learning. McCarthy's 4MAT System identifies four different learning styles. He notes that improved teaching and learning comes from instruction which uses strategies that relate to each learner's style preference. The learning styles in this system are the imaginative, the analytical, the common sense, and the dynamic.

The value for principals in identifying teachers' learning and teaching styles lies in the way this knowledge can be used to design highly effective teams and to identify the inservice and staff development needs of these teachers.

Conflict Resolution and Interpersonal Communication

Conflict management models exist for the purpose of proposing ways to manage conflict between individual and organizational needs. While there is no one best way to resolve conflict, principals and team leaders can minimize conflict by attempting to satisfy the concerns of the leader (to accomplish the task) *and* the individual (fulfilling the needs of group members). The role of the principal or team leader in conflict management is to lessen or defuse conflict between two or more parties. Analyzing the needs of the individual and the root of the conflict and then seeking resolution are essential to productive outcomes. Certain steps can be taken to minimize the potential of conflict and to promote positive results from group situations.

Dolan (1996) notes that a cooperative spirit among team members and the team leader is important, that the needs of the individual and those of the organization have to be met, that trust and respect must exist among all parties, and that good communication skills are necessary to promote cooperation. Principals and team leaders must be able to draw on a variety of skills to facilitate group work and to mitigate the potential for conflict. The leader must have a positive attitude and the human relations skills necessary to maintain harmony within the group and to keep the group goal-oriented. The needs of the organization and those of the individual are central to productive and harmonious group activity. Thomas (1976) presents five styles of conflict management that fall along the leadership needs continuum from unassertive to assertive and the individual's need continuum from uncooperative to cooperative. Five conflict management styles are presented in the Thomas model:

(1) Avoiding style: unassertive and uncooperative behaviors are exhibited to avoid conflict in hopes that individuals will remedy the conflict themselves or the situation will naturally defuse.

(2) Compromising style: the leader exhibits a balance between unassertive and uncooperative behaviors and uses negotiation to find solutions that are mutually acceptable.

(3) Competitive style: the leader exhibits assertive and uncooperative behaviors and places leadership needs over individual needs. Positional power is used to achieve the desired end.

(4) Accommodating style: the leader exhibits unassertive and cooperative behaviors and places the needs of the individual over the needs of the leader.

(5) Collaborating style: the leader exhibits assertive and cooperative behaviors with an emphasis on problem solving, joint resolution, and meeting the needs of both leader and individual.

Collaboration is the most effective way to resolve conflict since both sets of needs are deemed important, an integrative solution is sought, and consensus and commitment are stressed. Compromise is less satisfactory than collaboration because it results in temporary solutions to important problems.

Interpersonal Skills

Effective communication is at the heart of effective decision making. Good communication can reveal and eliminate many problems both within and outside the organization and promote organizational efficiency (Weick and Browning, 1986). Having good interpersonal skills makes the mission of the leader easier and facilitates both team and individual work efforts. Fisher (1980) finds that attitude toward group work is as critical as interpersonal skills and that a positive attitude toward teamwork is the foundation for team member effectiveness. The psychological "set" of open-mindedness toward teamwork and team members is imperative. Open-mindedness involves being sensitive to the values, attitudes, and behaviors of others regardless of how dissimilar they are from one's own. Interpersonally sensitive members are committed to the belief that the group process will fulfill both group and individual goals and that personal sacrifices of time and energy are necessary to fulfill the goals of the group and those of other members within the group. To Fisher, the feeling of responsibility to the group fosters group commitment and dedication to group and individual goals.

While there are many interpersonal skills described in the literature, there seems to be a nucleus of the more effective skills. These are trust, honesty, credibility, empathy, expertise, respect, candor, and support (Hoy and Miskel, 1996). Effective groups are then both task- and goal-oriented and work toward their goals with the membership embracing certain socio-emotional skills which facilitate group harmony and task completion.

TEAM PLANNING

Team planning is another characteristic of high performing middle schools and is valued by effective middle school principals who realize that team planning is an effective way to meet students' needs. Principals devoted to the team planning concept develop a scheduling configuration which allows for common planning periods on a daily basis so that team members can plan, review, and evaluate their instructional program. Principals in effective middle schools support team efforts by attending planning meetings to assist with special problems or provide leadership and moral support. Problems and issues which relate to team planning include student behavioral and emotional problems, individual student progress and evaluation, compatibility of team planning and student needs, curricular changes, enrichment and elective activities, advisement activities and home/school relations, and space and its scheduled utilization with regular and special needs teachers.

Planning jointly for instruction is most important in the middle school since its curriculum is more exploratory in nature than the elementary and high schools. Instruction is planned to show the natural relationship between subject disciplines in order to provide cohesive learning experiences for students through exploratory and elective courses, structured club programs, activity programs, and special interest courses. To facilitate this type of instructional program, principals must allow time for core curriculum teachers, reading and special education teachers, and exploratory and elective teachers to meet and plan together for a common group of students. Adequate planning time during the school day for teams is also important for teacher morale. When teachers have to plan before or after school or during their lunch breaks, team effectiveness suffers, the quality of work decreases, and teachers become resentful. The use of their personal time for common planning soon leads to frustration and a feeling that the principal does not appreciate their work or dedication.

Teacher Planning vs. Team Planning

Planning can be defined as creating mental maps that provide images of the future or constructing rational linkages to realize the end state in an effective and efficient manner. Teacher planning is an individual process where the teacher defines selected classroom goals and objectives and correlates instructional activities to these sequenced objectives in order to facilitate student learning as defined by the teacher for the specific discipline being taught. Little if any consideration is given to how this learning relates to the knowledge and skills learned by these students in other content areas.

Team planning, on the other hand, is constructed around interdisciplinary teams of teachers. MacIver (1990) notes that interdisciplinary teacher teams are the foundation for effective instruction in middle schools. (Chapter 5 will discuss more fully the interdisciplinary team concept.) Team planning is cooperative group work involving team members who teach the same group of students. They resemble small communities within the school. The principal schedules these team members so that they have the same planning time allocated to them in their daily schedules and are housed in the same area of the school. This allows them to plan instructional activities together that are coordinated, sequenced, and meaningful across curricular areas.

Team planning, like any team effort, is not easily done, nor is the idea of teamwork a natural one. As stated previously, teams and team members need certain skills and knowledge to function effectively. The principal's role in providing these essential elements is crucial. Selecting the right mix of teachers for a team is most important for effective and cooperative outcomes. Trust, honesty, and dedication to the middle school principles are the key factors which promote optimal team planning results. George and Lawrence (1982) relate that for team planning to exist in middle schools, common planning periods must exist in the teachers' schedules, teachers must have good interpersonal communication skills or opportunities for these skills to be learned, and teachers must learn how to plan for instruction as a team member as opposed to planning for individual classroom instruction.

Mechanics of Team Planning

The idea behind team planning is to meet the needs of the transescent in an environment of changing cultural attitudes and values where knowledge is constantly expanding and new life skills are being identified. Therefore, ongoing planning is the ultimate goal of team planning if there is to be a quality curriculum. Quality team planning progresses through the following stages.

Stage one of quality team planning begins with each team member keeping current in their respective fields of expertise. With this essential foundation, team members explore the areas of knowledge that are of the most worth to the transescent and how this knowledge can best be taught. George and Lawrence (1982) reinforce this concept when they stress the importance of first developing long-range goals for instruction and then modifying these goals as the planning process progresses. Next, teams develop objectives appropriate for meeting these goals. When goals and objectives for instruction are agreed upon, specific activities are developed to meet individual student needs. Most importantly, as the instructional units are taught, student work is used to assess the effectiveness of instruction and serves as the basis for future modification the instructional delivery system and content.

Stage two of team planning is matching the long-range goals and objectives with those of the school and school system. When these are matched, instructional units or themes are then identified and examined for continuity and interrelationships. Skills and concepts are then targeted for learning within units or themes to correlate with the objectives designated as goal achievement targets for each unit.

Stage three is identification of the special resources and teachers needed to support the instructional units. Community resources, special speakers, and field trips are all planning topics. Special projects and instructional activities are also identified and included to increase the probability of student success and achievement.

Stage four is where the team identifies exploratory courses and extracurricular activities which reinforce and enhance the knowledge and skill areas to be taught in the instructional units. Teachers of these courses and activities become part of the planning team and work with team members to provide continuity and enrichment in their programs. Here, modification of the goals and objectives of the instructional program and resources may be necessary to ensure that the needs and interests of the students are met.

Stage five is where all regular and special needs teachers function as a team to identify special learning materials to facilitate the instructional units and the needs of individual students within the learning community. Estimates of time and grouping arrangements are made to facilitate the learning of the unit goals and objectives. This information is then presented to the principal for designing a master schedule that will meet all grade-level teams' instructional program needs.

Stage six is the development of student assessment methods for each unit. Evaluation criteria and instruments are selected or designed and are carefully examined to ensure that the content which is to be tested is the content to be taught. Special projects and other student activities needing assessment are also discussed for performance criteria and assessment validity.

Stage seven is when the efforts of instructional planning are implemented in the classroom. Using the Deming (1986) quality admonishment that those closest to the problem should be allowed to solve the problem, teachers in their classrooms talk individually with their students about their interest in the units, the relevance of instruction to their lives, how this instruction relates to their personal goals and problems, how projects and learning activities can be adjusted to provide more meaning and learning, and any ideas students have to enhance the goals and objectives of the units. These suggestions, along with student assessment results, provide planning data for the next academic year and, because team planning is a continuous process, team members can make daily adjustments regarding their instructional goals and activities. For example, if more time is needed to cover one unit of study or for reinforcement or enrichment purposes, adjustments can be made. Likewise, if a unit is assimilated faster than the allotted time, the next unit of study can be started without disturbing the instructional schedule or teaching activities.

Stage eight is the evaluation of the team's performance, an essential component of the quality planning process. Evaluation of how well the team members work together is important to assess on a regular basis. Different assessments for work group effectiveness exist. George and Lawrence (1982) relate that group assessment instruments are most effective when groups have a high degree of trust, plan to stay together over an extended time period, and have mutual goals and objectives. These instruments identify strengths and weaknesses of work groups and can be used as a source for discussion on how to improve group effectiveness and interaction patterns. Most weaknesses are identified in terms of interpersonal problems and behaviors as a group, not as individuals. The group discusses these strengths and weaknesses and reaches consensus on how weak areas can be improved. The group agrees upon a plan of action for improvement and assessment of their progress. It is suggested that group performance evaluation take place at least twice a year.

Types of Middle School Planning

Different approaches to planning for instruction exist, but Brown (1988) notes that middle school teachers usually plan in a "nested" manner. They begin with yearly plans, then develop unit or theme planning packages, progress to weekly plans, and finally develop daily lesson plans.

(1) Yearly planning is long term in scope. Major goals and themes are identified which provide direction to the entire planning process. Goals and themes can be modified, added, or deleted as the planning progresses. Yearly planning provides sequence and coordination to concepts being taught, provides an estimate of materials and instructional activities needed for the year, and delineates the space requirements and instructional time blocks needed for teaching. Textbooks and curriculum guides serve as resources.

(2) Unit or theme planning involves the development of interconnected concepts and skills that are identified during the yearly planning process. These units are usually two to three weeks in length. Content is determined by the identification of which knowledge is of the most worth to students based on interests, needs, and relevancy. Objectives are developed for each of the sub-areas within the theme, and learning materials and activities are identified and correlated to each of the learning objectives.

(3) Weekly planning revolves around the instructional themes. Weekly planning is more flexible than yearly or theme planning in that instructional pacing depends on student progress in mastering the goals and objectives of the unit. Special activities or materials can be introduced to provide enrichment or to reinforce learning. Independent or group work can be used to promote remediation or provide special interest area projects. Student homework assignments and evaluation methods are planned, but are tentative and are based on how well daily lesson plans progress. Detailed weekly planning also provides information for substitute teachers and allows for last minute changes in the school's schedule.

(4) Daily planning provides step-by-step directions for instruction with objectives clearly defined and correlated to student activities. Daily plans allow teachers to prepare for next-day instruction, to make a smooth transition from the previous day's work into the new material to be covered, and to assign homework and evaluate student progress. Daily lesson plans are largely a function of student readiness to progress.

TEAM TEACHING

Team Teaching Is Not

Team teaching is not "turn teaching," where one teacher takes a turn with other teachers in teaching large groups of students. Turn teaching is departmental instruction which lacks the following essential components of team teaching: collaboration among professionals on instructional goals, objectives, activities, teaching strategies, and student needs; and an integrated curriculum which helps students connect concepts and knowledge to real life.

Team teaching is not interdisciplinary team teaching which will be discussed in Chapter 5. Briefly, interdisciplinary team teaching includes teachers from the four major content areas as well as teachers of art, music, physical education, vocational education, guidance, and exploratory courses and extracurricular activities. This teaming practice facilitates cooperation, coordination, and communication among all teachers as they teach their intact group of students interconnected themes or units of instruction across the entire curriculum. Interdisciplinary team teaching evolves from regular team teaching; it is but a small step to take from regular team teaching, but it is not synonymous with team teaching.

Team Teaching Is

Team teaching is a structural organization in which two or more teachers pool their talents, expertise, interests, and instructional resources and take joint responsibility for meeting the needs of the students and the instructional program. Teaming maximizes the strengths of teachers and allows them to work flexibly with individuals, small groups, and large groups. Properly conceptualized and implemented, team teaching facilitates the academic growth of students, connects core courses with relevant and practical examples and activities, and allows for more effective and efficient use of space, resources, and teaching time. The major strength of team teaching lies in utilizing the varied talents of the teaching staff while addressing the social, emotional, physical, and intellectual needs of the transescent (Irvin, 1990).

The major elements of team teaching are a common team planning time, adequate space for both large and small group instruction, and a heterogeneously grouped set of students. Epstein and MacIver (1990) relate that team teachers without common planning time are much less effective than those with common planning periods. Most desirable is a daily common planning period for teamwork and an independent planning period for each teacher to plan instructional activities. Adequate space is needed for various grouping configurations, and students should be heterogeneously selected in order to promote a sense of well-being among students, enhance their attitudes toward school and themselves, and provide a feeling of security and friendship.

Team teachers must be able to deal with management issues and interpersonal conflicts. Good communication skills and positive working relationships are, therefore, necessary. This is especially important when team teaching is used as a transition from a departmentalized to an interdisciplinary instructional approach. Beane (1990) notes that moving from a departmentalized structure to an interdisciplinary curriculum and teaming configuration is not easy since the departmental approach has long existed. The negative aspects of the departmental approach include a territorial mind-set, a lack of coordination between the teaching of subject areas, an emphasis on classroom control and student discipline rather than on the needs of students, and the autonomy of the individual teacher as the instructional entity. Team teaching can break down these barriers and ease the transition into a middle school program with a total interdisciplinary curriculum and instructional team configuration.

Team Teaching Configurations

The most rudimentary teaming structure is the two-teacher, two-subject approach which groups either language arts and social studies teachers or mathematics and science teachers. These teachers plan and develop instructional activities for their subject fields and then share their plans. Both teachers teach the material to their two groups of students. Here, the relationship between the two content areas is demonstrated and students are able to see the connection between the knowledge and skills taught in the two subjects during a double-period block of time.

Two-teacher teams can also teach the four content areas by dividing the areas into one set composed of language arts and social studies and the other set composed of mathematics and science. Each teacher will plan for a content set, share plans, and teach all four subjects to both student groups in both a double-period time block and one or more weekly four-period time blocks. This configuration lends itself to unit or thematic teaching with important concepts and skills from all four areas taught around one theme.

Another teaming arrangement is made up of multiple teachers teaching multiple subjects. This is an extension of the two-teacher, two-subject approach. In this configuration, reading, art, music, and physical education teachers can be part of the planning and teaching. This approach takes a high degree of coordination but can be the precursor to interdisciplinary teaming which calls for the integration of core subjects, exploratory and enrichment courses, and extracurricular activities into well-planned units.

TEAMING IS NOT FOR ALL TEACHERS

Some teachers are highly effective in self-contained classrooms and do not wish to be part of team instruction. The purpose of teaming is to capitalize on the strengths of teachers, but some teachers' strengths lie in departmentalization and they should not be forced into team teaching. Other teachers enjoy planning with others, expressing new ideas about the improvement of instruction, and sharing the benefits of team teaching. Sometimes teachers are reluctant to team teach because they do not want to relinquish their independent authority over instruction. Whatever the reason, teachers should not be made to team teach since their presence on the team will likely produce counterproductive results.

BENEFITS OF TEAM TEACHING

(1) Through its emphasis on interconnectiveness, team teaching can better meet the social, emotional, physical, and intellectual needs of students than self-contained or departmentalized classrooms. Teachers also benefit from teaching in teams due to the social, emotional, and intellectual growth and satisfaction provided by the instructional team environment.

(2) Learning and teaching activities can be more creative and challenging for both students and teachers. When instruction is integrated into themes, learning becomes more relevant for students, and teachers are more challenged to develop new and exciting ways to coordinate and teach subject matter in a meaningful way.

(3) Teaming allows teachers to make decisions and solve problems about the curriculum and instruction. Teams empower teachers to infuse quality education into the classroom by designing an instructional program which is best suited for their students and their team members. By allowing those closest to the problem to solve the problem, quality outcomes are assured.

(4) Teams determine the amount of instructional time needed for content mastery. They develop their own teaching schedule and provide these time blocks to the principal for master scheduling.

(5) Team teaching allows teachers to teach in areas of interest and to work and learn together as they share different strengths and learn new knowledge and skills. Teams also provide a support network for teachers.

(6) Teams also provide students with a close-knit support group since groups of students see the same teachers more often and for more con-

centrated time periods. Students have a better opportunity to know their teachers and, in this way, their individual needs can be better served.

CONSIDERATIONS ABOUT TEAMING

(1) The teaming concept must have the complete support of the principal. Principals must provide the necessary moral and fiscal support as well as time and facilities for teacher teams to plan and execute their instructional programs. Principals are the facilitators of the entire process and they lend their knowledge and skills to teacher teams as active and dedicated members of the team-teaching effort.

(2) Principals must provide daily common planning time for teachers and, ideally, independent planning time as well. Without the necessary planning time, team teaching will fail.

(3) Adequate space must exist or be provided for large and small group instruction. Ideally, this space should be in close proximity to each team member for ease and timeliness of use.

(4) Team teaching is not without interpersonal conflict. Principals must provide the necessary training to teachers to work as team members and to resolve team and individual conflict. Left unattended, conflict can create strong and lasting negative feelings which impact the efficiency and effectiveness of team instruction.

(5) Teams and team members need to regularly evaluate their progress. Principals have the responsibility of ensuring that these evaluations take place and of providing assistance to both the team and individual team members.

TEAMS, TEAM BUILDING, TEAM PLANNING, TEAM TEACHING: CASE STUDIES

Without question, building quality, high performing interdisciplinary teams and providing adequate team planning time are essential to promoting the goals of the middle school. Wayne Watts, principal of Edwards Middle School (National School of Excellence, National Blue Ribbon School and six-time Georgia School of Excellence); Joan Akin, principal of Creekland Middle School (Georgia School of Excellence and winner of the International Inviting School Award); and George Dougherty at Oglethorpe County Middle School (Georgia School of Excellence and a University of Georgia Laboratory School) all agree that high performing teams—producing effective, intended goal-oriented results—have certain characteristics in common:

- clear vision as to what interdisciplinary teams need to accomplish and the purpose of their being
- goal oriented to achieve the intended results
- high expectations for themselves and other team members
- competent in group dynamics and conflict resolution skills
- adequate team and individual planning time to do their work effectively
- the full support and backing of the principal in making decisions and solving instructional problems

In Georgia, middle school principals must schedule eighty-five minutes a day for team and individual planning. Watts notes that flexible block schedules provide the most efficient use of time for core academic and exploratory teachers to plan together. Academic and exploratory courses are arranged by grade level at Edwards Middle School (EMS) in Rockdale County and some common planning time exists for both exploratory and core teams during the core block. However, to accommodate interexploratory team planning, special scheduling arrangements have to be made. These exploratory teachers, for example, have extended lunch periods and thirty minutes at the end of the school day when core teachers are busy with advisee/advisor responsibilities. Watts emphasizes the importance of principals knowing the results of weekly team meetings and stresses the importance of "attending team-level meetings on a drop-in basis." His assistant principals, he says, rotate attendance at team meetings on a regular basis to serve as resource people and as facilitators of instruction. Each team is required to complete a weekly team meeting record (see Figure 4.1) and provide a brief outline of team activities designed to meet the child-centered, academic goals of the school.

Each team has a list of five focus questions to stimulate discussion and maintain constancy of purpose. Watts believes Deming's principle (1986) of constancy of purpose for teams at Edwards Middle School can best be achieved by teams regularly addressing the following questions:

- What were the strongest and weakest achievement areas of the school last year?
- How is the team structure being used to improve student achievement?
- If teams promote student achievement, why are we not achieving at our expected levels?
- When was the last time you talked about student achievement at your team meeting?

ROCKDALE COUNTY MIDDLE SCHOOL
TEAM MEETING DOCUMENTATION RECORD

Week of _____

School _____ Grade _____

Record number of minutes spent daily for the following:

Activity:	Mon	Tues	Wed	Thurs	Fri	Total
A. Meeting with Resource Person						
B. Common Student Problems 1. Academic 2. Behavior						
C. SST						
D. Instructional Strategies						
E. Parent/Teacher Conferences						
F. Student/Teacher Conferences						
G. Distribution of Materials						
H. Progress Reports, Report Cards, Permanent Records, etc.						
I. Team Projects						
J. Miscellaneous						

Comments: _____

_____

Team Leaders   Signature of Team Leader

1. _____ 5. _____
2. _____ 6. _____
3. _____ 7. _____
4. _____ 8. _____

FIGURE 4.1.

- When was the last time you analyzed your students' test scores to see where their strengths and weaknesses were, and what plans have you made to address those weaknesses?

Block scheduling with flexible time modules, encompassing from two to five class periods, is a must for "cohesive team planning," says Watts. Block scheduling facilitates team planning and instruction by allowing teachers to have control over their own instructional planning time. When teachers are teamed together, planning is an ongoing occurrence. Teachers plan over lunch, they plan in the halls, and planning becomes a part of professional life. At EMS, the principal provides planning time which exceeds that called for by the literature. Epstein and MacIver (1990) and Wiles and Bondi (1993) call for a minimum of two hours per week of common team planning time with a daily time period being most desirable. Epstein and MacIver found that only 30 percent of the schools surveyed having interdisciplinary teams provide a daily time period for team planning. The eighty-five plus minutes that EMS teachers have contributes to their effectiveness by allowing "a truly coordinated and goal-oriented team of teachers," says Watts. Instructional programs which are fragmented in scope and lack vision and constancy of purpose fail to be as productive as those which have these qualities. "Without [adequate] team planning time, teams simply cannot be effective," reports Watts. His basic philosophy is this: "Team success equals teacher success, and teacher success equals student success. A student's success is the result of successful teaching."

Another factor supported by the literature (Epstein and MacIver, 1990; Jacobs, 1991) which is practiced at EMS is the ongoing support provided each of the three grade level teams by the principal. Watts notes that a fine line exists between "supporting teacher teams and directing their work efforts." Support is providing continuous encouragement, resources, and time and freedom to do their jobs. Directing is telling and at times demanding teams do certain things. When principals become too directive, teams cease to function as a cohesive unit and become little more than individual teachers who strive to satisfy the administrator's wishes. One can, however, be supportive and directional at the same time, says Watts, if one defines direction as being goal-oriented and providing an "environment of support" for teacher teams. Environmental support is providing teams with seriousness of purpose through helping them remain focused on their purpose and by developing a collegial relationship with each teacher through a "helping and caring relationship with them as individuals, not as employees."

An example of administrator support at EMS occurred when grade level teachers, needing supplementary materials for their thematic units, discussed external ways to purchase them. Visiting the team planning session and hearing the discussion, Watts found central office monies to order the materials in time for them to be beneficial to current instruction. When teachers realize that administrators are facilitators, that "we're all in this together," planning time becomes even more effective.

Building strong interdisciplinary teacher teams is the most essential factor in promoting long-term team effectiveness, says Joan Akin. Getting the right mix of teacher personalities together is "absolutely essential" for such teams. "The team philosophy of the middle school can be taught, the goals and objectives of the interdisciplinary curriculum can be learned, and new teaching styles can be learned and acquired to match team needs, but," she adds, "conflict among team members sometimes cannot be resolved." Both Watts and Dougherty note that when personality conflicts cannot be resolved after much discussion with both the teacher and other team members, two practical solutions remain: first, see if the personality will mix with other existing teacher teams and second, bring these teachers to the realization that middle school interdisciplinary team teaching is not for them and their talents can best be utilized elsewhere.

The important first step in team building, Akin says, is to hire new personnel with the personalities of the team members in mind. Dougherty agrees and, using the same hiring practices as Akin and Watts, allows teacher teams to help make decisions about whom to employ. Each principal does the initial screening of applicants, but defers to team decisions on hiring should a conflict of applicant choice occur. Dougherty observes that when teacher teams actually choose a team member, they commit themselves to making their decision successful. Having a vested interest in new team members, teacher teams work more closely with new personnel to ensure their success as teachers and as team members. Watts notes that one teacher team established a peer coaching network with other teacher teams to assist a new team member in strengthening certain classroom skills.

Screening initial applicants for team positions is done similarly by these three principals. The three most salient indicators of potential success are questions aimed at assessing the following: (1) the applicant's dedication to the child-centered philosophy of the middle school; (2) the applicant's work philosophy and "team mentality"; and (3) the likelihood of the applicant's blending into, being compatible with, and fostering the climate of the school. Another question often asked is the applicant's definition of team teaching. "Often," Watts says, "I receive a definition of 'turn teaching' for team teaching. When applicants think team teaching is simply a method of instruction which brings two or more teachers together to take turns teaching a group of students, I question their understanding of the interdisciplinary approach to middle school education. This usually raises a concern about the applicant's preparation and triggers more probing questions about the depth of their middle school training."

No formal personality assessment instruments are used by these principals to add to their informal assessment of applicants. However, Watts believes principals should receive more formal training in the various types of available personality assessment instruments and their strengths and weaknesses for middle school educators. While all three agree such instruments can add pieces of information to the hiring process, all say that getting to know the applicants as individuals, personally determining their educational philosophies and ascertaining the ways in which they interact with others are good, reliable gauges of potential success. As Dougherty states, "After being a principal for more than twenty years, you get to be a pretty good judge of character."

Good communication within teams and across grade level teams is important to sustain the teaming approach to instruction. Providing inter-grade level information flow among all grade level teams is important for keeping teams informed of curricular problems and revisions. At EMS, an academic teacher from each grade level, six through eight, sits in on teacher team meetings at each of the other grade levels. Representatives from the exploratory teacher block and a school counselor also sit in on each of the three grade level teams' meetings. This representation allows for a constant dialogue among teachers representing all curricular areas. Problems confronting particular teachers, students, or grade level teams are discussed as well as problems with the curriculum. New ideas in instruction are shared, and possible revisions in thematic and units are filtered back to each grade level team. This vertical communication process is a particular help to exploratory teachers who often feel disassociated from core curriculum teachers. Moreover, representation on vertical core teams allows these teachers to understand other teams' problems and to discuss concerns and issues of mutual interest. Watts believes that if the interdisciplinary curriculum is to promote effective instruction, "then all faculty and support personnel need to work collaboratively through a school-wide communication network."

Dougherty uses a Schoolwide Instructional Team (SIT) at Oglethorpe County Middle School to improve communication "between and among the faculty, administration, and community" (see Figure 4.2). The SIT is a decision-making group made up of a faculty representatives and the school principal. Each member of the SIT is assigned a small number of faculty members with whom the member meets monthly to receive input to take before the SIT and to report to them the decisions made by the SIT.

Akin uses a School Leadership Team made up of advisory representatives from all instructional areas (see Figure 4.3). In addition to other assigned responsibilities, these representatives meet monthly with administrators and regularly with a group of teachers in their assigned instructional areas to facilitate the communication process.

Watts notes that teacher teams are made up of teachers—human beings with similarities and differences. Often, he says, conflicts or problems which exist on one team may be resolved by other teacher teams who have experienced similar problems or conflicts. Sharing ideas and resolving problems strengthen all teams and serve to bring the total faculty closer together.

Schoolwide Instructional Team (SIT)
Oglethorpe County Middle School
1996-1997

Purpose - We will improve learning opportunities for students through shared governance and improved communication between and among the faculty, administration, and community.

Limitations - The following areas are excluded from consideration by the SIT:

    1)   Personnel matters
    2)   Normal administrative functions

Team Composition -

3	A representative from each grade level: 6th, 7th, and 8th
1	Exploratory, HPE, Chapter, Media, ISS representative
1	Special Ed, Teacher Aides representative
1	School counselor
<u>1</u>	School principal
7	Total Members

Team of Office - Elected members will serve for two years. The chairperson and recorder will be selected by SIT members for a one year term. The principal is an ex-officio member.

Faculty Input - Each team member will be assigned a small group of faculty members called a Liaison Group to meet monthly for receiving input, discussing issues, and reporting team decisions. Liaison Group members are asked to submit items in writing to their Liaison Group leader for consideration using a standard form. The liaison chairperson will then set the agenda based on each group's list of important items for the SIT meeting where actual and final decision making will occur.

    As a general rule, anyone identifying a concern, problem, or issue is expected to also recommend a proposed course of action to bring about improvement.

Decision-Making Process - The SIT will deal with items on its agenda in the priority the team thinks appropriate. Each team member has one vote. If consensus is reached concerning how to respond to the item, it will be carried out. At least a 5 to 2 majority will be accepted for approval of a course of action. If there is no consensus, the item will be reconsidered at the next meeting. If consensus is still not reached, it will be dropped from the agenda.

FIGURE 4.2. Oglethorpe County Middle School schoolwide instructional team.

Team cohesiveness and productivity are the expected results of building grade level teams. Good working relationships, fostered through open and honest communication among team members, are vital for successful team teaching and intra-grade level instructional cohesiveness, reports Watts. Good horizontal communication becomes a key concern for effective principals. Watts believes that grade level teams need to communicate regularly about issues and concerns, and he has teams at EMS schedule regular grade level team meetings to coordinate the instructional programs. Student problems are also discussed, as well as needed materials for the following year. The school counselor, principal, and exploratory teachers are important members of each grade level team and provide valuable input as resource and problem-solving personnel.

Akin, at Creekland Middle School, whose teams function in a similar manner, notes the important role teams play in fostering school climate. Teacher teams serve as microcosms of the school as a whole and embody the school climate through the individual teachers who comprise each team. A danger, however, is for teams to assume too much of an independent identity which is often fostered through high levels of inter-team competition. Too much pride in performance outcomes can lead to inter-grade level team conflict which can destroy the cohesiveness and constancy of purpose necessary for effective interdisciplinary team instruction. Competition among grade level teams is natural, but the level of competition must be put in perspective. A positive outcome of excessive team competition is the likelihood of bringing together teams lacking the necessary cohesiveness to be

---

LEADERSHIP TEAM REPRESENTATIVE

PRIMARY FUNCTION - TO SERVE AS AN ADVISORY REPRESENTATIVE ON THE SCHOOL LEADERSHIP TEAM AND TO REPRESENT ALL STAFF MEMBERS IN A SPECIFIED AREA.

Major Responsibilities:

- Serve as a mentor to teachers new to the school
- Conduct productive area meetings on a regular basis
- Help assigned area set and accomplish goals
- Keep written summaries of area meetings and activities
- Maintain continuity and clear communication within assigned instructional area
- Promote high involvement from each group member
- Work within your instructional area to provide attractive hall displays
- Collect and monitor emergency lesson plans
- Assist with property and material inventories
- Work with administrators to facilitate class coverage when needed
- Help plan and schedule extra-curricular activities
- Attend regular monthly meeting with administrators
- Coordinate procedures that are consistent within area
- Develop attendance goals and lead plans that focus on good attendance
- Help plan and carry out Awards Day activities
- Coordinate development and implementation of behavior management plan for area
- Help with materials order and distribution

FIGURE 4.3. Creekland Middle School's leadership team.

effective; however, the role of the principal in keeping competition at a level which is educationally beneficial to students is an important one, Akin says. She notes that such a role often requires the use of both diplomacy and positional authority. The important thing is to be involved in team meetings and extracurricular activities so that the principal "can sense when competition begins to go beyond that healthy range." At that point, says Akin, the principal must refocus teachers on the goals of middle school education.

Some teams "can become little fiefdoms, assume too much autonomy, and really enjoy their empowerment," says Watts. The danger here is a mind-set of superiority which works against horizontal and vertical communication and fosters an attitude that school board policy can be ignored or circumvented if it works counter to the goals of the team. One way to keep autonomous teams from developing is the principal's modeling of expected behavior. Watts uses faculty meetings to model behavior expected from all teacher teams. He begins each faculty meeting by stating, "There are some negotiable issues and some non-negotiables. Negotiables are open for discussion and resolution, non-negotiables are policy and we have to work within the boundaries." Watts reminds all teams that if board policy hinders the goals of the school that it is his responsibility to work with the superintendent to explore ways to achieve school goals while working within the boundaries of board policy. By frequently sitting in on team meetings, principals can "easily assess the level of autonomy of each team and gently remind them of the negotiables and non-negotiables," states Watts. Reminding teams frequently that their decision-making power and effectiveness lies in instructional and curricular decisions which impact the classroom keeps teams focused on their mission and keeps them away from areas outside their decision-making prerogatives.

Akin and Watts concur that teacher teams composed of teachers with good human relations and conflict management skills will facilitate the effectiveness, harmony, and communication flow within teams. The practical approach to promoting team harmony and professionalism is the use of "common courtesy and common sense rules of good human behavior," relates Akin. Treat people with respect, dignity, and worth, says Watts, who models the theory Y management behaviors of McGregor (1960) and who inservices his teams on McGregor's theory X and theory Y management principles. Showing common courtesy, being polite and understanding, and tolerating others' views with respect when they conflict with one's own are essential and rudimentary skills. Watts uses the analogy of teacher teams viewing each team member as one of their students, and treating each team member as they would that student. The same goes for principals. When teachers become forceful, too independent with others, two things generally happen, says George Dougherty. "Either the peer group brings them back to reality or I [the principal] have to remind them of the essentials of good human relations." If personality conflicts develop throughout the team relationship which cannot be mediated or satisfactorily resolved, teachers are then assigned to other teams. "Rarely," says Dougherty, "do I have to seek a transfer or take other measures."

Conflict management skills are important in resolving inter-team tension. Watts notes the value of teachers having such skills but finds that most teachers did not acquire them in their teacher preparation programs. Since these skills are essential in promoting effective team outcomes, teachers are provided inservices on conflict resolution skills by the school counselor where they are provided supplemental reading materials, and they are encouraged to attend professional conferences and workshops on resolving conflict. A practical book on conflict resolution is Richard Maurer's (1991) book entitled *Managing Conflict: Tactics for Administrators.*

The more informed team members are of conflict resolution skills, the more resources they have to mediate disagreement quickly and amicably. Most conflicts focus around one of three issues: individual interest, individual right, and power. At the interest level, egos are usually involved as well as basic needs issues. Here, Watts says, a knowledge of Maslow's needs hierarchy (1970) is helpful in seeking solutions to conflict. The issue of the rights of individual teachers is not a needs issue but one of entitled rights as perceived by teachers. Power issues focus around individuals trying to dominate each other or the team with the intent of getting their way. Conflict is not a random or erratic action but an active state with specific patterns of behavior. With sufficient knowledge about conflict, sources of conflict can be analyzed and steps taken to resolve the disruptive behavior.

There are many generic causes of conflict among a team of teachers, but the most common causes center around the following:

- unclear team goals
- unclear roles team members are to play
- communication barriers
- egos
- personal interests/needs
- need to succeed or dominate
- unresolved conflicts from previous encounters
- lack of trust

Some of the generic causes of conflict, such as unclear team goals, role identity for team members, and the need to dominate, can be lessened or eradicated by having teacher teams develop their own goals and set of operating procedures. For example, teams can rotate team leadership responsibilities yearly and have a secretary and an assistant leader position. Team goals can be posted in a designated meeting room and a team bill of duties and responsibilities can be drafted which clearly specifies team member obligations.

The issues of ego, trust, personal gain, communication barriers, and unresolved conflicts are usually more difficult to resolve because they are situation-specific. Watts believes conflict arising from personal interests or needs results from teams having misplaced their focus on maintaining a sense of community to achieve the goals of middle school education. Usually peers within the team will realize this and will seek to resolve the conflict by refocusing the team on student needs.

"Egos are like fleas, they come with the dog," says Watts. Dealing with bruised or inflated egos takes real "people skills" on the part of team members, and treating people with respect and value and acknowledging their worth and contributions to the team from time to time does much to lessen this conflict area. Like students, team members need genuine praise and reward which is a primary responsibility of the team leader.

Unresolved conflict and lack of trust are two of the more difficult issues confronting teacher teams. Unresolved conflict usually results from antecedents which, depending on the time factor involved, may run deep with emotion. One of the main purposes of providing teachers with conflict resolution skills is to deal with conflict immediately so antecedents do not exist. Most unresolved conflicts need the attention of the team leader. Often, the conflict antecedents are known and problems can be resolved. However, if emotions are deep, resolution is not reached, and behavior is disruptive to the team, the principal needs to meet with the parties involved and resolve the issue through mediation, first, or positional power, second.

Trust is built on consistent, reliable performance. Peer pressure helps mediate conflict resulting from the unrealized potential and unfulfilled promises of teachers. Here, the team leader's appeal to professional integrity and the need for all teachers to work together as a team to meet their obligations is a powerful tool to build and sustain trust.

Finally, communication barriers can cause team conflict which, for the most part, is unnecessary. Communication barriers have several sources and usually reside within the individual. Many teachers find it difficult to express their opinions openly and honestly. Couching words or not expressing their true feelings can lead to internal conflict which can trigger feelings of resentment or passive-aggressive behavior toward others. Other teachers are too open and honest and their words or poor choice of words cause resentment or hurt feelings. In teams, since open communication is essential, a good guide to use is the following: "One can say almost anything about anyone as long as it is phrased nicely." Thinking before speaking, choosing words carefully, being tactful, and realizing one's own bias are good fundamental tools for communication.

Akin and Watts both encourage their teams to "focus on problems, not on personalities" and to make sure other team members "understand what you mean, not just what you say." Clear and concise English and getting to the point without placing blame on team members is important in breaking down communication barriers. Dougherty believes that emotional issues triggered by deep feelings on certain issues or personal needs often cause communication-based conflict. Addressing the emotion or the need first allows others to more clearly understand the problem and is the precursor to resolving the real problem at hand, says Dougherty.

REFERENCES

Bales, R. F. and F. L. Strodtbeck. 1951. "Phases in Group Problem Solving," *Journal of Abnormal and Social Psychology*, 46:485–495.

Beane, J. A. 1990. *A Middle School Curriculum: From Rhetoric to Reality*. Columbus, OH: National Middle School Association.

Brown, D. S. 1988. "Twelve Middle School Teachers' Planning," *The Elementary School Journal*, 89:69–87.

Deming, W. E. 1986. *Out of the Crisis*. Boston, MA: MIT University Press.

Dolan, G. K. 1996. *Communication: A Practical Guide to School and Community Relations*. Belmont, CA: Wadsworth Publishing Company.

DuFour, R. and R. Eaker. 1992. *Creating the New American School: A Principal's Guide to School Improvement*. Bloomington, IN: National Education Service.

Dunn, R. 1991. "Rita Dunn Answers Questions on Learning Styles," *Educational Leadership*, 48:15–19.

Epstein, J. L. and D. J. MacIver. 1990. *Education in the Middle Grades: National Practices and Trends*. Columbus, OH: National Middle School Association.

Fisher, B. A. 1980. *Small Group Decision Making*. Second edition. New York: McGraw-Hill.

Garner, H. G. 1988. *Helping Others through Teamwork*. Washington, DC: Child Welfare League of America.

George, P. and G. Lawrence. 1982. *Handbook for Middle School Teaching*. Glenview, IL: Scott, Foresman and Company.

Getzels, J. W. and E. G. Guba. 1957. "Social Behavior and the Administrative Process," *School Review*, 65: 423–441.

Goloy, K. 1982. *Learning Patterns and Temperament Styles*. Fullerton, CA: Manas-Systems.

Hoy, W. K. and C. G. Miskel. 1996. *Educational Administration: Theory, Research, Practice. Fifth edition*. New York: McGraw-Hill.

Irvin, J. L. 1990. *Reading and the Middle School Student*. Boston: Allyn & Bacon.

Jacobs, H. H. 1991. "Planning for Curriculum Integration," *Educational Leadership*, 49(2):27–28.

Jung, C. G. 1971. *Psychological Types*. (H. G. Baynes, Trans. Revised by R. F. C. Hull). *The Collected Works of C. G. Jung, Vol 6*. Princeton, NJ: Princeton University Press. (Original work published in 1921.)

Larson, C. E. and F. M. LaFasto. 1989. *Teamwork: What Must Go Right/What Can Go Wrong*. Newbury Park, CA: Sage.

Lezotte, L. W. 1991. *Correlates of Effective Schools: The First and Second Generation*. Okemos, MI: Effective School Products, Ltd.

MacIver, D. J. 1990. "Meeting the Needs of Young Adolescents: Advisory Groups, Interdisciplinary Teaching Teams, and School Transition Programs," *Phi Delta Kappan*, 71(6):458–464.

Maeroff, G. 1993. "Building Teams to Rebuild Schools," *Phi Delta Kappan*, 74:512–519.

Maslow, A. H. 1970. *Motivation and Personality*. Second edition. New York: Harper and Row.

Maurer, R. E. 1991. *Managing Conflict: Tactics for Administrators*. Boston: Allyn & Bacon.

McCarthy, B. 1991. "Using the 4MAT System to Bring Learning Styles to School," *Educational Leadership*, 48:31–37.

McGregor, D. 1960. *The Human Side of Enterprise*. New York: McGraw-Hill.

Morris, G. B. 1985. "Perspective: A Futuristic Cognitive View of Leadership," *Educational Administration Quarterly*, 21:7–27.

Myers, I. B. 1980. *Gifts Differing*. Palo Alto, CA: Consulting Psychologists Press.

Myers, I. B. and M. H. McCaulley. 1985. *Manual: A Guide to the Development and Use of the Myers-Briggs Type Indicator*. Palo Alto, CA: Consulting Psychologists Press.

Purkey, S. C. and M. S. Smith. 1983. "Effective Schools: A Review," *Elementary School Journal*, 83:427–452.

Scheidel, T. M. and L. Crowell. 1964. "Idea Development in Small Discussion Groups," *Quarterly Journal of Speech*, 50:140–145.

Schmoker, M. J. and R. B. Wilson. 1993. *Total Quality Management Education: Profiles of Schools That Demonstrate the Power of Deming's Management Principles*. Bloomington, IN: Phi Delta Kappa.

Spady, W. G. and D. Marshall. 1991. "Beyond Traditional Outcome Based Education," *Educational Leadership*, 49:23–26.

Thomas, K. 1976. "Conflict and Conflict Management," in *Handbook of Industrial and Organizational Psychology*, M. D. Dunnett, ed. Chicago: Rand McNally, pp. 889–936.

Tuckman, B. W. 1965. "Developmental Sequences in Small Groups," *Psychological Bulletin*, 63:384–399.

Wade, C. and C. Travis. 1990. *Psychology*. New York: Harper and Row.

Weick, K. E. and L. D. Browning. 1986. "Argument and Narration in Organizational Communication," *Yearly Review of Management of the Journal of Management*, 12:243–259.

Weller, L. D. 1995. "Principals and Quality Performance: Getting in the Backdoor," *The TQM Magazine*, 76(1):13–16.

Weller, L. D. and S. H. Hartley. 1994. "Total Quality Management and School Restructuring: Georgia's Approach to Educational Reform," *Quality Assurance in Education,* 2(2):18–25.

Whitaker, K. and M. Moses. 1990. "Beyond the Rhetoric of Restructuring." Paper presented at the annual meeting of the University Council of Educational Administration, Pittsburgh, PA.

Wiles, J. and J. Bondi. 1993. *The Essential Middle School.* Second edition. New York: Macmillian Publishing Company.

Wilkinson, A. M. and M. M. Smith. 1995. "Team Recruitment, Team Building and Skill Development," in *Teamwork Models and Experience in Education,* Howard G. Gardner, ed. Boston: Allyn & Bacon.

Zaleznick, A. and D. Moment. 1964. *The Dynamics of Interpersonal Behavior.* New York: Wiley.

CHAPTER 5

The Principal and the
Interdisciplinary Curriculum

Instructional leadership of high quality is essential if the middle school is to accomplish its goals. The principal is the key instructional leader who must design an instructional program that will address the diverse needs of the adolescent learner. It is in designing, scheduling, and staffing the interdisciplinary curriculum that principals demonstrate the leadership necessary to make their middle schools a school of excellence.

This chapter will explore the leadership patterns and practices of highly successful principals as they promote quality learning through the integrated curriculum and the use of interdisciplinary teams. A case study of effective middle school practices will be presented as well as pitfalls to avoid in developing this curriculum. This chapter will specifically address the following questions:

- What are the generic leadership beliefs and skills which promote effective curriculum and instructional management restructuring?
- Why is a culture of participatory governance an essential part of the integrated curriculum?
- What is a true middle school core curriculum?
- What is a true middle school integrated curriculum?
- What is the rationale for building an integrated curriculum and why is it important for the particular needs and characteristics of the adolescent?
- What are the major adolescent needs and characteristics that need to be addressed when building a developmentally responsive curriculum?
- How can the integrated curriculum best address and infuse the goals and mission of the exploratory curriculum, the electives curriculum, and the social curriculum? What is the role of the principal?

- What are the scheduling and staffing needs that have to be considered?
- How do principals and teachers best go about deciding on themes for integrated instruction?
- What are the learning activities and instructional resources which facilitate theme teaching and learning? What is the role of the principal and the role of teachers in deciding these issues?
- How should interdisciplinary teams be organized and what are their specific duties and responsibilities for making sure the themes are taught as originally planned?
- What is the role of the principal in this effort?
- How are the action plan curriculum, the curriculum planning wheels, and the Wiles-Bondi Mapping Model used? What is the role of the principal and the role of teachers in making these decisions?
- How can the impact of the integrated curriculum and interdisciplinary team teaching be evaluated to assess their impact on student learning and other adolescent development characteristics?

THE ROLE OF THE PRINCIPAL

Instructional leadership of high quality is essential to effective middle schools' goal achievement. Although the literature on leadership is replete with theory on and characteristics of effective middle school leadership in curriculum development, certain essential knowledge and behaviors must be displayed by the middle school principal. These are as follows:

(1) There must be vision and knowledge of what a true middle school can and should be. This requires a firm understanding of the research-based literature on the need for the various components of the middle school, the reasons why a middle school is needed for this particular age group, and the major characteristics (social, emotional, physical, and intellectual) of the transescent learner. Vision is required to take the principal's middle school beyond the traditional practices found in some middle schools. Education can always be improved upon and vision is the driving force behind the development of new and innovative programs and practices.

(2) Initiative is required for principals to put vision and knowledge into practice. High energy, self-motivated leadership drives the initiative to excel, to act, and to achieve. Self-confident that their decisions and actions will yield success, these principals believe their actions will make a difference and provide the quality outcomes they desire.

(3) Empowered teachers and effective communications are the mechanics

which drive the vision and sustain the initiative. Empowering teachers to make decisions and solve problems about instruction and curricular matters is part of the leadership role of the effective middle school principal. Here, teachers are allowed to lead, be creative, and have the freedom to fail without fear of reprisal. Principals support and encourage teachers through communication which is both overt and covert. Communication stimulates teacher action and determines the survival of the vision and curriculum initiative. Overt communications comprise good and effective use of oral and written communications. Having the skills to persuade teachers to embrace the vision and sustain its goals is all-important. If principals are weak in these areas, they should enroll in programs or courses designed to develop such skills. Covert communication is the principal's use of modeling behaviors and body language to reinforce on a daily basis the vision and beliefs held by the principal. Every action of the principal either reinforces or undermines this vision and these beliefs. Some principals never learn that as the leader of the school they are *always* center-stage.

Major Challenges for the Principal

Challenge number one in building an interdisciplinary curriculum is to provide a solid core curriculum of basic skills and content for all students. The core is largely dictated by state and local standards for mastery in the areas of science, mathematics, social studies, language arts, reading, and special education. Principals and teachers must design an instructional delivery system that places skills and content knowledge at the center of major themes or units which are responsive to adolescent problems, needs, and concerns. A developmentally responsive curriculum is designed with the characteristics of the early adolescent in mind which helps students understand in meaningful ways their experiences both in school and out. This allows them to relate their personal problems, needs, and concerns to those of the exterior world. This task is best accomplished through interdisciplinary teams wherein teachers of various subject areas modify and correlate their content to related units or themes which are taught across subject areas to the same group of students.

Challenge number two for the principal is to provide leadership for the restructuring of the core curriculum so that the various subject areas, exploratory courses, and elective activities are blended into these common themes or units. This type of curriculum planning calls for the use of interdisciplinary teaming and teaching, with teachers being more concerned with helping students learn central concepts and skills than with the equal distribution of instructional time blocks among subject areas. During such planning, teacher teams relate school skills and knowledge to the social and emotional needs of the learner which, through teamwork and cooperative learning, will foster good human relations skills and the notion of interdependence.

Challenge number three for the principal is to move teachers first to accept and then adopt an integrated curriculum model and the interdisciplinary team teaching approach to deliver the instruction program. At the heart of the challenge is the principal's leadership ability to convince teachers that this approach will meet the unique needs of their young adolescent learners and that through teaming, teachers will be able to capitalize on their strengths and skills; fulfill new interests and apply ancillary expertise; and design and create curricular themes, programs, and instructional materials.

THE CURRICULUM

What Is Curriculum and What Is Instruction?

Curriculum is a planned and taught program developed by a school with goals and objectives for learners to master. Instruction is the various teaching activities and methods used to implement the curriculum. In the middle school, instruction may be defined as teaching methods and teaching activities designed to help students understand themselves and their surroundings, master the content and skills deemed essential for middle school youth, and provide experiences for individual exploration and of personal self-interest to each student (George and Alexander, 1993).

Responsiveness of the Curriculum

The curriculum should respond to the nature of the learner, the society in which the learner functions, and the knowledge and skills most appropriate for the age of the learner. Lounsbury and Vars' observation (1978) that the nature and needs of the learner are the primary building blocks of the curriculum is still true today. In essence, when middle school curriculum is being developed, the focal question should be, "What are the characteristics of the transescent learner?"

The Interdisciplinary Curriculum

An interdisciplinary curriculum is a vast departure from the traditional middle school curriculum which is subject-matter oriented, centered on academics, and focused on a core of basic courses with few other subjects or electives available to students. This subject- or discipline-centered approach to education reflects that of the university and high school curricular model which is fragmented in nature, with each discipline or subject providing its own set of knowledge and skills. The call for curricular integration was endorsed by the Carnegie Council (1989) and the CREMS (1990) national survey. Briefly, the Task Force on the Carnegie Council on Adolescent Development recommended in a report entitled *Turning Points* that middle school educators blend the core courses of English, mathematics, science, and social science with fine arts and foreign languages and that middle school students "should learn to think critically through mastery of an appropriate body of knowledge, lead a healthy life, behave ethically and lawfully, and assume the responsibilities in a pluralistic society" (Carnegie Council, 1989, p. 42). The Center for Research on Elementary and Middle Schools (CREMS) at Johns Hopkins University, which surveyed a total of 2,400 middle school principals in 1991, found that the traditional middle school "was paying little attention to creating learning opportunities that are more responsive to the characteristics of the young adolescents" (CREMS, 1990, pp. 3–4). The Center argued against retaining a subject-centered, discipline-based curriculum and called for the adoption of an interdisciplinary curriculum which integrates knowledge and skills across subject area lines. The Center stated that such a curriculum should be centered around compelling social and personal issues, with emphasis on making the curriculum responsive to and meaningful for the needs and concerns of the transescent learner.

Middle school principals are challenged to develop a curriculum which takes an expansive view of program organization and to organize this curriculum around themes or units of instruction which directly relate to the world of the young adolescent. Beane (1992) notes that since one of the purposes of the middle school is to provide the learner with a general knowledge base, theme or unit organization of the curriculum is a natural outcome. To Beane, themes become a new "core" curriculum with thematic units replacing the traditional subject area disciplines. This new way of thinking about a curriculum core will effect change in students' learning because it will fuse personal concerns and social issues with concepts and knowledge that are developmentally appropriate and relevant to the world of the young adolescent. This curriculum will enable students to see the world as a whole by helping them "put together in some meaningful way the many bits and pieces of experience both in school and out" (Vars, 1992, p. 67).

How to Build an Interdisciplinary Curriculum

An integrated curriculum comes from either a restructuring of the existing curriculum or the building of an entirely new program of study. Drake (1991) describes this process as evolutionary, with team planning and teaching efforts slowly dissolving subject area boundaries through changes in commonly held assumptions and beliefs about teaching content. This evolutionary process, Drake says, goes from discrete subject areas to a correlation of content across subject area borders, to a blurred mix of subject area skills and content, and finally to the development of thematic units which entirely replace discrete subject areas. Jacobs (1991) recommends curriculum action plans for developing an integrated curriculum. Action plans and action research methods are used to experiment across and within grade levels to assess and refine the newly implemented themes of instruction. Like Deming's continuous improvement model (1986) to promote quality outcomes, action research is used to develop an interdisciplinary curriculum based on pilot testing and data regarding what is effective and what is not. The curriculum planning wheels model, espoused by Palmer (1991), is also effective in building an interdisciplinary curriculum. Planning wheels allow teachers to make connections across subject areas by allowing teachers to view their particular subject area as the center of a wheel and other subjects and curricular activities as spokes which radiate from its center. In this way, teachers make logical and natural correlations with other curricular programs and subjects while focusing on their own subject as a point of reference.

Curriculum mapping is another model for building an interdisciplinary program. The Wiles-Bondi Curriculum Mapping Model is a vertical model which includes sequenced topics or content areas within an academic discipline and specifies learning objectives and skills to be mastered. From these major concepts or content areas across disciplines, logical connections are made and serve as the basis for theme building. Themes fit logically into a grading period and vary in length from two days to two or more weeks. Emphasis is placed on making logical connections between all content concepts which are relevant to each theme, and these concepts are sequenced in such a way that learning is relevant to students' inner and outer world relationships (Wiles and Bondi, 1993). In mapping an integrated curriculum, the cooperation and dedication of the school's interdisciplinary teams are essential to success since mapping requires more than the correlation and resequencing of content and concepts. Themes also have to be fused in such a way as to provide the necessary skills and knowledge for students to make connections between and among subject areas and then apply this knowledge to larger issues. Teachers cannot be concerned with equal time being given to their specific subject areas in all thematic units but, instead, must concentrate on providing learning experiences which are meaningful to students.

BUILDING YOUR OWN CURRICULUM

Essentials for Middle School Staff Members

Curriculum construction requires careful planning, individual teacher effort, and input from parents, students, and community members. In addition, there are needed essentials from the professional staff: dedicated commitment and sustained leadership from the principal; recognition from teachers that subject content is a means to an end, not an end in itself; and skills for all staff members in group conflict management and group decision making. The principal must set in place a planning and communication process which will allow teachers to view their subject areas in the broad context of student needs and will arrange training, staff development, and inservices for teachers in conflict management and group decision making.

Stages of Curriculum Development

In middle school curriculum development, the learner is the primary consideration. Lounsbury and Vars (1978) stress that within this curriculum all students should have the following:

(1) One adult who personally knows and cares for them and is responsible for helping them face the problems of maturation.

(2) The opportunity to meet these problems head-on and have continued guidance and support as they meet and deal with these challenges.

(3) The opportunity to progress through learning experiences at their own rates through a continuous sequence of learning activities and materials.

(4) Access to a variety of learning experiences which are both required and chosen.

Some of the groundwork in curriculum development is laid by federal, state, and local requirements; and the laws, codes, and policies of these three levels of government provide the framework for curriculum building. Within this mandated framework a cadre of professionals, with input from parents, students, and community members, develop the local curriculum. The stages of curriculum development for a middle school interdisciplinary curriculum follows.

Stage 1: Curriculum construction begins with the philosophy and goals of the local district. These elements will later be blended into the interdisciplinary curriculum themes as the nucleus of the instructional program. At this stage, the curriculum development committee simply identifies and formalizes their existence.

Stage 2: The principal, classroom teachers, reading and technology specialists, counselors, special education teachers, parents, and community members who make up the curriculum committee begin their planning by examining the traditional academic disciplines and existing programs currently being taught in the school. Student input may come from either representation on the committee or through questionnaires, informal interviews, and records kept by teachers concerning the interest and relevancy of previously taught curriculum content.

Stage 3: The philosophy and goals of the middle school concept and the nature and needs of the middle school learner are identified and discussed. Beane (1993) states that a focus on common concerns within the personal and social environment in which students live is essential to a strong integrated curriculum. The nature of the learners, their social and personal concerns, the needs of developing transescents, and the relevancy of academic knowledge are identified as the major criteria for the selection of content and skills which will occur in the next stage.

Stage 4: Based on the criteria agreed upon in the previous stage, the committee identifies skills and content to be covered in the curriculum. Theme or unit construction is not yet a concern. Their construction will be based on the essential skills and knowledge appropriate for the middle school learner as identified at this stage. As Beane (1990) points out, constructing thematic units without first identifying the essential skills and knowledge content necessary for middle school youth may lead to the omission of something important for the sake of forcing learning activities into the confines of a theme. Content and skill selection focus on how much information by subject area and program needs to be incorporated into the interdisciplinary curriculum. The scope of a curriculum is *how much* of a content area needs to be taught. The question "What knowledge is of the most worth?" becomes central to scoping the curriculum and the committee arrives at the answer to this question at this stage.

Stage 5: Theme identification then results from the interrelationship between the needs of the learner, the social and personal concerns of the learner, and the essential skills and knowledge to be taught. Consequently, this step relates *what* is to be taught to the themes or units which are the *methods* by which it is to be taught. The identification of thematic topics can be accomplished in several ways. One way is to use chapters or a combination of chapters within textbooks, research findings from the professional literature, and workshop and professional conference materials. Another way is through teacher brainstorming sessions. Often, teacher-made materials provide excellent ideas for topics. Beane (1990) provides a list of issues that could be the basis for theme development in the middle school.

(1) The interdependent network of people from neighborhood to the global level

(2) The diversity of cultures from neighborhood to the global level formed by race, social customs, gender, and other factors

(3) The environment, its diminishing resources, its relationship to man and animals, and our interdependency in preserving our planet

(4) The political process and structure of government and human relations and the role individuals, groups, and cultures play in government oppression, renewal, and preservation

(5) The economic and commercial system and its impact on the individual, groups, and cultures; its relationship to power; its inequitable distribution; and its relationship to personal and family security

(6) The role of technology in society and its impact on the individual, the family, and the workplace

(7) The self-destructiveness of drugs, crime, suicide, street gangs, and teenage pregnancy

Questionnaires are a good way to assess student needs and interests. The results should be compared with those themes identified by teachers, parents, principals, and community members and adjustments made. Beane (1990) maintains that because the transescent is concerned with issues that surround them as "real people living out real lives in a very real world" (p. 39), the macro world has direct and relevant implications for the micro world of the preadolescent.

When topics or themes are identified, committee members evaluate the following: (1) their relevancy to the criteria set forth in Stage 3; (2) the overall interrelatedness of the themes; (3) and the inclusion of local and state curricular goals and mandates.

Stage 6: Content teachers then take the essential knowledge and skills identified in Stage 4 and examine them in terms of how this content can be developed within the thematic units. Here, teacher expertise is key to the success of each unit. Reading teachers, music teachers, art teachers, technology specialists, and teachers of exploratory and extracurricular courses or programs relate their instructional content to each unit. Within each unit, teachers identify subtopics and skills and aim for both relevance and a smooth transition for students from one learning experience to another.

Stage 7: Next, teachers must sequence the units, and place them in the order in which they will be taught. In the middle school, integrated curricular building is done across all three grade levels (sixth, seventh, and eighth grades). This requires the participation of representatives from each of these grade levels to ensure continuity across the curriculum. Process criteria vary for sequencing topics and can be selected from among the following: the basic concepts and skills learners must master before they can be expected to progress to more difficult levels; learner interest and how it must be aroused before students become actively involved in the learning process; and the intellectual development of the transescent. Here, the learning theory of Piaget (Inhelder and Piaget, 1958), discussed in earlier chapters, becomes an important concern. The stages of intellectual growth of this age child provide direction for learning hierarchies within the topics. The developmental level of the student influences whether topics should go from the concrete to the abstract or from the general to the particular. Sequencing decisions are left to those who build the curriculum; however, for the transescent all three of these criteria are important in promoting the goals of the true middle school. It is suggested that topics be sequenced and scoped with each of these three criteria in mind.

Stage 8: Teachers will now specify the learning activities and instructional materials to be used to teach the objectives within the identified themes and subthemes in the interdisciplinary curriculum. Here, principals and teachers use research findings and their expertise to determine those activities and materials which will have the most impact on students' learning the predetermined knowledge and skills within each thematic unit. Technology specialists can recommend computer programs, slides and filmstrips, and instructional games for drill and practice, demonstration and tutorial, and simulation activities. Special education and reading teachers can recommend learning strategies and materials that emphasize interaction, writing, and grouping. Other teachers may focus on the use of independent study, cooperative learning, lecture, case studies, peer tutoring, and other activities appropriate for learning content and skills within themes. Each learning activity must be tied to specific objectives and must be targeted for those students whose learning preference responds best to that particular type of instruction.

Stage 9: The last stage is the pilot testing of the thematic units. The principal schedules or assigns groups of students to teachers to test the effects of the thematic units, instructional materials, and learning activities for learning effectiveness on a long- or short-term basis. Results are studied and teachers modify the curriculum as needed. Hamm and Adams (1994) note that using thematic units and an integrated curriculum is the only way to expose the learner to the whole curriculum with all the necessary enrichment, skills, and knowledge each curricular segment has to offer. Wright, Sorrels and Granby (1996) report that teaching a curriculum based on thematic units has been so successful that several colleges are teaching their prospective teachers how to plan for and implement instruction with themes. Miller

(1992) found that the development of thematic units prepares teachers for both typical and atypical students. Besides being learner effective, thematic units are economically feasible and adaptable to various instructional environments (Wigle and Dudley, 1993).

Barriers to Building an Interdisciplinary Curriculum

Several barriers exist to building a successful integrated curriculum in the middle school. Each barrier can be surmounted though some are more difficult and take more time than others. The leadership of the principal is the key to overcoming these barriers and each barrier must be actively addressed.

(1) An integrated curriculum may be resisted by parents, teachers, and community members. Parents, teachers, and community members are "academics-oriented," the cry of "back to basics" is a popular argument for core subject emphasis, and students are performing poorly on standardized tests. According to Carroll and Carroll (1994), all of these things reinforce the need for a no nonsense curriculum teaching the 3R's. Lewis (1990), however, believes that in middle schools, the reform of the curriculum is the *key* to improved student achievement. Past reform efforts have focused on all other aspects of the middle school with varying degrees of success. According to researchers, a change to an interdisciplinary curriculum may be a more effective approach to enhance student learning and increase scores on achievement tests. The principal, therefore, must educate the school's publics on the necessity of an interdisciplinary curriculum and must involve parent and community members in planning and developing the interdisciplinary program if the curriculum is to be successful. Providing open and honest communication to these publics regarding the goals and objectives, values and beliefs, and advantages of the curriculum keeps them informed of the school's efforts to provide students with a quality education. Carroll and Carroll (1994) relate that public and parental support is more likely when they are kept informed and have representatives to express their concerns. Principals, by appointing parent and community members to the planning committee and by keeping the larger populations informed through newsletters, open forums, and media releases, can build and sustain widespread support for an integrated curriculum.

(2) Teachers are subject matter–oriented. Few have been exposed to the philosophy behind the integrated curriculum or the planning strategy necessary for implementing such a curriculum. Teachers may also see an integrated curriculum as a weakening or watering down of their sub-

ject fields. Principals must provide the necessary training, resources, and time for teachers to become acquainted with the philosophy and goals of an integrated curriculum. Teacher fears about the "watering down" of subject content must be recognized and addressed through an educational program of inservices and staff development opportunities which are well-planned and practical in scope.

(3) Teachers may feel they do not have adequate time to plan for and implement an integrated curriculum. Gaining consensus on content and skills to be taught, identifying and sequencing themes for instruction, and pilot testing the units and the instructional materials take teacher time and effort. Providing adequate planning time for teachers during the school day is a top priority for principals committed to the successful implementation of an interdisciplinary curriculum. Ideally, teacher teams should have at least one hour per day to work together and one hour per day to work independently. Principals need to build this time into the master schedule and also provide time for teachers to benchmark other middle schools using an integrated curriculum. By providing substitute teachers, principals free their staff to visit other middle schools and learn from other teachers what facilitates the planning and implementation process. Weller (1993) notes that for teachers and principals alike, nothing has more credence than the word of one professional to another. Peers have mutual trust and will associate freely since they have common interests, concerns, and objectives. Moreover, benchmarking forms a peer network through which information can be regularly exchanged. Such mutual learning experiences strengthen all who are involved.

(4) Without ongoing assessment and evaluation, the interdisciplinary curriculum will fail in its objectives. Principals have the primary responsibility of making sure that each stage of the curriculum building process is evaluated and that these results are then used to refine the planning process and the instructional delivery system. Planning sessions must be evaluated from both a group-dynamics and a product-outcome perspective. The curriculum must be evaluated for relevancy, for the inclusion of state and local mandates, for the appropriateness of learning materials and activities, and for academic content and skills. Pilot testing the new curriculum with selected teachers and students is required in order to assess the overall effectiveness of the thematic units. All of these serve as a basis for curriculum refinement. Outcomes which should be assessed include teacher attitudes and satisfaction with the units and learning activities, student attitudes and satisfaction, and the instructional impact on student learning. As Beane (1992) argues, stu-

dent attitudes and learning outcomes must be the primary concerns of teachers and administrators. If a curriculum fails to excite and stimulate the students, fails to provide meaning in their lives, and fails to challenge them to explore the new and different, then the curriculum is not responding to the needs of the transescent learner.

(5) The social and political aspects of teams can present interpersonal problems which can thwart the goals of the interdisciplinary curriculum. Principals can do much to alleviate these problems by providing teachers with staff development programs focusing on conflict management, group dynamics, interpersonal relations, and problem-solving skills. Teachers having similar interests, who like each other and share the same educational philosophy, should be teamed together when possible.

THE INTERDISCIPLINARY TEAM

The idea of integrating subject matter through interdisciplinary themes is not new. Wiles and Bondi (1993) relate that over the past four decades, "common learnings" from the core subjects have been fused into themes or units for instruction. What *is* new to the middle school is the flexibility of interdisciplinary themes which allows teacher teams, through their expertise, to weave together a variety of subjects into creative patterns of instruction. The goal of the interdisciplinary curriculum and the interdisciplinary team is to enable students to see the interrelationships among subjects as they are presented comprehensively and cooperatively by subject-matter specialists. Such an approach negates the fragmentation students find in regular classrooms where each teacher teaches in an area of expertise with little or no regard for what is being taught in the classroom next door.

The use of interdisciplinary teams in middle schools has increased over the past three decades. MacIver (1990) reported that 42 percent of middle schools had interdisciplinary teams in grades 6–8 by 1990, and the Center for Research on Elementary and Middle Schools (CREMS) reported 40 percent of America's middle schools using this type of teaming in 1990. Approximately 25 percent of the schools using these teams had grade configurations of K–8, K–12, and 7–12. George and Alexander (1993) note that growth in the number of interdisciplinary teams in middle schools is increasing but is not used to the extent called for by many theorists.

What Is an Interdisciplinary Team?

Interdisciplinary teams are organized around teachers representing the four traditional content areas of science, social studies, mathematics, and language arts as well as teachers who specialize in reading, special education, art, music, and physical education. Teachers on the same team teach the same group of students, have the same planning time and the same teaching schedule, and are housed in one area of the school. In essence, they form a small community or a small school within a school. Team members work closely together to plan for instruction, implement the curriculum through a variety of instructional strategies and learning materials, and evaluate student learning outcomes and the curriculum.

A more specific definition of interdisciplinary teaming is presented by George and Alexander (1993) who state that there are four essential organizational components of integrated teams: students who are grouped together in one way or another; a group of teachers who plan, teach and evaluate students and the curriculum together; and a group of teachers and students who have the same schedule and are housed in the same area of the school. When all four components exist, the school has an interdisciplinary team organization which serves as the most distinguishing feature of a true middle school.

Interdisciplinary teams meeting these criteria can have their work facilitated by two additional components: block scheduling and adequate space for small and large group instruction. Block scheduling allows teams the flexibility within time blocks of two or more class periods to plan for instruction, have more control over the instructional environment, and spend more time with students. Space is also an important factor in interdisciplinary teaming. Housing teacher teams in the same part of the building allows them the opportunity to interact with each other and their students and have varied group instruction. Having space to conduct large group demonstrations and lectures as well as space for small group discussion and seatwork in one area of the building is time-saving and convenient, and it reduces the likelihood of student misbehavior.

Rationale for Interdisciplinary Teams

The research literature (Beane, 1990, 1992; Alexander and McErwin, 1989; MacIver, 1990) notes the importance of integrated curriculum teams in fulfilling the mission of the true middle school and the many advantages for both teachers and students. For teachers the benefits of interdisciplinary teams include the following:

(1) A higher sense of efficacy and greater job satisfaction
(2) Increased collegiality among teachers and a reduction in feelings of teacher isolation
(3) Increased enthusiasm about teaching and planning functions
(4) A greater sense of control over their professional lives through decision making and problem solving concerning instruction and curriculum

(5) More positive and frequent interactions with parents
(6) More of an inclination to use developmentally appropriate instructional activities and materials
(7) A willingness to try new approaches to teaching and use new and varied instructional strategies

Students also benefit from interdisciplinary teams (Arhar, 1992; Fenwick, 1992; MacIver, 1990; George and Alexander, 1993). Student benefits include the following:

(1) A climate of intellectual, social, emotional, and physical development exists for students which makes transition from elementary to middle grades easier and less threatening
(2) Students have at least four teachers who know them personally and are aware of their individual problems and their learning strengths and weaknesses
(3) Students have collective support from teachers as they take on responsibilities, develop self-reliance, explore their freedom, and learn to take responsibility for personal choices
(4) All students are exposed to the same quality standards and expectations for academic success and experience social interactions that are supportive and developmentally appropriate
(5) Students are surrounded by teachers who give them personal recognition and praise both as individuals and as group members
(6) Through an atmosphere of support, praise, and recognition, students have fewer discipline problems and are less likely to drop out of school

Interdisciplinary teams have additional strengths for promoting the goals of the true middle school. When team members function as student advisors, the ratio of advisor to student will range from 10 to 20 students which allows teachers to meet with students independently on a daily basis (James, 1986). By including reading teachers and special education teachers as part of the integrated team, team members have direct access to knowledge of students with specific learning problems, and strategies can be constantly designed and redesigned to meet their needs. Robinson (1991) argues that this type of instruction for special needs students is an alternative to pull-out programs which result in fragmented and disjointed learning. Robinson calls for "collaborative consultation" which is based on the objectives of parity among all participants, the understanding that all teachers can learn more effective ways to teach students, and a student-centered approach to instruction. Robinson notes that the middle school concept and integrated team teaching can best accomplish these objectives.

Including both core subject and exploratory teachers as members of the interdisciplinary team ensures instructional continuity regardless of the content covered by these teachers. For example, teachers of art, music, and physical education help plan thematic content and then teach correlated skills and knowledge to the same group of students. As team members, they provide support and assistance to students by having a first-hand understanding of their learning needs and personal problems.

Home-school communication is better facilitated with interdisciplinary team instruction. Communication with parents tends to be more positive, more frequent, and more informative. Because team members have extensive contact with each student, their conversations with parents are more specific concerning special needs and problems. This allows both parents and teacher to work more effectively to assist the student (Hawkins and Graham, 1994). Communication between teachers and administrators is also enhanced through integrated teaming. Principals, as ex-officio team members, will meet with teams as time permits. Through these meetings, principals get to know both teachers and students—as well as the instructional program—on a more personal level. Moreover, in large middle schools, team leaders who serve on school councils or school advisory committees meet regularly with the principal to discuss mutual concerns and student performance. Erb (1995) found that in middle schools where teaming occurs and where teams meet on a regular basis with principals, "life for teachers, students, and administrators tends to be more satisfying" (p. 184).

Interdisciplinary teams foster a supportive environment for students. Erb (1995) relates that "interdisciplinary teams represent a major advance in school organizational structure for creating a safe environment where each student is well known by each adult and by the student's peers on the team" (p. 185). Teams promote a sense of community in which students and teachers interact socially, where expectations for student success are high, and where students are cared about as unique individuals. Teaming has a positive impact on students through the formation of positive relations with the school, teachers, and peers, and results in higher levels of student self-esteem.

Characteristics of Effective Interdisciplinary Teams

The way teachers work within teams impacts the effectiveness of the team's planning and instruction. The characteristics of effective interdisciplinary teams include the following components:

(1) Teams have a student-centered approach to instruction.
(2) Team members are committed to achievement in academics and assist students in a variety of ways to help them succeed academically.

(3) Team members make behavioral expectations known to their students and expect good citizenship and behavior. They model this behavior and post rules and regulations that are fair and equally enforced among all students.

(4) Teams have their own sense of community or unity among teacher members and the students they teach. These teams behave as though they are a school-within-a-school and they participate in competitions and socialize within their own team membership.

(5) Teams have close and frequent contact with parents in both reporting student progress and involving parents in school activities. Team members see themselves "as having a 'customer relationship' orientation," and think of themselves as "providing a service to parents rather than doing them a favor" (George and Alexander, 1993, p. 256).

(6) Teachers are high on student praise and reward and are willing to try the new and the different to bring successful experiences to students. They take risks, are not afraid to fail, and learn from their mistakes to improve their instruction, the curriculum, and student learning.

Responsibilities of the Team Leader

The demands and responsibilities placed on interdisciplinary teams require team decision making and problem solving throughout the school year. Teachers must have not only the authority to make these decisions but the trust, confidence, and support of the principal if integrated teaming is to succeed. Although principals serve as advisors and facilitators to these teams, leadership roles reside within the team's membership in general and in its elected or appointed peer representatives in particular.

The tasks of team leaders vary from school to school, but the quality of leadership they provide has a high impact on the kinds and quality of programs and activities teacher teams provide their students. Interdisciplinary teaming requires the use of several such teams throughout grades 6–8. While the principal is responsible for the overall coordination of the interdisciplinary team program, team leaders represent their respective teams in school-wide team council leadership forums which are held at regular times throughout the year and are conducted by the principal. Team leadership meetings form the nucleus of the school's governmental organization and address problems confronting the whole school as well as those problems confronting their respective teams. Leadership teams assist the principal in making school policy, building the master schedule, determining budget allocations, and making decisions about the curriculum (George and Alexander, 1993). Collaborative leadership of this nature does not necessarily mean that interdisciplinary teams function within a site-based management approach. It does mean that a culture of collaboration exists within the school whether it is called a leadership team, a leadership council, a quality circle, or a school improvement team. However, principals of site-based managed and TQM schools often delegate authority to team leaders to make policy decisions, plan the yearly schedule, and make decisions regarding teacher education and promotion criteria.

In schools where team leaders are not part of a collaborative governance structure, team leaders are usually appointed by the principal and have specific duties and responsibilities. George and Alexander (1993) report that the general duties of an interdisciplinary team leader are as follows:

(1) Speaking for the team when interaction with the principal is necessary.
(2) Functioning as a peer teacher.
(3) Coordinating the overall functions of the interdisciplinary team.
(4) Preparing paperwork for field trips, the ordering of supplies, and the team budget.
(5) Scheduling and conducting team meetings and promoting cooperative relations among team members.
(6) Coordinating teacher aide and volunteer assignments.
(7) Motivating and challenging the team to pursue the goals of the middle school.
(8) Assisting teachers with classroom problems.
(9) Keeping informed of the most recent research and trends impacting middle school education and keeping team members informed of these trends and issues.

Effective and ineffective characteristics of team leaders are reported by George and Alexander (1993). Effective team leaders have the following abilities:

(1) They are good organizers and effective managers of time.
(2) They have excellent communication and human relations skills.
(3) They keep the team focused on their goals and those of the school.
(4) They build and maintain cooperation, morale, and commitment within the team.
(5) They influence and persuade others.

Ineffective leaders have the following weaknesses:

(1) They are poor at delegating responsibility.
(2) They do not maintain a positive attitude toward work and goal completion.

(3) They do not always represent the feelings of the team when talking with administrators.

The Principal's Role

The role the principal takes in sustaining effective interdisciplinary teams is crucial to their success. As discussed above, principals are role models, facilitators, consultants, and suppliers of time and resources so teams can do their jobs effectively. However, George and Alexander (1993) note that the following specific behaviors on the part of the principal are central to team effectiveness:

(1) Helps individual teams develop their goals each year
(2) Provides common planning time blocks in the master schedule
(3) Empowers teams to make decisions
(4) Provides staff development for teams based on their needs and interests
(5) Provides block scheduling for teams to have the needed flexibility to make teaming instructionally successful
(6) Requires all teachers to be members of teams
(7) Allows teams to have input in the selection of new members
(8) Evaluates each team's efforts and accomplishments as well as the efforts and accomplishments of each teacher in meeting the team's goals and objectives

Regardless of how strong team leaders are in fulfilling their roles, principals must guard against depending too much on these teacher leaders. Erb (1995) notes that teachers are teachers first and that they lack certain expertise and training in leadership skills and theory. Principals cannot relinquish their leadership responsibility to teachers and depend totally on team leaders to provide effective leadership. Such dependence can lead to teacher frustration, the feeling of being taken for granted, and team dysfunction. It is the principal's role to make sure that each teacher shares in the work of the team and takes responsibility for the quality of that work.

Teacher team members can facilitate the team process and assist the team leader in the following ways:

(1) Be open and honest in team discussions and display professional courtesy and respect to all team members.
(2) Take the initiative in volunteering for work assignments without waiting to be asked or assigned by the team leader.
(3) Be punctual, pay attention, and do not disrupt team meetings with personal concerns or information not relevant to the task of the team.

(4) Focus on issues and problems and not personalities when solving team problems.
(5) Be willing to see and understand different perspectives of team members and look for common ground to reach an agreement that will satisfy parties engaged in dispute.
(6) Support the team decision and do so with a positive attitude.

The importance of the role played by the principal in building the interdisciplinary curriculum and implementing interdisciplinary teams is paramount to the success of this instructional design. Providing vision, empowering teachers, and believing in the interdisciplinary curriculum are essential foundations. Generating enthusiasm among teachers and providing inservice for teachers for curriculum building and effective team outcomes are crucial. Principals must provide teachers the necessary time, support, and resources needed to have an effective interdisciplinary program. Instituting block scheduling, providing adequate planning time for teachers, and offering instructional assistance facilitate the goals of the interdisciplinary curriculum and team instruction.

THE INTERDISCIPLINARY CURRICULUM: CASE STUDY

"The interdisciplinary curriculum is only as strong as the individual team members who make up each one of the interdisciplinary teaching teams," says Dr. George Dougherty, principal of Oglethorpe County (Georgia) Middle School. A Georgia School of Excellence, Oglethorpe County Middle School (OCMS) is known for its quality instruction and a rich learning environment fostered by the team approach to integrating thematic units across core academic and exploratory courses. Serving as a laboratory school for the University of Georgia's Department of Middle School Education, OCMS not only has a curriculum that is developmentally responsive to transescents' problems, needs, and growth patterns but also a curriculum which has strong academic core content in science, mathematics, language arts, social studies, and reading.

How does a middle school develop a strong interdisciplinary curriculum? According to Dougherty, there is no single, set answer but rather a combination of factors which is essential.

First among the essentials is strong principal leadership which rests on a foundation of genuine personal belief in and commitment to the benefits of the interdisciplinary curriculum. Without this deep, driving personal belief the chance of success is slight.

Second, says Dougherty, is "talking-up the merits of the interdisciplinary curriculum with teachers and parents, with enthusiasm, every chance you get." In faculty meetings, in informal conversations in classrooms and halls, and in formal meetings, Dougherty reinforces the importance of an interdisciplinary curriculum. He also provides professional literature and conference material to teachers. Dougherty believes strongly in Deming's principles (1986) that leadership for quality begins at the top, through the principal, and that the need for education and reeducation is vital in order for teachers to change. Usually, a group of teachers will become interested in the idea of an interdisciplinary curriculum and seek more information. Agreeing with Weller (1995), this can become the "spark that sets things in motion" and the principal's role will shift to being the facilitator rather than the catalyst of change. Providing substitutes for these teachers to attend national conferences, local workshops, and benchmarking other middle schools is essential. Benchmarking, Dougherty says, is a valuable quality tool which allows teachers to visit middle schools having an interdisciplinary curriculum in order to see firsthand how the curriculum is structured and implemented. Here, teachers learn from their peers the do's and don'ts of interdisciplinary curriculum development "from practitioners who have far more credibility than textbook theory."

The role parents play in adding impetus to adopting an interdisciplinary curriculum can be crucial. Tact, however, must be used in stimulating parental interest and support in this effort. Being open and honest with teachers about stimulating parent interest through PTO programs and literature disseminated at parent-teacher conferences creates additional teacher interest and provides reassurance that the principal is not trying to circumvent teachers in the decision-making process. "Sometimes," Dougherty says, "parental enthusiasm is the necessary stimulus to get teachers motivated to try new things."

Third, a forum for disseminating conference and benchmarking information has to be provided. According to Dougherty, this is best done through a faculty meeting where teachers "can share their excitement with their peers and receive direct, honest information from reliable sources." This excitement will then spread through informal teacher discussions with peers and others will soon develop an interest in the interdisciplinary curriculum. Once this momentum begins, the principal has to quickly capitalize on this force by allowing others to investigate for themselves the attributes of the program. Dougherty says, "Monies, somehow, can be attained and the experienced principal knows the budget and the superintendent."

"Next, and this is vital," Dougherty says, "interdisciplinary team teaching and adequate team planning time are essential to having a successful interdisciplinary curriculum." Developing team teaching configurations, whether by grade level or through progressive teams (teams which have the same group of students as they progress from sixth through eighth grade), can be discussed and agreed upon as well as the other necessary components of team building and team teaching. Building interdisciplinary core academic teams with exploratory and elective teachers included as team members fosters a sense of community and unified purpose among all team members from the start. Core teachers, in particular, will grow to understand the value of having these non-core teachers as team members when they begin the development of thematic units and the correlation of course content with appropriate developmental strategies across curriculum areas. Having the school counselor involved in the early stages of team building is also important from both a practical and an educational perspective. Practically, the counselor can facilitate meetings among teachers who have difficulty buying into the team approach to instruction and mediate conflict between teachers as the teams solidify. From an educational perspective, the counselor keeps the teams focused on the child-centered philosophy of the middle school and assists team members in providing developmentally appropriate content and skills for transescents as they move from sixth through eighth grade. Dougherty says that here "the job of the principal is to be a resource person, a cheerleader, a supplier of any and all things teachers need to get going."

Fifth, agreeing upon curriculum structure and content can become a heated topic of debate, but "friction can be minimized by reminding teachers of the basic purpose of a curriculum and the goals and objectives of a true middle school," Dougherty says. Keeping teachers focused on the need to develop a planned set of common goals to ensure that students will both realize and actively experience the relationships among the disciplines and exploratory courses is an important job of the principal. Dougherty relates the importance of the principal actively helping teachers to develop a curriculum which is holistic in scope and developmentally appropriate, and at the same time allows for students to have coherent interconnections among all curriculum areas. "But," he warns, "teachers have to do the real development work themselves if they are to take pride in ownership of the outcome and, thereby, have a personal commitment to making it [the curriculum] a success."

Curriculum structure depends on teacher team preferences. Dougherty notes that many structural models are available but stresses the importance of first exploring the applicability of those models found during benchmarking visits as well as those presented at conferences and workshops. However, "providing too many models of curriculum structure for teachers to consider can cause frustration and indecision, and stop the momentum. It is important to remind teachers that structure can be adjusted or changed later after the operational model has a trial run." Dougherty suggests a conceptual framework which allows teachers to broaden their traditional, discrete subject-centered approach into a delivery format which is responsive to the needs of adolescents. Here, a fusion between the essential knowledge and skills of core academic content areas "with the content and skills adolescents need to successfully meet the challenges and problems confronting them in their daily lives and to prepare them for responsible citizenship" is necessary.

What such an approach does, says Dougherty, is force teachers to question the content of the core academics and exploratory courses. Teachers realize that if fusion is to take place they must first assess what knowledge and skills are most essential in their own subject areas. This becomes an important and valuable exercise in curriculum evaluation. Textbooks, an important issue to discuss with teachers, says Dougherty, are often the major source of teacher-taught knowledge and skills and define for many teachers what is important. This is particularly true in the academic core subjects of language arts, mathematics, social studies, science, and reading. The research material supports Dougherty's assertion. Woodward and Elliott (1990) report, for example, that "dependence on textbooks as opposed to use of textbooks is an issue at the core of professional practice" (p. 180) and that approximately 90 percent of all types of classroom instruction is textbook influenced. Depending on textbooks for core curriculum content allows writers and publishers as opposed to teachers to determine what knowledge is of the most worth. Consequently, textbooks, for the majority of teachers, become the legitimate knowledge source and structure of the curriculum. Dougherty believes that getting teachers to realize that textbooks are merely an information source, a guide for learning, is an important step in helping teachers realize that their own professional judgment should dictate relevance and importance of content. Woodward and Elliott found that several factors contribute to high textbook use. Teachers with less than five years' experience rely more on textbooks than do more experienced teachers; limited supplementary materials or access to these materials increases the dependency on textbooks; and a lack of adequate planning time and a lack of adequate class time to teach required content contribute to textbook dependency.

This is not to say that textbooks lack value or relevance, but that textbooks and teacher guides should be used as an instructional source while teacher judgment about importance and relevance of curriculum content should dictate the core curriculum and the interdisciplinary curriculum. Dougherty states that "having teachers who develop much of their own instructional materials and deviate from textbook structure offer examples to other teachers is an effective way to get teachers to trust in their own professional training and judgment." Often, teachers lack knowledge of what their peers are doing instructionally, Dougherty says, and when teachers are forced to examine core content and discuss content relevance, new ideas and energies begin to emerge. While this can be a time-consuming process, teaming core teachers by grade level with similar disciplines greatly facilitates the process. Exploratory teachers follow the same process with grouping based on content similarities, when possible. For example, health, physical education, and home economics teachers can be grouped to discuss content relevance.

Determining relevant content can be accomplished in a variety of ways. However, the work of Ralph Tyler (1950), often affectionately referred to as "the Grand Old Man of Curriculum," has particular relevance to building an interdisciplinary middle school curriculum. First, instructional goals should be based on the knowledge and characteristics of the learner. Here, knowledge of the principles of the true middle school and the various developmental processes of transescents come into play. Second, selection of relevant content will be based on an understanding of the society and environment in which the learner exists. Third, content will be selected based on the goals of the school and society. Figure 5.1 presents a model for curriculum analysis.

Sixth, each team now reports their findings to all teacher groups. A grand course content matrix is constructed by content area and grade level which lists the knowledge, skills, and concepts to be taught. When general consensus is reached, copies of the matrix are distributed to all teachers and it forms the basis for the thematic unit design which provides linkages between course content and the goals of the interdisciplinary curriculum.

Each grade level team, along with exploratory teachers and the school counselor, now develops themes and units of instruction which are content-relevant and developmentally appropriate for the preadolescent. Beane (1990) notes the primary importance of this step being the careful examination of the "common elements" of personal, social, and emotional development of the transescent. Curriculum themes, he states, should result from a blend of knowledge and skills with these common elements. At Oglethorpe County Middle School, Dougherty relates, teachers, upon their yearly self-review and evaluation of the effectiveness of their team planning, instruction, and thematic content, noticed an increase in discipline problems resulting from student disagreements with their peers and student frustration over their inability to resolve conflict amicably. Reading and language arts teachers took the lead in suggesting that a theme across all grade levels be developed focusing on conflict resolution. A task force was appointed representing grade six through eight teachers, an exploratory teacher, and the school counselor to explore existing material on conflict resolution and propose a school-wide, theme-based curriculum. Incorporat-

Curriculum Analysis Model

Instructional Goals

- Knowledge
- Skills
- Concepts
- Generalizations

Knowledge of True Middle School Principles

- Documentation to guide all aspects of learning
- Organized knowledge and skills
- Knowledge of personal development activities
- Exploration
- Preparation of students for high school
- Responsive to developmental characteristics of the learner
- Focused on learning needs of students
- Guidance and counseling by teachers
- Positive school climate
- Flexibility in instruction
- Promotion of student self-concept
- Involvement of community and parents

Knowledge of the Transescent

- Responds to needs of physical development
- Responds to needs of intellectual development
- Responds to needs of social-emotional development
- Responds to needs of moral and ethical development

Select Knowledge and Skills

- Needs of the middle school learner
- Most important knowledge and skills to meet goals of the school and society
- State and local education requirements

FIGURE 5.1. Curriculum analysis model.

ing commercially produced videos and texts, teachers developed thematic units for each grade level which were sequenced for knowledge and skills. This joint faculty project later led to the development of a Peer Mediation Forum started by eighth grade teachers and students.

Originally made up of eighth grade student volunteers, the Peer Mediation Forum has expanded to include sixth and seventh grade students. Trained in a two-day workshop in conflict resolution and mediation procedures by the school counselor, student mediators preside over peer disputes at all grade levels. Students requesting issues to be mediated drop a Request for Mediation Form into a mailbox outside the counselor's office. The form states the names of the parties involved, the date and nature of the issue, and any supporting information a student may want to include. Mediation time is scheduled by the counselor, usually within one or two days of the request, and is conducted in a formal, serious atmosphere with set policies and procedures provided to students in advance of the hearing. Student findings are binding on both parties and a contract is signed by both students agreeing to abide by the decision of the mediators. Student discipline problems have decreased by more than 80 percent with few students repeating the mediation process for similar type infractions.

Another example of teacher initiative in developing their own interdisciplinary curriculum at Oglethorpe County Middle School is the inclusion of a theme on Research Methods and Study Skills. Here, sixth grade teams took the lead in developing a unit on teaching students quantitative research methods and study skills. Teacher teams noticed students lacked these basic skills in preparing papers and projects and in studying for tests. Seventh and eighth grade teams adopted the unit with the research part of the unit being sequenced in these grades and with study skills being periodically reinforced at these grade levels. An Environmental Issues theme was developed from teacher and student interest and, in part, as a result of the Research Methods theme. Students who wished to explore topics relating to ecology lacked the fundamental skills necessary to conduct the research and the growing student interest in ecology stimulated teacher interest in developing an instructional theme on ecology.

Health, a state-required thirty hour course, was expanded to a nine week course at Oglethorpe County Middle School due to teacher team requests. An increase in student pregnancy rates and drug abuse promoted teachers to reexamine the health curriculum and, as a result, the content was redesigned with parental input. Dougherty says the program is "a no holds barred approach to sex and drug education. Anything students want to know, we cover, and we answer any and all questions." The result is a decrease in student pregnancy from 4 a year to 1 or zero a year.

The principal's role in these examples directly relates to Dougherty's leadership philosophy: "As a a facilitator, I provide the time, support, and resources necessary to these teacher-leaders to do their job." Examples such as these, he maintains, directly support Deming's quality philosophy principles (1986) of continuous improvement and constancy of purpose. Dougherty also believes that successful principals have to "develop a mind-set that teachers are talented professionals who want to do their best and have the best interests of the students at heart." With this mind-set, you give teachers freedom to do their job, make decisions, and solve problems that impact instruction. "After all," asks Dougherty rhetorically, "is this not what quality education and the effective schools research is all about?"

"You see," says Dougherty, "if you treat people with respect and dignity, treat them as professionals having creative potentials, they respond in kind. More good ideas are generated than we have time and resources to implement," he states. Dougherty believes his open meetings with teachers, which take place three times a year, do much to improve teacher morale and "cross pollenize" ideas for curriculum revitalization. His occasional informal "chats" with teacher teams and with individuals on a one-to-one basis serve as idea stimulation sessions for instructional improvement. Dougherty sums up by saying that "principals as leaders can do only so much. Clock hours and management constraints limit the amount of time a principal can spend on instructional leadership. You have to make that *faith leap* that teachers are leaders and can and will make the right decisions for their students."

Eighth, developing themes using corresponding instructional units for the interdisciplinary curriculum "is situation specific," according to Dougherty. "The guidepost for theme and unit development is relevancy to student lives. [Using] theory for unit development is one thing, but themes must come from student needs or problems they have or will face." An example, he says, is the theme on conflict resolution and the expansion of the health curriculum to meet real-life, current problems of students.

While themes for interdisciplinary units can come from a variety of sources, the goal is to make themes conceptually flexible which allows teachers to pull content from various knowledge and skill areas and to weave them together in a creative way to meet student needs. "Once teachers see the opportunity to apply their creativity to theme and unit development, they become self-motivated; they have fun in taking on this new challenge." Getting themes developed in a timely manner depends on a clear purpose and focus. Often, teams tend to get "bogged down" in discussing issues of specific academic content, or the importance of key skills or concepts to be covered in their specific fields. This is unproductive, leads to unresolvable issues, and causes frustration among all teachers. "Too much frustration can stop momentum and cause teachers to seriously question the value of the interdisciplinary curriculum," says Dougherty. He suggests having meeting agendas which clearly state the purpose of the meeting and provide targets for accomplishing certain key tasks. This meeting agenda format can be used for developing thematic units with modifications. First, state the purpose of the meeting which is developing interdisciplinary themes with a working definition of a theme.

Next, have a school calendar which clearly specifies the number of instructional days, by week and month, excluding holidays and other non-school days. This provides teachers with an index of instructional time to plan the number and content of thematic units. Third, teachers must ask themselves what knowledge is of the most worth to students for later academic success and to successfully confront current life problems. Figure 5.2 presents a theme and unit meeting agenda for developing an interdisciplinary curriculum. The curriculum then guides the developmental processes of students in the following ways:

- Themes cut across and make creative connections among all content area curricula.
- Students are exposed to knowledge and skills from different perspectives with each exposure having value in itself.
- Themes and units contain content which is of interest to students.
- Themes and units have correlated real-life learning experiences to apply classroom knowledge and skills in order for students to make mental and physical connections across subject areas.

Dougherty relates that principals must emphasize the importance of themes being "motivational in nature." Catchy, descriptive titles arouse student interest and describe the content linkage. Such a theme might be Mother Nature and Her Step-Children: Industry, Economy, Society. Next, themes need to have concepts which link subject areas so students can make connections between the need for or impact of one content area or part of a content area on other areas. An example of such concept linkages might be how the ecology impacts local industry which in turn impacts the economy and subsequently social life in the community. Skills then have to be identified within the units for students to learn. Skills depend upon the concepts being taught and the instructional goals of the unit. In the ecology example, map reading, demographic chart reading, and social statistics about the community would be taught with a focus on students being able to make interdisciplinary connections. Active learning could be done through community surveys, interviews with officials, and so on. Many models exist for curriculum building by themes. These include the Wiles-Bondi Curriculum Mapping Model (Wiles and Bondi, 1993), the Yinger Model (Yinger, 1980), and the Tyler Model (Tyler, 1950).

Finally, the thematic curriculum has to be pilot tested for effectiveness. Several options exist and selection will depend on grade-level team preferences. If themes were developed for sixth grade only, the results of pilot testing may serve as a basis for expanding the curriculum to grades seven and eight. If all three grades are involved, pilot test results can be compared

```
┌─────────────────────────────────────────────────────────────────────────────┐
│                                                                               │
│        Theme and Unit Meeting Agenda for Developing Interdisciplinary Curriculum │
│                                                                               │
│  Directions:      This agenda is a guide to assist you in developing themes and units for the interdisciplinary │
│                   curriculum. Complete the requested information on the agenda form. Use additional paper │
│                   when needed. Please return a copy to me [the principal] after each work session. │
│                                                                               │
│  Team: _____        Date:_____          │
│                                                                               │
│  Theme:           A student-motivating, descriptive topic or phrase which links component parts or units to │
│                   make connections across subject areas.                      │
│                                                                               │
│  Unit:            Subtopics within the theme which are based on learner goals and objectives and allow │
│                   students to make connections across subject areas through integrated concepts, skills, │
│                   and active learning.                                        │
│                                                                               │
│                                    School Calendar                            │
│                                                                               │
│  Instructional Days for:                                                      │
│                                                                               │
│  •      September    18         November    20         January    22          │
│  •      October      22         December    18         February   21          │
│  •      March        20         April       19         May        20          │
│                                                                               │
│  (See attached copy of school calendar for specific days of each week school is not in session.) │
│                                                                               │
│  Number of Days for Theme Instruction:        _____  │
│                                                                               │
│  Theme Name: _____ Number of Thematic Units:        _____  │
│                                                                               │
│                                      Unit Names                               │
│                                                                               │
│  Unit:         _____ │
│                                                                               │
│  Student Goal(s):_____    Student Objectives:_____   │
│                                                                               │
│  _____        _____         │
│                                                                               │
│  _____        _____         │
│                                                                               │
│                                     continued                                 │
│                                                                               │
└─────────────────────────────────────────────────────────────────────────────┘
```

FIGURE 5.2. Theme and unit meeting agenda for development of an interdisciplinary.

Concepts Taught by Subject Areas*

Subject Area: _____   Concepts Taught: _____

Skills Taught by Subject Area*

Subject Area: _____   Skills Taught: _____

_____

_____

*Note: Teachers can best determine concepts and skills by asking themselves what knowledge is of the most worth for student success in academics and in confronting real-life problems. Teacher observations and students surveys are good data sources.

Instructional Materials and Resources Needed

List all instructional materials and resources needed for all units under each theme. Prioritize each category for principal use in ordering and scheduling each team's request.

Materials (e.g. reference books, commercial kits, etc.):

1. _____   4. _____

2. _____   5. _____

3. _____   6. _____

Resources (e.g. guest speakers, field trips, etc.):

1. _____   4. _____

2. _____   5. _____

3. _____   6. _____

continued

FIGURE 5.2 (continued). Theme and unit meeting agenda for development of an interdisciplinary.

176

```
                              Evaluation

List specific ways and measures each team will use to evaluate the effectiveness of each unit within the
theme. Units should be evaluated by teachers and students, and include both cognitive and affective
assessment. For example, teachers' recorded observations or logs of student interest and student test
scores may be used. Student surveys and informal discussion may serve as evaluation data.


Unit: _____


Cognitive Assessment: _____        Affective Assessment:_____

_____                 _____

_____                 _____
```

FIGURE 5.2 (continued). Theme and unit meeting agenda for development of an interdisciplinary.

between grade levels for effectiveness in meeting the goals and objectives of the units and student cognitive and affective development.

The practical idea of developing thematic interdisciplinary curriculum "is for teachers to enjoy their work, to have fun in creatively developing the curriculum, and to continuously improve the themes and units to meet their students' needs," Dougherty says. After the first year, teams work together in more cohesive groups, instructional strategies and materials are improved, and teachers become more adventurous in applying their creative talents. Planning time, Dougherty states, is essential to interdisciplinary team planning, curriculum evaluation, and revision. Principals *must* schedule teacher teams with daily planning time blocks to assess and revise the thematic units as they are being taught. "This daily planning time truly promotes the quality principles of continuous improvement and sustains constancy of purpose," relates Dougherty, which is central to an effective interdisciplinary curriculum.

REFERENCES

Alexander, W. M. and C. K. McErwin. 1989. "Schools in the Middle: Progress 1968–1988," in *Schools in the Middle: A Report on Trends and Practices*. Reston, VA: National Association of Secondary School Principals.

Arhar, J. M. 1992. "Interdisciplinary Teaming and the Social Bonding of Middle School Students," *Middle School Journal*, 20(3):24–27.

Beane, J. A 1990. *The Middle School Curriculum: From Rhetoric to Reality*. Columbus, OH: National Middle School Association.

Beane, J. A. 1992. "Turning the Floor Over: Reflections on a Middle School Curriculum," *Social Studies Review*, 28(1):38–41.

Beane, J. A. 1993. *A Middle School Curriculum from Rhetoric to Reality.* Second edition. Columbus, OH: National Middle School Association.

Carnegie Council on Adolescent Development. 1989. *Turning Points: Preparing American Youth for the 21st Century.* New York: Carnegie Corporation of New York.

Carroll, S. R. and D. Carroll. 1994. *How Smart Schools Get and Keep Community Support.* Bloomington, IN: National Education Service.

Center for Research on Elementary and Middle Schools. 1990. "Implementation and Effects of Middle Grades Practices," *CREMS Report* (March). Baltimore, MD: Johns Hopkins University Center for Research on Elementary and Middle Schools.

Deming, W. E. 1986. *Out of the Crisis.* Boston, MA: MIT University Press.

Drake, S. M. 1991. "How Our Team Dissolved the Boundaries," *Educational Leadership*, 49(2):20–22.

Erb, T. O. 1995. "Teamwork in Middle School Education," in *Teamwork Models and Experience in Education*, H. G. Garner, ed. Boston: Allyn & Bacon, pp. 175–198.

Fenwick, J. 1992. *Managing Middle Grade Reform—An "America 2000" Agenda.* San Diego, CA: Fenwick and Associates, Inc.

George, P. S. and W. M. Alexander. 1993. *The Exemplary Middle School.* Second edition. Fort Worth: Harcourt Brace Jovanovich College Publishers.

Hamm, M. and D. Adams. 1994. *The Collective Dimensions of Learning.* Norwood, NJ: Ablex.

Hawkins, M. and D. Graham. 1994. *Curriculum Architecture: Creating a Place of Our Own.* Columbus, OH: National Middle School Association.

Inhelder, B. and J. Piaget. 1958. *The Growth of Logical Thinking from Childhood to Adolescence.* Translated by Anne Parsons and Stanley Milgram, New York: Basic Books, Inc.

Jacobs, H. H. 1991. Planning for Curriculum Integration. *Educational Leadership*, 49:(2):27–28.

James, M. A. 1986. *Advisor-Advisee Programs: Why, What, and How?* Columbus, OH: National Middle School Association.

Lewis, A. C. 1990. "Getting Unstuck: Curriculum as a Tool of Reform," *Phi Delta Kappan*, 71:534–538.

Lounsbury, J. H. and G. E. Vars. 1978. *Curriculum for the Middle School Years.* New York: Harper and Row.

MacIver, D. 1990. "Meeting the Needs of Young Adolescents: Advisory Groups, Interdisciplinary Teaching Teams, and School Transition Programs," *Phi Delta Kappan*, 71(6):458–464.

Miller, P. S. 1992. "Segregated Programs of Teacher Education in Early Childhood: Immoral and Ineffective Practices," *Topics in Early Childhood Special Education*, 11(4):39–52.

Palmer, J. M. 1991. "Planning Wheels Turn Curriculum Around," *Educational Leadership*, 49(2):57–60.

Robinson, S. M. 1991. "Collaborative Consultation," in *Learning About Learning Disabilities*, B. Y. L. Wong, ed. San Diego, CA: Academic Press.

Tyler, R. W. 1950. *Basic Principles of Curriculum and Instruction.* Chicago: University of Chicago Press.

Vars, G. F. Spring 1992. "Integrative Curriculum: A Deja Vu," *Current Issues in Middle Level Education*, 1(1):66–78.

Weller, L. D. 1993. *Total Quality Management: A Conceptual Overview and Applications for Education*. Athens, GA: College of Education, The University of Georgia.

Weller, L. D. 1995. "Principals and Quality Performance: Getting in the Backdoor," *The TQM Magazine*, 7(1):20–23.

Wigle, S. E. and R. E. Dudley. 1993. The Integrated Methods Model and Secondary Preservice Teacher Education Programs," *Action in Teacher Education*, 15(3):52–55.

Wiles, J. and J. Bondi. 1993. *The Essential Middle School*. Second edition. New York: Macmillan Publishing Company.

Woodward, A. and D. L. Elliott. 1990. "Textbook Use and Teacher Professionalism," in *Textbooks and Schooling in the United States*, D. L. Elliott and A. Woodward, eds. Eighty-Ninth Yearbook of the National Society for the Study of Education, Part I. Chicago: University of Chicago Press, pp. 178–193.

Wright, E., R. Sorrels and C. Granby. Spring 1996. "A Five-Year Journey: Integrating Teacher Education Methods Courses," *Action in Teacher Education*, 28(1):39–47.

Yinger, R. J. 1980. "A Study of Teacher Planning," *The Elementary School Journal*, 80:107–127.

CHAPTER 6

Intramural Athletics: Promoting Quality Middle School Goals

Effective middle school principals know that meeting the physical needs of middle school students is crucial to their success as learners and to their social, emotional, and mental development. These principals know that their students' physical and emotional health are directly related to their intellectual development. Quality physical activity programs cannot, therefore, be planned and conducted in isolation of these other factors. These programs must focus on the physical concerns and needs of the adolescent and provide experiences in which students can compete, succeed, and develop a healthy life style.

This chapter will provide curriculum and scheduling examples of quality middle school physical education programs and intramural programs. A list of intramural activities will be provided as well as a list of considerations for staffing and scheduling the intramural programs and selecting an intramural director. A program planning guide will present goals, objectives, and methods and through a case study, the philosophy of a true middle school intramural program will be presented.

This chapter will focus on the following questions.

- Why is the physical activities component of the middle school curriculum important to the intellectual, social, and emotional development of adolescents?
- What is the role and what are the responsibilities of the principal in providing a quality intramural program?
- How do the physical development activities specifically complement the interdisciplinary curriculum and facilitate the intellectual, social, and emotional development of students?
- What are the key components of a quality middle school physical

education program and what are the essential considerations a principal must face when providing leadership in developing this instructional curriculum?

- Why are interscholastic activities inappropriate for the adolescent learner?
- How can principals best transform an interscholastic program into an effective intramural program?
- What are the guiding principles underlying an effective intramural program and what facilities, resources, and equipment are necessary to promote such a program?
- How do you build an effective intramural program? How do you go about planning the program, staffing the program, and selecting intramural activities? What is the role and what are the responsibilities of the principal in making the activities successful?
- How does a principal ensure the maximum use of the adviser/advisee concept in the intramural program?
- What are the criteria and the considerations for selection of an intramural director?
- How is the impact of the intramural program evaluated?

THE NEED FOR INTRAMURAL PROGRAMS

Central to the middle school philosophy is the idea of intramural athletics and physical activities which help all students develop a healthy life style. This contrasts with the interscholastic sports found in the traditional junior high school where physical activities are mainly for those having more highly developed athletic skills. These highly competitive athletic programs are not developmentally appropriate for transescent learners who are already under the pressures of physical, emotional, intellectual, and social development. Middle schools must focus on physical programs designed to help students understand their bodies and intramural programs designed to foster wide participation which allows all students to excel to their capacity and to receive personal satisfaction and recognition for their achievement and individual progress. Wiles and Bondi (1993) relate that an intramural program is an outgrowth of the physical education program and that such a program will be quality-oriented, well-planned, and focused on the physical needs and concerns of the adolescent so that it can "assist the student in physical, mental, and social development" (p. 91).

Effective middle school principals know that meeting the physical needs of the transescent is crucial to their success as learners and to their social, emotional, and mental development. Students' physical and emotional health are directly related to their intellectual development, and physical activity programs are just as important as other programs making up the middle school curriculum. Quality physical activity programs, therefore, cannot be planned and conducted in isolation of other school activities as they are an essential part of the interdisciplinary curriculum and integrated team approach to instruction.

Transescent Development and Intramurals

The need to be successful physically is especially true for boys during this time of preadolescent development. Success in physical activities promotes social acceptance and, for some, a chance to excel in their innate areas of strength and talent. During the age span from ten to fourteen years, actual physical growth tends to be well ahead of muscular strength with rapid skeletal growth spurts causing a lack of coordination. The more mature males in this age group are better coordinated and have increased muscle size and strength which allow them to excel over their more slowly developing counterparts who run slower, have less stamina, and are less capable of long spurts of endurance. In adolescent bodies growing at such a rapid rate, psychomotor currents to the brain are often slow and are not constant from one individual to the next. Aggressive play and roughness among boys increase with the onset of puberty. Since students mature at different rates and times, contact sports and other highly competitive sports are not for all transescent males because the increase in the competitive spirit and the concern over winning and losing impact the development of the self-concept (George and Lawrence, 1982).

Girls, on average, begin puberty two years ahead of boys at about age 10½. Like boys, but about two years earlier, girls begin their growth spurts and muscle and skeletal development. Both girls and boys are concerned with body image and a positive body image correlates with positive self-concept. Girls especially need reassurances that their lack of coordination is temporary and that they can experience success in some physical activity. intramural activities take into consideration the low endurance found in both male and female transescents and moderate the intense prolonged physical activity often found in competitive sports which may damage students physically. Girls have equal opportunities to participate and excel in intramurals and to develop their physical talents more so than in the male-dominated sports programs of the traditional junior high school. Through a strong intramural program boys and girls compete on the same teams, learn and practice good sportsmanship, and develop recreational interests and lifetime sports skills for adulthood.

How Intramurals Complement Other Middle School Programs

Physical activity programs complement and enrich the other middle school programs which focus on the social, emotional, and cognitive development of middle school youth. At times, the physical needs and concerns of middle school students are their most important concerns. Physical ability, personal appearance, size, and strength all impact peer group acceptance. Self-concept and confidence are closely tied to the perceived societal norms of peers and impact the transescent's cognitive performance in other subjects. Positive and negative learning experiences and confidence in learning ability also directly impact cognitive performance. When learners have a choice in what type of experiences they will participate in and when these experiences are related to future use and value, learning becomes more effective. A strong, well-planned intramural program offers transescent students all of these advantages.

Why Interscholastic Programs Are Inappropriate

Interscholastic programs, compared to intramural programs, are inappropriate for middle school youth since they are exclusive in nature and incompatible with the developmental characteristics of the transescent age learner. Moreover, interscholastic programs are mostly adult-directed, and they consume an inordinate amount of resources that could be better utilized for the benefit of all students rather than for the esoterically skilled few.

Interscholastic activities have a highly competitive orientation with emphasis on winning at the expense of participation, enjoyment, and skill development. Parents or other adults coaching these activities place winning before participation and those students who do not succeed or "measure-up" to the skill level or the emotional maturity level desired by the adult will not be allowed to participate. Students who do not succeed in this area may develop negative feelings about self-concept and self-esteem which may diminish their liking for sports and other physical activities in general.

Highly intense competition may also cause emotional damage to students. Many students lack the emotional maturity to compete at an intense level until they reach adolescence (usually around age 15). Often the pressure to excel under difficult and demanding situations at this early age can lead to failure which not only impacts the self-concept of the student, but the attitude directed toward the student from peers and adults (Kindred, Wolotkiewicz, Mickelson and Coplein, 1981).

THE PRINCIPAL'S ROLE IN BUILDING AN INTRAMURAL PROGRAM

A strong intramural program is the result of a strong physical education program and is a primary responsibility of the principal. Intramural programs which excel infuse the goals and objectives of the physical education program into a multi-activity program geared to the interests of students, not adults. As with other curricular programs, the physical education program must be student-focused and the education of the whole learner remains the most important consideration. Ideally, the physical education program should stress the Greek concept of soundness of mind and body. Therefore, students should have access to the activities and resources necessary to develop the basic skills and positive attitudes for lifelong physical activity and sound physical and emotional health. As the leader of the middle school, the principal must provide instructional leadership in meeting these goals and objectives.

Principals enhance the quality of the physical education and intramural programs in a variety of ways. First, the quality of the staff is central to the quality of the programs within the middle school. Staff must be hired and maintained who are knowledgeable of and committed to the educational philosophy of the middle school concept and they must be fully aware of the unique needs and developmental characteristics of the transescent learner.

Second, the type of scheduling selected by the principal is crucial in that it must allow adequate planning and instructional time for teachers and adequate activity time for students. The use of block scheduling can best facilitate the needs of both teachers and students.

Third, the effective use of existing facilities in and around the school is important in developing quality programs in physical education and intramurals. Scheduling adequate time for the use of the gym, auditorium, and cafeteria is essential. Time for recess and extended lunch breaks allows the use of playing fields and surrounding land and wood areas. With proper and adequate adult supervision these outside areas can provide places for physical activities for all students through a variety of programs.

Fourth, the role of the advisor/advisee program, the guidance counselor, and the intramural director can be maximized. The use of parents, teachers, and community members must be broadened to assist in supervising, conducting, and officiating these activities. A word of caution is necessary to those including non-trained middle school staff in any of these activities. The philosophy of the middle school must be fully explained to these adult volunteers and they must clearly understand that intramural activities are designed to educate the whole child, enhance self-esteem, promote positive attitudes and wide participation, foster healthy emotional and social development, and promote good sportsmanship while providing a positive athletic and recreational experience for each student. Intense competition which emphasizes winning above all other considerations is not the goal of the program.

Organization of the Intramural Program

The organization of the intramural program primarily depends upon the needs and interests of the students, the building facilities, and the existing equipment and the amount of money available to purchase new equipment. Student and teacher surveys can provide information regarding student needs and interests while teachers and the physical education staff can assist the principal in designing the intramural program based on existing facilities and equipment. Program design must take into account the objectives of maximal participation of all students; the development of fundamental skills and knowledge; the maximal use of facilities, staff, and time; the maximal number of activities that can be offered based on student needs and interests; and the organization of teams by grade-level ability and skill level (Wiles and Bondi, 1993).

Student and teacher surveys do not have to be lengthy or elaborate in design to be effective. For students the essential information needed for developing an intramural program focuses on these questions: What are the activities of interest to the student? Why is the student interested in this activity? What does the student expect to learn from the activity? Each student in each grade completes the survey, as seen in Figure 6.1, and the results are used as a basis for curriculum development. While the activities listed by students will provide course offering information, the reasons for student interest and what they expect to learn are important for course content. By having students relate exactly why they are interested in an activity and what they want to learn, the principal can provide teachers with information to give the students what they want and expect from the course. This quality feature coincides with Deming's philosophy (1986) that to satisfy customers you must first ask customers what they want and second, provide them what they want and more, if possible.

Teacher surveys are somewhat different from student surveys, but they can also be short in length. These surveys are important for staffing the intramural program. Figure 6.2 presents an example of such a survey. This survey can be modified slightly for parent and community member use.

The time of the day intramurals are scheduled is important since a goal of the program is maximal student participation. Students should be able to participate in one or more activities weekly and these should include individual, dual, and team-oriented activities. Scheduling time for these activities is the principal's responsibility. They should be scheduled before and after school, during recess, and in conjunction with daily blocks of time al-

Student Intramural Interest Survey

Harrison Middle School
Harrison, Georgia
May, 1996

Directions: Write the activities you would like to participate in at school under the Activity column. Tell why you
would be interested in participating in the activity under the Interest column. Tell what it is you want to
learn from the activity under the Learn column. You can list as many activities as you want. Look at the
example before completing the survey.

Example:

Activity	Interest	Learn
1. Basketball	It's fun and I want to play as well as my friends.	I want to be able to dribble and shoot hook shots like the pros.

Name: _____
Grade: _____
Homeroom Teacher: _____

Activity	Interest	Learn
1.		
2.		
3.		
4.		
5.		

FIGURE 6.1. Student intramural interest survey.

located for physical education. The utilization of parent and community member volunteers with expertise in coaching, advising, judging, and assisting regular school staff has to be considered when intramural activities are planned.

INDEPENDENT STUDY, GUIDANCE, AND THE ADVISOR/ADVISEE PROGRAMS

Intramural activities need to be planned to coincide with topics covered by regular classroom teachers, the guidance staff, and the advisor/advisee

Teacher Intramural Activity Survey

Harrison Middle School
Harrison, Georgia
May, 1996

Directions: In the space provided below, please list those intramural activities in which you have interest in
teaching, your qualifications/experience, and the days of the week you are available to teach the activity
after regular school hours. Also, specify the season of the year you would be willing to teach the activity.
Rank order your choice of activities to help the program committee know your highest to lowest interest
areas. Place a checkmark beside the activity you would be willing to co-teach with another teacher.

At the end of the survey, list the activities you would be willing to serve as an official, scorer, timekeeper,
etc.

Name: _____

Activity Interested in Teaching	Qualifications Experience	Days Available	Season of Year
1.			
2.			
3.			
4.			
5.			

Please list the activities and duties for which you would be willing to serve as an official, scorer,
timekeeper, etc.

1.			
2.			
3.			

FIGURE 6.2. Teacher intramural activity survey.

program. For example, independent study topics can be supervised by teachers and can focus on intramural activities or sports. Students can research the history of an activity or sport and/or spend time developing a basic skill in an activity of interest. In some middle schools, an independent study activity period is scheduled school-wide as part of the school's integrated curriculum. The idea of independent study is to allow students to work individually and explore areas of high personal interest. When intramural activities are scheduled during the school-wide activity period, students receive maximal benefit from the goals of independent study *and* the intramural program.

Guidance counselors can assist students in choosing which intramural activities to participate in and when. Guidance personnel, along with teachers, know the needs and maturation levels of their students and can help students make proper choices based on physical, social, and emotional levels of maturation. Comprehensive guidance programs in effective middle schools assist students in understanding their physical growth patterns and body changes. Students are provided instructional materials and time to discuss the particular needs and problems associated with their physical and emotional development and what *they* expect to learn from intramural activities (Riemcke, 1988).

Advisor/advisee programs also play an important role in strong physical education and intramural programs. In the advisory program, teachers serve as advisors to groups of students and focus on helping students with their social and emotional development. Working closely with counselors, teachers assist individual students in identifying and resolving their personal socio-emotional problems as they progress through preadolescence. While working with their assigned groups, teachers have the opportunity to discuss topics specifically related to students' social and emotional development. Included in these topics are issues concerning teamwork, sportsmanship, leadership behavior, etiquette, cooperation and sharing, and conflict resolution. When time is scheduled for the advisor/advisee program as part of the regular classroom time block and is not just a weekly occurrence or merely tacked on at the end of the school day, teachers and students have the opportunity to discuss relevant matters on a continuing and consistent basis. During the advisor/advisee time, the goals of the intramural program can be supported by allocating time for students to sign up for intramurals and to discuss the rules and regulations of each activity, the philosophy behind intramurals, safety procedures, and the use of equipment (Wiles and Bondi, 1993).

The Director of Intramurals and the Intramurals Committee

Although responsibility for developing an intramurals program ultimately rests with the principal, a continuing and comprehensive program needs direct leadership and coordination. Wiles and Bondi (1993) advocate using a director and committee to coordinate intramural activities. The overall responsibilities of planning, organizing, and scheduling these activities will then reside with the director who is a physical education teacher. Arranging for officials, advertising sign-up procedures, developing safety regulations, and providing adequate equipment are all part of the director's responsibilities. The committee, consisting of parents, members of the physical education staff, teachers from all grade-level teams, and students from each grade level, has the responsibility of selecting appropriate activities by grade level and developing the necessary procedures to evaluate the program and reward and recognize students and volunteers.

FUSION OF THE INTRAMURAL PROGRAM WITH PHYSICAL EDUCATION

The philosophy of the physical education program and that of the intramural program should be similar. The basic beliefs are as follows:

(1) Students' physical well-being and their social and emotional concerns are the primary concerns of the entire intramural staff.

(2) Students enjoy maximal participation with the goals of developing fundamental skills, knowledge, and interest in a wide variety of activities and sports.

(3) Students learn recreational and lifelong activities and sports.

(4) Students (boys and girls) participate equally in individual, dual, and team activities, with no one group of students dominating any activity or sport due to advanced physical and/or skill development.

(5) Students are taught good sportsmanship and wellness practices and are assessed on their individual progress. They participate in activities which best meet their unique needs and capabilities. Intramural time can also be used to help students strengthen skills learned in physical education classes.

(6) A variety of instructional materials, independent study activities, and discussion groups supplement the learning gained through participation in the physical activities.

(7) Students enjoy success and receive both intrinsic and extrinsic rewards for individual and team accomplishments. Students have the opportunity to practice leadership skills and take responsibility for their own actions as team members.

Physical education time blocks can be arranged to coincide with advisor/advisee time blocks and if scheduled, should be done so by grade level. In this way, students will receive maximal exposure to activities and sports, will be able to compete by grade level, and will have the benefit of the supervision and instruction of both their advisor and physical education teacher. Safety is always a key concern in physical activities and proper supervision is essential for the protection of students. Some activities may be too risky for students to engage in even with adequate adult supervision. For this reason, as well as others, broad representation on the intramural committee is important to allow for maximum input regarding the safety factor of activities and sports offered in the program.

APPROPRIATE INTRAMURAL ACTIVITIES

While offerings should originate primarily from the interests of students, and be deemed developmentally appropriate by teachers, parents, and intramural committee members, offerings will be limited by the facilities, the equipment, and the expertise available to conduct the intramural activities. Activities vary from school to school, but generally include some or all of the following.

Sports	Activities
Basketball	Chess
Badminton	Dancing
Bowling	Kickball
Field Hockey	Ping-Pong
Golf	Roller Skating
Gymnastics	Self-Defense
Soccer	Swimming
Softball	
Tennis	
Track	
Volleyball	

Evaluation of Intramural Programs

McMillan (1996) notes that the purpose of evaluation is to "make decisions about the effectiveness or desirability of a program" (p. 12). To evaluate programs, one has to collect information and then use that information to make decisions. However, certain desired criteria have to exist so as to compare performance with those objectives or standards. In some instances, clearly defined criteria exist with measurement instruments readily available to assess performance. For example, standardized tests of achievement with high validity and reliability assess student achievement on a particular subject from one year to the next with an expected amount of grade-level growth being the expected outcome of instruction. In other instances, evaluation criteria are not as clearly defined, or as accurately measurable as testing for student academic (cognitive) performance. This is often the case when one attempts to evaluate student growth in the affective domain and, to a lesser degree, in the psychomotor domain.

Assessing intramural program outcomes depends on the goals and objectives of the school's program in general, and the goals and objectives of each of the activities in particular. The evaluation of each intramural activity, when taken together, provides a composite picture of the overall success of the intramural program. From an evaluation perspective, the goals and objectives of the intramural program become the overriding criteria by which each activity is then evaluated. This does not preclude situation-specific course criteria such as skill development in physical education classes or cognitive objectives in other intramural activities. These can and should be evaluated, but the central question to address when evaluating the intramural program is: What is the overall purpose of the program?

Again, the intramural program has several objectives, but focuses on providing a broad array of activities in which all students can participate which meet their current needs and interests; which promote social, physical, cognitive, and emotional development; and which are meaningful learning experiences that promote enjoyment. To assess these ends, the assessment instrument will have to focus on the affective rather than the cognitive or psychomotor domain. Ideally, students should evaluate each activity at its conclusion for its value and in meeting the stated objectives of the activity.

Figure 6.3 presents a sample student survey to assess student attitudes toward an intramural activity. With affective evaluation instruments, the emphasis is on assessing student perceptions and feelings rather than knowledge or skill development. When students' evaluation results are taken together, they provide an index to judge the effectiveness of the overall intramural program.

Teacher assessment of the intramural program (Figure 6.4) is equally important and, like the student evaluation instrument, should be administered after each activity. The individual and combined teacher responses serve as an evaluation of how well the principal and the intramural planning team met the needs of teachers. This data can be used for future planning with more specific information being gained through informal discussions with teachers.

When principals have the results of these evaluation instruments, they have data to make program decisions which are much more sound than decisions made on intuition. These data serve as sources of information which can be presented to parents, the community, and the superintendent regarding the effectiveness of the program's outcomes in meeting its objectives. Informal feedback from teachers, parents, and students is a source of evaluation data as well. Combined, this information provides a current index of overall satisfaction with the program and should be used to plan future program activities.

PROMOTING A QUALITY INTRAMURAL PROGRAM: A CASE STUDY

The philosophy of a true middle school intramural program can best be

Student Intramural Activity Assessment Instrument
Harrison Middle School
Harrison, Georgia
_____, 1996

Directions: Please read each statement carefully and then circle the number which best describes how you feel about each of the questions. It is important that you express your real feelings about what the question asks so we can make the activities more enjoyable and beneficial for you.

		Almost Never	Some of the Time	Most of the Time
1.	This class was fun and exciting.	1	2	3
2.	I learned what I wanted to learn.	1	2	3
3.	The teacher held my interest in this course.	1	2	3
4.	I could apply what I learned in the class to my life outside of school.	1	2	3
5.	The teachers allowed me to participate in class activities.	1	2	3
6.	I enjoyed personal success in this class.	1	2	3
7.	The teacher allowed me to explore my own interests in this class.	1	2	3
8.	I learned more from this activity than I expected.	1	2	3
9.	I developed new interests as a result of being in this class. If yes, what are they? List them:		Yes	No
10.	As a result of this class, I did an independent/ group project in another class. If yes, what topic did you study and in what class? Topic:_____ Class: _____		Yes	No
		Low	Medium	High
11.	Overall, I rate the value this class had for me as:	1	2	3

FIGURE 6.3. Student intramural activity assessment instrument.

captured by the program at Gilmer Middle School, Ellijay, Georgia. Wesley "Wes" Clampitt, principal of this Georgia School of Excellence, believes the intramural program must focus on providing successful experiences for all students, allowing all students to participate in whatever activities they choose, and coordinating intramurals with the physical education program. The physical education department at Gilmer plays a key role in helping the principal coordinate an intramural program that is as diverse as school re-

Teacher Intramural Assessment Instrument
Harrison Middle School
Harrison, Georgia
_____, 1996

Directions: Please read each question carefully and provide as much information as you wish on each question. Please be specific in your answers and use extra paper if necessary. Circle either **Yes** or **No** and then comment based on your Yes/No answer.

Name: _____

1.	Does the intramural program enhance the climate of the school?	Yes	No
2.	Did you have sufficient materials to teach the activity?	Yes	No
3.	Was your room/space large enough to accomplish the goals and objectives of your class?	Yes	No
4.	Did you have sufficient assistance in conducting your class from judges, officials, scorers, etc?	Yes	No
5.	Did you have sufficient time to teach your class?	Yes	No
6.	Did you have sufficient time to plan for your class?	Yes	No
7.	Did you have sufficient assistance from the principal or members of the intramural planning committee in teaching your activity?	Yes	No

8. How could we make the intramural program more responsive to the needs and interests of the students?

9. How can the principal/planning committee be of greater assistance to you in making your job easier and your class more effective?

FIGURE 6.4. Teacher intramural assessment instrument.

sources and teacher expertise will allow. Intramurals at Gilmer Middle School "not only focus on enhancing the development of the physical skills of the students, but teach sportsmanship, the value of teamwork, and the rules and basic principles of the intramural activities," Clampitt says.

Intramurals at Gilmer are not strictly allocated to physical activity. Developing mental processes through the core academic curriculum is closely correlated with the intramural program. Clampitt says, "You never know what will spark a student's interest, and our philosophy is to let that interest take that student as far as it can." Advancing student interest through intramurals is evidenced by students participating in wrestling who suddenly develop an interest in researching its Roman and Greek origins and exploring its history through independent study within the social studies core. Track and field events trigger interest in the history of the Olympics and the historical roots and development of these various track and field events. Interest in health, nutrition, and exercise are correlated with the health class and serve as independent study or topics for group investigation. Hiking, an exploratory course, but also part of the physical education program, provokes interest in botany and geology which serve as independent study or group projects. "Whenever academics can be tied to intramurals, teachers are encouraged to help students make direct connections and fuse academic learnings and physical learnings with skill development," states Clampitt.

Topics found in the advisor/advisee program often dovetail with the intramural program and teachers are encouraged to spend advisor time talking about good sportsmanship, fair play, and the reason for rules and regulations. In middle schools, Clampitt says, it is essential that students be able to connect the importance of what is learned in the classroom to what they do in their everyday lives. The idea of promoting soundness of body along with soundness of mind is a guiding principle.

Facilities and staffing of intramural programs are key concerns for principals. At Gilmer Middle School, facilities not used for intramural activities are hard to find. The gym, stage, cafeteria, classrooms and conference rooms, outdoor playing fields, and surrounding mountain woods and trails provide intramural areas for the curriculum. Staffing is done through teachers and parent and community volunteers skilled in areas they instruct. "The mind-set at Gilmer Middle School is that if students are interested in an activity then it is the principal's responsibility to respond to that interest," notes Clampitt. Student surveys, teacher and parent interests, and available staffing provide the basis for curriculum development for the intramural program. Staffing the intramural program is no particular problem for Clampitt who requires staff members to be fully qualified to teach each activity. All teachers at Gilmer are involved in the intramural program and teach either an activity individually or team teach with other teachers. Parents and community members serve as judges, referees, and scorekeepers. Clampitt notes the importance of a teacher-dominated program by saying that while intramurals provide healthy competition for all involved, "the essentials of the program are to develop skills, gain an understanding of the rules and regulations of the activities in which they are involved, learn good sportsmanship behavior, and have fun while being successful."

Intramurals, as part of the physical education program, are primarily conducted during this time block with some activities extending into the enrichment course time blocks and others conducted after school. Students "compete" in teams against other teams both within the physical education time block and after school for community members and parent convenience. All competition must be concluded by five thirty to ensure students have adequate time to do their required schoolwork.

There is no limit on the number of teams on which students may participate, and students are excused from practices with no penalty when conflicts occur with other school activities. Clampitt notes the importance of being child-centered and understanding these natural conflicts as an essential part of teaching intramurals.

In a school of approximately 850 students, fifty faculty members, and two counselors, the intramural curricular offerings at Gilmer are comprehensive. These include the following: cheerleading, aerobics, soccer, softball, basketball, golf, tennis, field hockey, flag football, dancing, chess and checkers, badminton, hiking, table tennis, wrestling, hunter and gun safety, tee shirt painting, gymnastics, volleyball, cross country, and walking class.

Some team activities are scheduled with other middle schools but they are low-key and informal in nature with every student having a chance to participate fully in each activity. The value lies in students having a chance to interact with those from other schools and to develop new friendships. Planning these outside activities as well as those which are school-based rests jointly with the chair of the physical education department and the principal. Transportation, Clampitt says, is the major obstacle to interschool intramural programs. With questions of liability and child safety, the school bus is the best and safest means to transport students. However, he says, Gilmer has to compete with other county schools in reserving an already limited number of buses.

It is important, says Clampitt, that teachers have high interest and skill/knowledge in the activities they teach. For example, the teacher in charge of Hunting and Gun Safety is a state certified instructor. Those teaching other skill areas are certified in their discipline, have had prior experience in the activity, or have had college or continuing education classes.

Equally important is a planning guide that all teachers use as they plan their intramural activities to serve as a constant reminder of the goals and objectives of the intramurals program. Planning guides can be as simple or as elaborate as the principal or intramural coordinator deems necessary. To Clampitt, "simplicity is best since lengthy and lofty plans are not as likely to be used as those which are short," but the guide carries the salient points for teachers to include in their planning and teaching. Planning goals include the following:

- Activities should be designed to provide individual student success and enjoyment and should be child-centered in scope.
- Activities should allow for students to progress at their own rates, according to their own abilities, and students should learn team and individual skills for immediate satisfaction and lifelong pleasure.
- Activities should allow for the development of leadership skills, the importance of cooperative effort, and good sportsmanship conduct.
- Activities should promote inquiry into the cognitive domain and the importance of school learning to real life situations.
- Activities should stress individual growth, good health and fitness habits, and the value of physical fitness.

By emphasizing the fact that all students are encouraged and allowed to participate in the intramural program, Clampitt relates that special education students get much enjoyment in participating in these activities where they can excel, enjoy success, and receive recognition from their peers. For example, in wrestling where individual performance is vital to team success, these special students have the opportunity to demonstrate their talents and take pride in their team contributions. Students assessment is based on individual accomplishments in relation to their progress and in accordance with their own capabilities. In many activities, students set their own goals with input from teachers. This makes goal attainment both individually challenging and realistic. Some activities are evaluated with non-letter grades and are supplemented with individual progress reports and parent conferences. When letter grades are given, student limitations and individual attainment goals are the criteria for assessing student performance. As Clampitt says, "One student may have the ability to achieve only 40 percent of what another student can achieve. But if that 40 percent is achieved, they get the top grade."

Successful intramural middle school programs have certain factors which contribute to their effectiveness. "The role of the principal in these successful programs is crucial," states Clampitt, and relates that the following steps need to be taken to ensure program effectiveness:

(1) Offer full support and commitment to the program. This can be done by scheduling time for intramurals in the physical education and exploratory course time blocks, regularly attending teaching planning and evaluation meetings, providing adequate space and equipment for each activity, and being the primary public relations person for the

goals and objectives of intramurals with teachers, students, and parents. "Enthusiasm from the principal is motivating and catching," says Clampitt.

(2) Coordinate the intramural program with the physical education program. Principals need to work with the chair or team leader of the physical education component to coordinate curriculum offerings and events both within and between schools. Teachers from the exploratory block need to be represented with the school counselor serving as an advisor to maintain the middle school perspective. "This is so vital for program focus," relates Clampitt, who says, "it's easy for teachers to get off track."

(3) Make sure the program is child-centered and meets the needs of students. Surveys to students, parents, and teachers as well as informal feedback provide the basis of the intramural curriculum. The overriding goal of intramurals is for students to enjoy success while learning new skills and knowledge as they physically and cognitively develop. Therefore, student interest and fusing physical learning and cognitive learning opportunities are major considerations.

(4) Ensure that program activities stress participation for all and not competition for a select few. Intramurals build self-esteem and stress good sportsmanship and the value of teamwork. While teachers are central in promoting these objectives, both teachers and the principal have the responsibility to remind parents of the objectives of the program lest parents try to take over the program by stressing competition and winning over participation and learning. "Continuously reminding parents of the goals of the program through newsletters and parent-teacher conferences and highlighting the positive effects of the intramural program at PTO meetings keeps the goals of the program in perspective," notes Clampitt.

(5) Help keep teachers child-centered by developing a program planning guide for intramural activities. The guide should be developed by school-wide teacher representatives, the principal, and the school counselor. The guide should be published in the school handbook for student and parent information and should serve as a reminder to teachers who plan and conduct activities or when new activities are developed for the curriculum.

(6) See that the intramural activities are evaluated annually. Since many student development areas lie in the affective domain, informal assessments such as teacher, parent, and student observations which are recorded and annotated can serve as evaluation data. In cognitive and skill areas, traditional measures can provide the needed information. It is important that yearly activities planning be based on this data and not on intuition.

(7) Ensure that qualified and enthusiastic teachers, parents, and community members are responsible for all activities. If those conducting the activities are poorly qualified or motivated, students will not receive the instruction they deserve. Moreover, when teachers lack enthusiasm about an activity, they may serve to turn some students away from an area where they have latent skills and high potential. "When teachers can volunteer for activities and courses, and not be recruited or assigned to these duties, they have the dedication and interest necessary to make a quality intramural program," Clampitt states.

REFERENCES

Deming, W. E. 1986. *Out of the Crisis.* Cambridge, MA: MIT University Press.

George, P. and G. Lawrence. 1982. *Handbook for Middle School Teaching.* Glenview, IL: Scott, Foresman and Company.

Kindred, L. W., R. J. Wolotkiewicz, J. M. Mickelson, and L. E. Coplein. 1981. *The Middle School Curriculum: A Practitioner's Handbook.* Second edition. Boston: Allyn & Bacon, Inc.

McMillan, J. H. 1996. *Educational Research: Fundamentals for the Consumer.* Second edition. New York: Harper Collins.

Riemcke, C. 1988. "All Must Play—The Only Way for Middle School Athletics. *Journal of Physical Education and Dance.* March 1988, pp. 82–84.

Wiles, J. and J. Bondi. 1993. *The Essential Middle School.* Second edition. New York: Macmillan Publishing Company.

CHAPTER 7

A Quality Advisor/ Advisee Program

The importance of an effective and comprehensive advisor/advisee program as part of the quality-oriented school guidance program in middle schools is gaining rapid recognition and acceptance. Student advisement is important at the middle school level to ensure that each student receives regular, compassionate, and supportive counsel from a concerned adult about academic progress, adjustment to school, and personal concerns. While this does not replace professional counseling, it does provide a consultation system in which to give students immediate assistance to problems and concerns. Central to the success of this program is the school principal. The principal must understand and believe in the principles and benefits of the advisor/advisee concept, develop a comprehensive guidance program to support the other middle school programs, and schedule time and provide resources and inservice training for teachers to be competent advisors.

This chapter will include the most common pitfalls principals face in developing and implementing an advisor/advisee program and offer examples of successful programs using a variety of scheduling approaches and activities. Case studies will be provided showing the positive aspects and results of advisor/advisee programs.

This chapter will center around the following questions:

- What are the primary goals and objectives of an advisor/advisee program?
- How can the advisor/advisee program blend in naturally with the middle school guidance program?
- What is the role of the principal in planning, organizing, and sustaining an effective advisor/advisee program?
- What are the major considerations and concerns in planning and organizing an effective advisor/advisee program?

- What are the major benefits of this program to teachers, students, parents, administrators, and the educational environment?
- What type of scheduling works best for this program and what resources are needed to ensure the success of an advisor/advisee program?
- What are some of the organizational and scheduling patterns and topics/themes associated with quality advisor/advisee programs?

MIDDLE SCHOOL GUIDANCE PROGRAM

The guidance program in effective middle schools coordinates a wide array of services and programs designed to help students cope with their specific and diverse problems. Guidance programs provide counseling services and coordinate support services from psychologists, psychiatrists, social workers, and community programs. These services focus on student problems involving self-esteem, peer relations, physical changes, and emotional health. The advisor-advisee program is part of the guidance component and in it teachers serve in counseling and advising capacities focusing on students' social, emotional, and cognitive development (Wiles and Bondi, 1993). In short, the guidance program in the last decade has changed in the middle school from providing professional counseling to highly troubled students and being responsible for parent contact and student records to a comprehensive student support services program coordinated by guidance personnel. In this capacity, *guidance*, the noun, is the act of directing, while *counseling*, the verb, is recommending or advising.

Guidance programs in effective middle schools embody the middle school philosophy of child-centeredness. They provide students with experiences which foster the healthy development of the self-concept and the knowledge and skills necessary for positive learning experiences as they develop physically, intellectually, emotionally, and socially (Alexander and George, 1981). Providing counseling to students is central to the goals of the total guidance program, but it is only a part of the array of services provided. Counseling, providing advice and counsel to the student, requires the involvement of parents, teachers, administrators, and trained guidance personnel. Each of these groups is vital to the overall success of the counseling component, with each group making significant contributions to the healthy development of preadolescents (Wiles and Bondi, 1993).

Parents play an important role in counseling their children within the home environment. Cole (1988) relates that the guiding attitude of parents significantly impacts the self-concept of the child and that many parents lack a basic understanding of the counseling act and the skills to counsel effectively. To maximize the contributions parents make to the healthy development of their children and to the overall guidance program of the middle school, programs need to be conducted for parents by the principal and guidance staff in order to assist parents in making effective contributions. Meyers (1985) relates that good parent counseling skills can be fostered through comprehensive training sessions which provide professional assistance and literature on parenting; the total developmental process of transescent youth; the guidance services available within the school and community; and the role of teachers, administrators, and guidance staff in meeting the social, emotional, physical, and intellectual needs of the child.

Principals, according to Cole (1988), provide the necessary leadership to make the overall guidance program effective. Working in conjunction with the guidance staff, principals support and facilitate the guidance program by providing the time, space, and resources needed to effectively coordinate all activities within this student service component. Most importantly, principals serve as counselors themselves by providing moral support and advice and taking on the role of confidant and friend to students. Working closely with the guidance staff, the principal helps plan and implement parent counseling programs, counseling inservice programs for teachers, and an evaluation component for the overall performance of guidance services.

Guidance personnel in middle schools have the primary duty of coordinating the guidance services with some duties bordering on administration. However, most of their specific tasks will be from the counseling perspective. George and Alexander (1993) note that guidance counselors act as resource suppliers by providing materials or personal assistance to teachers and parents needing specific help. Guidance staff also act as advisors to teachers by providing ongoing assistance and research information on advising skills and techniques and conducting periodic training sessions for teachers and administrators.

Teachers in effective middle schools are the key element in the success of the counseling component of the guidance program. The teacher-student relationship is the starting point of the student-centered philosophy of the middle school, with teachers being trained to interact personally with students on a daily basis and to assist them with their social, emotional, and intellectual development (Merenbloom, 1982). Having a caring and responsible adult who is personally empathetic to each child's needs and problems is crucial to the child's development. Therefore, the primary counseling responsibility rests with the instructional staff with whom students are most personally and frequently associated (Cole, 1988).

To best meet the counseling needs of students at the middle school level, many principals have initiated the advisor/advisee program. The philosophy of this program meets the need of having a caring, empathetic adult who can provide personal and immediate assistance to each student as each confronts the problems of transescent development.

ADVISOR/ADVISEE PROGRAM

Advisor/advisee programs are part of the middle school's mission to be developmentally responsive to preadolescent behavior and growth patterns. Teachers, serving as student advisors, act as student advocates and assist students by making the transition into adolescence less stressful through positive academic, social, and personal experiences (MacIver, 1990). Advisor/advisee programs are designed to assist both the individual student and groups of students. The Carnegie Task Force on Education of Young Adolescents (1989) calls for teachers to provide advice and assistance and to personally monitor the academic and social development of the small group of students to whom each teacher is assigned. National studies (Cawelti, 1988; Alexander and McEwin, 1989; CREMS, 1990; MacIver, 1990) show that the implementation of advisor/advisee programs in middle school programs are on the rise with Cawelti reporting 29 percent, Alexander and McEwin reporting 39 percent, and the *CREMS Report* reporting 66 percent implementation. With its obvious benefits for middle school youth and with the student-centered philosophy of the middle school, it is surprising that more widespread implementation of the advisor/advisee program is not in effect.

RATIONALE FOR ADVISOR/ADVISEE PROGRAMS

The emphasis on close teacher-student relations with friendly, caring, and knowledgeable teachers dedicated to the middle school concept is central to the true middle school philosophy. Keefe (1991) points out that the purpose of the advisor/advisee program for teachers, to serve as friends, advocates, and mentors for the preadolescent, coincides with the role of the middle school teacher, and that serving as both teacher and advisor is a natural fit.

One purpose of the advisor/advisee program is to foster a closer personal relationship between student and teacher. Ideally, a student-teacher bond will develop which will help make each middle school student's transition from childhood to adolescence more rewarding and less stressful. As the early transescent matures, a reliance on peers and taking responsibility for their own actions increase. However, during this time, the need for a close relationship with an adult is essential. When teachers in middle schools develop a warm, friendly, and open relationship with their students, students feel free to place their trust in these adults and express their concerns and problems more candidly. Teachers have the opportunity to get to know their students personally and the personal warmth and respect generated in such groups are beneficial to the teacher as well as the student. In advisee groups, teachers see the positive impact they make on students and receive immediate feedback on how their efforts make a difference in the lives of their students (Myrick and Myrick, 1990).

Advisor/advisee relationships provide an avenue for discussing issues of direct importance to students. Often, student concerns focus around problems of a social and emotional nature and they need specific help on how to deal with these issues that affect them immediately and personally. Teachers as advisors can help students analyze their emotions and assist them in applying social problem-solving skills to their emotional entanglements.

Peer pressure and peer group influence on transescents can have both a positive and negative effect. Peer group relationships often break down and cause students to have feelings of alienation and loneliness. Advisor/advisee groups provide a peer support group, a "home base" where students feel safe, welcome, and accepted by their peers. Capelluti and Stokes (1991) relate that a feeling of security is provided by advisor/advisee relationships that is essential for combating the fear of the new experiences in middle schools. Fear thwarts student learning, inhibits maximal cognitive and affective development, and causes distractions in attention. Advisor programs provide the security, affection, and belonging essential to the transescent's healthy development.

Advisor/advisee groups also provide for individual counseling for students. While counseling in this capacity cannot, nor is meant to, replace professional counseling by guidance personnel or through other professional services, it does serve as a front-line effort to assist students with the more common and less critical problems of preadolescence. In schools with only one or two counselors with case loads of 300 or more each, counselors cannot adequately meet the needs of each student on a daily basis. Teachers, on the other hand, have a first-hand knowledge of the student's academic progress, family background, and social and emotional level of development (Myrick and Myrick, 1990).

Within advisor/advisee groups, students can learn about and apply the mechanics of the democratic process. Making group decisions about intramural competitions and nominating and electing student representatives to school programs are a few ways students learn about representative government. Discussions about equality, justice, and law, as well as the importance of character, personal responsibility, and integrity, are appropriate topics for group exploration. Middle schools with effective advisor/advisee programs report improvement in school discipline problems as a result of these programs. George and Alexander (1993) relate that "on numerous occasions, teachers have told us that students who have a place, time, and person to assist them in 'centering' themselves, a situation which encourages the appropriate expressions of feelings of frustration, hurt, and sorrow, are much less likely to be found venting these feelings in regular classrooms" (p. 203).

Additional research by MacIver (1990) shows a reduction in student dropout rates as a result of advisor/advisee programs which provide strong academic and social support. Advisor programs also allow students to develop socially and contribute to a positive school climate through the reduction of classroom disruptions and the development of better working relationships with teachers and principal. Finally, Fenwick (1992) and Arhar (1992) relate that interdisciplinary teaming, teacher advisory programs, and school climate impact positively on student dropout rates and student self-concept.

When principals schedule advisor/advisee sessions daily, time exists for school announcements, special grade level activities, intramural events, and school-wide projects or meetings. Special laboratory-learning projects can be undertaken at this time or time can be allocated for community involvement programs. Engaging in activities as a group at one specific time builds friendship and fosters the development of teamwork and citizenship skills (George and Alexander, 1993).

Finally, the advisor/advisee relationship promotes the goals of the affective curriculum. Schools have been expected to take on more responsibility for the general welfare of children. Messick and Reynolds (1992) point out that entitlement programs require the offering of assistance to low-income children with special needs and information and prevention programs on such social concerns as sex education and drugs. Societal concerns also focus on the need for schools to teach values, character education, and the principles of truth and integrity. The affective domain of education must focus on the social and emotional development of students and teach students how to effectively interact with others, how to deal with their feelings and the actions of others, and how to address problems and concerns impacting their lives in an acceptable way.

Perhaps the best way to ensure that the goals of an advisor/advisee program are achieved is through modeling and leadership. In this context, all who are involved in the advisor/advisee relationship must assume leadership responsibilities by modeling to the students the behaviors and content taught within the program. Teachers, parents, principals, counselors, and community members involved in these activities must serve as role models in their behavior and in their interactions with students.

The Affective Curriculum

Teaching the affective curriculum is a significant part of middle school education and this curriculum should be fused with the core and exploratory curriculum. However, the components of the affective domain can be taught independently as part of the goals of the advisor/advisee program.

The basis for affective curriculum development rests with the work of Krathwohl, Bloom and Masia (1964). Their taxonomy of the affective domain outlines curriculum principles and a delivery system under a hierarchy of affective components that are correlated to the cognitive domain which, when taken together, provide students with a more complete set of skills, knowledge, and behaviors to be learned. Among the components of the affective domain to be taught are attitude development, character development, values and valuing, sensitivity to others' beliefs and feelings, and responsibility for one's choices and decisions.

Categories of the affective domain, from lowest to highest, consist of receiving, responding, valuing, organization, and characterization. Each of these affective levels is presented in Figure 7.1 along with their cognitive domain counterparts from lowest to highest level of achievement.

The application of the constructs of the advisor/advisee program holds great importance for assisting students with their social and emotional development. In scheduled advisement time, teachers have the opportunity to relate the affective constructs to a wide variety of student problems and concerns. When advisor/advisee topics are introduced, both hierarchies should be used for a more comprehensive approach to instruction. As seen in Figure 7.1, receiving and knowledge are the beginning points of the domains' hierarchy with each serving as the initial intake construct which will then serve as the basis for further construct development. Here, the students possess knowledge after receiving it and deal with it mentally or emotionally in their respective ways. Responding and comprehension are next in the hierarchy and relate to the behaviors of complying and understanding. Valuing and application connote the act of a continuous behavior or the application of theories or ideas generally. Organization and analysis and synthesis relate to the placement of the value on a personal value scale and the understanding of the importance of particular ideas and concepts as they relate to a whole. These ideas are then synthesized into a new whole or generalization. Characterization and evaluation are at the pinnacle of the hierarchies. Characterization is the makeup of the total patterns of one's behavior or the total value or worth of something relative to one's specified criteria. Evaluation is the act of carefully criticizing or examining something to determine its worth or merit. At this highest structure of the two domains, the information or knowledge is evaluated for its meaning or worth and then

Hierarchies from Lowest to Highest Levels	
Affective Domain	Cognitive Domain
Receiving - being aware of, observing, or being conscious of something. This does not imply specific discrimination or recognition of the object being observed, but the object does have an effect, whether or not it can be verbalized.	Knowledge - knowing facts, information, terms, basic understanding of methods, criteria, and theories and generalizations.
Responding - willing to comply or obey, acquaint, accept, or in any way react to the stimulus. Enjoyment, appreciation, or pleasure or another emotional behavior which shows satisfaction exists.	Comprehension - the lowest level of understanding that includes translation, interpretation, and exploration.
Valuing - realizing that a thing or behavior has worth both for the individual and the social order. One has taken on a belief or attitude, the behavior is displayed consistently, and the behavior is displayed because one believes in and is committed to the value, not because one must comply or obey.	Application - use of abstractions in particular situations or the generalization of abstractions to various theories, general ideas, and procedures.
Organization - the structuring of values which are internalized into a value system at the level of importance each value holds. Some values are discarded while others become rearranged in the value system as new ones are acquired or old ones omitted.	Analysis and Synthesis - analyzing the hierarchy of ideas or concepts and understanding the relationships among ideas in a systematic way. Synthesizing several ideas or concepts and placing them into a whole or combining parts into a structure not evident before.
Characterization - consistent behavior and belief over time, the prediction of one's behavior and the characteristics of that behavior which make up the total philosophy of life and view of the world.	Evaluation - judging the value of something for a specific purpose. Judging the ideas, concepts, methods, etc. relative to satisfying accepted criteria.

FIGURE 7.1. Adaptation from Krathwohl, Bloom, and Masia (1964). Correlation of the affective and cognitive domains.

characterized (taken into and arranged in one's internal value system) by taking action.

Under the rubric of the affective domain lies the moral development of students. Determining what is right and wrong through interactions with peers is an important part of transescent life. Making choices and being responsible for these choices at this time are difficult for these students. Choices about engaging in sex, drugs, and joining gangs prone to violence are choices of right and wrong and need exploration. The development of morals is an internal conflict compounded by the physical, social, and cognitive changes taking place.

Principals and teachers need to be aware that moral development, like cognitive development, is a progression of stages and the student's moral development is closely aligned with the cognitive development stages (Kohlberg, 1981). Kohlberg, influenced by Piaget's work (1977) on moral and cognitive development, developed a social cognition of moral judgment consisting of three levels with each level having two developmental stages. Kohlberg's social cognition theory on moral judgment is as follows:

(1) Level I: preconventional
   • stage 1: punishment and obedience
   • stage 2: individual instrumental purpose and exchange
(2) Level II: conventional
   • stage 3: mutual interpersonal expectations, relationships, and conformity
   • stage 4: social system and conscience maintenance
(3) Level III: postconventional and principled
   • stage 5: prior rights and social contract
   • stage 6: universal ethical principles

Moral development, the progression through these six stages, is to a large degree determined by one's intellectual development. Most transescents are at stages 2, 3, and 4 in the moral development theory (Kohlberg, 1980) while in the cognitive development theory (Piaget, 1977) the preadolescent is in either the concrete operations thought stage or the formal operational thought stage.

Stage 1 of Kohlberg's theory looks at obedience as a behavior to avoid punishment, and what is right to the individual is largely determined by what the individual can get away with without punishment. Stage 2 looks at behavior as serving one's own interests or the needs of others for a personal benefit or reward. At stage 2, individuals are usually egocentrical, and personal desires usually dictate behavior. Good and bad are consequences of their behavior with right and wrong impacting the nature of their relationship with others. Usually these "others" are those having a close relationship with the individual. Groups are secondary in consideration in stage 2. Group members become important only when any one or more of the group members are considered important to the individual. Therefore, acting in the best interests of the group depends on whether or not group action is best for the individual and/or the significant other(s) in the group.

Stage 3 evidences groups as being more important to the individual. "Good" and "bad" are now viewed in terms of what the group determines is good and bad. Groups include the family and peers, and individuals become sensitive to the values and attitudes held by the group. At this stage, individuals have a sense of the community and its values and norms. Middle school students for the most part are in stage three of Kohlberg's (1980) model and this idea is important for further development. If students do not fully master stage 3 during the middle school years (realize the importance of groups and identify with group values, attitudes, and norms), they may never reach levels 4, 5, and 6 which is the understanding of the need for social order and the universal principles of justice and morality which are at the higher stages of moral development. The concepts and responsibilities of citizenship along with the moral duties of the citizen are central to stage 3 and are the foundation for further development. George and Alexander (1993) note that stage three is very important for middle school teachers in that they are assisting in the moral development of their students by providing and emphasizing group work and teaching loyalty, duty, citizenship, and responsibility.

Stage 4 is when the individual views the choice between good and bad acts as a responsibility or duty which transcends their own personal wants. This stage of development calls for an understanding of the importance of a social order, a greater good, which comes before personal benefit and the wishes of the group. In stage 4, the individual develops to a level where the good of the school, community, or state are placed before the self and the group and realizes that such action must exist if these larger entities are to survive.

Moral development for middle school students can be assisted in various ways by teachers, administrators, parents, and school guidance counselors. First, modeling moral behavior is a major part of teaching moral behavior. Second, rewarding positive behavior among students is a way to ensure that such behavior will continue. Third, small group work within classes (advisor/ advisee sessions, clubs, and intramurals) provides a teaching-learning forum for students. Group discussions in these learning environments, as well as role playing exercises, help students through developmental stages as they explore the rationales behind group and community values, norms, rules, laws, and the concept of the greater good. Fourth, exercises involving choices, both social and academic, and the responsibilities of these choices foster moral development. Finally, community projects can assist students in seeing beyond the personal and group benefits of their involvement and they will gain a sense of belonging to the community as they realize that their efforts as individuals contribute to improving the lives of many people.

TYPES OF ADVISOR/ADVISEE PROGRAMS

Cohesion among advisors in planning and implementing advisement programs is essential. Wiles and Bondi (1993) maintain that one way to achieve continuity and consistency is to establish the advisor/advisee program as part of the interdisciplinary team concept which provides integrated instruction among the core, exploratory, and extra activities curriculum. Beane (1993) relates that when teacher advisement programs become part of interdisciplinary teaming, a smooth instructional transition among affective, cognitive, and psychomotor domain constructs takes place. Moreover, teams teach a common group of students, are able to interact with their students on a daily basis, get to know the students personally, and have regular contact with parents. This thorough knowledge of the students and their family backgrounds makes team teachers "better prepared to address the needs of the whole child and to help guide the student through his or her own life experiences" (Wiles and Bondi, 1993, p. 94).

The two types of advisor/advisee programs which are most common are the large group and the one-on-one programs. The choice of the program type should reside with the teachers who are primarily responsible for the planning, implementation, and success of the program. Principals act as facilitators in the selection, development, and implementation of the program by providing time, resources, and advice.

Daily Large Group Programs

Daily meetings with groups of 10 to 15 students for approximately 30 to 45 minutes at the beginning or end of the school day is one approach to establishing an advisor/advisee program. The advantage of having group meetings first thing in the morning is having time to discuss problems and concerns of students prior to the start of the academic day. Announcements and other administrative requirements can also be accomplished early. Variations of scheduling are school-specific, but a variety of scheduling options exist to accommodate the needs of both students and teachers (James, 1986).

Two examples are found in George and Alexander (1993). The first begins the school day with 30 minutes allocated for announcements, administrative housekeeping, and a formal or informal advisement session. The last 15 minutes of the day is spent with student groups in informed advisement where teachers interact individually with each student or continue discussions from the morning session.

The second example begins with a 25-minute block of time structured around counselor-prepared objectives and materials for use two days a week. Teachers and students decide what topics to focus on the other three days with one of the three days allocated as "silent day where students may read, write, or study silently, while the advisor uses the time to interact quietly with individual students" (George and Alexander, 1993, p. 207).

Some programs extend the advisor/advisee time throughout the day, with teachers meeting with each student individually on a weekly basis, and with structured programs at the beginning or end of the school day. Some advisement programs meet for 30 minutes during the middle of the day with structured and unstructured programs. In some programs, time during the week is allocated to intramurals, club activities, and independent study. As George and Alexander (1993) note, programs differ but the commitment and support from the school leadership make the difference between successful and unsuccessful advisement programs.

One-to-One Programs

Individualized one-to-one programs usually provide teacher teams with one period per day for advisement. This is not in lieu of a teacher planning period. Interdisciplinary teams of teachers meet with their students at different times during the day during which teachers are free to advise on a one-to-one basis and build a strong personal bond with each student. Students are usually in physical education classes or in exploratory or extracurricular courses and are pulled out of these classes to meet with the teacher. Scheduling regular time during the day also allows for guidance counselors and parents to meet with teachers without disrupting teachers from their classroom duties (George and Alexander, 1993).

A variation of the one-to-one advisement program is one which allows a teacher to work with a small group of students (5 to 10) throughout the week while the rest of the teacher's advisees attend physical education or applied arts classes. On a weekly basis, each student has one small group advisor/advisee session and four classes of physical education or applied arts. Some programs operate on both a small group basis and a one-to-one basis and this is best accommodated through block scheduling. Teacher teams have expanded time blocks in their advisor/advisee program to conduct either small group sessions or individual sessions. Some principals expand the time blocks for team instruction which allows time for group advisement or individual counseling while the rest of the group is involved in other activities. One middle school, relates George and Alexander (1993), built their entire curriculum around an advisory system which stressed child-centered learning and adult support. The advisee program is both group- and individual-centered, with group meetings in the morning and time for individual sessions in the afternoon prior to the close of school. In another middle school, teachers meet with small groups of students in the morning and during lunch break. One middle school principal scheduled a conference period three out of five mornings for teachers to meet individually with their advisees while the fourth morning of the week was scheduled for teachers themselves to discuss the problems of students and to meet with parents and the guidance counselor.

DESIGNING AN ADVISOR/ADVISEE PROGRAM

The vision for an effective advisor/advisee program is twofold: first, to provide education in the affective domain which will lead to the healthy socio-emotional development of the transescent and second, to provide time for activities which will "lead to growth-producing interpersonal relationships between teachers and students" (George and Lawrence, 1982, p. 174). Wiles and Bondi (1993) expand the vision of the advisor/advisee program by adding that the teacher as advisor assists students with their overall maturation process, is the chief advocate for the student, is a role model, and is the academic advisor for the student. Keefe (1991) adds that advisor/advisee programs should promote a positive, safe, and orderly learning environment for the student. Squires, Huitt, and Segars (1984) found in their research on effective schools that learning environments called for by Keefe are promoted by teachers and principals who emphasize academics, care about their students' well-being, and consult with students regularly about their academic and social problems. Lunenburg and Ornstein (1996) relate that schools which have safe and orderly environments and care about the development of the "whole student" have principals with child-centered philosophies who consistently model this behavior. Advisor/advisee programs should be designed with this vision in mind.

Organization of the Program

School staff members need to first determine whether a daily group advisement program or a one-to-one program best suits the needs of their students and teachers. Keefe (1991) cautions that regardless of the program design, both group and individual advisement must take place in order to have a sound, comprehensive program. George and Alexander (1993) relate that the daily group advisement program seems popular but that "experience has not yet been broad enough to indicate whether either design (daily group or one-to-one) is superior" (p. 213). The choice remains school-specific, but the following considerations can help the school's staff determine which program is best for their students:

(1) Group advisement primarily focuses on advising groups of students on a daily basis while one-to-one advisement time is more limited.

(2) Daily group advisement builds a sense of group safety and a support network but does not build as strong of a personal relationship with a caring adult as the one-to-one program.

(3) Daily group advisement lends itself to topics or themes for discussion while the one-to-one program is more individualized in scope and can be more time-consuming for the teacher.

(4) Daily group sessions allow for group interaction with peers in a safe environment, and a variety of viewpoints and personal problems and solutions can be explored. Group interactions can address several student problems at once and allow teachers more time to concentrate on students with other concerns or those students needing more specialized attention.

(5) Daily group sessions do not provide for the highly personal adult relationship deemed necessary for transescents that one-to-one programs provide, but they do allow teachers to address a wider variety of student problems to a greater number of students.

LENGTH OF ADVISEMENT PERIOD

Programs vary, but 25 to 45 minutes per day at the beginning of each day seems to be the norm. Time allocated for advisement can also be distributed throughout the day, during lunch break and at the end of the school day. Advisement time can also be scheduled during blocks of time allocated for interdisciplinary team teaching. Most middle schools prefer that teachers meet daily to decide how the advisement schedule is to be arranged (Epstein and MacIver, 1990).

Groups of 10 to 30 students are assigned to teachers as advisees with the most common assignment criteria being grade level placement; however, an equal number of students from grades 6 though 8 can also be assigned to teachers for advisement (Keefe, 1991). Teachers can remain with the same group of students throughout the students' middle school experience or teachers can be assigned a new group of advisees yearly.

ACTIVITIES IN AN ADVISOR/ADVISEE PROGRAM

Advisors are not meant nor should they be expected to replace the skilled functions performed by guidance counselors. Teachers should not be expected to fill the role performed by parents or the church; however, teachers as advisors do teach values that are within the prerogative of the school's domain. George and Alexander (1993) suggest that values such as honesty, integrity, loyalty, love of country, respect for individual rights, cleanliness, and punctuality are values to be taught by middle schools.

Guidance counselors and other professionals can provide the inservice training necessary for the teacher-advisor role. MacIver (1990) relates that inservice training should be on-going to assist teachers in their role as advisors, but that some essential skills are necessary at the implementation stage of the program. These include good listening skills, conflict management skills, open-ended questioning skills, group dynamics, and problem-solving skills. The major role of the principal in conducting inservice programs for teachers is to provide the necessary time and fiscal resources for teacher training. Principals themselves should be active participants in these inservice sessions and may even conduct some of the necessary training. When the advisor/advisee program is fully implemented, the principal should provide a budget for the needed instructional materials for teachers and guidance personnel. Additional tasks of the principal include making sure teachers have the necessary materials to conduct each advisement session throughout the year; communicating with the superintendent, board members, and the community about the goals, objectives, and content of the advisement program; and evaluating the program's progress in meeting its goals (Vars, 1989).

Guidance personnel, teachers, and administrators should plan the year's advisement program. Some middle schools include parents, community members, and students in the planning process as well. While program emphasis should be on topics and activities leading to the socio-emotional and cognitive development of the student, some advisement programs also include topics addressing the psychological development of the preadolescent. Fenwick (1992) relates that programs can be based on school-wide themes, can be grade-level specific, or can be advisee-group specific. Ideally, school-wide monthly themes are developed by a committee, have correlated materials and activities, and are designed to cover one or two daily advisement sessions with the remaining three or four sessions allocated for student interest topics. The importance of each middle school developing its own advisement themes cannot be stressed too highly. Canned programs developed for commercial distribution or programs imposed by central office administrators are not as successful as those which are school-developed.

Guidance personnel play a key role in helping teachers select and/or develop advisement materials. Often the guidance staff is the major supplier of materials used in the advisement sessions. Teachers are more apt to have a positive attitude about the advisor/advisee program when they do not have to spend a great deal of time preparing materials and activities for each session. When adequate assistance is not provided to teachers, they often view these responsibilities as additional work placed on top of an already demanding workload. Some teachers may view this extra work as "picking up the slack" for guidance personnel and doing their work for them. Attitudes such as these will defeat the purpose and effectiveness of the advisor/advisee program (Lounsbury and Clark, 1990).

Monthly themes and activities, developed by a representative committee, should be bound into book form and include all necessary supporting materials for teachers to use in the classroom. Teachers, however, need the freedom to deviate from these prescribed materials and supplement them with their own should they decide to do so. Flexibility, not rigidity, is the key to successful advisement. George and Alexander (1993) specifically point out that success, in a large measure, depends on "teachers seeing themselves as free to pursue their own activities in a mode that feels safe" (p. 228). Teachers also need to feel comfortable in discussing the various topics associated with socio-emotional problems of students as the program unfolds. Therefore, resource material of various kinds and references to additional materials should be included in the resource guide to advisement. Here, guidance personnel can be of great value in their practical and professional expertise in providing books, articles, videos, and other materials to assist teachers.

TOPICS FOR ADVISEMENT

Topics and/or themes appropriate for advisor/advisee programs abound and choice depends on the needs of the school, teachers, and students. When possible, topics or themes should correlate to those of the interdisciplinary team to provide continuity between the cognitive and affective domains. Some middle schools develop topics or themes that run across grades 6 through 8 with each grade level focusing on different constructs within the affective domain. Other middle schools explore topics in depth at a specific grade level with subsequent grade levels expanding on the topic or having different topics to explore altogether.

Topics or themes can be divided into strictly socio-emotional topics with those relating to cognitive topics housed within the interdisciplinary teams. Topics can be further delineated to address self-knowledge, the student as an individual, and group-knowledge or the student as a group member. The role and responsibilities of individuals as group members and the part they play in making group problem solving and decision making effective are of crucial importance in today's global market competition and students need to understand the importance of teamwork in the work place (Weller, 1996). Presented below are a list of possible topics for both individual and group exploration which relate to the socio-emotional curriculum.

Self-Knowledge	Group-Knowledge
1. Self-Concept	1. Conflict Management
2. Responsibility	2. Problem Solving
3. Prejudice	3. Decision Making
4. Values	4. Values
5. Attitudes	5. Trust
6. Tolerance	6. Prejudice
7. Character	7. Goal Setting
8. Integrity	8. Family Responsibilities
9. Honesty	9. School Responsibilities
10. Trust	10. Community Responsibilities
11. Valuing Diversity	11. Citizen Responsibilities
12. Decision Making	12. Friendship Responsibilities
13. Human Relations Skills	13. Peer Groups and Pressure
14. School Rules	14. Group Dynamics
15. Goal Setting	
16. Friendship	
17. Career Awareness	
18. Choices	

Some middle schools have the same advisor assigned to the same group of students as they progress through grades 6 through 8. Having the same students allows teachers to develop a strong personal relationship with their students and parents, and teachers who serve as advisors to the same group of students over three years provide more continuity in the goals of the affective curriculum.

Through group advisement sessions, students also have the opportunity to participate in a variety of functions which serves to further bond the group and allow the individual to excel. Taking field trips together, having rap sessions, participating in school-wide activity days, having indoor and outdoor games (bike, chess, basketball tournaments, and softball games), participating in intramurals, and participating in community projects are examples of advisor/advisee activities.

Benefits to Students

Students benefit from the advisory program in a variety of ways. These benefits include the following:

(1) Provides a group a home base of safety and security.
(2) Provides a caring adult advocate.
(3) Provides one caring adult to help each student with both academic and personal problems.

(4) Helps students solve their own problems and understand other people better.
(5) Helps students learn how to manage time, take responsibility for their own actions, and make sound decisions.
(6) Provides opportunities for students to learn how to function as group and team members and to respect the rights, feelings, and thinking of others.
(7) Helps students understand themselves, feel good about themselves, and build confidence in their own abilities.

Benefits to Teachers

Teachers, like students, benefit from the advisor/advisee program. These benefits include the following:

(1) Get to know students on a more personal level.
(2) Get to know parents on a more personal level.
(3) Get to participate more with students in social and intramural activities.
(4) Help students mature socially and emotionally.
(5) Get to work with a small number of students on academic and personal problems.
(6) Get personal satisfaction from students looking to them as a friend, confidant, and advocate.

Successful advisor/advisee programs need the full commitment and cooperation of the principal, teachers, parents, and guidance personnel. The advisor program takes a team effort of full participation and support. The principal has to be the program's chief advocate and support the program through scheduling adequate time, showing personal participation, and providing the necessary inservice training and fiscal resources needed to prepare teachers to undertake their advisor role. Teachers are the key to advisor/advisee success. They must be well prepared for their role as teacher-advisor, feel comfortable in that role, and receive the moral and fiscal support necessary to do their jobs. Guidance personnel act as coordinators of the advisor/advisee program, act as peer instructors to teachers, and provide research and other material to teachers as they continuously lend moral support. Parents are also vital to the program's success and are a home extension of the advisor/advisee program. They mirror teacher efforts in the classroom by role modeling and reinforcing the goals and objectives of the program with their own children.

ESTABLISHING AN ADVISOR/ADVISEE PROGRAM: CASE STUDIES

The goals of the advisor/advisee program vary from school to school.

However, the program's importance and relevance to the middle school philosophy and the transescent seems to be without question. The literature supports the importance of the advisor/advisee program with the most pressing call made in *An Agenda for Excellence*, published by the National Association of Secondary School Principals, which states that middle schools "should institute student advisement programs that assure each student regular, compassionate, and supportive counsel from a concerned adult about his or her academic progress, adjustment to school, and personal adjustment" (1985, p. 4). The Carnegie Council in *Turning Points* (1989) also strongly recommends the advisor/advisee program for middle schools so all students are known personally by one adult, have their socio-emotional needs met and skills developed, and are provided a sense of security from feeling wanted and appreciated for who they are. Despite the benefits of the advisor/advisee program, its acceptance has been rather slow with some middle school principals.

Principals wanting to begin an advisor/advisee program face several challenges and many are situation-specific. Walker Davis, principal of West Jackson Middle School in Jefferson, Georgia, is currently laying the foundation for implementing an advisor/advisee program. Davis, who has implemented several advisor programs in other middle schools, notes the importance of having an accepting attitude from parents and community members toward the advisor/advisee program. From a practical aspect, he states, this is crucial to success "since some look upon advisor/advisee programs as fluff, non-academics, and wasted time. Many have the mind-set that time in school should be strictly for academic work." The key is to "inform and educate" the parents and community about the advisory program well in advance of implementation. Laying the groundwork is crucial and begins with the principal and school counselor introducing the need for counselor assistance and the benefits of the advisor/advisee program, gradually, at PTO meetings and through informal discussions with parents and community members. Davis comments that "introducing new programs takes time for the need to sink in, takes education, and takes a real determination on the part of the principal."

Having a modified version of an advisor/advisee program already in existence helps. At West Jackson Middle School, Davis, along with concerned teachers, developed the PALS program (Positive Attitudes for Life Skills) to promote student success. Several students in grades six through eight were below grade level in reading and mathematics and, as a result, had difficulty in being successful in other subjects. Many of these students received little positive reinforcement from home since rural Jackson County has a 50 percent functionally illiterate adult population. Davis, who chairs the county's Adult Literacy Program and received a state grant to fund a county-wide adult reading education program, believes the school and home must reinforce each other in promoting student success and parents who lack the basic skills cannot provide the needed home support to ensure student success.

Students in the PALS program are selected by teachers (one student is selected from each class), referred to the counselor for testing and conferencing, and assigned to a teacher different from those the student has for classroom instruction. The rationale is that students need an adult role model who serves as a surrogate parent, friend, and confidant separate from the classroom authority figure. Each teacher is assigned only one student. The teacher meets with the student daily for thirty minutes and, serving as the student's "champion and tutor," discusses the student problems and concerns, and focuses on attitude adjustment, school discipline, attendance, violence, and academics. Assistance is provided daily in strengthening reading and math skills. Over 85 percent of these students have shown a decrease in discipline and attendance problems and an increase in their reading and mathematics skill levels. "Statistics like these go a long way in convincing outsiders and teachers that an advisor/advisee program is needed to benefit all students, not just target populations," Davis says.

But what about the actual implementation of an advisor/advisee program? Davis says the next step is "to convince the entire faculty of the merits of the advisor program." He agrees with Henderson and LaForge (1989) that it's easy to get teachers to agree on the relevance and importance of such a program. They see its worth, but achieving consensus and getting their full support is another matter. Teachers have several real-life concerns that have to be addressed up front and to their satisfaction.

At West Jackson Middle School, the school-wide leadership team is the basic governing body for curriculum and instruction and will make the decision on whether or not to implement an advisor/advisee program. Davis believes both the leadership team and the faculty will want to explore the advantages and disadvantages of the program and know more about the theoretical underpinnings and what the research reports about the advisor program. With this information at hand, he has developed a plan to implement an advisory program contingent on the approval of the school's leadership team. The implementation plan consists of the following steps.

Step One: Prior to the leadership team making a formal decision, the process of educating the faculty is the essential first step. To clear up myths, misconceptions, and fallacies about the advisory program, Davis will hold a faculty meeting to talk about the advantages and disadvantages of teacher advisement. Research literature will be provided for teachers to read and the results of the PALS project will be presented and discussed. Davis says that while he will accent the positive aspects, he will be truthful in his approach and present the drawbacks of the program as well.

Teachers must know that the decision to implement the program will be made by them, but that the principal is pro-advisor/advisee and is committed to support fully every aspect of the program. It is also important to let teachers know that program implementation can take place first on a pilot-test basis using teacher volunteers instead of having school-wide adoption. Results of the pilot project can then serve as a decision point for further discussion. Davis states, "Teacher attitude is the most important variable for introducing an advisor/advisee program. If they view the program as valuable and not a burden on their already overcrowded schedules, the chances of success are high."

Step Two: During a time frame of three to four weeks, additional literature will be provided to teachers on the advisor/advisee program. Teachers will be encouraged to discuss their concerns with the principal and members of the leadership team with more information-giving meetings scheduled upon teacher request.

Step Three: This step involves the use of a consultant and the question of expense. Often teachers will want to know more about a program than the literature can provide and will have questions which are directly practitioner-oriented rather than research or theory-oriented. A pitfall principals can make, says Davis, is not providing information teachers really need to make informed decisions. Through informal talks, feedback from leadership team representatives, and a teacher questionnaire principals can know the specific concerns of their teachers. This data serves as the basis for hiring consultants who can tailor their program to the needs of the teachers and not the perceived needs as assessed by the principal. Data also provides a good indication of teacher feeling on whether or not they want to adopt the program.

If teachers need more information from a practitioner's viewpoint before they are ready to make a decision, an outside consultant, well-versed in both theory and practice, can directly address teacher concerns. Ideally, a counselor and one or more teachers from schools having successful advisor/advisee programs should be used with their presentations tailored to the specific needs of the faculty. Having the practical questions addressed alleviates much unfounded anxiety and speculation.

Should the leadership team decide to implement the advisor program, consultants are necessary in getting the program off to a sound start. The credibility of the consultants is essential to the success of the training programs.

Step Four: A year-long inservice program is advisable to orient and prepare teachers thoroughly for implementation, with consultants providing structured presentations as inservice proceeds. Davis also believes in the value of *benchmarking,* a quality improvement tool where teachers visit and study schools having exemplary advisor/advisee programs. Talking to other teachers, finding out what works and what does not, is central to the success of any improvement program.

The importance of using models of existing teacher-advisor programs as resource material cannot be over-emphasized, especially when examples come from schools with similar student and staffing demographics. Key components of the inservice program are the teaching of guidance skills and the development of useful advisor materials. The role of the school counselor as program coordinator and as teacher mentor needs to be fully explained, and teachers have to know that continuous support will be provided by both the principal and the counselor to design advisor activities and provide the necessary resources for program success. Davis emphasizes the importance of teachers having a highly positive attitude toward the advisor/advisee program ensuring that "they fully understand their role to be that of an advisor and not that of a teacher."

Step Five: The design of the advisor/advisee program must take into account the time teachers have to adequately advise students and how students will be grouped for advisement. Davis believes thirty minutes, three times a week is adequate for student advisement and if implemented, it will be conducted during a "homeroom period" scheduled specifically for that purpose. Depending on the grade level block schedule, homeroom will be scheduled at the beginning or ending of the day. Teachers will be assigned students they do not teach and activities will be designed for both group and individual advisement. The curriculum will emphasize life skills, social and emotional development, and personal problems and concerns of the preadolescent. Activities and materials will be teacher-developed through release time, by grade level, with a separate budget for supplies. The counselor will coordinate program development, supply teachers with the materials, and instruct teachers on how advisor/advisee materials should be used and activities should be implemented.

Developing a program within these parameters is beneficial for both teacher and student alike, Davis maintains. For teachers, thirty minutes, three times a week, is not taking too much of their instructional time and, since the emphasis is on providing a quality advisement program, "teachers will have time to prepare without the advisement sessions becoming too much of a routine—just another thing for teachers to do." Also, by developing the activities and materials ahead of time, the program is already planned for teachers to implement.

Students benefit from this scheduling design in much the same way as do teachers. The advisor/advisee program allows students to get to know another adult role model, one who is their friend and champion, and one who has a genuine interest in their well-being and personal development. By meeting three times a week, program activities are not merely a routine, but time to explore problems and concerns and topics of interest to them as transescents. Moreover, students will interact with different age-level peers and expand their circle of friends. When students are confronted with personal problems that disrupt their school lives or with tragic, personal events, the advisor is a trusted friend who will be there to provide counsel and understanding.

The advisor/advisee program at Edwards Middle School in Conyers, Georgia, is built around personal exploratory topics and is based on the philosophy that students should receive regular supportive counsel from a concerned adult role model who has the students' best interests at heart, says Dr. Wayne Watts, principal. At Edwards, advisor/advisee time is scheduled twenty minutes per day, five days a week, with grade-level teacher teams being responsible for assigning their own cadre of students to teacher team members for advisement. In this way, students get to know another adult role model, one who may be able to "relate or identify more closely with certain students' needs and backgrounds." The use of block scheduling, with flexible time modules, at Edwards allows teachers to expand advisee time into core academic or exploratory time to pursue topics of interest to students or address individual student problems as the need arises. This option provides an important dimension needed in advisor/advisee programs where student group interest should remain high, content continuity is essential, and teachers need to bring closure without interruption in order to sustain interest and maximize the effectiveness of the program. Figure 7.2 presents an example of a block schedule with advisee time interspersed with core and exploratory courses.

The advisor/advisee program, Watts relates, is designed to supplement, not supplant the guidance program at Edwards. Teachers cannot nor do they want to serve as professional counselors; they are advisors, friends, and confidants of students and provide individual or small group assistance in

Grade 6 Teams ½		Grade 7 Teams ½		Grade 8 Teams ½	
Block	Time	Block	Time	Block	Time
Advisor/Advisee	20	Core 1	60	Core 1	50
Core 1	50	Core 2	60	Core 2	60
Core 2	50	PE/Exploratory	115	Core 3	60
PE/Exploratory	115	Lunch	30	Lunch	30
Lunch	30	Advisor/Advisee	20	Advisor/Advisee	20
Core 3	60	Core 3	50	Core 4	50
Core 4	60	Core 4	50	PE/Exploratory	115

FIGURE 7.2. Advisor/advisee schedule in block modular form.

helping students with their academic work as well. In academics, teacher advisors serve as tutors to individuals and groups of students and they keep up with each student's academic progress. Having close contact with students, advisors work with core academic and exploratory teachers to help students achieve success. Both sets of teachers work with parents to promote a close working relationship and support network for their students. Often, Watts says, teacher-advisors will take the initiative to call parents and arrange a conference to discuss concerns or problems which surface during advisement time and are unrelated to academic performance. Quick, prompt action frequently resolves issues before they distract the students from their academic work. Many times, prior to implementing the advisor/advisee program, student academic problems resulted from social-emotional problems which were related to conflicts within the home or with peers, with poor academic performance being the symptom rather than the cause of the problem.

The curriculum, to Watts, is the most important aspect of a good advisor/advisee program and the role the principal plays in curriculum development is central to its overall success. Strong curriculum is based on student interests and needs. Students are surveyed yearly for topics of interest to them for the advisor program and teachers have the flexibility within the existing curriculum to incorporate topics of immediate interest or ones focusing on current school or community events. Teachers also provide topics for the advisor/advisee program in yearly planning sessions with the counselor or principal. Principals need to reinforce the importance of the program by attending yearly planning sessions and quarterly teacher team evaluation meetings designed to assess the impact of each year's program and to make curriculum alterations if necessary.

Positive teacher attitudes toward the advisor/advisee program are essential for its success from a delivery standpoint, Watts says. If teachers are excited about the curriculum and view the program goals as an important part of the overall middle school mission, "they place that needed extra attention and energy into their efforts that separate the mediocre from the superior." To Watts, the teacher advisor program adds to the quality-oriented curriculum and promotes the positive climate which permeates Edwards Middle School. Often units within core academic topics coincide with topics covered in the advisor/advisee curriculum with their respective content reinforcing each other. In certain instances, core academic time is devoted to teacher advisor topics or serves as a natural carry-over from discussions in the advisor program. Watts says, "In fact, this is one of the planning concerns teachers have in developing their yearly core curriculum and advisory program—can there be a fusion of curriculum?" This fusion, to Watts, makes both programs more meaningful to students and teachers alike.

The quality of school life is enhanced at Edwards as a result of the teacher-advisor program. Student morale and self-esteem are higher, students are more courteous to peers and teachers, and vandalism is virtually non-existent with students learning the need to respect the rights and property of others. Parents comment on the safe and orderly environment of the school and report that when their child feels safe and secure at school they can concentrate on academics, have a good feeling about school, and not worry about uncontrollable behavior of peers. Watts points out that a chain reaction takes place when students are happy and successful at school. When students feel safe and secure, and are successful, parents are pleased and content, teachers are happy and intrinsically rewarded, and the principal intuitively knows the school is a place of learning and success for students.

Continuous counselor involvement in the advisor program also serves to keep teacher interest high. Watts makes the advisor/advisee program a top priority for the counselor. The counselor attends all team meetings; provides suggestions to teachers on how to approach and handle sensitive, personal student problems; and is a continuous resource person for teachers. A teacher resource section is maintained by the counselor and teachers are encouraged by the principal to attend workshops and conferences deemed helpful in their role as student advisor. When new teachers are hired, the counselor provides an orientation session outlining the goals and objectives of the advisor/advisee program and provides copies of past years' curriculum. New teachers are provided special assistance by teacher team members in introducing advisor/advisee topics through joint planning efforts and team teaching large group advisement sessions.

Topics for the advisor/advisee program are presented in Figure 7.3. Topics were developed from student and parent surveys, teacher interest, and principal and counselor recommendations. Some topics are sequenced while others are grade-level specific. Advisor/advisee programs can be highly successful and beneficial to students, parents, and teachers if the principal avoids some of the more common pitfalls in developing and sustaining the teacher-advisor program. Dr. Wayne Watts and Dr. George Doughtery, principal at Oglethorpe County Middle School in Lexington, Georgia, agree that principals can avoid failure if they do the following:

(1) Principals must personally believe in the worth of the advisor/advisee program, be committed to training and sustaining the program with adequate personal enthusiasm and funding, and make the teacher-advisor program a primary responsibility of the school counselor.

(2) Principals must provide adequate fiscal resources and planning time for teachers and the counselor to develop and update topics for the advisory program.

TOPIC	GRADE	GOALS
Study and Research Skills	Grades 6-8	Teach students sound study and research skills to succeed in school.
Time Management	Grades 6-8	Teach students skills to maximize the use of their time in school and at home.
Resolving Conflict	Grades 6-8	Teach students how to resolve conflict with peers and adults.
Teams: Responsibilities as Individuals and Team Members	Grades 6-8	Teach students the responsibilities of team membership, team work, and their roles as individuals.
Career Opportunities	Grades 6-8	Teach students the value of work and the many jobs people have that contribute to our daily life.
Academic Responsibility	Grades 6-8	Teach students the value of school work to later life and their responsibilities as students for learning.
Parent and Child Care	Grades 6-8	Teach students the responsibilities of parents in providing adequate economic, psychological, and health care for children.
Middle School and You	Grades 6-8	Teach students the goals of the middle school, the curriculum, the activities available, and responsibilities of good student citizenship.

FIGURE 7.3. Advisor/advisee topics.

(3) Principals must provide teachers with a thorough understanding of the goals and objectives of advisory programs through research literature and a well-planned orientation program designed for practitioners which emphasizes the program's benefits and allows teachers to benchmark successful schools.

(4) Principals must provide time and resources to adequately train teachers in their role of advisor by using the school counselor as the primary resource person.

(5) Principals must continuously show program support by attending teacher meetings and planning sessions and play an active role in these activities as a resource person and motivator.

(6) Principals must allow teachers to develop program topics that are of interest to them, their students, and the students' parents if teacher enthusiasm for the advisor program is to be sustained.

(7) Principals must provide adequate time within the school schedule to plan for and conduct teache-radvisor activities.

(8) Principals must allow teachers to have input regarding student grouping configurations within grade levels and, along with the school counselor, assist teachers in teaching and advising students on sensitive, personal, and highly controversial issues and problems.

(9) Principals should encourage teachers to pilot test advisor/advisee programs on a grade-by-grade basis before fully implementing a teacher-advisor program across all grade levels.

REFERENCES

An Agenda for Excellence. 1985. Reston, VA: National Association of Secondary School Principals.

Alexander, W. M. and P. S. George. 1981. *The Exemplary Middle School.* New York: Holt, Rinehart, and Winston.

Alexander, W. M. and C. K. McEwin. September 1989. *Schools in the Middle: Status and Progress.* Columbus, OH: National Middle School Association.

Arhar, J. M. 1992. "Interdisciplinary Teaming and the Social Bonding of Middle Level Students," in *Transforming Middle Level Education: Perspectives and Possibilities.* J. L. Irvin, ed. Needham Heights, MA: Allyn & Bacon, pp. 139–161.

Beane, J. A. 1993. *A Middle School Curriculum from Rhetoric to Reality.* Second edition. Columbus, OH: National Middle School Association.

Capelluti, J. and D. Stokes. 1991. *Middle Level Education: Programs, Policies, and Practices.* Reston, VA: National Association of Secondary School Principals.

Carnegie Council on Adolescent Development. 1989. *Turning Points: Preparing American Youth for the 21st Century.* New York: Carnegie Corporation of New York.

Carnegie Task Force on Education of Young Adolescents. 1989. *Turning Points: Preparing American Youth for the 21st Century.* Washington, DC: Carnegie Council on Adolescent Development.

Cawelti, G. November 1988. "Middle Schools a Better Match with Early Adolescent Needs, ASCD Survey Finds," *ASCD Curriculum Update.* Alexandria, VA: Association for Supervision and Curriculum Development.

Center for Research on Elementary and Middle Schools. 1990. "Implementation and Effects of Middle Grades Practices," *CREMS Report* (March). Baltimore, MD: Johns Hopkins University Center for Research on Elementary and Middle Schools.

Cole, C. G. 1988. *Guidance in Middle Level Schools: Everyone's Responsibility.* Columbus, OH: National Middle School Association.

Epstein, J. L. and D. J. MacIver. 1990. *Education in the Middle Grades: National Practices and Trends.* Columbus, OH: National Middle School Association.

Fenwick, J. 1992. *Managing Middle Grade Reform—An "America 2000" Agenda.* San Diego, CA: Fenwick and Associates, Inc.

George, P. S. and W. M. Alexander. 1993. *The Exemplary Middle School*. Second edition. Fort Worth, TX: Harcourt Brace Jovanovich College Publishers.

George, P. and G. Lawrence. 1982. *Handbook for Middle School Teaching*. Glenview, IL: Scott, Foresman and Company.

Henderson, P. and J. LaForge. 1989. "The Role of the Middle School Counselor in Teacher-Advisor Programs," *The School Counselor*, 36:348–349.

James, M. A. 1986. *Advisor-Advisee Programs: Why, What, and How?* Columbus, OH: National Middle School Association.

Keefe, J. W. 1991. "Advisement," in *Instructional Leadership Handbook*. J. Keefe and J. Jenkins, eds. Reston, VA: National Association of Secondary School Principals.

Kohlberg, L. 1980. *Recent Research in Moral Development*. New York: Holt.

Kohlberg, L. 1981. *The Philosophy of Moral Development: Moral Stages and the Idea of Justice*. San Francisco: Harper and Row.

Krathwohl, D. R., B. S. Bloom, and B. B. Masia. 1964. *Taxonomy of Educational Objectives: The Classification of Educational Goals. Handbook II: Affective Domain*. New York: David McKay Company, Inc.

Lounsbury, J. H. and D. C. Clark. 1990. *Inside Grade Eight: From Apathy to Excitement*. Reston, VA: National Association of Secondary School Principals.

Lunenburg, F. C. and A. C. Ornstein. 1996. *Educational Administration: Concepts and Practices*. Second edition. Belmont, CA: Wadsworth Publishing Company.

MacIver, D. 1990. "Meeting the Needs of Young Adolescents: Advisory Groups, Interdisciplinary Teaching Teams, and School Transition Programs," *Phi Delta Kappan*, 71(6):458–464.

Merenbloom, E. Y. 1982. *Developing Effective Middle Schools through Faculty Participation*. Columbus, OH: National Middle School Association.

Messick, R. G. and K. E. Reynolds. 1992. *Middle Level Curriculum in Action*. White Plains, NY: Longman.

Meyers, J.W. 1985. *Involving Parents in Middle Level Education*. Columbus, OH: National Middle School Association.

Myrick, R. and L. Myrick. 1990. *The Teacher Advisor Program: An Innovative Approach to School Guidance*. Ann Arbor, MI: ERIC Clearinghouse on Counseling and Personnel Services. ERIC Document Reproduction Service No. ED 316 791.

Piaget, J. 1977. *The Essential Piaget*. New York: Basic Books.

Squires, D. A., W. G. Huitt, and J. K. Segars. 1984. *Effective Schools and Classrooms: A Research-Based Perspective*. Alexandria, VA: Association for Supervision and Curriculum Development.

Vars, G. F. January, 1989. "Getting Closer to Middle Level Students: Options for Teacher-Advisor Programs," in *Schools in the Middle: A Report on Trends and Practices*. Reston, VA: National Association of Secondary School Principals.

Weller, L. D. 1996. "Return on Quality: A New Factor in Assessing Quality Efforts." *International Journal of Educational Management*, 10(1):30–40.

Wiles, J. and J. Bondi. 1993. *The Essential Middle School*. Second edition. New York: Macmillan Publishing Company.

CHAPTER 8

Leadership for At-Risk Students and Remedial Education in Middle Schools

At-risk is a term that applies to learners who are not successful in the learning environment despite the effective utilization of staff and resources. This usually results from the lack of the necessary intellectual, emotional, and/or social skills needed to take advantage of the educational opportunities available to them. Middle school principals, as instructional leaders, must develop programs and provide training to teachers to make both school and staff more developmentally responsive to students.

This chapter will provide lists of characteristics and examples of student profiles which tend to place students at-risk of failure in school. Examples of interdisciplinary team teaching and scheduling to address the problems of at-risk students will be presented. Examples of special training programs for remedial teachers as well as diagnostic instruments to assess at-risk and remedial students will be presented. Case studies of principals who have effective at-risk and remedial programs will be presented as well as common pitfalls to avoid.

This chapter will focus on the following questions:

- What is an at-risk student and what are the generic characteristics of at-risk students?
- What are the major generic factors contributing to at-risk students?
- What are four primary causes which contribute to at-risk students and what can teachers, parents, and principals do to alleviate these factors?
- What are some of the different learning styles of at-risk students and correlated teaching styles teachers can use to accommodate and remediate these students?
- What is the role of multiple intelligence in addressing the at-risk problem and in providing remediation activities?

229

- What is the role of the middle school principal in providing programs and activities to meet the needs of at-risk students?
- How do an interdisciplinary curriculum, team teaching, and an advisor/advisee program lend themselves to assisting at-risk and remedial students?
- What is remedial education and how does one best identify-diagnose students needing remediation?
- What are the components of an effective remediation program and what are the responsibilities of principals, teachers, and parents in maximizing the effectiveness of this program?

AT-RISK STUDENTS

"At-risk" is a term generally applied to learners who are not successful in the learning environment despite the effective utilization of staff and resources. While at times all students run the risk of failure, most students, as a result of their positive experiences in schools, develop into young adults who have a healthy self-concept and a positive attitude toward school. At-risk students, however, are apathetic toward school, have poor motivation, show underachievement, and are below average for their grade levels.

At-risk students have also been identified in the literature as disadvantaged or educationally disadvantaged. Educationally disadvantaged children are those having experiences in school, home, and community which negatively impact their development and impair their success (Pallas, Natriello, and McDill, 1989). Environmental variables which impact students who are considered disadvantaged or at-risk include home, community, personal, and cultural backgrounds which impact a student's attitude, behavior, and probability of success in school (Messick and Reynolds, 1992). Identifying characteristics associated with disadvantaged or at-risk students include those who are members of minority groups, those who speak English as a second language, gifted or highly talented but unchallenged students, children of parents abusing drugs, latchkey children, children from poverty-level families, and children under stress or living in highly stressful situations. Students with one or more of these environmental factors are considered at-risk or educationally disadvantaged and the likelihood of their dropping out of school before completing high school is greater than for other students.

Data from a national survey of 25,000 eighth graders in 1,000 public and private schools indicates that 53 percent of these students had no risk factors, 26 percent had one risk factor, and 20 percent had two or more risk factors (Hafner, Ingels, Schneider, Stevenson, and Owings, 1990). Students with two or more risk factors are six times more likely not to graduate from high school than those with no risk factors. Multiple risk-factor students are twice as likely to be in the lowest achievement test quartile.

CONTRIBUTING FACTORS

Single-Parent Families

Kowalski (1996) reports that in 1990, traditional families accounted for fewer than one-third of the family population with single-parent family configurations and gay couples on the rise. From 1980 to 1990, there was a 41 percent increase in single parent families with black children being four times more likely and Hispanic children two times more likely than white children to be raised by single parents. Eighty percent of single-parent families are headed by women, the birthrate among unmarried white women is increasing, and the number of children living with single, never-married mothers increased from 1970 to 1990 by 678 percent (Hodgkinson, 1991). Because many single mothers are primarily responsible for raising their children, many of these children grow up economically disadvantaged. Children raised by single mothers (about 15 million in 1990) have about one-third the income as those of two parent families. Moreover, 50 percent of single mothers live in poverty (Kirst and McLaughlin, 1990). Minority children are more likely to be retained a grade level and perform below grade level on achievement tests. More than 2 million of these children spend two or three hours daily without adult supervision and preschoolers are read to an average of only two minutes a day during weekdays and three minutes a day on weekends (Carroll and Carroll, 1994).

The term "time deficit" is applied to both single-parent children and two-parent children and connotes the decrease in the amount of time parents spend with their children. This risk factor becomes quite evident when viewed as a statistic: children from 1960 to 1990 have lost 10 to 12 hours (a 40 percent decrease) in parent contact time per week (Hewlett, 1991). This is attributed to the increased employment of single mothers, increased demands of employment (the forty-hour work week now averages fifty-two hours), and the stress induced by the job which allows little time for parents to concentrate on their children at day's end.

Poverty

Poverty correlates with race, ethnicity, and gender as variables affecting the ability to learn. Hodgkinson (1991) reports that 40 percent of all those listed as poor are children, with one out of every five children living in poverty. This makes children poorer than any other age bracket in America. By race, 44 percent of black children live in poverty, 37 percent of Hispanic children live in poverty, and 14 percent of white children live in poverty. Poverty is not restricted to urban areas. It is even more prevalent in rural America with almost one-fourth of rural children (50 percent higher than for urban children) living in poverty.

Children in poverty have higher rates of poor health, developmental disabilities, teenage mothers, and school dropouts, and lower academic achievement. Many of these children lack health insurance and have infrequent dental and physical examinations (Kirst and McLaughlin, 1990). Twenty-one percent of these children live in public housing. Homelessness is correlated with race, gender, and age with 30 percent of the homeless being children. Most homeless families consist of women with two or more children under age 5. Homeless children have more health, psychological, and school problems than those living in family homes. School problems include absenteeism, dropout, and low self-esteem (Hodgkinson, 1991).

Diversity

America is becoming a more diverse nation. From 1980 to 1990, approximately 50 percent of the population growth was nonwhite. Approximately one-fourth of the population of America is of minority status (Ward, 1994) with blacks representing 12 percent of the population and Hispanic and others representing 8.4 percent and 3.6 percent respectively. Kowalski (1996) notes that a large part of the minority population growth is due to fertility rates which are highly correlated to race and socioeconomic status. Economically disadvantaged groups have the highest birth rates. With the increased immigration rates, especially among Asian and Hispanic groups, an increase in minority group children is likely for some time to come.

While demographic data is helpful in identifying at-risk students, such factors alone will not identify all at-risk students. Other indicators of at-risk students also exist and must be considered by educators before a more accurate assessment can be made.

CHARACTERISTICS AND BEHAVIORS

Student characteristics and school-related behaviors are also associated with at-risk students. Ogden and Germinario (1994) list the following characteristics and behaviors as placing students at-risk of failure:

(1) Problems of attendance
(2) Retention in grade level
(3) School suspensions
(4) Two or more years below grade level

(5) Not participating in extracurricular activities
(6) Placement in special programs

Middle school principals identify at-risk students as those who are frequently sent to the office, attend school infrequently, have court appearances, move frequently, have primary care responsibility for siblings, or have consistent trouble with law enforcement agencies (Bergmann, 1989). Messick and Reynolds (1992) add that students who have low self-esteem, feel alienated, have below grade-level reading and mathematics skills, evidence emotional or physical problems, have financial needs, are pregnant, or "lack a bonding with school" (p. 149) are at-risk of failure and dropout.

Precocious sexual activity places students at-risk as well. Hodgkinson (1991) relates that more students under sixteen are becoming high-risk pregnancy candidates. Every day 40 teenage girls give birth to their third child, teenage mothers are more prone to give premature birth which contributes to low birth weight and correlates with learning difficulties, and one-fourth of all sexually active teenagers will be infected with a sexually transmitted disease before high school graduation. Substance abuse, both alcohol and illicit drugs, is on the increase with middle school students. Alcohol is becoming an increasing problem, with many students beginning to drink during grades 6–9. Use of illicit drugs is also evidenced in grades 6–9. Johnson, O'Malley, and Bachman (1988) found that 56 percent of high school graduates began drinking in the middle school grades and 19 percent began using drugs during their middle school years. Messick and Reynolds (1992) note that co-dependency exists in the middle grades and that substance abuse signs include "sudden changes in behavior or mood, listlessness or sleeping in school, loss of weight or appetite, loss of interest in physical activity, poor academic performance, inability to get along with peers, and expressions of not belonging at school" (p. 149).

Such student characteristics and behaviors provide an overall profile of those who may be at-risk of school failure or dropout. However, Ogden and Germinario (1994) suggest "that it may be more beneficial to examine general descriptors of a student's profile to establish parameters for determining the nature of risk" (p. 70). They maintain that research has provided for a synthesis of a student's profile through the analysis of four major factors: "self-concept, alienation, lack of school success, and student learning style" (p. 70).

Self-Concept

Self-concept plays a key role in the physical, cognitive, social, emotional, and moral development of the transescent. Specifically, self-concept is related to student educational outcomes such as grades, test scores, and a positive attitude toward school in general. When students feel better about themselves, they have a more positive outlook on life and do better in school. For this reason alone, middle school educators must provide ways for transescents to build a healthy self-concept, feel pride in themselves and their school, and feel that they can be successful in their school activities (Ogden and Germinario, 1994).

Of specific value to middle school educators is the work of Marsh (1990). His research indicates that there are two major dimensions of the self-concept which are the multifaceted dimension and the hierarchial dimension. The multifaceted dimension has three separate self-concept areas: nonacademic self-concept, math/academic self-concept, and verbal/academic self-concept. Each of these three areas has several facets which are part of an individual's self-concept. In the nonacademic self-concept, there are the self-concepts of physical ability, physical appearance, peer relationships, and parent relationships. The math/academic and verbal/academic self-concepts involve the academic disciplines listed in their descriptors as well as the facets of school, geography, history, the sciences, foreign language, and economics/business. Parent relationships play an important part in all three dimensions and they specifically impact the facets of biological sciences, economics/business, and school. As middle school students progress to adulthood, the number of facets in their self-concept develops which is a result of their being directly exposed to these facets. For example, a student could not have a self-concept about the physical sciences until introduced to one or more of these sciences.

The hierarchical dimension addresses the individual's own perception about these facets and their own performance within the confines of these facets. Perceptions, according to Marsh (1990), are greatly impacted by how others view the performance of the individual within the facet and the type of reinforcement the individual receives while engaging in facet activities. Behavior also plays a part in self-concept development of a facet through the attitude or perception one takes toward it. For example, is the facet viewed as hard, easy, fun, laborious, personally rewarding, or personally threatening?

Self-esteem becomes the sum total of the dimensions of self-concept and the self-concept facets under each of the three dimensions. When all of these self-concept factors are taken together, the result is the general self-concept held by the individual.

Alienation

Alienation from school is attributed to a lack of school success. Central to the cause of alienation is a student's being or feeling disengaged from school itself. Engaging that student in the school and in the classroom will decrease the sense of school alienation the student feels. Ogden and Germinario (1994) suggest that schools and classrooms employ practices which promote a sense of membership and belonging and which involve students on a daily basis in activities which make students feel truly valued as part of a group or team. These authors state that "common practices associated with grouping patterns, discipline and attendance policies, school regulations, school curriculum, and special class placement may be rooted in good intentions, yet they may, in fact, lead to increased feelings of isolation and lack of belonging" (p. 70).

Feelings of alienation can best be alleviated by making students feel that they are important and that their personal contributions are of high value and are greatly appreciated. Hackman (1996) relates that students who are given responsibility and enjoy success feel valued by their peers and teachers. When teachers reward these students openly and point out the importance of their work to the class and/or school, students not only take pride in their own personal contributions but in making contributions to others. This promotes a high sense of belonging and a feeling of personal worth. Schools and classrooms can also foster a sense of belonging and membership by allowing students to participate in community projects, practice cooperative learning in the classroom, and act as peer tutors. In this way each student has a chance to exhibit personal strengths to others in ways that will yield success and recognition.

LEVEL OF SCHOOL SUCCESS

Success in middle school is vital to a healthy self-concept, a feeling of worth and belonging to a group, and a positive attitude toward the future. Success breeds success. Most often, school success is thought of as academic success. However, there are different kinds of success and different ways individuals can be successful. Athletics, music, art, writing, theater, and dance are just a few ways students can be successful beyond academics.

A key component of success is being viewed as successful in the eyes of peers and adults. Despite the fact that transescents seek autonomy, they also seek group approval. Parents play a key role in rewarding the successful efforts of their children and in providing tasks where their children can enjoy success and not suffer ridicule or expressions of parental displeasure.

Peer groups significantly influence transescent behavior. Peer groups can positively influence the transescent by providing friendship, belonging, and rewards. The negative influences of peer groups which hold negative values and norms and reward deviant behavior can and do work against the accepted definitions of success. Peer groups are cliques of students with similar interests, backgrounds, and values. Peer groups are often the primary source of information about sex and, next to parents, are most powerful in the socialization process. Ogbu (1985, 1992) notes that for minority students, status in the peer group comes not from exhibiting positive traits or behaviors but from promoting the goals of the clique. These peer groups exert pressure on their members *not* to achieve good grades, and research suggests that in some minority groups, those who adopt behaviors leading to school success are open to criticism and isolation from the group. Ogbu states that within such groups students who have a positive attitude toward academics are put down by their peers as "acting white." Pressure of this nature compounds the problems of those students who already evidence one or more risk factors. Schools also play an important role in promoting success among students. McPartland and Slavin (1990) report that school failure sends a message of rejection to students and contributes to a sense of poor self-worth. Having a firm grasp of the basic academic and social skills is important to academic success, and those who lack this essential foundation meet with failure and frustration. Students who are performing a year or more below grade level, have behavior problems, have low socioeconomic status, or who have been retained in prior grades are at high risk of further failure and dropout.

Doing away with organizational patterns such as tracking can disperse cliques and allow for new peer group assimilation. A comprehensive exploratory program with a variety of extracurricular activities can also disrupt cliques by providing a wide array of challenges for at-risk students with an adult role model who is in daily contact with these students and can assist them with their learning and personal problems. Teacher-advisors can also help at-risk students set personal goals, both academic and social, and help the student achieve these goals and thereby receive personal satisfaction and experience success. MacIver (1990) notes that the use of interdisciplinary teaching teams and advisor/advisee programs provide a supportive academic and social environment in which transescents, both at-risk and those with no risk factors, can enjoy success.

The effective schools movement research variables have positive effects on low achieving children as well as those children having no academic problems. MacIver (1990) and Squires, Huitt, and Segars (1984) note that time on task and consistent and fair discipline practices assist social and academic development. Squires et al. (1984) found that principals and teachers who create a school climate in which success is expected, academics are emphasized, and the environment is safe and orderly evidence academic success among all students. In effective schools, reading, writing, and mathematics are emphasized and classrooms are conducted in a businesslike environment. Time on task is emphasized, school rules are strictly enforced, and students know what behaviors are expected of them. Students are actively engaged in academic work, teachers help students set goals which they can achieve, and teachers provide constant rewards for achievement. Moreover, students are expected to master their work and graduate from high school. Students feel that teachers care about them as individuals and about their academic progress, and students believe that academic success results from hard work rather than luck.

At-risk students need structure, clear rules and expectations, and directed teaching. At-risk students have developed counterproductive behaviors which need to be reshaped through instructional programs which provide a warm, supportive, and confidence-building environment (Blumenthal, Holmes, and Pound, 1991) and at the same time provide high involvement, high reinforcement, and personalization (Henson, 1993). By providing structure and empathy and helping these students set realistic achievement goals, at-risk students gain self-confidence and success which contribute greatly to attitude change. Blumenthal et al. (1991) also note that at-risk students need a certain amount of free time (at least 30 minutes a day) to discuss their problems or general concerns. An advisor/advisee program provides for this need to dialogue with adults and peers.

According to Squires et al. (1984), student success is clearly related to school climate, which is, in turn, related to leadership. In effective schools, three leadership variables are important for success: modeling, feedback, and consensus building. Modeling expected student behavior is an important part of sustaining the school's climate. Modeling also sets the tone for teachers and parents who are expected to support the emphasis placed on student success, academics, and a safe and orderly environment. Principals provide praise and feedback to teachers and students on their accomplishments and success. Principals practice "leadership by walking around," being visible, observing classrooms, and talking to teachers and students about their problems and concerns. Consensus building is a result of vision. Vision, developed jointly among teachers and administrators, provides the agreed-upon direction and goals of the school's educational program. Principals have the responsibility to move teachers and students toward the school's vision through the evaluation of their progress and performance.

LEARNING STYLES

The work of Gardner (1993), Armstrong (1994), and Dunn and Dunn (1979) points out that students learn differently and have their own preferred learning styles. Moreover, the research indicates that teaching to the learning styles of students enhances student learning. Ogden and Germinario (1994) relate that research suggests at-risk students have predominant learning styles that differ greatly from traditional teaching styles. At-risk students are prone to have poor or fair auditory and visual learning capabilities and the use of more multi-sensory learning activities for at-risk students would increase learning. A variety of teaching strategies not only helps at-risk students, but increases learning for all students.

While the research of matching teaching strategies with learning styles is still progressing, findings seem positive. Thought should be given, however, to the following considerations: Good and Stipek (1983) found that a particular style of learning that a student may find motivating may not be consistent with the student's ability or prior knowledge and sometimes a mismatch may be effective. Second, there is no single dimension for learners which is clear enough to prescribe a *single* learning activity. Third, uniform classroom instruction is often more effective than individual student prescription because such instruction matches the skills of the teacher. Good and Brophy (1987) found that teachers, especially inexperienced ones, find it too difficult to teach to a variety of student learning styles.

Research shows, however, that consistently matching instruction to the preferred learning style of the student increases academic achievement, reduces truancy and discipline problems, and promotes a more positive attitude toward school (Henson, 1993). Work by Geisert and Dunn (1991) found gains in student achievement when knowledge and skills are introduced through the student's strongest learning style and reinforced through those styles of a less preferred nature. Dunn and Dunn (1979) identified five learning styles:

(1) Environmental which includes sound, light, temperature, and design
(2) Emotional which includes motivation, persistence, structure, and responsibility
(3) Sociological which includes colleagues, self, pairs, team, and varied
(4) Physical which includes perceptual, intake, time, and mobility
(5) Psychological which includes analytic, global, cerebral preference, reflective, and impulse

Matching teaching style with learning style can also be accomplished through personality-type matching between teacher and students. Thelan (1960) found these matches to produce greater student satisfaction with classes and that students are more attentive to learning.

What seems to offer the most promise to promote learning in all students is a combination of teacher-directed strategies, learner-directed strategies, and individualized instruction. Teachers should consider the content to be covered when selecting the strategies.

Teacher-directed strategies are those managed by the teacher and are most appropriate for teaching facts, basic skills, concrete concepts, and generalizations. These strategies provide for little interaction between teacher and learner or learner and learner, and they include lecture (telling and explaining while students record information in the manner presented), direct instruction (explaining information in small steps with an occasional check for student comprehension), demonstration (engaging students in viewing and hands-on learning rather than just hearing information), and recitation (asking teacher imposed questions with only teacher-student interaction).

While teacher-directed strategies can be effective in promoting learning, Berryman (1993) notes that these are passive learning strategies, they limit student input, and they contradict what is known about how people learn. The problem is that these strategies are used too often with very little student-directed strategy intervention. Berryman also states that teacher-directed strategies reduce time for student exploration of new and varied activities, thwart discovery learning, fail to teach students responsibility for their own learning, and lead to motivational and classroom-control problems.

Learner-directed strategies allow students to manage their own learning and to participate in their own learning. These strategies require more instructional time but are more effective in teaching abstract concepts and generalizations and developing higher order thinking skills. Roleplaying allows students to act out ideas and events as they express themselves in character roles. This allows students to connect with the content as they relieve frustrations, show creativity, and develop an appreciation for other points of view. Problem solving presents students with a challenge, and they are required to think through the solution and explain the procedures/logic behind the solution. This can be done on paper either individually or in small groups, or it can be done in whole class instruction through brainstorming. Brainstorming is a quality education tool and is most effective when teachers monitor the process. The idea is to identify the basic problem, propose ideas for solving the problem, select the best idea to solve the problem, and then implement the selected idea and monitor the results. Cooperative learning is another way to involve students in learning. Braddock and McPartland (1993) found cooperative learning to increase academic achievement, foster positive attitudes toward school and other racial groups, and promote positive peer group climates for learning.

Learner-directed teaching strategies are used by teachers who believe students can learn on their own and will take the responsibility for their own learning. These teachers provide learning opportunities that are challenging, exciting, meaningful, and rewarding. Active learning is a way to stimulate interest and motivation and make school an important part of the transescent's life (Epstein and Salinas, 1992). Berryman (1993) found that when classrooms provide instruction which simulates the real workplace by providing characteristics of authentic work environments, students demonstrate gains in both academic and social growth. Authentic classrooms provide for extrinsic and intrinsic rewards, instill pride in work and the quality of work performed, provide enjoyment, and develop interpersonal relations skills which are important to job performance and success.

Individualized learning and independent study also promote learning for all students (Henson, 1993). These approaches to learning make school more meaningful for students. Independent study allows students to choose their own topics, have a liberal amount of time to complete their work, and remediate without penalty. Contract grading is another approach used with success for at-risk students since it provides both structure and freedom of choice. Students set their own goals based on teacher expectations with careful monitoring by the teacher regarding individual student progress. When parents are involved in contract grading, students receive home support and monitoring as well.

Individualizing instruction is part of the true middle school concept, but with class sizes of 25 to 30 students teachers find this practice difficult at best. Compounding the issue of class size is the wide array of student abilities. One approach to individualizing instruction is ability grouping or tracking students, even though arguments exist against this kind of group instruction. Heterogeneous grouping, with its diverse student abilities, often results in teacher-directed activities exclusively which have a negative impact on students. First, those students who are not being academically challenged by such activities become bored and are in danger of finding school unrewarding. Second, when teachers set academic expectations too high, students not able to meet those standards become discouraged, may lose the motivation to learn, and risk successions of failure which negatively impact their self-esteem (Henson, 1993).

Ability grouping by subject is one way to alleviate the negative results on students from heterogeneous grouping. Here, students are grouped by ability by subject with teachers teaching to their students' ability levels yet having the leeway to challenge them without causing frustration or discouraging their motivation to learn and succeed. Grouping of this type could place a student in as few as one group (ability level constant in English, science, social studies, and mathematics) or up to four groups depending on the student's ability levels in the core subjects. The use of interdisciplinary team teaching can greatly enhance the ability grouping practice in the middle school.

In intraclass grouping, another tracking procedure, teachers have more time to spend with low achievers or low-ability students. Good, Reyes, Grouws, and Mulryan (1990–1991) found that when classes are divided into ability groups, higher ability groups tend to work alone and can be given more creative challenges requiring divergent thinking and problem solving. This allows teachers to spend more time with low-ability students needing more monitoring and guidance. Brophy (1983) notes that low-ability groups within classrooms can achieve if teachers hold high expectations for their success. Brophy suggests that teachers, when working with low achievers and at-risk students, constantly reward and reinforce learning, praise students for success no matter how little the progress, provide appropriate challenges for their abilities, and turn failures into positive learning experiences.

The use of computers is another way to individualize instruction. Computer programs promote drill and practice and provide for problem solving, simulations, tutorial, and games. Alessi and Trollip (1991) found computer assisted instruction (CAI) enhances the education of students because they are actively involved in the learning process and their success motivates them for further learning. The varying levels of instruction make CAI ideal for ability variation and independent study, and CAI guides the learner while providing immediate feedback about the student's learning progress.

Mastery learning and using behavioral objectives are two other ways to individualize instruction. The mastery learning model developed by Benjamin Bloom, known as Learning for Mastery (LFM) is "teacher-paced and group-based. In other words the teacher leads the lesson and the class as a group follows" (Henson, 1993, p. 153). According to Henson, most other mastery learning models are student-paced and individually based. In these other models, students control the amount of time needed to master the learning, there is remediation and assessment without penalty to the students' grades, and evaluation is based on pre-set criteria. Cunningham (1991) found that for mastery learning to have an impact, there must be congruence between the content taught, the teaching strategies used, and the material evaluated. Additionally, there must be formative evaluation, wherein students are provided on-going feedback designed to enhance learning.

The use of behavioral objectives which are measurable and coincide with learner capabilities can promote student learning. Planned activities which address learning style preferences and which are based on these behavioral objectives are jointly determined by teacher and student. A pretest is given at the beginning of study with formative tests occurring periodically throughout the individualized instruction. Teacher monitoring, feedback, and corrective action are crucial to success. Posttests determine whether or not mastery has been attained for the successful completion of study. Remediation is only for those objectives or parts of the objectives students failed to complete satisfactorily. As with other individualized learning methods, the behavioral objectives approach is student-paced, can accommodate a variety of ability levels, and can provide success and challenge without unnecessary frustration and failure.

BUILDING A PROGRAM FOR AT-RISK STUDENTS

The task of educators in the 1990s has become more difficult than in past decades with the increasing demands to become more responsive to the needs and expectations of parents and society. Rapid changes in our social, economic, and political arenas are creating new tensions in our social order and, in turn, our schools. Changes in family structure, shifts in values, and the growing numbers of students with varied socioeconomic backgrounds call for new and better ways to meet these challenges and responsibilities (Toepfer, 1996). Ogden and Germinario (1994) note that the diversified student population with its growing numbers of at-risk and educationally disadvantaged students presents difficult challenges for educators whose mission is to provide the best possible education for all students.

Schools must take the lead in providing ways to help all students succeed in school and life despite the pressures and disadvantages they bring to school. The task is not easy, but neither is it unattainable. Ogden and Germinario (1994) suggest that efforts in early prevention and intervention at the pre-elementary and elementary school levels are necessary to adequately assist at-risk students. Programs which educate parents on the importance of regular health care, proper diet, reading to their children on a consistent basis, and having creative play sessions with their children are one measure schools can take toward early prevention. Toepfer (1996) calls for cooperative planning efforts among elementary schools, middle schools, and high schools to build into their curriculum and learning experiences those essentials necessary to increase the potential for high school graduation and to challenge students to the fullest levels of their abilities, develop lifelong learning skills, and learn how to solve problems impacting their own lives. Central to these curriculum and learning experiences is the need for students to learn at their own pace, enjoy continuous success in schoolwork, and receive regular rewards and recognition for their accomplishments. Toepfer notes that success in school, especially in the early years, correlates with high school graduation. He also points out that many social problems stem from those who have little education: "High school completion rates hinge upon how prior school experiences fit student needs given the changing conditions of our society. While most students reach legal school-leaving age during high school, they often make the emotional decision to drop out between third and eighth grades" (p. 45). Those with no marketable skills contribute to high unemployment, increase the number of people living in poverty, and make up more than 80 percent of prison inmates.

Today's middle school educators are asked to take on more of the role of parents than their counterparts of decades ago. The increase in violence in society and in the home impacts all students. The shift in societal values and the natural stress of transescent maturation compound the problems both facing and encountered by students. These include substance abuse, gangs, prejudice and racism, poverty, pregnancy, and crime. Parents who work and single parents who have little time to spend with their children and have poor parenting skills often look to teachers and administrators for help in teaching their children many of the skills and values which were once the prerogative of the home. Because of these societal, economic, and family pressures, many students are at-risk of failure. These problems confront both low income, minority families as well as well-educated, middle class white families. Middle schools, for these reasons, must enhance their instructional and support programs to meet the multiple needs of individual students as they progress toward adolescence.

Identifying At-Risk Students

Toepfer (1996) emphasizes that identifying the nature of at-risk factor(s) for each student is the important first step in designing a program for at-risk students. Toepfer states, "The current 'at-risk' label can have an insidious punitive impact. The 'at-risk' designation can focus upon ethnic, poverty, racial, and social class realities alone. Instead, we need to identify the behaviors of individuals which put them 'at-risk' while specifying 'of what' these individual young adolescents are 'at-risk' " (p. 47). The educational goals for at-risk programs should be based on our educational obligations to provide learning, care, and understanding to these transescents rather than concerns with labeling students as having certain or general at-risk characteristics.

Targeting factors contributing to making students at-risk should be done consistently as students progress through school. Reviewing student records from previous years, teachers and principals can keep informed of any changes in demographic and school-related variables which place students in an at-risk category. Advisor/advisee programs in middle schools and interdisciplinary teaching teams can both maximize and simplify this effort. Many teachers need inservice programs to sensitize them to the various indicators which identify at-risk students. This is especially true for young teachers whose academic preparation may not have adequately prepared them for diagnosing at-risk children beyond the standard socioeconomic descriptors.

PROMOTING RESILIENCY

Improving the school success rate of students who experience at-risk factors can be accomplished through promoting "resilience" among students. Winfield (1991) uses the term resilience to describe those students who have defied the odds for school failure despite certain hardships. These students recover from or adapt to life's stresses and problems; lead healthy, stable lives; and succeed academically.

Research studies by Benard (1993) and reported in Reed, McMillan, and McBee (1995) found that one-third to one-half of the children experiencing at-risk factors early in their lives overcome these conditions and become successful in school. Certain beliefs, attitudes, and behaviors promote resiliency in middle school students. These are, according to Reed et al. (1995), as follows:

(1) Believing that they are in control of their behaviors, that their choices influence their lives, and that self-control of their destinies comes from within
(2) Engaging in constructive hobbies or other activities at school or church in their spare time
(3) Avoiding children who are a negative influence and encouraging others to do the same
(4) Having an important relationship with an adult who provides trust, recognition, support, and direction
(5) Setting goals for themselves and possessing a sense of self-efficacy

An analysis of the above characteristics reveals environmental traits (having a significant relationship with an adult who provides support and direction; having outside hobbies; and participating in activities at school, church, and community organizations) coupled with personal traits (self-efficacy, goal setting, personal responsibility, and optimism) lead to resiliency. Garmezy (1991) identifies three conditions which characterize resiliency in children: personal attitudes and beliefs; sound ties with the family; and adult caring, support, and direction from outside the family.

Implications for Principals and Teachers

Using the research on student resiliency, middle school teachers and principals can develop a program designed to prevent the effects of at-risk factors. Many of these elements are part of the true middle school philosophy and are found in the effective schools research.

(1) Provide a safe, orderly school environment with adult relationships for students which provide care, support, and direction for each student.

(2) Provide for programs which foster community and parent involvement, and encourage parents to support and become actively involved in the education and problems of their children. Special programs for parents on how to assist their children through the difficult period of transescence and on good parenting skills are a way to get parents involved.

(3) Provide programs for students which foster moral and ethical development, goal setting, and responsible citizenship. This emphasis on the development of the affective domain can help students gain internal control and self-efficacy, and take personal responsibility for their lives.

(4) Provide students with a school environment that expects and demands student academic success and quality work, and teachers who make learning exciting, challenging, and personally meaningful.

(5) Provide activities which demonstrate that success in school comes from hard work rather than luck. Offering rewards and encouragement, emphasizing time-on-task, and matching student abilities with learning activities provide students with evidence of success and feelings of personal accomplishment and satisfaction. Success in academics or other activities builds self-esteem and self-confidence, and the positive behaviors and attitudes which lead to success in the present are the same attributes needed for future (lifelong) success.

(6) Provide developmentally responsive educational programs and a wide variety of exploratory courses and extracurricular activities to stimulate student interest in sports, hobbies, clubs, the fine arts, and other such areas where students can attain personal enjoyment and enrichment.

(7) Provide instructional activities which call for the use of cooperative learning to promote academic and interpersonal success.

(8) Provide a classroom atmosphere where teachers treat students with respect, trust, and love. Being patient and open-minded, yet firm, demonstrates caring and support. School rules are enforced fairly and evenly and are posted in classrooms and explained to the students at the beginning of the school year.

(9) Provide for a smooth transition from elementary school to the middle school. Most dropouts decide to leave school in the later elementary grades or in the middle school years. Good counseling programs, advisor/advisee programs, interdisciplinary teaching teams, and programs which educate and encourage parents to support their children and inform them of the key role they play all help in this transition.

Programs That Work

In studying programs at the best schools for at-risk students, Ogden and

Germinario (1994) discovered some general characteristics of effective programs in elementary and middle schools. According to these authors, these programs are "comprehensive and intensive" (p. 72), they begin with ways to identify at-risk students, and they provide instructional strategies and school programs which promote success in school. These programs help students become self-motivated, create interest in continued learning, and alleviate feelings of isolation. Principals are the major driving and sustaining force behind these successful at-risk programs. Their leadership and belief in creating programs for at-risk students are essential for program success and teacher commitment.

According to Ogden and Germinario (1994) successful at-risk programs have the following components:

(1) Teachers are trained to teach their academic disciplines but are also trained by school guidance counselors in teaching in the affective domain.

(2) Teachers give strong, personal attention to students and "create a feeling of nurturing and belonging that is often absent from the home and school experiences of at-risk students" (p. 72).

(3) Teachers encourage parental support and involvement. "Special care should be given to accommodate access to the school for the parents of at-risk students. Parenting classes, home visits, and a recognition of parental responsibilities in educating their children are examples of bringing parents into the mainstream" (p. 72).

(4) Teachers are trained in identifying at-risk factors and the intervention strategies necessary for student success.

(5) Teachers take the time and use their skills "to build relationships of trust and respect with at-risk children and their families" (p. 72).

(6) Teachers implement programs for at-risk students as they are designed, carefully monitor student progress, and regularly evaluate the program's impact.

(7) Teachers have assistance from professional personnel in the community such as social workers, psychologists, substance abuse counselors, and medical professionals.

(8) Teachers have principal, superintendent, and school board support and are given the necessary resources to carry out the goals of the at-risk program.

Suggestions from national study councils and organizations should be utilized in the development of an at-risk program. The Accelerated Schools Project (cited in George and Alexander, 1993) recommends developing at-risk programs which focus on promoting high expectations from teachers and parents for student success, setting specific rules and regulations for students to follow in classrooms and deadlines for projects and homework, and expecting that all students in the school can and will be brought to a certain level of competency through a common core academic program. Many of these components are found in the research on effective schools.

Results from the Effective Parenting Information for Children (EPIC) organization (cited in George and Alexander, 1993) found at-risk students to have positive gains in self-confidence and self-concept, and improved behavior in school when teachers concentrated their efforts in the following areas: building self-esteem and self-concept, enforcing rules and regulations and instructing students on their rights and responsibilities as well as those of others, and teaching decision making and problem solving skills.

The Council on College Level Services (1991), in an effort to have more at-risk middle school children enroll in advanced placement courses in high school, advocates that middle school teachers and administrators work with their high school counterparts to develop a curriculum which utilizes individualized instruction and learning materials, individualized learning plans for students, diagnostic instruments to assess student learning preferences and skill levels, and mentoring groups. Mastery learning models, contract grading, and computers are a few of the ways to individualize instruction. This program is specifically designed to address the cognitive growth of disadvantaged minority students.

Dropout prevention programs, such as the Syracuse Stay in School Partnership Project (cited in George and Alexander, 1993), focus on preventing at-risk students in middle schools from leaving school early. This is a collaborative program involving schools, a university, and the state department of education. The goal is to keep these students in school for high school graduation. Pulling students out of the classroom, it is thought, further isolates students already alienated from school. All students receive instruction within the classroom with more diversified teaching techniques and learning materials to increase interest and to provide challenges based on their abilities. Peer tutoring programs provide assistance from "friends" in a nonthreatening atmosphere, and "teachers form peer support groups around at-risk students so that the students develop positive interaction patterns (friendships)" (George and Alexander, 1993, p. 19).

Cooperative effort between parents, administrators, teachers, and students is deemed an essential part of helping at-risk students stay in school. George and Alexander (1993) describe one program using this joint approach. Students and their parents attend a two-evening seminar at the beginning of the school year which "is designed to involve student and parent(s) in 'contracting' for school improvement. Session one focuses on (1) identifying the problem at school, (2) getting organized at school and home, and (3) developing a realistic action plan to which both make a commitment" (p. 20). The second session focuses on improving the self-esteem of children, testing procedures and helpful hints, and reviewing the contract with the parent and the student to make sure the problem has been clearly identified and that both parties have a realistic plan to solve it.

The Role of Extracurricular Activities in Programs That Work

In the best schools research, particular care is given to providing students with a wide array of extracurricular activities that extend student learning opportunities. In these enrichment activities, both teachers and administrators become actively involved, and through their involvement, the idea of cooperation and teamwork is fostered among students (Ogden and Germinario, 1994). Extracurricular activities are limited only by facilities and fiscal resources, available scheduling time, and the number of adults with expertise and time for supervision. Examples of extracurricular activities are intramural programs consisting of a variety of team and individual sports; a fine arts program of band, chorus, drama, art, drawing, dance, and creative writing; and clubs centered around foreign language, drama, math, chess, gardening, ceramics, stocks and bonds, and the computer. Many of these activities can be developed into mini-courses and become part of the exploratory curriculum and the physical education program. Principals, teachers, parents, and community members participate in these activities as sponsors, judges, referees, coaches, and team members. These adults model sportsmanship, fair play, and team spirit.

Extracurricular activities can also be designed to help specific student populations although participation should not be limited to those found to be at-risk. These activities, be they clubs or mini-courses, should be directed by qualified professionals. Topics can include food and nutrition, prenatal and infant care, child abuse, parents with substance abuse problems or who are incarcerated, study skills, and the role and responsibilities of siblings charged with primary care (Reed et al., 1995).

SUBSTANCE ABUSE PROGRAMS IN PROGRAMS THAT WORK

Substance abuse in society and in schools is growing despite massive efforts to curtail it. Ogden and Germinario (1994) report the following research on substance abuse (p. 83):

(1) Two-thirds of all teenagers will use drugs before high school graduation.

(2) Teenagers can become addicted to drugs in less than six months.

(3) Most unwanted teen pregnancies result from one or both partners being under the influence of a substance.

(4) Substances are involved in two out of three suicides. Suicide is the leading cause of death among middle school students.

(5) Substance abuse is a major contributor to school failure and dropout.

Schools cannot ignore substance abuse, but they cannot be expected to solve the problem alone. Parents and community agencies must assist schools in their efforts to prevent student use of drugs. Principals and physical education teachers can design a health and physical education program designed to educate students on the harmful effects of drugs which includes community agencies and parents as part of the instructional team (Kowalski, 1996). Ogden and Germinario (1994) believe the problem of substance use to be so complex that a multifaceted approach may be more effective. In these programs, principals must take the lead in designing and coordinating program goals and objectives. At the same time, teacher support and cooperation are essential for success. They list the following components of an effective program:

(1) Training the entire school staff to be knowledgeable of the signs of substance use

(2) Teaching the negative impact of drugs on the individual, the family, and society

(3) Creating and strictly enforcing policies which send the message to students, parents, and community that drug use will not be tolerated

(4) Having procedures in place to work with parents and community agencies when students are caught using drugs

(5) Teaching decision making, free-choice, and conflict resolution skills to students to help them resist peer and peer group pressure to use drugs

(6) Providing opportunities for students and parents to seek help for students or their peers using drugs

(7) Providing help and support (on an individual and a group basis) for students seeking to refuse drugs and for those returning from treatment

As with any other school-related program, parent involvement and support is critical. The school should involve parents in the formation of drug prevention policies in order to ensure parental cooperation. Educational programs on drugs for parents should be conducted annually as should an evaluation of the success of the drug prevention program. Parent training should be identical to teacher training so as to provide a comprehensive knowledge of drugs, their dangers and effects, and the signs of drug use.

Parents who have a thorough understanding of the need for and the content of the program are more likely to assist their children and the school in combating drug use. Community and law enforcement agencies should take part in the drug education program.

Remedial Students

Remedial education in the middle school can be defined as a structured process which identifies the educational, social, and emotional needs of students, and then provides adequate and relevant programs and experiences to address these needs. Remediation may be needed for those students who are willing and able to learn, but have difficulties which are different from those of special needs children. Remediation may also be needed for students having social and/or emotional problems which impact their ability to function to full potential in the cognitive domain. Remedial education, therefore, is based first on correct diagnosis and then on remediation of what went wrong.

Research indicates that remedial measures are successful when solid teaching principles are applied in a positive learning climate which continuously rewards success and effort. Essential to successful remediation efforts are enthusiastic teachers who are patient and caring, who use the experience and expertise of other teachers, who use teacher teams to reinforce remedial work, and who have the full support of the principal who must provide the necessary time and resources to accomplish the task. However, it must be emphasized that the primary component for successful remediation is the teacher who acts as the learning style diagnostician, has a thorough knowledge of the basic principles underlying the learning process, and is familiar with a wide variety of teaching techniques.

Remediation becomes necessary when students fail to learn the material presented by the teacher be it through lecture, inquiry, demonstration, reading, or any other teaching method. Learning occurs when experiences match the needs of the student, when the content is relevant to the values held by the student, and when there is a relationship with the student's previous experiences (transfer of training). The learning environment has an important impact on student learning as does the student's ability to see the present and future value of the learning experience (Dunn and Dunn, 1979).

Other factors associated with learning include the student's readiness to learn and the time it takes the student to learn newly presented material. Piaget (1973) notes that readiness to learn and the time required to learn depend on a mixture of variables. These include the student's cognitive stage of development; physical and social maturity; past learning experiences; value system; the importance and relevance placed on learning; and the support received for learning from peers, parents, teachers, and friends. The self-concept is also important in learning. If students perceive they can learn and they have been successful in prior learning, they will learn. Being able to make choices among different learning activities also promotes student learning. The ability on the part of the teacher to diagnose the learning style preference(s) of the student can greatly facilitate remedial instruction.

Remedial teachers in the middle school must keep in mind that transescents are between the concrete operations stage and the formal operations stage. Although the formal operations stage encompasses ages 11 through adult, only about 15 percent of middle school learners reach this stage by age 14 (Milgram, 1992). Consequently, learning, for the most part, needs to be compatible with the concrete operations stage which allows students to think logically about concrete objects and be directly involved with the learning content. Active learning techniques, including videos, manipulatives, and instructional activities that are not too abstract, are most appropriate for the majority of middle school students. In addition, peer interaction facilitates the learning of basic concepts and generalizations and promotes the social development of transescents as well. (See Chapter 1 for a more in-depth discussion of cognitive development in the transescent.)

METHODS FOR REMEDIATION

An instructional method called adaptive instruction which is used for regular instruction by some teachers can also be effective for remediation. Adaptive instruction occurs when the teaching activities are adapted to the needs of students. Although difficult to facilitate in large classes, adaptive instruction targets the capabilities of the learner through materials that allow students to pace their own learning and that appeal to their interests. Students help set their own learning goals and take part (with the teacher) in evaluating their own progress. Adaptive instruction builds on the strengths and knowledge of the learner, caters to the student's learning style, and focuses on the interest of the learner, all of which are important in remedial efforts (Strother, 1985).

Reciprocal teaching is another technique which can be successfully used to remediate student learning. This technique is very effective with small groups or pairs of low-achieving students in middle schools (Palinscar and Brown, 1984). Interacting with peers, they learn to respect the opinions and ideas of others and work together to achieve a common goal. Used primarily with reading, students enhance their comprehension by asking each other questions and clarifying problems as they read and then forming questions and summarizing what they have read.

Comic books and sports magazines are effective remedial reading materials for middle school youth. Used to stimulate initial student interest in reading and in some cases address the ability level of the student, comic books, sports magazines, and similar materials can be used effectively to increase comprehension and sustain interest in reading. The *Classic Series* of Dell Comic Books provides a rudimentary historical foundation for social studies and English and sparks interest in history and literature.

Chapter I programs and other federally funded programs provide remedial teachers in reading and mathematics for both elementary and middle schools. Formally known as Title I, Chapter I is a pull-out program where small groups of students are taken from regular classrooms into separate rooms for remediation. Several problems, however, seem to exist with this approach to remedial work. First, these slow learners are labeled as such because of the nature of the program itself and second, gains made in elementary school tend to dissipate by grade six or middle school. Some critics also say the program is disjointed in that remedial instruction often does not coincide with regular classroom instruction (Allington, Boxer, and Broikou, 1987).

In a national survey, basal readers were found by Irvin and Connors (1989) to be the most popular way to teach remediation in reading for sixth, seventh, and eighth grade students. Basal programs also have their critics (Peters, 1990) who maintain that emphasis is placed on stories, not content, and that these programs are more skills-oriented than other programs. However, it is because of these criticisms and others that basals are valuable for remediation. These programs are developmentally appropriate for varying ability levels, emphasize basic skill development, have workbooks and enrichment materials, and provide tests at the end of study units.

Mastery learning models are also effective in remediation. Henson (1993) notes that mastery learning models allow teachers of remedial students to diagnose the learning difficulty, provide for student-paced learning that is individually based, allow for adequate time for the student to master the material, provide for frequent testing evaluation of student learning, and provide enrichment materials for reinforcement or alternative learning strategies. Mastery learning, as already noted, is an effective teaching technique suitable for all students, not just those who are at-risk.

Peer teaching or tutoring is another way to provide remediation in the classroom. Walberg (1990) notes that in this approach highly effective learning results for both the tutor and the tutee. Not only do students increase learning in academic contents, but they improve self-confidence, human relations skills, and attitude toward learning. Another positive attribute of peer tutoring is the individualized instruction students receive. Students become more involved in their own learning and learning becomes less threatening since peers are more understanding of mistakes and learner difficulties. Cross-age or multi-age tutoring works equally well and can be accomplished in middle schools with various grouping configurations such as a school-within-a-school approach or with representatives of students at different grade levels on one team (George and Alexander, 1993). These authors present the "Four Ts of Tutoring" discussed by Smith (1980) which carefully outline a four-phase model clearly delineating the tutoring responsibilities of the peer and the role of the teacher:

(1) Testing—the teacher matches the learning skills of the tutor to those of the tutee to make sure the tutor's skills are "slightly" higher than the tutee.

(2) Training—the teacher discusses with the tutor the learning characteristics of the tutee, the materials to be used for tutoring, how the tutee should behave in the learning environment, the importance of pacing and positive reinforcement, and the need for understanding of the learner's difficulties and frustrations.

(3) Tutoring—the tutor begins actual instruction after the training process ends. Instruction lasts for approximately 30 minutes and consists of three parts: presentation, recitation or drill, and practice.

(4) Translating—tutors evaluate the session through answering a series of questions designed to assess the effectiveness of the lesson.

Smith (1980) notes that tutors gain as much from the "Four Ts of Tutoring" as the tutee through listening, speaking, writing, reading, and teaching.

Learning centers or stations have been part of middle school instruction for years for fast learners and for enrichment, but they can also be used with learners needing remediation. They can be used for alternative learning activities, additional in-depth work, reinforcement, and motivation; and they can be teacher-supervised or peer-supervised. Wiles and Bondi (1993) note that "a learning *station* implies *how* a student learns (auditory, visual, kinesthetic), whereas a learning *center* implies *what* the student will learn (grammar, fractions)" (p. 117). Combining both station and center activities can greatly facilitate the remedial process.

Learning activity packets (LAPs) can be used effectively for remediation. The basic components consist of pretest, objectives, learning and enrichment activities, and posttest. Some LAPs have individual objective completion tests for students who need help on individual objectives, or students may work through each objective in the packet. LAPs are ideal for teachers who work with several students needing remedial work since the objective completion tests allow teachers to constantly monitor the progress of several students at once.

Computers and their various programs are effective for drill and practice because they are individually paced, have different levels of difficulty, and provide test questions and answers for immediate feedback. Records of student responses and test scores are recorded for teacher monitoring and progress evaluation. It should be noted that the effectiveness of computer-assisted instruction lies in the quality of the programs used for instruction and not in the computer hardware itself.

Simulation, according to Magney (1990), provides cognitive, motivational, and attitudinal benefits for students who use computers for regular, remedial, or reinforcement/enrichment learning. Most simulations reinforce memorization and promote problem solving as they allow learners to live out roles or solve a variety of problems. One advantage of simulation which is highly appropriate for remediation is the repetition aspect which allows learners to repeat the experience several times without teacher supervision. The "what if" factor allows for different conditions and alternative situations which promote learner motivation.

Mentor programs provide students with skilled, caring adults who can make learning relevant to real life situations. Parents, retirees, and community members provide general tutoring or specific expertise tutoring to students needing remediation or enrichment and reinforcement (Wiles and Bondi, 1993).

Matching instruction to individual learning styles is a key factor in making remedial work successful for middle school students. In the area of multiple intelligences (MI), Armstrong (1994) relates that "teachers and administrators need to serve as 'MI strength detectives' in the lives of students facing difficulties in school" (p. 138). Students with difficulties in school often do not succeed because of limitations in specific intelligence areas and they will bypass these obstacles by using their more highly developed or preferred intelligence. The use of MI Theory is just as applicable for regular classroom instruction as it is for remedial work with the difference being in the way the remedial work is carefully tailored to the needs of the student or small groups of students. Armstrong, in his *Multiple Intelligences in the Classroom*, provides examples of MI remedial topics for teachers, as well as a guide for developing remedial strategies which are compatible with lesson plans and units of instruction for regular classrooms.

Identifying and matching instruction with the learning styles of students and the teaching styles of teachers for remedial work has been a topic of the work of Dunn (1991). Dunn notes the importance of having teachers, tutors, or mentors with teaching styles which coincide with the learning styles of their students to maximize instructional efforts. On the other hand, O'Neil (1991) notes that teachers must redesign their instruction and "learn" new styles for effective instructional outcomes.

The work on psychological type by Jung (cited in Johnson, 1987) is relevant to remedial work with students in the matching of the instructional mode and activities with the four primary mental processes of individuals (sensing, intuition, thinking, and feeling). Drawing on the work of Jung, Johnson states that each person has a preferred way of receiving information that is developed in early life. As one matures, one relies on the preferred mental process more and more for informational intake. Behavior patterns develop and can be grouped into one of sixteen different types of behaviors. The psychological types differ in the way each type prefers to learn and teach. For example, *extroverts* prefer to be active and learn while speaking or doing while *introverts* reflect on and analyze data internally. *Sensory learners* need direct contact and learning comes from manipulation, while *intuitive learners* make leaps in learning and intuitively "know." *Thinkers* are rational and enjoy logical analysis while *feelers* become emotionally involved and take values into consideration when making decisions. All sixteen of these psychological behavior patterns which are formed from the different combinations of these preferences have important implications for both teaching and learning in remedial and regular classroom settings.

LEADERSHIP FOR AT-RISK STUDENTS AND REMEDIAL EDUCATION: CASE STUDIES

Mary Anne Charron, principal of Trickum Middle School in Lilburn, Georgia, is a research-oriented administrator with a vision whose philosophy concerning at-risk students and programs at Trickum encompasses and coincides with much of the literature-based descriptors of what it takes to meet the needs of at-risk students. At Trickum Middle School, a National Blue Ribbon School, a National School of Excellence, and a four-time Georgia School of Excellence, at-risk students in the eighth grade are identified by their scores on the Iowa Test of Basic Skills, teacher referrals, and previous school performance records. These students, approximately twenty-five, are then assigned to two teachers in a self-contained classroom where they receive concentrated instruction in reading and writing, the two essential skills for success. Daily instruction in social studies and science supplement the other two core courses with exploratory activities assigned to meet state middle school requirements.

The Success School, as it is called, has its own budget and raises additional monies through school- and parent-assisted programs. Students are motivated to succeed through teacher praise, recognition by peers, and a special incentives program which allows for pizza parties, field trips, and other social-oriented rewards honoring student achievement within the goals and objectives of the Success School.

Central to the success of this program are its teachers. Charron is quick to point out that the positive mind-set, the devotion of these teachers to their students, is the essential factor which creates the climate for student learning and success. Teachers, Charron maintains have to "really want to help these students, go the extra mile, and believe these students can and will succeed given time, effort, and constant opportunities to succeed." Many of these students have low self-esteem, lack positive home role models, have a history of poor academic performance, and display a poor attitude toward school. For the most part, this negative attitude stems from a lack of school success, and the initial challenge is to build a program oriented around praise, success, and self-esteem. "Nothing succeeds like success," Charron says, "and these teachers begin from day one to focus on building positive self-esteem."

Success School teachers are laudably unique in many ways. They use diagnostic measures as a basis to plan their curriculum and they know each student personally. Through personalization, they get to know the students' backgrounds, their personal problems and concerns, and their learning strengths and weaknesses. Skilled in a variety of teaching and student learning strategies, including Howard Gardner's Multiple Intelligences theory, these teachers team together to meet the students' individual needs in the truest sense. For example, both individualized and group learning play a major role in their instruction. Peer tutoring and healthy group competition stimulate learning and rewards are provided to all students for their effort and accomplishments. While individual success is praised and is important, group work, promoting the need for and the importance of cooperative effort, is equally praised and is an important part of the instructional repertoire.

The use of technology, according to Charron, plays a major role in helping at-risk students succeed. Computers and computer programs are a "major plus in the success of these students," she states. Trickum's business partnership with Apple Computers, Inc. creates a school-wide technology team whose members include Success School teachers. Computer software is used to monitor the progress of at-risk students as they advance through learning modules which are teacher-selected for each individual student. Computers serve as a primary and reinforcing teaching tool depending on the student's need and skill level. Whether it's the use of technology or teacher-led instruction, the emphasis is on student success; reward and praise; and promoting a positive, highly supportive environment for students. Charron adds that teachers can be task-oriented, stress the importance of academics, and have no-nonsense classrooms "if they set the stage from day one." Firm yet caring, serious about learning yet rewarding and praising, Success School teachers promote these attributes with their at-risk students and find an eager and responsive audience.

"Parental support is essential for maximum success of any at-risk program" Charron relates. A structured parent involvement program at Trickum Middle School complements the efforts of the Success School program. Parents are introduced to the goals and objectives of the program prior to the beginning of school through a structured orientation program conducted by the teachers and the principal. The theme of cooperative effort between the home and school is stressed with information provided on how parents can reinforce the objectives of the school in a home environment. Program activities vary based on parent interest, but usually include the following topics:

- parental skills essential for promoting responsibility, building student self-esteem, and emphasizing the importance of school and learning
- home environment variables which reinforce school goals which include the importance of doing one's best and completing homework on time (Parents can promote these goals by scheduling quiet time and providing space and materials for their children to complete school assignments.)
- respect for the rights of others, others' property, and the talents, skills, and contributions of others
- characteristics of the middle school learner and their needs and concerns as they develop physically, emotionally, socially, and intellectually
- peer relationships, the influence of peers and peer groups, and the duties and responsibilities of good citizenship
- parents as tutors, as "friends," as confidants, and as counselors

Communication between teachers and parents is essential in this mutual support network for students. Teachers take the responsibility for having daily or weekly contact with parents via telephone calls, notes, or face-to-face contact either at school or at home. Parents are urged to maintain ongoing communication with the teachers and the school counselor, who is an important member of the at-risk team.

Often, at-risk students need instruction in good study habits, the role of good citizenship, and self-discipline. Self-discipline is a key factor in school and life success. Self-control is taught and is based on understanding the limits of one's rights and freedom and the respect for the rights of others, including teachers and other adults. Rights and responsibilities of students and others are emphasized through the enforcement of school rules and through modeling by teachers. Topics of freedom, rights, and responsibilities are areas of discussion and study and focus on applying school rules to students' conduct. Emphasis is placed on the following:

- respect for rights of others to learn, to be safe, and to be free to express their ideas and opinions

- respect for private and public property
- appropriate conduct for settling disputes, disagreements, and different points of view
- courteous and appropriate behavior

Study habits include the importance of personal commitment and pride in doing one's best, completing work on time, and the value of individual and group success through hard work and accepting responsibility for one's own learning. Setting personal goals, managing one's time, and commitment to tasks through the setting of personal priorities are additional habits taught to at-risk students. These habits, also taught to parents, are central to promoting student success. Classroom and home environments which are conducive to learning demonstrate respect for and the importance of education. Charron comments that parents are encouraged to look at school as their child's work. When parents view school in the same light as they do their own work, "our job becomes easier because parents can make a direct connection between the importance of their work habits and those habits students need in order to succeed."

Plans are being made to expand the Success School downward to grades seven and six. Why start an at-risk program at grade eight? Charron responds that with a county-wide no social promotion policy, it's important that eighth grade students have the skills necessary to move on to grade nine with their peers. Resources and classroom space are also considerations she must take into consideration when expanding the Success School. Additional and adequate instructional materials and self-contained space in a school with over 1,600 students are major factors to be resolved in program expansion. In addition, the number of teachers who are willing to teach these at-risk students is an all-important matter that must first be resolved.

Getting teachers to understand the need for and support a special program like the Success School is not difficult. However, staffing the program is another matter. To get the Success School funded and staffed took some time. Charron's approach was to first talk with individual teachers with the help of her three assistant principals, stressing the need for a program designed to help at-risk students. Well-versed in the research literature, she and her administrative staff presented the advantages for students who received special, indepth instruction from teachers who were both interested in teaching these students and adequately funded to do so. The topic was discussed on a broader level at both faculty meetings and at interdisciplinary teacher team meetings in order to create interest and provide fact-based information.

At the same time, the need to assist at-risk students was a topic of consideration for the school's School Improvement Planning Committee comprised of teachers representing core academic teams from each grade level, exploratory teacher representives, special education teachers, a school counselor, and the principal. Charged with developing the school's yearly improvement plan, this committee explored the research on at-risk students, investigated the processes used to identify these students, and studied successful at-risk program configurations. Their recommendation was developed and was based on the specific needs of Trickum Middle School students. The plan was then brought to the school's governing body for consideration and final approval. Staffing the program was accomplished by calling for teacher volunteers. The volunteer process was a crucial component in that teachers had to want to work with at-risk students. They would be expected to teach reading, writing, and mathematics skills as well as science and social studies. Charron maintains that success comes from having the right combination of teachers who are well-versed in subject matter and skill development techniques, know how to use and apply technology, know how to use both individualized and group instruction strategies, and have the necessary fiscal and material resources. Finally, she adds, "administrator support and continuous commitment to the program are essential." Teachers in this program need adequate funds, moral support, and appreciation for their difficult work. All of this has to come from the principal and the administrative team.

West Jackson Middle School's principal, Walker Davis, relates that their Jackson Ultimate Motivation Program (JUMP) "is to provide a positive learning environment to at-risk students in which positive self-esteem is developed through continuous success and, as a consequence, a more positive attitude toward school and learning." This program, along with their PALS program (Positive Attitude for Life Skills) discussed in Chapter 7, provides a two-pronged approach to helping at-risk students achieve. Davis notes the PALS program emphasizes the development of affective characteristics and working with immediate personal problems, while JUMP students develop self-confidence through an emphasis on success in academics. Building and monitoring good self-esteem are important parts of the program. Davis states, "To be successful in anything you have to feel good about yourself and about others and that boils down to having a healthy self-esteem."

Students eligible for the JUMP program are those who score at or below the twenty-fifth percentile on the Iowa Test of Basic Skills (ITBS) for reading and mathematics, are recommended by teachers, have a documented history of behavior problems, may or may not have been retained at a grade level, and have an interview and a recommendation from a school counselor. There are no special education students in the JUMP program since the two programs have separate missions. Davis views students in the JUMP program "as those who are in intensive care. They need constant, personal attention from qualified and caring professionals to get them back into the regular schooling process. Special education students, on the other hand, are on a life-support system which is often turned off when they exit school. Intensive care gets JUMP students ready for a healthy re-entry into the regular classroom."

The JUMP curriculum is based on the individual and collective needs of students and is academically oriented. Test scores on the ITBS and teacher and counselor records serve as the basis for program planning which is done yearly to "personalize the at-risk program," says Davis. "Programs based on intuition just won't work. The value lies in truly knowing the student." An Individual Plan for Improvement (IPI) is designed for each student based on reading and mathematics levels. Students assist the teacher, paraprofessional, and school counselor in developing their IPI goals to help them be more responsible for their own learning and to make these goals realistically attainable. Monies are available for supplementary materials; however, standard textbooks and teacher-made materials form the nucleus of instruction. Emphasis is first placed on gaining student confidence through the successful completion of small tasks or projects. Often, this means the teacher helps students apply prior knowledge to real-life situations rather than using abstract or unfamiliar examples. Computers and software provide students with individual enrichment and tutorial work with computer programs selected for each student based on their IPI. "Enthusiasm and success must be attained from day-one if the program is to reap its expected rewards. Students must get excited about learning and find it fun. Learning must be personally meaningful if you are to get their attention. That's the real key."

There are approximately 30 students in the JUMP program. They come from grades six, seven, and eight and are taught in a self-contained classroom with a teacher and a paraprofessional who is trained specifically to help at-risk students. Students participate in physical education and exploratory classes with their grade level peers and they are assessed by their respective teachers of these classes. Instruction in the core academics is provided by the JUMP teacher who works closely with each student's respective teacher team.

As students work on their academic skills, they also work on building self-esteem. PALS teachers work closely with the JUMP staff to provide on-going information about student problems and concerns and these two groups of teachers work together to develop topics and materials for use in the affective part of the curriculum. This close working relationship pays high dividends, says Davis. The affective curriculum includes topics such as conflict resolution, rights and responsibilities, respect for property and individual freedoms, study skills, school rules and regulations, and good citizenship and social behavior. Independent study and group work teach the importance of individual work and effort and its application to teamwork and cooperative coexistence. Guest lectures are provided by representatives from different community agencies. An official from the police department, for example, talks to students about of the individual in society and respect for the rights and property of others.

Strong parent involvement is a part of the JUMP program. As at Trickum Middle School, parents receive an orientation on the goals and objectives of JUMP and are encouraged to be active partners in ensuring their children's success. Parents are surveyed regarding their interests in learning how to help their child succeed at school, with other topics decided upon by the teacher, school counselor, and principal. Program activities vary from year to year based on parent needs and interests, but usually include the following:

- characteristics of the transescent learner as they develop socially, emotionally, physically, and intellectually
- parental responsibility to help their child to be successful in school (this includes positive reinforcement for school success, the importance of school for life success, regular time and place for homework, and daily inquiry about performance at school and issues which cause conflict or distract them from schoolwork)
- parents as friends and confidants (the importance of frequent informal chats, doing things together, and helping students with homework and school projects are important for building a sound communication system between parent and child)

Members of the JUMP staff communicate constantly with parents through telephone calls, letters, and conferences (both at school and in the home). When problems arise, parent, student, teacher, and counselor meet to resolve the issue which may or may not be contractual in nature. This approach helps to teach the students responsibility for their own actions, addresses the real problem of the issue rather than the symptom, and lets the student know that home and school are united in providing assistance.

Davis also notes the importance of the teachers who are responsible for teaching these at-risk students. "Teachers who show personal excitement, who care, who can empathize with these students, and who can be firm in their interactions with them are an important part of a successful program." Teachers, he adds, must really enjoy working with these special needs students and maintain a classroom where learning is fun, exciting, and relevant, but at the same time serious and task-oriented. The teacher is responsible for setting the atmosphere, must work well as a team member, and must be highly skilled in teaching the basics. Davis says that at West Jackson Middle School, "the object of the at-risk program is to get these students into a regular environment as quickly as possible with the necessary skills and confidence to function with their peers."

REFERENCES

Alessi, S. M. and S. R. Trollip. 1991. *Computer-Based Instruction, Methods and Development*. Englewood Cliffs, NJ: Prentice Hall.

Allington, R. L., N. Boxer, and K. Broikou. 1987. "Jeremy, Remedial Reading, and Subject Area Classes," *Journal of Reading*, 30:643–645.

Armstrong, T. 1994. *Multiple Intelligences in the Classroom*. Alexandria, VA: Association for Supervision and Curriculum Development.

Benard, B. 1993. "Fostering Resiliency in Kids," *Educational Leadership*, 51(3):44–48.

Bergmann, S. 1989. *Discipline and Guidance: A Thin Line in the Middle School: What At-Risk Students Say about Middle Level School Discipline and Teaching*. Reston, VA: National Association of Secondary School Principals.

Berryman, S. E. 1993. "Learning for the Workplace," in *Review of Research in Education, Vol. 19*. L. Darling-Hammond, ed. Washington, DC: American Educational Research Association, pp. 343–401.

Blumenthal, C., G. V. Holmes, and L. Pound. 1991. "Academic Success for Students At-Risk," in *Youth at Risk*. R. C. Morris, ed. Lancaster, PA: Technomic Publishing Co., Inc.

Braddock, J. H. and J. M. McPartland. 1993. "Education of Early Adolescents," in *Review of Research in Education, Vol. 19*. L. Darling-Hammond, ed. Washington, DC: American Educational Research Association., pp. 135–170.

Brophy, J. 1983. "Classroom Organization and Management," *Elementary School Journal*, 37:110–113.

Carroll, S. R. and D. Carroll. 1994. *How Smart Schools Get and Keep Community Support*. Bloomington, IN: National Education Service.

Council on College Level Services. 1991. *Advanced Placement Pre-High School Initiative Committee Summary and Recommendations*. New York: The College Board.

Cunningham, R. D. 1991. "Modeling Mastery Teaching through Classroom Supervision," *National Association of Secondary School Principals Bulletin*, 75(536):83–87.

Dunn, R. 1991. "Rita Dunn Answers Questions on Learning Styles," *Educational Leadership*, 48:15–19.

Dunn, R. and K. Dunn. 1979. *Teaching Students through Their Individual Learning Style: A Practical Approach*. Reston, VA: Reston Publishing Company.

Epstein, J. and K. Salinas. 1992. *Promising Programs in the Middle Grades*. Reston, VA: National Association of Secondary School Principals.

Gardner, H. 1993. *Multiple Intelligences: The Theory in Practice*. New York: Harper Collins Publishers, Inc.

Garmezy, N. 1991. "Resiliency and Vulnerability to Adverse Developmental Outcomes Associated with Poverty," *American Behavioral Scientist*, 34(4):416–430.

Geisert, G. and R. Dunn. 1991. "Effective Use of Computers: Assignments Based on Individual Learning Style," *The Clearing House*, 64(4):219–223.

George, P. S. and W. M. Alexander, 1993. *The Exemplary Middle School*. Second edition. Fort Worth, TX: Harcourt Brace Jovanovich College Publishers.

Good, T. L. and J. Brophy. 1987. *Looking in Classrooms*. Second edition. New York: Harper and Row.

Good, T. L. and D. J. Stipek. 1983. "Individual Differences in the Classroom: A Psychological Perspective," in *Individual Differences and Common Curriculum*. G. D. Fenstermacher, ed. Eighty-Second Yearbook of the National Society for the Study of Education, Part I, Chicago: University of Chicago Press.

Good, T. L., B. J. Reyes, D. A. Grouws, and C. M. Mulryan. 1990–1991. "Using Work-Groups in Mathematics Instruction," *Educational Leadership*, 47(4):56–62.

Hackman, D. C. 1996. "Student-Led Conferences at the Middle Level: Promoting Student Responsibility," *National Association of Secondary School Principals Bulletin*, 80(578):31–36.

Hafner, A., S. Ingels, B. Schneider, D. Stevenson, and J. Owings. 1990. *National Education Longitudinal Study of 1988: A Profile of the American Eighth Grader*. Washington, DC: U.S. Department of Education, Office of Educational Research and Implementation.

Henson, K. T. 1993. *Methods and Strategies for Teaching in Secondary and Middle Schools*. Second edition. White Plains, NY: Longman.

Hewlett, S. A. 1991. *When the Bough Breaks: The Cost of Neglecting Our Children*. New York: Basic Books.

Hodgkinson, H. 1991. "Reform versus Reality," *Phi Delta Kappan*, 72:623–627.

Irvin, J. L. and N. A. Connors. 1989. "Reading Instruction in Middle Level Schools: Results of a US Survey," *Journal of Reading*, 32:306–311.

Johnson, L. D., P. M. O'Malley, and J. G. Bachman. 1988. "Illicit Drug Use, Smoking, and Drinking by America's High School Students, College Students, and Young Adults," *Department of Health and Human Services Publication No. ADM 89–1062*. Washington, DC: Government Printing Office.

Johnson, V. R. 1987. "Learning Styles and Instructional Strategies," *Science Scope*, 10:12–14.

Kirst, M. W. and M. McLaughlin, M. 1990. *Rethinking Children's Policy: Implications for Educational Administration*. Bloomington, IN: Consortium on Educational Policy Studies (Indiana University).

Kowalski, T. J. 1996. *Public Relations in Educational Organizations: Practice in an Age of Information and Reform*. Englewood Cliffs, NJ: Merrill.

MacIver, D. 1990. "Meeting the Needs of Young Adolescents: Advisory Groups, Interdisciplinary Teaching Teams, and School Transition Programs," *Phi Delta Kappan*, 71(6):458–464.

Magney, J. 1990. "Game-Based Teaching," *Education Digest*, 60(5):54–57.

Marsh, H. W. 1990. "A Multidimensional, Hierarchical Model of Self-Concept: Theoretical and Empirical Justification," *Educational Psychology Review*, 2:77–172.

McPartland, J. M. and R. E. Slavin. 1990. *Increasing Achievement of At-Risk Students at Each Grade Level.* Policy Perspective, Office of Educational Research and Information, United States Department of Education.

Messick, R. G. and K. E. Reynolds. 1992. *Middle Level Curriculum in Action.* White Plains, NY: Longman.

Milgram, J. 1992. "A Portrait in Diversity: The Middle Level Student," in *Transforming Middle Level Education: Perspectives and Possibilities,* J. L. Irvin, ed. Boston, MA: Allyn & Bacon, pp. 16–27.

Ogbu, J. U. 1985. "Research Currents: Cultural-Ecological Influences on Minority School Learning," *Language Arts,* 62(8):60–69.

Ogbu, J. U. 1992. "Understanding Cultural Diversity and Learning," *Educational Researcher,* 21(8):5–14.

Ogden, E. H. and V. Germinario. 1994. *The Nation's Best Schools: Blueprints for Excellence. Volume 1, Elementary and Middle School.* Lancaster, PA: Technomic Publishing Co., Inc.

O'Neil, J. 1991. "Making Sense of Style," *Educational Leadership,* 48:4–9.

Palinscar, A. S. and A. L. Brown. 1984. "Reciprocal Teaching of Comprehension—Fostering and Monitoring Activities," *Cognition and Instruction,* 1:117–175.

Pallas, A., G. Natriello, and E. McDill. 1989. "The Changing Nature of the Disadvantaged Generation: Current Dimensions and Future Trends," *Educational Researcher,* 8(16):16–22.

Peters, C. W. 1990. "Content Knowledge in Reading: Creating a New Framework," in *Reading in the Middle School.* G. C. Duffy, ed. Second edition. Newark, DE: International Reading Association, pp. 63–80.

Piaget, J. 1973. *The Psychology of Intelligence.* Totwa, NJ: Littlefield, Adams.

Reed, D. F., J. H. McMillan, and R. H. McBee. 1995. "Defying the Odds: Middle Schools in High Risk Circumstances Who Succeed," *Middle School Journal,* 27(1):3–10.

Smith, L. 1980. "A Model for Cross-Age Tutoring," *Middle School Journal,* 9:26–27.

Squires, D. A., W. G. Huitt, and J. K. Segars. 1984. *Effective Schools and Classrooms: A Research-Based Perspective.* Alexandria, VA: Association for Supervision and Curriculum Development.

Strother, D. B. 1985. "Adapting Instruction to Individual Needs: An Eclectic Approach," *Phi Delta Kappan,* 67:308–311.

Thelan, H. 1960. *Education and the Human Quest.* New York: Harper & Row.

Toepfer, Jr., C. F. 1996. "Caring for Young Adolescents in an Ethnically Divided, Violent, Poverty-Stricken Society," *Middle School Journal,* 27(5):42–48.

Walberg, H. 1990. "Productive Teaching and Instruction: Assessing the Knowledge Base," *Phi Delta Kappan,* 71:470–478.

Ward, J. G. 1994. "The Demographic Politics and America's Schools: Struggles for Power and Justice," in *The New Politics of Race and Gender.* C. Marshall, ed. Washington, DC: Falmer Press.

Wiles, J. and J. Bondi. 1993. *The Essential Middle School.* Second edition. New York: Macmillan Publishing Co.

Winfield, L. F. 1991. "A Conceptual Framework," *Education and Urban Society,* 25(1):2–11.

CHAPTER 9

Schedules and Scheduling
for Quality Education

Scheduling of any kind is effective only to the extent that it helps support the mission and objectives of the school in which it occurs. Scheduling in the middle school is not only a method to organize instructional time to serve students but is the single most important component in the overall effectiveness of the school. Consequently, in quality-oriented middle schools, the schedule must fit and serve the program rather than the program fit and serve the schedule. Flexible time, within time blocks, is the most effective and efficient way to serve the needs of the interdisciplinary curriculum, team teaching, the advisor/advisee program, the exploratory program, at-risk and remedial students, and the other components of a quality-producing middle school. Flexible scheduling and block scheduling, or variations of the two, serve to bridge the gap between the elementary self-contained classroom with teachers structuring instructional time slots and the rigid, departmental approach of the high school which forces the instructional program into 50 or 55 minute time slots. The five most common middle school schedules are flexible scheduling, modular scheduling, flexible modular scheduling, block scheduling, and flexible block scheduling.

Since there is no one "right" way to design a flexible or flexible block schedule for the middle school, principals must consult with teachers on how best to schedule programs for *their* middle school. Consequently, the right schedule ultimately depends upon the complex needs of the students and the variety of instructional opportunities that is to be provided.

This chapter will provide examples of how the major components of the middle school fit into the five most common types of schedules found in effective, quality-producing middle schools. Charts and lists showing the major and minor considerations needed for scheduling will be presented as well. Samples of different scheduling configurations will be presented and pitfalls to avoid will accompany this section. Case studies of scheduling in effective middle schools will also be presented.

This chapter will focus on the following questions:

- What are the major purposes of scheduling?
- Why is selecting the right schedule important for middle schools?
- What are the primary concerns principals must consider when developing a schedule?
- Who should be involved in making scheduling decisions?
- What are the different kinds of scheduling configurations found in effective middle schools and why are they effective?
- How can these different scheduling configurations be developed?
- How can scheduling configurations be evaluated to determine if they meet the needs of students, teachers, and program demands?

QUALITY EDUCATION

The quality management theory of W. Edwards Deming (1986) holds that the practices of management and the structure of the organization, more than the people who work within the organization, cause the problems which decrease the organization's level of quality and service. Management is the cause, Deming (1993) says, of 90 percent of all the problems in an organization while the work force is responsible for only 10 percent of the problems. Deming notes that in education, one of the problems is the structure of the school and the ineffective use of the work force. Fragmentation of effort and lack of adequate time to perform work tasks lead to loss of quality outcomes. Canady and Rettig (1995a) relate that scheduling procedures are a valuable resource, and ones which are not often used, to promote quality instruction in schools. Depending on the type of school schedule used, the concerns of fragmented efforts and lack of adequate time to perform quality work functions become moot. A well-designed schedule ensures a more effective use of time, space, and both material and human resources. Such a schedule helps solve problems related to providing a smooth transition between comprehensive instructional programs, and it can accommodate new and varied instructional practices.

The major challenge today for those middle school principals seeking to instill the quality management principles of Deming (1986) is to know how to provide the necessary balance between the core curriculum, the exploratory curriculum, and the extracurricular activities program to meet the unique learning needs of their diverse student population (Erb, 1995). Quality instruction in middle schools comes about through the application of

Deming's Fourteen Points for Quality Management which makes the school more responsive to the needs of the customer (student) through inter-disciplinary teaching teams, self-managed work teams, and shared decision making. The key component in fostering collaborative leadership and promoting quality instruction in middle schools is providing teachers and learners the necessary time to meet the goals and objectives of middle school education.

Scheduling for Quality

Scheduling creates the organizational system which drives the instructional programs housed within the school. Jenkins and Jenkins (1995) note that when the instructional programs within a school do not deliver their expected outcomes, "chances are the problem lies within the system and not with the people doing the work" (p. 7). Infusing the quality philosophy into the middle school means that principals must believe in the middle school philosophy; identify the needs of their teachers, students, and parents; and help design a program that is developmentally appropriate for their students. This may mean altering or changing the scheduling practices currently in place.

Schedules reflect an arbitrary division of a school day into time blocks. In dividing up the instructional time, teachers and administrators must focus on how programs can best be scheduled to facilitate the goals of the middle school. George and Alexander (1993) suggest units of time should be varied in length and the manipulation of these time units should be based on how teams of teachers can function most effectively. *Time*, in scheduling middle school programs, can be thought of as blocks, periods, and modules. Combinations among these three time units can vary and can provide a wide array of different scheduling configurations. For example, modules, small time units, can be combined into a period or more, and periods can be combined into blocks, the largest time unit. Modules can also be combined into one or more time blocks. There is no *one* superior way of combining time units for a middle school program, but there is one "right" way of scheduling for each individual school. The right way is the best way for the school, its teachers, its instructional program, and its students.

Involving the Staff in Quality Scheduling

In quality middle schools, the total school staff is involved in scheduling. Craig (1995) relates that when middle school staff members are actively involved in developing a flexible or block schedule they realize that "time, which is budgeted by a schedule, becomes the embodiment of educational priorities" (p. 18) and the facilitator of quality instruction. When teachers help the principal develop the school schedule, they not only take ownership and responsibility for the effective use of time, but they learn to manipulate time units or modules within the schedule to meet their instructional needs and the instructional goals of the school. Craig points out that unless teachers are familiar with the scheduling process and assist in setting curricular priorities for the schedule, the effective use of flexible or block scheduling will not be realized.

Maximizing Time to Support Learning

The importance of time in the learning process is reinforced in a report disseminated by the National Commission on Time and Learning (1994) entitled *Prisoners of Time* which states that "time is learning's warden" (p. 7). The Commission's report leaves little doubt that American education is a prisoner of time and that schools have held time schedules constant within schools while letting learning activities vary. In general, schools have provided time slots through their scheduling procedure of one standard 45 to 50 minute time module per instructional unit for teachers to impart knowledge to and develop skills in students. "The rule, only rarely voiced, is simple: learn what you can in the time we make available" (p. 7). The Commission goes on to report that in the time made available for learning, "it should surprise no one that some bright, hard-working students do reasonably well. Everyone else—from the typical student to the dropout—runs into trouble" (p. 7). The Commission, after investigating the relationship between learning and scheduled time for learning in schools, found "the degree to which today's American school is controlled by the dynamics of the clock and calendar . . . surprising, even to people who understand school operations" (p. 7).

The report also notes that schools typically offer a six-period day with approximately 5.6 hours per day of classroom instruction. Regardless of how simple or complex the subject, an average of 51 minutes per class period exists, no matter how well or how poorly students learn the lesson. Schedules in schools dictate "how administrators oversee their schools, and how teachers work their way through the curriculum. Above all, it governs how material is presented to students and the opportunity they have to comprehend and master it" (National Commission on Time and Learning, 1994, p. 8).

The call for more effective use of time in schools is not new. During the 1980s, some educators and national legislators proposed not only a longer school day but a longer school year and pointed to the findings of the 1983 National Commission on Excellence in Education. *A Nation at Risk*, the

Commission's report, triggered the first wave of the school reform movement as a result of its focus on the principal as leader; international data on educational achievement; and a series of philosophical questions about the structure, mission, curriculum, and methods of schooling. The belief was that excellence in education and restoring America's rightful place in the world economy could be attained by improving the quality of education in America through higher academic standards, more rigorous testing, and a longer school day. Rossmiller (1983) relates that 60 percent of the time in a school day is used for instruction while Gilman and Knoll (1984) place that figure at less than 30 percent. Karweit (1985) relates that students spend only 38 percent of the school day on academics. While the actual time spent on instruction and academic activities per school day may lie somewhere among these percentages, even the highest rate of 60 percent is a highly discouraging finding. Canady and Rettig (1995b) state that many of the proposed curricular innovations of the past two decades have failed primarily because of a lack of time and space within the school to allow innovations to mature into positive effects. Canady and Rettig report that many educators, frustrated with the lack of promised gains from new programs, concluded that more than any other variable "the schedule was the problem" (p. 4).

The National Commission on Time and Learning (1994) made certain recommendations to guide school scheduling practices. One was that schools should be organized around the kind and type of learning which is to take place and not around time itself. Another recommendation was that schools need to look at time as a factor which promotes learning and not as a boundary to learning. Yet a third recommendation was that schools should provide more time for academic instruction and adequate time for teachers to plan for and achieve the goal of student learning. These recommendations seem valid in light of the criticism of current scheduling practices.

One such criticism is that current scheduling practices provide fragmented learning experiences. Pullout programs disrupt classroom instruction and take students away from one learning environment and place them into another environment. Students who are pulled out of classes often miss important material, teacher explanations, class discussions, and the instructional continuity of the lesson. Pullout programs also stigmatize students, open the way for ridicule from other students, and lower the self-concept of the students themselves. Schedules which divide daily instructional time into 50 minute periods, with each core subject being taught by one teacher, provide students with unconnected pieces of knowledge and allows little time for indepth study (Canady and Rettig, 1995a).

Traditional scheduling procedures can also exacerbate discipline problems in middle schools (Canady and Rettig, 1995a). First, according to Canady and Rettig, frequent class changes during the day allow time for students to congregate in hallways, bathrooms, and commons areas where problems frequently arise. Second, having teachers responsible for 100 to 180 students a day contributes to the impersonal nature of the school's climate. When teachers lack the opportunity to get to know students personally, the ability of the teacher to help students with the root causes of their problems is greatly diminished and disruptive behavior reoccurs. Third, short instructional periods provide little time for teachers to help students with the social and emotional problems which lead to disruptive behavior. With such short instructional periods, teachers view time spent on discipline problems as time taken away from instruction and, with little patience, send students to the office for corrective action. Here, students miss instruction and often the behavior of the student is not changed but only temporarily altered. Next, schedules that do not allow for interdisciplinary team teaching make any teaming efforts more difficult. Finally, short learning periods work against the middle school concepts of self-paced learning and indepth exploratory learning. Short time periods benefit those who learn quickly while penalizing those who do not, with the lower achieving students falling further behind as the school year progresses. Short time periods also leave little time for the individualized instruction and remedial work which are essential for at-risk students. Finally, some students just need more time than others for learning to "sink in." Traditional scheduling procedures work against the goal of a successful school experience for all students despite the quality of the teaching staff and the curriculum.

SCHEDULING IN THE MIDDLE SCHOOL

Developing the middle school schedule is ultimately the responsibility of the principal. Since the school's schedule is the very foundation of the entire instructional program within the school, however, it needs to be constructed jointly by teachers and administrators. Two important considerations should guide the development of the school's schedule: first, the schedule must meet the special needs of the middle school learner, and second, it must provide the necessary time and space for the instructional programs deemed essential to accomplish the school's goals. Middle grades schedules also serve as a transition between the large, daily block schedule of the elementary school which is determined mainly by the classroom teacher and the departmentalized, small time units or periods found in high schools and determined by administrators.

In middle schools, schedules should be developed by both teachers and administrators for the sole purpose of promoting the goals and objectives of the middle school philosophy. Providing flexibility within time blocks in middle grades schedules is most important.

Essential Considerations for Middle School Scheduling

(1) Time and space are the two most salient considerations principals have to consider when developing a middle school schedule. While the principal can be creative in the use of space, time is a limited commodity. The importance of developing a schedule which is driven by the instructional programs housed within the middle school cannot be overemphasized. The schedule serves as the quality foundation upon which all other programs are built. Efforts in other areas to achieve quality in the instructional program will fall short of the mark if the schedule does not provide adequate time and space. Scheduling, therefore, is the essential means to achieve the essential ends.

(2) If the schedule is the essential foundation for quality middle school programs, what are the essential ends? Ends are the educational priorities determined collaboratively by teachers and administrators. Program priorities are a result of jointly determining which of the components of the true middle school philosophy are most important and are to be addressed within the school. Priorities translate into goals and goals are derived from the values and philosophy held by middle school educators. Just as it is important to individualize instruction based on the specific needs of the learner, it is equally important to individualize the middle school schedule based on the needs of the learner and the educational goals of the individual school.

From a practical standpoint, collaborative decision making is essential to a workable, educationally effective schedule at the middle school level. Principals as educational leaders have many areas of responsibility that require a variety of expertise and demand vast amounts of time. They cannot be expected to be knowledgeable in all subjects concerning the content to be covered, the skills to be taught, or the instructional materials and activities which best facilitate learning in these areas. In addition, Lunenburg and Ornstein (1991) relate that many principals lack the ability to develop an effective schedule, which is one of the practical skills associated with school leadership. For these reasons, principals must depend on the assistance of their teachers in order to build an efficient and effective schedule.

(3) Interdisciplinary team teaching is the most important component of the effective middle school philosophy and is the foundation upon which scheduling is built (Weller, Brown, Short, Holmes, Deweese, and Love, 1987). Other components of the middle school philosophy which will need to be prioritized by the principal and the teachers at each school are the exploratory curriculum; the advisor/advisee program; the grouping of students for instruction (a school-within-a-school or heterogeneous, homogeneous grouping); the community involvement program; the in-

tramural program; and time for individual teacher and team planning. Goals will vary from school to school and may vary from year to year. Variation in goals depends upon how well the educational program fits the needs of the middle school learner or may reflect a change in priorities based on research findings reported nationally or conducted within the school itself through action research. What is important is that priorities and goals are reviewed annually, preferably in the spring so the fall schedule will accurately reflect the change in school goals.

Realistically, the schedule represents the philosophy and mission of the school. Current programs which have been in practice over a long period of time may no longer reflect the current priorities of the staff or adequately meet the needs of its students. However, parents and members of the community may not look at program change in the most positive way. For this reason, parent and community representatives should be involved in an advisory capacity when scheduling changes are made to reflect program changes. Whether the committee is designated as a standing or an ad hoc committee is a decision of the principal; however, it is important that representation does exist and that proposed changes in the schedule be made known to parents and the community at large. This is especially true in middle schools which plan to discontinue interscholastic athletics in favor of a strong intramural program.

(4) Flexibility within the school's schedule is an important factor. This allows teacher teams the freedom to make decisions about how best to teach their students and how much emphasis, time-wise, should be placed on various subjects. Freedom to manipulate the amount of time spent on particular subjects or thematic topics on different days is equally important since students learn at different rates and through different learning preferences.

When schedules are devised around teacher teams, teachers have the ability to make decisions and solve problems that directly impact their students and themselves. In this sense, middle school schedules allow for teacher empowerment where the need for empowerment is most important. Teams also need the flexibility to lengthen or shorten thematic units, teach to large and small groups of students, have guest speakers which require the presence of all students in one or more grade levels, or have regular class instruction with correlated time modules for independent study and/or remedial work.

Flexibility in scheduling design is also beneficial to students. Weller et al. (1987) points out that students are free from a lock-step schedule which promotes fragmented learning, boring repetition, and the standard classroom seating arrangement which places students in a passive learner mode and lends itself to lecture when transescents need active learning and freedom of movement. Administrators, too, reap rewards: with flexible scheduling there tend to be fewer discipline problems (Canady and Rettig, 1995a); teachers have more control over their professional lives and find work more rewarding (Weller and Hartley, 1994); and both human and material resources are used more effectively (George and Alexander, 1993).

(5) Deciding how the units of time will be allocated and arranged in the schedule is up to the middle school teachers and administrators. Principals should note that this may be a potential source of conflict among teachers. Even though program priorities have been established (see Chapter 5, "The Principal and the Interdisciplinary Curriculum"), when it comes time to place the number of instructional minutes beside the subject, some teachers will insist that the time frame is too short while others will insist that it is too long. Also, some teachers will want to insert subjects or programs not on the original priority list. While this conflict is natural enough, principals have to remind teachers that the priorities decided upon represent the essential components of *their* middle school and those subjects which did not make the priority list are considered luxury items to be included if time and space permit. Here, the wise use of time modules, combined in period or block form, can alleviate much of the conflict by allowing some of the luxury items to be included. While compromise is important in reaching solutions to conflict arising over subject or program inclusion in the schedule, budgetary limitations imposed from the central office may stop such conflict from arising. Monies (or the lack of) to fund programs or subjects (hiring new or additional teachers and buying additional instructional material), no matter how educationally worthy, ultimately dictates the curriculum in any school system.

There is little debate over the importance of the traditional core courses in the curriculum—English, mathematics, science, and social studies—and the need for students to receive daily instruction in these areas. The debate over the continuation of reading from the elementary school curriculum into grades six and seven, however, still exists as does the debate over the amount of instructional time to be spent on physical education and health. These courses are an important part of the elementary curriculum and careful consideration should be given to them as priority subjects for the middle school. Some middle schools retain reading as part of the curriculum while some have reading teachers and reading pullout programs to assist those students reading below grade level. Physical education is part of the effective middle school program, as is the intramural program which provides physical activity and basic skill development. Health, and its many related topics, can be taught separately or, as it is done more commonly in middle schools, the subject and its related topics can become part of the exploratory program. How much time is allocated to these subjects, and others, is a matter for compromise among the stakeholders based on the priorities that they have established and which they believe best reflect the philosophy of the true middle school.

(6) Computers and computer software play an integral part in middle school scheduling and can greatly facilitate this time-consuming, complex task. However, since every middle school schedule should be tailored to its students' needs, packaged computer software will provide a template only. Often, principals are faced with modifying or adding information to the computerized schedule. Depending on the size of enrollment and the number of teachers and subjects offered, scheduling modifications can take several hours of work. This problem can be mitigated somewhat by having a seven- or eight-period day instead of a six-period day. Generally, a seven-period day has fifty minutes per period compared with a fifty-five minute period for a six-period day. As mentioned before, breaking the day into smaller time units ultimately allows for greater flexibility. The principal first looks at the enrollment figures for special courses such as band and those in the exploratory curriculum, which meet less frequently and have the fewest students, and determines the number of sections needed for each subject by grade level. This process is the same for required courses. For example, when determining the number of sections needed for each class, the number of students is divided by the desired class size to get the required number of sections needed for every class which meets daily. This figure is matched to the number of teachers who can teach the classes. When teachers are in short supply for a subject, options to the principal are these: Ask to hire new teachers or part-time teachers, over-size class sections, enroll only those who signed up early for the class, or cancel the class. When principals involve their staff in the decision to schedule, cancel, or over-size classes, teachers are more willing to support the outcomes.

Next, student schedules with conflicts are isolated and then matched to the greatest extent possible with those sections already scheduled. Sometimes, student requests for subjects cannot be honored. This can be a function of lack of space, teachers, or time.

Planning times for teachers on interdisciplinary teams are then scheduled and time for the advisor/advisee program is determined. Blocks of time for core courses work well with planning time arranged within the core blocks. In scheduling, the bottom line is that all students, for each unit of instructional time, must be accounted for.

For many principals and teachers, flexible scheduling represents a paradigm shift. Traditional scheduling provides the security of the known and the workable. Six-period schedules are also easy to develop, but they do not provide preadolescent learners a variety of enrichment subjects, time for multi-group activities, exposure to different teachers with different strengths and expertise, or varied learning activities. Flexible scheduling requires the support and commitment of teachers who may be required to change their teaching styles; to work as team members; and to make decisions about the use of instructional time, content coverage, and when, where, and how instructional activities and materials will be used. To some teachers, these responsibilities are both frightening and unwanted.

Principals have the responsibility of educating their teachers about the positive aspects of flexible scheduling. Often, teachers fear the unknown and change to a different schedule will be initially resisted because of lack of information as to how flexible scheduling will impact them and their students positively. While workshops and training sessions play an important role in providing the needed information about the positive aspects of flexible scheduling, on-site visits or benchmarking schools having flexible schedules remains the best way to convince teachers of the attributes of flexibility in scheduling.

Principals can also facilitate the scheduling process by allowing teachers to make certain decisions within the time frames they are provided. Typically, core subject teams of teachers can make decisions about how the school day should be organized once the set times for lunch, exploratory courses, advisor/advisee time, band, and physical education are established. Empowered teachers will decide when core subjects will be taught within allocated time periods or blocks, which teachers will teach which subjects, and how students will be grouped for instruction. By empowering teachers to make these decisions, the quality-promoting practice of Deming (1986) is operationalized: Let those closest to the problem solve the problem. They are the ones who know the problem best.

SPACE AND SCHEDULING IN MIDDLE SCHOOLS

Building the ideal schedule for meeting the unique needs of the transescent learner would mean the eradication of many obstacles. One major obstacle confronting middle school principals is the lack of adequate space or space which lends itself to the middle school philosophy. The ideal situation for any principal is to be able to assist in the design and construction of a new middle school. Since few principals have this luxury, space in existing buildings must be utilized to maximum efficiency. George and Alexander (1993) observe that with a little creative effort and help from teachers and the central office, "exemplary middle schools can function beautifully in all kinds of physical plants" (p. 407). Each building has its own advantages and disadvantages with the key to success being the creative use of the building's space to meet the needs of the school's schedule.

Programs Needing Space

Although scheduling practices differ from one middle school to another, there are certain key aspects of the middle school philosophy that are essential in an effective program. Adequate space is needed for an advisor/advisee program, various sized grouping patterns of students, independent study, interdisciplinary teams of teachers, library and media facilities, the exploratory program, physical education and intramurals, and laboratories.

Space in middle schools, like schedules, should be used to keep students, by grade level, in the same part of the school as much as possible. Teacher team conference rooms, supplies, and other materials needed for instruction should be close to the teachers' assigned wings or block of classrooms.

ACADEMIC LEARNING TIME

According to Squires, Huitt, and Segars (1984), effective schools research on academic achievement found significant relationships between student achievement and student behaviors of *involvement, coverage,* and *success. Involvement* is the amount of time the student is actually involved in learning. *Coverage* is both the appropriateness of the content covered by the student based on prior mastery and the appropriateness of the content based on the evaluation instrument to be used to assess student achievement. *Success* is how accurately students complete their work. A significant finding of the research based on involvement, coverage, and success is "that more is not always better; that the appropriate levels [of success] may depend on grade level, subject area, and student characteristics; and that the appropriate levels are different from what we might expect on the basis of current practice" (Squires et al., 1984, p. 14). These authors go on to say that Academic Learning Time or ALT "is defined as the amount of time that students spend actively working on criteria-related content to a high rate of success. . . . Certainly, there is room for improvement in most classrooms in terms of these critical student behaviors" (pp. 14–15).

Time spent on instruction and its relationship to curriculum density—the quantity of content students are expected to learn over a certain time frame—was investigated by Stallings (1980) and Rosenshein (1979). The greater the density, the more difficulty students will have in mastering the content. Therefore, if curriculum content of high density is to be learned, it must be accompanied by adequate time for high rates of learning to take place. Successful academic learning time exists when student achievement rates match time on task. Rosenshein found that the maximum use of class time for direct instruction through well-organized activities facilitates student achievement, as does careful consideration of student needs and interests. When the school's schedule allows teachers the flexibility to adequately address these impact variables, academic learning time is increased.

The effective and efficient use of time on task correlates to student achievement, but so does the total amount of time allocated for learning. The most effective way to improve student achievement is to lengthen the time spent on instruction and provide activities which keep students on-task, build on their prior knowledge and skills, and appeal to their interests (Purkey and Smith, 1983). Scheduling is the foundation for the maximal use of learning time. Through flexible scheduling teachers can arrange the needed time for direct instruction and correlated activities and, at the same time, allow students the necessary time for engagement time or time on-task in order to be successful at learning (Weller et al., 1987).

TYPES OF SCHEDULING

The instructional program of the middle school should be agreed upon by the principal and teachers and designed to meet the unique needs of the pre-adolescent learner. This program dictates the kind of scheduling procedure to be used within the school. The schedule is constructed to fit the requirements of the instructional program and is not constructed for any other purpose. The temptation for some principals, for ease of scheduling, is to let the schedule dictate the kind of programs and time modules allocated within each instructional program. Part of the middle school philosophy is to individualize and meet the special needs of the learner. There is no better way for the middle school principal to begin to model this behavior than by setting in place a process to develop a school schedule which addresses these needs and this philosophy.

Self-Contained Schedule

While the self-contained schedule is not often used in today's middle schools, some self-contained classrooms do exist and are found primarily in those middle schools which have grade five in the middle grades configuration. Arguments for self-contained classrooms for grade five focus on the age of the learner which research indicates still needs a strong "home base," a single, loving teacher who represents a mother or father image. These students are generally far enough behind sixth grade students in their physical, emotional, social, and cognitive development to place them at a disadvantage in a middle school program (Alexander, Williams, Compton, Hines, and Prescott, 1968).

The instructional rationale behind the self-contained classroom is solid for certain student age groups, but the instructional practices that take place within the self-contained classroom are questionable. Criticism, according to Alexander et al. (1968) focuses on the lack of subject integration which leads to a fragmented curriculum and the lack of teacher expertise in certain areas of instruction which causes the teacher to emphasize one or two areas depending on the strength(s) of the individual teacher. For teachers, isolation from their peers often leads to professional stagnation, complacency, and burnout.

Traditional self-contained schedules are easy to develop with every teacher teaching the same subject at the same time, by grade level. A variation of self-contained scheduling for fifth grade or for grades six through eight places greater emphasis on teacher-made decisions regarding the use of instructional time, strategies, and activities. In this variation, decisions on instruction are made based on the interests and needs of the students; however, freedom of choice is still greatly restricted by the confines of the classroom.

Scheduling and instruction depend on different factors such as lunch, recess, the availability of special subject teachers and programs, and other available uses of the school's common facilities. With a self-contained schedule, time is fixed for all students on a daily basis and deviation from this fixed time is rare. Within the self-contained classroom, both group and individualized instruction take place and teachers decide how much time will be allocated to core and non-core subjects such as art, music, and physical education and health. When a self-contained grade five is housed in a true middle school, students may go to art, music, foreign language, and physical education classes taught by subject area teachers. Self-contained students may or may not have learning centers, learning activity packets, and time for independent study depending on the importance the teacher places upon these activities.

It is important to have activities for both large group instruction, small group work, and individualized instruction in a self-contained classroom. Free time, time for students to work on projects or pursue interests of their choice, is an important part of the schedule. Time should be available for independent study, learning center activities, and computer assisted instruction. Sometimes home base activities are planned and time should be allocated for these whole class events either at the beginning of or at the end of the day. Activities such as these prepare these fifth grade students for a smooth transition into the middle school where students will take more responsibility for their own learning experiences.

Figure 9.1 presents an example of a self-contained classroom schedule for fifth grade students. Variations of this schedule depend upon the teachers and the principal as they strive to meet the goals of the school and school system.

Flexible Scheduling

Flexible scheduling is scheduling that accommodates the requirements of the middle school program and is a developmentally responsive approach to making the curriculum respond to the special needs of the transescent learner while providing both a subject-centered and an exploratory curriculum. Flexible scheduling, with flexible time units, lends itself to interdisciplinary team teaching; advisor/advisee programs; cooperative learning and individual student work; various student grouping configurations for in-

Time	Class Schedule
8:00 - 8:30	Home Base Activities
8:30 - 9:30	Math and Science (whole group instruction and small group work)
9:30 - 10:15	Individualized instruction in Math and Science and/or Independent Study
10:15 - 11:15	Language Arts and Social Studies (whole group instruction and small group work)
11:15 - 12:00	Individualized instruction in Language Arts and Social Studies and/or Independent Study
12:00 - 12:30	Lunch
12:30 - 1:00	Recess
1:00 - 1:45	Free Time (work on Independent Study/Group Projects/Silent Reading)
1:45 - 2:45	Art, Music, Physical Education/Health, and Foreign Language
2:45 - 3:45	Home Base Activities/Small Group Projects/ Independent Study/Individualized Instruction

FIGURE 9.1. Example of a self-contained classroom schedule.

struction; and community youth activity programs and intramurals. Weller et al. (1987) relate that flexible scheduling also has the following advantages:

(1) Allows for different time allotments for different subjects based upon the nature and time requirements of the subjects

(2) Allows for differences in time needed to master certain concepts and skills, by subject and skill area

(3) Allows for adequate time for remedial work and independent instruction

(4) Allows teachers to arrange class size based on the nature of the subject or the type of instructional activities used to teach the lesson

(5) Allows for daily class schedules of students to differ from day to day and allows for subjects to meet at different times and days during the week and for different lengths of time

(6) Allows a wide choice of subjects and activities for students to choose from to address their special interests

(7) Allows for teachers within interdisciplinary teams to group students for large-group, small-group, and independent study activities

The overall advantage of flexible scheduling is that teachers and students are allowed choices in what they will do and how and when they will do it. The exploratory nature of transescents, their potential creativity, and their complex needs are addressed and enhanced through flexible scheduling.

FLEXIBLE SCHEDULING OPTIONS

When looking at flexible scheduling options, two important considerations present themselves to principals seeking quality educational outcomes. First, which scheduling design best meets the curricular goals of the school and second, which design best accommodates the programs necessary to meet the unique needs of transescents as they move toward adolescence. With these considerations in mind, the following examples of flexible scheduling options are presented: flexible modular scheduling, block scheduling, and flexible block scheduling. These different scheduling procedures have their own strengths and weaknesses; however, they all serve to bridge the gap between the elementary self-contained classroom and the rigid, departmental approach of the high school.

Flexible Modular Scheduling

A module is a period of time which can be divided into different lengths of time—fifteen, twenty, or thirty minutes or longer. The fewer the number of minutes in the modules, the more flexible their use. Modules of different time lengths can be either added together or divided into two or more separate modules. Modules are particularly effective when combined with interdisciplinary team teaching so instructional time can be arranged as needed to present material in a variety of subjects. Modules also allow for student schedules to change from day to day and they permit flexibility in the grouping of students. For example, modules of thirty minutes can be divided into two, fifteen-minute time periods, or two or three modules of thirty minutes can be combined into time periods of sixty or ninety minutes. In combining three modules of thirty minutes, students can receive forty-five minutes of instruction, fifteen minutes of individual teacher assistance or peer tutoring, and thirty minutes for independent study or small group work. By dividing or combining modules of time, teams of teachers make the time fit the needs of the instructional program and their students.

Figure 9.2, a basic modular schedule design for one grade level, shows the simplicity of modular scheduling and its potential for flexibility. This schedule utilizes forty, 10-minute modules which can be reorganized in a variety of ways to meet the instructional needs of students. For example, time units or modules can be rearranged so that mathematics and science can be taught in the morning and language arts, social studies and reading can be taught in the afternoon. Time allotments can also be rearranged to allocate time for the advisor/advisee program, unified arts, and exploratory courses.

Figure 9.3 shows the organization of grades 6, 7, and 8 within another variation of the flexible-modular scheduling design. The time for basics, mathematics, social studies, reading, language arts, and science is arranged according to the needs of the interdisciplinary teams. Often, trial and error is the best way to find the optimal schedule. Teachers and the principal will find that several discussions are necessary to arrange the "best" schedule for each grade level. In Figure 9.3, the schedule is divided into fourteen modules of 30 minutes each. Rearranging these modules into different time periods will allow for more flexibility depending on the required amount of time needed for the day's lessons.

Figure 9.4 provides another example of flexible-modular scheduling. This schedule is more intricate than the previous examples and represents a more detailed picture of flexibility in curriculum and instruction. Again, courses by grade level are arranged and divided into time modules through teacher and principal coordinated efforts. Changes in the schedule for different days of the week or for longer or shorter time modules for each subject are decided upon by teacher teams. For example, the advisor/advisee program may be shifted to the end of the day with core courses arranged to begin during the first part of the day. Within the core curriculum, field trips

Time	Module	Class Schedule
8:30	1	Homeroom/Advisor/Advisee Program
8:40	2	
8:50	3	
9:00	4	
9:10	5	
9:20	6	Language Arts
9:30	7	
9:40	8	Social Studies
9:50	9	
10:00	10	Reading
10:10	11	
10:20	12	
10:30	13	
10:40	14	
10:50	15	
11:00	16	
11:10	17	Lunch
11:20	18	
11:30	19	
11:40	20	
11:50	21	
12:00	22	Math
12:10	23	
12:20	24	Science
12:30	25	
12:40	26	Lab Classes
12:50	27	
1:00	28	
1:10	29	
1:20	30	
1:30	31	Physical Education
1:40	32	
1:50	33	Unified Arts
2:00	34	
2:10	35	
2:20	36	Exploratory Courses
2:30	37	
2:40	38	Individual Projects
2:50	39	
3:00	40	Small-group Activities

FIGURE 9.2. Middle school modular schedule.

Time	Module	6th	7th	8th
8:30	1	Homeroom	Homeroom	Homeroom
8:45	2		Basics	Physical
9:15	3	B		Education
9:45	4	A		Unified Arts
10:15	5	S	Physical	Basics
10:45	6	I	Education	
11:15	7	C	Unified Arts	Lunch
11:45	8	S	Lunch	B
12:15	9	Lunch		A
12:45	10	Physical	Basics	S
1:15	11	Education		I
1:45	12	Unified Arts		C
				S
2:15	13	Exploration	Exploration	Exploration
		Individual	Individual	Individual
		Projects	Projects	Projects
2:45	14	Advisor/Advisee	Advisor/Advisee	Advisor/Advisee

FIGURE 9.3. Flexible-modular schedule.

can be arranged or students needing special help or groups needing more time to complete projects can have extra time without disturbing the entire school schedule.

Block Scheduling

Block scheduling is allocating large blocks of time to a subject or a group of interdisciplinary subjects. One can conceive of block scheduling as merely combining time modules to form blocks, or more traditionally, the combining of periods to form blocks. The flexibility resides in the fact that blocks of time can vary in length and can be interchangeable, depending on the needs of the students and the curriculum. Moreover, within each block of time, freedom exists to organize units of time to better facilitate subject matter coverage and student learning. The term "flexible-modular block scheduling" derives from the time-unit flexibility found within the time blocks.

Most middle schools incorporate some form of block scheduling procedure where the core courses are housed within time blocks for longer periods of instruction (Wiles and Bondi, 1993). Flexible block scheduling is an important part of the interdisciplinary team teaching concept since time blocks allow teacher teams to teach the same group of students (often called schools-within-a-school or communities), teams have the same planning time, and teams are provided the needed flexibility for team members to vary their instructional activities and the time needed for these activities to meet student needs. Block schedules also promote the team's mission of providing content connections among the disciplines or the use of topics or

Time	M	6th	7th	8th
8:30	1	Homeroom	Homeroom	Homeroom
8:45	2	Advisor/Advisee	Advisor/Advisee	Advisor/Advisee
9:00	3	Reading	Unified Arts	Math
9:15	4	English	Physical	Science
9:30	5	Creative	Education	Lab Classes
		Writing		
9:45	6	Foreign Language	Individual	
			Projects	
10:00	7	Social Studies	Group Counseling	
10:15	8		Language Arts	
10:30	9		Creative Writing	Individual
				Projects
10:45	10		Foreign Language	Group
				Counseling
11:00	11	Individual		Unified Arts
		Projects	Social Studies	Physical
11:15	12	Group Counseling		Education
11:30	13	Unified Arts		
11:45	14	Physical		
12:00	15	Education		Lunch
12:15	16			
12:30	17	Lunch	Lunch	Language Arts
12:45	18	Math	Math	Social Studies
1:00	19	Science	Science	
1:15	20	Lab Classes	Lab Classes	Foreign Language
1:30	21			
1:45	22			
2:00	23			
2:15	24	Elective	Elective	Elective
2:30	25	Exploratory	Exploratory	Exploratory
2:45	26	Courses	Courses	Courses
3:00	27			

FIGURE 9.4. Modular schedule.

themes for instruction. Because all teachers on the same team teach the same group of students, block scheduling promotes close student-teacher relationships which enhance interpersonal communications and supplement the goals of the advisor/advisee program. Varying time units within the time blocks also allows for large and small group instruction and time for remedial work and independent study. George and Alexander (1993) relate that block scheduling, when used in conjunction with interdisciplinary team teaching, promotes peer coaching among teachers which improves their teaching skills and provides a support network to help first-year teachers strengthen their teaching abilities.

Block scheduling is affected by certain variables which must be considered if students are to move uninterrupted as a group throughout the school day. Wiles and Bondi (1993) relate that the most important considerations for block scheduling include the following:

(1) There must be enough special teachers to offer the essentials of a true middle school (physical education, exploratory courses, guidance program, unified arts, and enrichment and remediation). Without these special teachers, core teachers will have to assume additional responsibilities and may not have adequate planning time for the needs of interdisciplinary team teaching. Moreover, with an insufficient number of teachers, the goal of block scheduling (having blocks of students share common teachers, time, and space) may not be possible.

(2) Adequate space is necessary to have team instruction. Team space and common space as opposed to individual teacher "owned" classrooms is essential for group instruction within time blocks. Common space can be the use of the gym, lunchroom, or any other large area when not scheduled for use.

(3) Grouping students is an important consideration. This takes consensus between teachers and the principal on the different groupings of students that will exist for instruction. For example, will you use homogeneous and heterogeneous groups in all subjects? Will you use tracking for some core courses and not others? Will you use heterogeneous classrooms for instruction but ability groups for short-term courses or activities on a temporary basis? These questions impact student achievement and self-concept as well as the scheduling process itself.

Middle schools have the problem of scheduling students with diverse achievement levels. This diversity in ability is greater during the middle school years than at any other time in the schooling experience. Grouping students for instruction according to their skill levels is one way to meet the individual needs of students and keep students with the same teachers. Braddock and McPartland (1990) caution educators on the detrimental effects of excessive homogeneous grouping on student attitudes and achievement, but note the positive effects of ability grouping in reading, English and mathematics. Small groups of ability grouped students (10 to 15) for reading and mathematics instruction and larger groups of heterogeneously grouped students for instruction in science, social studies, and most other curricular areas are recommended. Grouping by ability should be done on total scores for academic achievement and not on I.Q. score. More information on homogeneous and heterogeneous grouping practices is provided in Chapter 11.

In ability grouping and heterogeneous grouping block schedules, the reading and mathematics teachers' schedules usually remain constant but groups of students change based on skill mastery or lack of skill mastery. A student's schedule is based on these skill groups and teacher teams move students from one skill group to another based on student mastery. In this type of schedule, homogeneous groups, except for special activities or to meet the special needs of certain students, do not exist outside of the groupings for reading and mathematics.

IMPORTANT COMPONENTS OF BLOCK SCHEDULES

Block scheduling should be built around the most essential components of the true middle school (Wiles and Bondi, 1993; Forte and Schurr, 1993). These components are as follows:

- Provide for an advisor/advisee program of 20 to 30 minutes daily.
- There is a basic/core course instructional time with interdisciplinary teacher team organization. Usually one teacher for each of the core courses teaches approximately 120 heterogeneously grouped students (30 students per teacher) for four periods/time modules, arranged concurrently, with a common planning and conference period for these teachers. Planning time is best achieved through parallel scheduling which provides large blocks of planning time through the scheduling of special teachers whose classes are also rotated by teacher teams. This frees core teachers for planning periods.
- Teachers have duty-free lunch.
- The exploratory program courses and physical education courses are shorter than core courses.
- Enrichment and remediation programs are scheduled so pullout practices are not used.
- Teachers have the flexibility and autonomy to group and regroup students to meet curricular and student needs.
- Teachers can utilize units of time within time blocks to vary the instructional time for any subject or learning activity, or for mini-courses. Teachers have the flexibility to arrange these time units or divide the units in ways which best promote learning.

TIME MODULES IN BLOCK SCHEDULING

Block scheduling is at the heart of the middle school with time units/modules being decided upon by teachers and the principal based on the objectives of the curriculum, the goals of the instructional program, and the needs of the students. (See Chapter 5, "The Principal and the Interdisciplinary Curriculum," for information on how these objectives, goals, and needs are determined.) Usually, time units vary from 30 minutes to 45 minutes to 60 minutes in length. Then throughout the year, each interdisciplinary team, consisting of one teacher for each core subject and sometimes the reading and special education teacher, decides how the time allocated within these blocks is used. Subjects within the unified arts, physical education, the exploratory curriculum, and other components of the middle school are also scheduled by time units. Within time blocks, each interdisciplinary team can schedule large and small group instruction; have heterogeneous groups, ability groups, or interest groups of students (students with a common interest in a subject); create uneven time periods when needed for instructional purposes; and have field trips, guest speakers, and community projects.

Examples of Block Scheduling

Block scheduling in its simplest form is presented in Figure 9.5. Within this schedule, teachers are permitted total freedom in organizing the academic subject areas to meet the needs of students.

Figure 9.6 illustrates how the interdisciplinary team teaching approach can be incorporated into the flexible block schedule. In this example, one hour per day is scheduled for team planning. Any variation of this schedule

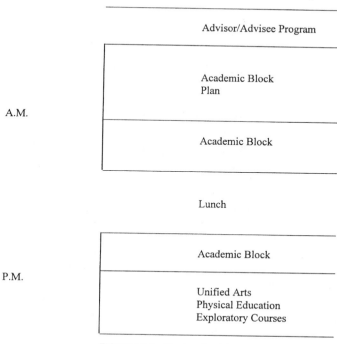

FIGURE 9.5. Block schedule.

HR Homeroom	Monday Homeroom	Tuesday Homeroom	Wednesday Homeroom	Thursday Homeroom	Friday
8:30		5 Teachers - 150 Students Math, Science, Language Arts, Social Studies Interdisciplinary Team Teaching Approach ACADEMIC BLOCK			
12:00	Lunch	Lunch	Lunch	Lunch	Lunch
12:30	Unified Arts	Physical Education	Unified Arts	Physical Education	Unified Arts
	TEAM PLANNING				
1:30	Advisor/ Advisee Meetings	Group Counseling	Peer- Tutoring	Teachers Option	Assembly Pep Rally
2:30	Explor. Courses	Explor. Courses	Explor. Courses	Explor. Courses	Explor. Courses

FIGURE 9.6. Block schedule.

can be made based on teacher and student needs. Again, any variation for any grade level can be applied to this basic block schedule.

The block schedule in Figure 9.7 is one provided by the Newport News Public School System and indicates the suggested percentage of time that could be allocated to particular subject areas. Each middle school in the system is free to adjust these suggested time allotments to facilitate coverage of course content and meet the needs of teachers and students.

In the block schedule labeled Figure 9.7, teachers have the freedom to adjust the time percentages suggested for subject coverage on any given day of any given week. This highly flexible approach to scheduling also allows teachers to switch times and amount of time core courses will be taught. By grade level, one teacher team member could spend an entire day conducting action research with one or more teacher team members, lengthening the instructional time for other subject area(s). The next day, the action researchers would extend their instructional time and free other teachers for research, additional planning time, or parent conferences.

A block schedule with mini or small time units is presented in Figure 9.8. Within these blocks, teacher teams can shift the order of instruction and allocate the number of minutes they choose to spend on each subject based on student needs. Emphasis on the exploratory program time block, as well as the time for small group counseling for each grade, is a decision made by teacher team members and the principal. Blocks of time can be shifted within grade levels from morning to afternoon.

Another type of schedule being used more frequently in middle schools is the four block schedule design. The popularity of this schedule lies in the rotation of its blocks by day, unit of study, or grading period. Canady and Rettig (1995a) maintain that the four block design reduces fragmentation in instruction because students spend about 90 minutes in language arts (one

Sixth Grade	Seventh Grade	Eighth Grade
Advisory Period	Advisory Period	Advisory Period
Academics	Academics	Group Guidance
Reading/Language Arts	Reading/Language Arts	Independent Projects
Mathematics	Social Studies	Academics
Science/Health	(37.5%*)	Social Studies
Social Studies		Reading/Language
(80%*)	Unified Arts	
	Exploratory Courses	Health/Physical Ed
Lunch	Physical Education	
Unified Arts	(25%*)	Lunch
Physical Education		Academics
Exploratory Courses	Lunch	Science
(20%*)	Academics	Mathematics
	Science/Health	
	Mathematics	Explor. Courses
	(37.5%*)	Unified Arts
		(The percent of time spent on basic skills varies with exploratory/elective courses chosen. A minimum of 50-60 percent of daily instruction is in basic studies.)

School day: 6 1/2 hours, including lunch.
*Indicates percentage of school day allotted to that area.

FIGURE 9.7. Block schedule.

Time	Grade 6	Grade 7	Grade 8
8:15 8:30	Advisor/Advisee	Advisor/Advisee	Advisor/Advisee
8:45 9:00 9:15 9:30 9:45 10:00 10:15 10:30 10:45 11:00 11:15	Basic/core Block (8:45-11:00) Reading English Math Lunch 11:00-11:30	Exploratory Curriculum Physical Education Reading Foreign Language Band Chorus (8:45 - 11:30)	Basic/Core Math English Reading Science Physical Education (8:45-12:30)
11:30 11:45 12:00 12:15 12:30 12:45 1:00 1:15 1:30	Exploratory Curriculum and Physical Education (11:30 - 1:30) PLAN (12:30 - 1:30)	Lunch 11:30 - 12:00 Small Group (12:00 - 12:30) Basic/Core Math Science Social Studies (12:30 - 3:15)	PLAN 11:30 - 12:30 Lunch (12:30 - 1:00) Social Studies (1:00 - 1:45)
1:45 2:00 2:15 2:30 2:45 3:00 3:15	Basic/Core Science Social Studies 1:30 - 3:00 Small Group Guidance (3:00 - 3:15)		Exploratory Curriculum (1:45 - 3:00) Small Group Guid. (3:00 - 3:15)

FIGURE 9.8. Block schedule with small time units of fifteen-minute modules.

block), 90 minutes in mathematics, and 90 minutes in science or social studies, which is rotated every other day, every other unit, or by grading period. The fourth time block of the day is allocated to physical education, unified arts and/or exploratory courses. The four block design also decreases the number of class changes and resulting discipline problems.

In addition to schedules grouping blocks of time, there are also schedules which group days. The 75-75-30 day schedule is a unique approach to scheduling in that it allows teachers maximum creativity in designing and teaching new courses. These courses are similar to mini-courses with time built into the schedule for remedial work, academic enrichment activities, and large and small group projects consisting of community service projects, research studies, and indepth independent study. Canady and Rettig (1995a) explain that having two 75-day terms allows students 150 days of academic instruction with interdisciplinary teams and 30 days of instruction in teacher-created courses which are focused on particular areas of academic content and designed to give the student more indepth knowledge of particular areas of student interest.

Another schedule which is gaining in popularity is the 35-(5)-35-(15)-35-(5)-35-(15) plan. "Each semester students attend regular classes for 35 days and have 5 days for reteaching and/or enrichment. They continue regular classes for 35 days and end the semester with 15 days for extended learning time or enrichment/electives" (Canady and Rettig, 1995a, p. 9).

SCHOOL-WITHIN-A-SCHOOL SCHEDULES

Scheduling a school-within-a-school, also known as a house plan or a school community, has been popular with some principals in large schools of 1,000 or more students. Other principals have tried this type of scheduling design and abandoned it due to frustration on the part of teachers and parents, and its inability to fulfill its promise of improving student self-concept and providing more individual instruction and closer relationships with caring teachers. As O'Neil (1995) points out, this school-within-a-school design suffered from the same problems which flexible block scheduling suffered from in the 1970s—time scheduled for independent study was not used productively, teachers failed to make adequate use of flexible time within blocks, and an increase in student disciplinary problems was attributed to this ineffective use of time. These problems stemmed from a lack of sufficient teacher training on how to use block time effectively, how to vary their instructional strategies, how to work within a team, and how to reorganize time modules within blocks to maximize time-on-task and student learning. Staff development, O'Neil maintains, is the key to making any flexible scheduling format successful.

School-within-a-school schedules provide for different learning houses or communities for students within the school itself. George and Alexander (1993) relate that any size middle school can use the house design to create an atmosphere of closeness, personal support, and individual attention for students. Each house has an interdisciplinary team of teachers teaching the four basic subjects who share common space for specialized instruction. Some learning communities are comprised of all one grade level while others are multiage grouped and house sixth, seventh, and eighth grades in each house. Principals and teachers jointly determine which grouping process is best for their curriculum and students.

Each school-within-a-school operates separately and fosters the atmosphere, relationships, and spirit of small schools. The principal becomes the instructional leader of each learning community and is responsible for the coordination and communication between each community. School councils made up of teachers from each house, along with the principal, make up the leadership team for the entire school. Each house has a lead teacher or coordinator who serves as team leader, instructional coordinator, and liai-

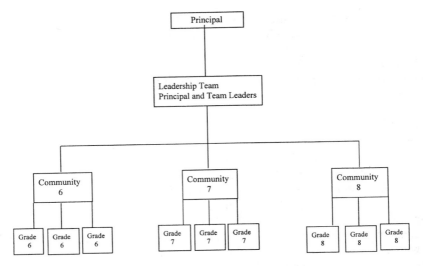

FIGURE 9.9. School-within-a-school organizational design.

son to the principal. Teachers and the principal work together to develop each community's schedule and they work within the same parameters of time, space, and priorities as do those who develop regular flexible block schedules. Figure 9.9 presents the organizational design of a school-within-a-school.

As represented in Figure 9.9, each community would have three groups of all one grade level with an interdisciplinary team of four teachers teaching approximately 120 students. Common space for large group instruction would be shared and block scheduling would accommodate the advisor/advisee program, the exploratory curriculum, and other components of the middle school. Special teachers such as art, music, physical education, guidance, and reading would be shared among the three communities.

SCHEDULING THE EXPLORATORY CURRICULUM

Exploratory courses are known as enrichment courses, mini-courses, or short courses that are of interest to middle school students. These may come about as a result of clubs and electives in the middle school or as an expansion of exploratory projects from the elementary school. Their goal is to stimulate interest and provide knowledge and skills in specific areas which appeal to the transescent and to exceed those experiences found in regular classrooms. These courses should address the wide range of cognitive, socioemotional, and physical differences found in preadolescents.

Courses in the exploratory curriculum are taught by teachers, parents, members of the community, and/or the principal. Short in duration, these courses provide instruction which lasts from three to nine weeks. The courses can be school-based or community-based. Some mini-courses may coincide with topics or themes in the core curriculum, while others may relate to the physical education and the intramural programs. Elective courses, part of the exploratory curriculum, are optional courses for student choice and often build on exploratory courses.

Building exploratory courses into a flexible block schedule is not difficult. The most important task is to determine which teachers will teach which courses and when they will teach them. The exploratory curriculum may be organized into thematic strands with correlated elective courses. Some schools have strands which consist of traditional exploratory courses; community activities; health, life, and environmental skills; and personal enrichment. These strands can change yearly based on student and teacher needs. Planning the exploratory schedule is best done by teacher teams and the principal, and course offerings depend on expertise, space, resources,

Period	Grade 6	Grade 7	Grade 8
1	CORE Courses	Exploratory/ Electives	Advisor/Advisee Program
2			CORE Courses
3	Advisor/Advisee Program	Band	Exploratory Courses
4	Lunch	Advisor/Advisee Program	CORE Courses
		Lunch	Lunch
5	Exploratory Electives CORE Courses	CORE Courses Physical Education	Elective Courses
			Band
6	Band		CORE Courses
7	Physical Education		Physical Education

Intramurals after school.

FIGURE 9.10. Exploratory block schedule.

and time available to teach the courses. Like the core curriculum, priorities must be set for exploratory and elective course offerings, with priorities usually defined by the number of students who pre-register for the courses.

Figure 9.10 presents a daily schedule for sixth, seventh, and eighth grade students with blocks for core courses and exploratory and elective courses for a seven-day period.

SCHEDULES AND SCHEDULING FOR QUALITY EDUCATION: CASE STUDIES

Scheduling methods and configurations vary at quality middle schools and are viewed as the most important facilitators of instruction. A schedule's configuration is directly correlated to the goals and philosophy of the middle school and it may incorporate any one of a variety of scheduling procedures. Flexible scheduling, within the block schedule design, is the choice of most principals who choose to incorporate the major components of the true middle school which include team teaching, the interdisciplinary curriculum, exploratory courses, the advisor/advisee program, and at-risk programs.

Principals in Georgia Schools of Excellence, as well as those named National Blue Ribbon Schools and National Schools of Excellence, employ flexible, modular block scheduling of one type or another. "Any other type of scheduling process would not allow us to schedule the components of a real middle school. You need the flexibility of the block," says Walker Davis, principal of West Jackson Middle School (WJMS). At WJMS, the school day for its 1,100 students in grades six, seven, and eight consists of seven periods, each fifty minutes long. This schedule is presented in Figure 9.11. "When building a schedule," Davis says, "you have to key off the popular electives of band, chorus, and the required time for physical education and lunch. When you schedule students in these time slots, the rest pretty much falls into place."

In grade six, those students electing to take chorus have it daily during first period (8:20 to 9:10), while the remaining sixth grade students, including those taking band, are scheduled into one of several exploratory courses. Period two, students who choose to do so take band, while other sixth graders are scheduled into exploratory courses. In Georgia, exploratory courses must be a minimum of six weeks in length with each student having a minimum of two courses in three of the four areas and one course in all four areas (vocational, foreign language, personal learning, and technology) during the three years of middle school education. During periods three through six at WJMS, sixth graders are scheduled in the core academic block with lunch being scheduled in between four blocks of time. Within the academic block, interdisciplinary teacher teams schedule their language arts, reading, mathemat-

	8:20 - 9:10	9:15 - 10:05	10:10 - 11:00	11:05 - 11:50	12:30	12:30 - 1:20	1:25 - 2:10	2:15 - 3:10	3:15
Grade 6	1 Chorus Explor.	2 Band Explor.	3	4	LUNCH	5	6	7 Phy. Ed. Health	← HOMEROOM

	8:20 - 9:10	9:15 - 10:05	10:10 - 11:00	11:40	12:35 -1:20	1:25 - 2:10	2:15 - 3:00	3:15
Grade 7	1	2	3 Band Explor.	LUNCH	5 Phy. Ed. Health	6	7 Chorus Explor.	HOMEROOM

	8:20 - 9:10	9:15 - 10:05	10:10 - 11:00	11:05 - 11:50	11:55 - 12:50	1:20	1:25 - 2:10	2:15 - 3:00	
Grade 8	1	2	3 Phy. Ed. Health	4 Band Explor.	5 Chorus Explor.	LUNCH	6	7	→

FIGURE 9.11. West Jackson Middle School schedule 1996–1997.

ics, social studies, and science in time modules which meet the needs of their sixth grade students. For example, mathematics may be scheduled from 10:10 to 11:00 A.M., but on a given day may last for only thirty minutes if a field trip is scheduled which addresses the objectives of the social studies and language arts curriculum, or if a guest speaker is presenting a special experiment as part of the science curriculum. The time lost on mathematics instruction will be made up the following day with less instructional time for one or all of the core courses requesting "loaned time" from mathematics. These flexible instructional time modules within the core block allow teams to schedule special events and adjust their core time sequence within the block without losing any instructional contact time.

Period seven for grade six is for physical education and health with the last fifteen minutes of the day serving as a homeroom period where teachers discuss with students topics in the affective domain and address the social and emotional problems of their students. Those students in the PALS program, discussed in Chapter 7, spend time with PALS teachers which supplements their self-contained classroom instruction held during the regular academic core block. Gifted and talented students are pulled out of the core academic block for mathematics and language arts at times teams plan to teach these subjects. Teacher planning time, both individual and team, is scheduled during first and second periods with seventh period used as planning time for teachers who teach both exploratory and academic core courses. Planning time for exploratory teachers exists during academic core courses, extended lunch periods, and homeroom time. For example, while not evident from Figure 9.11, the art teacher has sixth period (50 minutes), an extended lunch (50 minutes), and homeroom (15 minutes) for planning time which meets minimum standards of eighty-five minutes planning time per day.

Grades seven and eight students and teacher teams follow a similar schedule. Physical education, for example, is taught fifth period for grade seven and third period for grade eight which allows the three physical education teachers sixth period to plan for instruction and coordinate the after-school intramural program. Sixth period is also the planning time for most exploratory teachers who can plan together to coordinate their own programs and ensure curriculum alignment with the core academic teams.

At WJMS, computerized block scheduling is simplified by the heterogeneous grouping practice employed by the principal. Davis uses Iowa Text of Basic Skills scores, ethnicity, sex, and student discipline records to ensure that teams at all three grade levels have a random and even distribution of students. With the exception of a few students who are identified as gifted and talented and are taught by a certified gifted teacher in math and language arts through a pull-out program, teachers design their instruction for students who range from gifted to low achiever. This normal curve distribution of students has decreased discipline problems in the classrooms and school, and has promoted peer tutoring and cooperative learning in the classrooms. All of these have positive effects on student learning.

There are some pitfalls associated with flexible block scheduling, as Davis relates. One major hurdle is for a principal to think that adopting another school's schedule will solve the scheduling problems. "Each school's curriculum and student needs, as well as the available resources to fund exploratory programs and teachers, are unique and virtually dictate the scheduling configuration." While other block schedules may serve as models or templates, "you'll have to design your own based on what you have to work with," Davis says.

Another pitfall is the temptation not to "key-off" year-long elective courses such as band and chorus and required courses such as physical education. These must be scheduled first with all other considerations being secondary. Davis notes that this problem can be compounded when exploratory and/or elective teachers have to be shared with high schools or other middle schools. When this happens, principals at the respective schools have to negotiate teacher time with the added considerations of scheduling requirements for both schools and travel time for teachers. At WJMS, Davis has to share the band and foreign language teachers with the high school.

Another problem lies with exploratory teachers who may have to teach core academic subjects as well as an enrichment class. The funding available to hire exploratory teachers and the priority placed on academic courses limit the exploratory curriculum offerings and compound scheduling problems across grade levels.

Finally, no computer scheduling program alleviates the necessity to do some kind of hand scheduling. When computer programs are used they provide an overall scheduling matrix, by grade level and by subject, based on the student data requested by the scheduling program. Since student schedules are made prior to the beginning of each quarter or semester, adjustments have to be made by hand scheduling regarding student drop-adds, student failures, and student skill placement within electives such as band. These adjustments can be made easily based on the student's prior computerized schedule and teacher input.

Mary Ann Charron, principal at Trickum Middle School, uses flexible block scheduling for the 1,600 plus students in grades six through eight. Figure 9.12 presents the Trickum Middle School schedule which is a split-block, solid-block design.

In grades six and seven academic blocks are split by exploratory courses while grade eight has a solid block with exploratory courses at the end of the

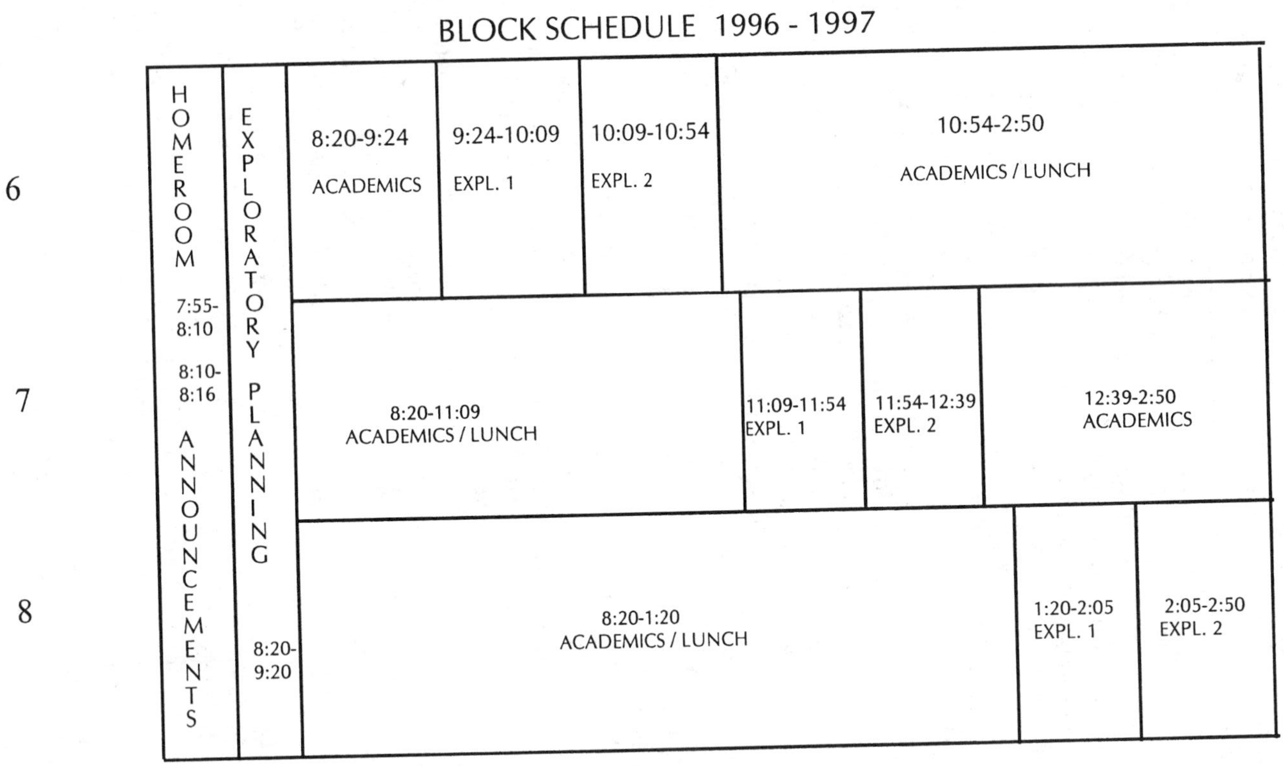

FIGURE 9.12. Trickum Middle School.

school day. Homeroom serves as advisor/advisee time, with exploratory teacher planning time scheduled prior to the beginning of the academic core block. In this way, comprehensive planning among all exploratory teachers can take place daily and at one time. Exploratory courses are forty-five minutes in length, lunch is twenty-five minutes, and the academic core has approximately four and one-half hours of instructional time.

At Trickum, the master block schedule is prepared by the principal who designates times for homeroom, exploratory teacher planning and instruction, and lunch. Teacher teams at each grade level schedule their own students within the academic and exploratory blocks for the year with assistance from school counselors, exploratory teachers, and the administrative team. Teacher teams are paid a stipend in the summer to assign their respective grade level students to these teacher teams based on heterogeneous student data supplied by the principal. Student information, by grade level, consists of student achievement scores on the Iowa Test of Basic Skills, ethnicity, discipline problems, sex, socioeconomic status, and special education status. Teacher teams schedule their own academic core sequence within their grade level time blocks with team planning time held during the exploratory time block. Hand scheduling is done by the administrative team for all drop-adds, students failures, and other reasons necessitating changes in students' schedules.

Charron believes that teachers know their students best and because they teach students as teams, they should have the opportunity to place students within teams that best meet the needs of the individual students. This "personalized" approach to scheduling has decreased student behavior problems, increased teacher morale, and contributed to a more positive school climate for students and teachers.

Gifted and talented students in mathematics are identified by the Iowa Algebra Aptitude Test and are taught separately by a certified gifted teacher during the regularly scheduled mathematics time for their grade level. Students in seventh and eighth grade needing instruction in geometry and trigonometry are taught by high school teachers, during first period, at the high school located a block away.

Edwards Middle School principal, Wayne Watts, develops his own master block schedule and believes "that if you develop the schedule from scratch you can truly meet the needs of teachers, students, and the curriculum. Canned [computer] programs can lock you into a mode of thinking and easily distract you from your main mission," he says. Watts practices a similar approach to student scheduling to that of Charron at Trickum Middle School. He generates heterogeneous lists of students, by grade level, achievement scores, ethnicity, disciplinary records, sex, and special education status, and allows teacher teams (academic and exploratory teachers, and school counselors) to assign students to their own teams. Teachers arrange content area according to their priorities within the time blocks allotted for core academic instruction and work with exploratory teachers during overlapping planning time to ensure continuity among thematic units of instruction.

The master schedule designates times for band (an exploratory block course), exploratory courses, physical education, and lunch. Teacher teams decide on times for gifted and talented instruction in language arts, while exploratory and physical education teachers organize the after-school intramural program. Gifted students are taught an accelerated curriculum by three certified gifted teachers in each of grades six, seven, and eight. These teachers provide instruction in the content area within the classroom in language arts.

Figure 9.13 presents the Edwards Middle School block schedule for the first semester. The second semester schedule is virtually a mirror image of the first semester. Variations usually center around instructional time module designations which appear alongside of classes on the schedule. Time changes reflect desired teaching times and are not fixed times since teams have fluid movement within each time block. Watts says these designated times are more for administrative student accountability purposes for emergency situations and for pull-out programs.

If the data in Figure 9.13 is arranged horizontally, the schedule more closely resembles a block, flexible-modular design. Figure 9.14 provides an example of Edwards Middle Schedule placed in block schedule form for Teams A/B for grades six through eight.

Watts notes some pitfalls to avoid when developing a master schedule. Some are similar to those expressed by principals in the preceding case studies and are listed to reinforce their importance. These pitfalls include the following:

- Schedule year-long elective and required courses first, such as band, chorus, and physical education and health. Watts calls these "single needs classes." When sharing exploratory or elective teachers with other schools, the scheduling process *must* be coordinated with the principal and teachers involved in joint-appointment; otherwise, there will be problems.
- Meet all federal, state, and school system requirements, such as those affecting special education students and state exploratory curriculum requirements. Watts notes that no matter how careful a principal is in scheduling, it is best to work with another school administrator who can serve as a double check on all scheduling procedures. He notes, "If an error can be made, it will be made, and scheduling is one area in which you need perfection." Checking grade level teacher team scheduling is a must. When conflicts or errors are found, make sure it

EDWARDS MIDDLE SCHOOL MASTER SCHEDULE

FIRST SEMESTER

RED SCHEDULE
GRADE 6
Teams A/B

8:25- 8:45	Team Time	20
8:45-10:20	PE/EX	95
10:20-11:35	Class I	75
11:35-12:05	Lunch	30
12:05- 1:05	Class II	60
1:05- 2:20	Class III	75
2:20- 3:20	Class IV	60

Teams C/D

8:25- 8:45	Team Time	20
8:45-10:20	PE/EX	95
10:20-11:35	Class I	75
11:35-12:50	Class II	75
12:50- 1:20	Lunch	30
1:20- 2:20	Class III	60
2:20- 3:20	Class IV	60

WHITE SCHEDULE
GRADE 7
Teams A/B

8:35- 9:25	Class I	60
9:25-10:25	Class II	60
10:25-12:00	PE/EX	95
12:00-12:30	Lunch	30
12:30-12:50	Team Time	20
12:50- 2:05	Class III	75
2:05- 3:20	Class IV	75

Teams C/D/E*

8:25- 9:25	Class I	60
9:25-10:25	Class II	60
10:25-12:00	PE/EX	95
12:00-12:20	Team Time	20
12:20-12:50	Lunch	30
12:50- 2:05	Class III	75
2:05- 3:20	Class IV	75

BLUE SCHEDULE
GRADE 8
Teams A/B

8:25- 8:45	Team Time	20
8:45-10:00	Class I	75
10:00-11:15	Class II	75
11:15-11:45	Lunch	30
11:45-12:45	Class III	60
12:45- 1:45	Class IV	60
1:45- 3:20	PE/EX	95

Teams C/D

8:15- 8:45	Team Time	20
8:45-10:00	Class I	75
10:00-11:00	Class II	60
11:00-11:30	Lunch	30
11:30-12:45	Class III	75
12:45- 1:45	Class IV	60
1:45- 3:20	PE/EX	95

Gifted I

Grade 8

Teams A/B	Class I
Teams C/D	Class III

Grade 7

Teams A/B	Class IV

Gifted II

Grade 6

Teams A/B	Class I
Teams C/D	Class II

Grade 7

Teams C/D	Class IV

LUNCH TIMES

Grade 6

Teams A/B	11:35-12:05
Teams C/D	12:50- 1:20

Grade 7

Teams A/B	12:00-12:30
Teams C/D	12:20-12:50

Grade 8

Teams A/B	11:15-11:45
Teams C/D	11:00-11:30

FIGURE 9.13. Edwards Middle School Master schedule 1996–1997.

Time	Grade 6 Teams A/B	Minutes
8:25-8:45	Team Time	20
8:45-10:20	Physical Education	95
10:20-11:35	Class I (Core Block)	75
11:35-12:05	Lunch	30
12:05-1:05	Class II (Core Block)	60
1:05-2:20	Class III (Core Block)	75
2:20-3:20	Class IV (Core Block)	60

Time	Grade 7 Teams A/B	Minutes
8:25-9:25	Class I	60
9:25-10:25	Class II	60
10:25-12:00	Physical Education and Exploratory	95
12:00-12:30	Lunch	30
12:30-12:50	Team Time	20
12:50-2:05	Class III	75
2:05-3:20	Class IV	75

Time	Grade 8 Teams A/B	Minutes
8:25-8:45	Team Time	20
8:45-10:00	Class I	75
10:00-11:15	Class II	75
11:15-11:45	Lunch	30
11:45-12:45	Class III	60
12:45-1:45	Class IV	60
1:45-3:20	Physical Education and Exploratory	95

FIGURE 9.14. Block schedule for Edwards Middle School.

is an error before discussing it with the teacher team. "one can be quickly embarrassed," he says, "if an error does not exist with their work, but with yours." If changes have to be made in team scheduling, discuss the changes with the team, use it as a learning situation, and do not unilaterally make the change if you want to maintain teacher confidence and sustain the idea of teamwork.

- Hand scheduling for last minute changes will always exist no matter what scheduling process is used. Double check your work with another administrator and be careful about balance in student numbers on teacher teams and keeping the student population as heterogeneous as possible within each team.
- To maximize block scheduling with interdisciplinary teams, Watts strongly suggests using "heterogeneous grouping through the bell curve distribution technique. The normal curve distribution allows an equal number of high, average, and low achievers to be placed in teacher teams and cuts down on classroom discipline problems." Like other quality-achieving principals, Watts provides a variety of information for teachers to use to group students both within and across grade levels.

From a practical point, Watts adds three additional pitfalls or considerations pertaining to block scheduling and teacher teaming. First, principals need to evaluate the effectiveness of the block schedule and team teaching approach. The best way to assess the merits of these variables is to take an attitudinal survey from parents and teachers. Watts uses informal assessment practices through teacher and parent feedback via telephone conversations, personal interviews, and attendance at teacher team meetings. By making notes and keeping a log, he can make the necessary adjustments or be able to present reasons why the overall components of block scheduling and interdisciplinary team teaching are making valuable contributions to learning outcomes. He also notes the value of having PTA meetings open for discussion regarding instructional issues and having a parent advisory council where instructional-related topics can be discussed.

Second, some teachers will not like block, flexible-modular scheduling while others may have difficulty adjusting to the flexible time within blocks. Usually these teachers "come into the fold" through peer pressure. Team members are generally patient and understanding and work with those having negative attitudes or adjustment difficulty. For the most part, he says, these teachers take the helpful suggestions of their peers and adjust. The other option for these teachers is to go to another school not practicing teaming or block scheduling.

The last consideration, Watts states, "has both a good side and a bad side and seems to be a common problem." Here, Watts is talking about teams that truly excel in instruction. They enjoy team teaching and have discovered the freedom of flexible block scheduling for promoting student achievement. Teacher teams can develop a deep interest in competing with other grade level teams for being the "best" performing team within their grade level. While competition is good and promotes the quality tenet of continuous improvement, too much competition can be detrimental. Teams need to share experiences, support each other, and display a cooperative attitude toward quality improvement. When, however, one team becomes overzealous and withholds information, instructional materials or other adopted improvements from other grade level teams in an effort to be "the best," trouble develops.

In such a situation, parents may begin to request that their children be enrolled in only that one particular team as word spreads throughout the school and community of student accomplishments resulting from being taught by "Team A teachers." Teacher peers within the grade level and school become resentful, morale suffers, and trust becomes an important issue. The principal can usually sense this overzealous competition by regularly attending team meetings and reminding team teachers of the purpose and mutual goals of teaming. This can lessen competition before it reaches the detrimental level. However, Watts says, when a team excels at a cost to other teams, the principal has two courses of action. First, counsel with the team members about the purpose of teams, the need for cooperation, and the importance of trust and hope this will change the team's behavior. Second, "disband the team by placing each member on another grade-level team and create a new grade level team composed of those teachers being displaced by 'Team A' members," he says. This spreads the competitive spirit around and usually results in general satisfaction.

Wesley Clampitt, principal at Gilmer Middle School, also uses block scheduling and interdisciplinary team teaching. Clampitt also assigns students based on heterogeneous grouping variables in grades six through eight. He, too, begins the scheduling process with the year-long elective courses and allows teacher teams to assign students to their respective grade level teams. Teams also devise schedules for the students on their team. Results of this process are higher teacher morale, a more positive school climate, fewer student discipline problems, higher student academic achievement, and wider use of peer tutoring and cooperative learning techniques. "These results," Clampitt maintains, "stem mostly from the flexibility and freedom teachers have within team scheduling and flexible blocks to switch students around to create a better mix of students with the 'right' teachers."

Gilmer Middle School practices multi-age grouping or "looping" with 60 percent of teacher teams in grades six and seven. Here, teacher teams are organized long-term, for three years, with students remaining with the same teacher teams as they progress from grades six through eight. Each grade level, six and seven, has four teachers with approximately 120 students who progress through the middle school curriculum with fewer discipline referrals, greater parent involvement, and higher student achievement than non-looping students at Gilmer. Clampitt hopes to have all teacher teams adopt looping but wants to move slowly, allowing successful student outcomes and teachers to spread the word among their peers. Looping was first introduced as a pilot project after a group of teachers became interested in the practice from reading journal articles and through conversations with other teachers in surrounding school districts.

The project began with one teacher team, in grade six, obtaining parental consent to try this new approach. Parents applied for the program and teacher teams randomly selected approximately 120 students to participate. Students were balanced according to achievement test scores, sex, ethnicity, socioeconomic status, and disciplinary problems. At the end of the second year, parents began to request that their children become part of the looping cohort, with fewer student openings than parent requests. "Success breeds success," says Clampitt. He points out that within four years two sixth and seventh grade teams have adopted looping and two more teacher teams in grade six are requesting a cohort schedule for next year. Parents still have the option to choose non-looping teams but most are requesting them since their children enjoy the benefits of remaining with the same peers and teachers, and parents feel more comfortable having the same teachers for their children all three years.

Although the pitfalls of looping are few, the principal should move slowly before engaging in this type of student scheduling. First, teachers themselves have to see the real value in looping and they must support the move to try it. Forcing looping on teachers will be counterproductive. Second, parents must be educated about the value and benefits of cohort teaming and should have a choice as to whether or not their children are assigned to such teams. Third, the principal must be willing to allow teacher teams the flexibility to assign, reassign, and schedule students to teams within the grade levels as students progress through grades six through eight. This latitude allows teachers to remain student-focused and truly meet the needs of each middle school child.

REFERENCES

Alexander, W. M., E. L. Williams, M. Compton, V. A. Hines, and D. Prescott. 1968. *The Emergent Middle School*. New York: Holt, Rinehart and Winston, Inc.

Braddock, J. H. and J. M. McPartland. April 1990. "Alternatives to Tracking," *Educational Leadership*, 47(7):76–79.

Canady, R. L. and M. D. Rettig. November 1995a. " Productive Use of Time and Space: The Power of Innovative Scheduling," *Educational Leadership*, 53(3):4–10.

Canady, R. L. and M. D. Rettig. 1995a. *Block Scheduling: A Catalyst for Change in High Schools*. Gradiner, NY: Eye on Education, Inc.

Craig, J. S. November 1995b. "Quality through Site-Based Scheduling," *Middle School Journal*, 27(2):17–22.

Deming, W. E. 1986. *Out of the Crisis*. Cambridge, MA: MIT University Press.

Deming, W. E. 1993. *The New Economics for Industry, Government, and Education*. Cambridge, MA: MIT Center for Advanced Engineering Study.

Erb, T. November 1995. "Middle Schools Require the Principles of Quality to Carry Out Their Mission," *Educational Leadership*, 27(2):2.

Forte, I. and S. Schurr. 1993. *The Definitive Middle School Guide: A Handbook for Success*. Nashville, TN: Incentive Publications, Inc.

George, P. S. and W. M. Alexander. 1993. *The Exemplary Middle School*. Second edition. Fort Worth, TX: Harcourt Brace Jovanovich College Publishers.

Gilman, D. A. and S. Knoll. 1984. "Increasing Instructional Time: What Are the Priorities and How Do They Affect the Alternatives?" *National Association of Secondary School Principals Bulletin*, 68:41–44.

Jenkins, K. D. and D. M. Jenkins. November 1995. "Total Quality Education: Refining the Middle School Concept," *Middle School Journal*, 27(2):3–11.

Karweit, N. 1985. "Should We Lengthen the School Term?" *Educational Researcher*, 14(6):9–15.

Lunenburg, F. C. and A. C. Ornstein. 1991. *Educational Administration: Concepts and Practices*. Belmont, CA: Wadsworth Publishing Company.

National Commission on Excellence in Education. 1983. *A Nation at Risk*. Washington, DC: US Government Printing Office.

National Commission on Time and Learning. 1994. *Prisoners of Time: Report of the National Education Commission on Time and Learning*. Washington, DC: US Government Printing Office.

O'Neil, J. November, 1995. "Finding Time to Learn," *Educational Leadership*, 53(3):11–15.

Purkey, S. C. and M. S. Smith. 1983. "Effective Schools: A Review," *Elementary School Journal*, 83:427–452.

Rosenshein, B. V. 1979. "Content, Time, and Direct Instruction," in *Research on Teaching*, P. L. Petersen and H. J. Walberg, eds. Berkeley, CA: McCutchan.

Rossmiller, R. A. 1983. "Time-on-Task: A Look at What Erodes Time for Instruction," *National Association of Secondary School Principals Bulletin*, 67:45–49.

Squires, D. A., W. G. Huitt, and J. K. Segars. 1984. *Effective Schools and Classrooms: A Research Based Perspective*. Alexandria, VA: Association for Supervision and Curriculum Development.

Stallings, J. December, 1980. "Allocated Academic Learning Time Revisited, or Beyond Time on Task," *Educational Researcher* (9):11–16.

Weller, L. D. and S. H. Hartley. July, 1994. "Teamwork and Cooperative Learning: An Educational Perspective for Business," *Quality Management Journal*, 4(1):30–41.

Weller, L. D., C. L. Brown, M. L. Short, C. T. Holmes, L. S. Deweese, and W. G. Love. 1987. *The Middle School*. Athens, GA: University of Georgia, Bureau of Educational Services, College of Education.

Wiles, J. and J. Bondi. 1993. *The Essential Middle School*. Second edition. New York: Macmillan Publishing Company.

CHAPTER 10

Leadership for Community and Home Involvement with the Middle School

Schools do not exist in a vacuum. The interaction between the school and its community is frequent and each has a significant impact on the other. Teachers, administrators, and staff personnel are community members as well and have an intimate and vested interest in school and community alike. At its best this relationship fosters mutual trust and goodwill between these two entities and this goal is an important part of the leadership role of the principal.

Communities which are well-informed of the mission of the school and its achievements are supportive communities. Consequently, a public relations (PR) program is important to create and sustain support, and every member of the middle school, including students, are part of the PR team. Getting community members and groups involved in the middle school is important for two-way communication and for community members to see first hand the quality of the educational program. The principal takes a proactive role in providing the necessary leadership, in communicating to the community through a variety of ways the needs, the strengths, and the mission of the middle school.

This chapter will present examples of how principals exercise leadership skills to create good public relations programs for their schools and personnel, how principals can be proactive in community relations activities, and how activities and programs can be used to get community members involved. An example of a well organized PR program will be presented, as well as an example of an organized youth service program which shows the variety of ways students can be involved in community life. Examples of effective parent programs and parenting seminars will be presented as well as ideas for maximizing parents as resources and partners in achieving the mission of the school.

Specifically, this chapter will address the following questions:

- What do effective principals do to create positive school-community relations?
- What kind of school-community relations programs and activities promote positive relations between these two entities?
- What are the roles of the principal, teacher, and staff members in promoting positive school-community relations?
- What kinds of activities can principals, teachers, and staff members be involved in to promote positive school-community relations?
- What are the characteristics and what is the organization of an effective youth service program?
- Why is it important to have parents involved in the school's mission and goals?
- What are the characteristics and organizational patterns of effective parenting and parent involvement programs?
- How can parents be used most effectively in the instructional programs of the school?

SCHOOL-COMMUNITY RELATIONS

Public Relations Defined

There are many definitions of school-community relations or public relations (PR) as it is identified in the literature. Kowalski (1996) relates that PR is both an art and a social science whose goals are to promote goodwill, to sell, to shape opinion and sentiment, and to persuade. Wilcox, Ault, and Agee (1992), after examining many definitions of PR, suggest that a definition can be arrived at through connecting six common words recurring in PR definitions:

(1) Deliberate—a conscious effort to persuade, influence, or promote a product or service
(2) Planned—a highly organized, goal-oriented planned activity
(3) Performance—a result of policy and practice leading to a change in behavior
(4) Public interest—a service to the community or its targeted public
(5) Two-way communication—a communication process which gives and takes information with a service end as a goal
(6) Management function—a responsibility of management or leadership and a variable in the decision-making function of administration

Another term which could be added to those of Wilcox, Ault, and Agee

(1992) is "public relationships" as used by Norris (1984) in the context of building close, trusting relationships with a variety of "publics" which make up the greater community. Building personal and solid relationships with these various groups is essential to achieving the goals of any organization be it corporate, education, or private sector–oriented.

Perhaps the most comprehensive and applicable definition of PR for educators is one given by Bagin, Gallagher, and Kindred (1994). They state that "constructive relationships between school and community are achieved through a process of exchanging information, ideas, and viewpoints and of which common understandings are developed and decisions made concerning essential improvements in the educational program and adjustments to the climate of social change" (p. 15).

The School's Image

The principal is the single most important person when it comes to establishing good school-community relations and building a strong public relations program. Farmer, Gould, Herring, Linn, and Theobald (1995) relate that the character and personality of the principal set the tone for the school's public relations program. And because the principal is the most visible educator the school has, the kind of personal interaction the principal has with community members will form the impression or image these constituents have about the school and the quality of its educational programs.

The importance of a good school-community relations program for middle schools is endorsed by the Carnegie Council on Adolescent Development whose 1989 report notes that part of a successful experience for middle school youth is a result of the student's opportunity to use the community as a learning laboratory. Shared responsibility for educating middle school students between the school and the community is a must and is achieved through a partnership between these two entities through collaboration on the part of both school and community leaders. The importance of a good school-community relations program is not new to the literature. Kindred, Wolotkiewicz, Michelson, and Coplein (1981) relate that one of the purposes of the original middle school movement was to develop programs with the community as part of the middle school's activities program. Community agencies were used to promote the goals of middle school education through their support of the school's programs in health, physical education, and recreation.

Community support for the ideals of middle school education is important if middle schools are to realize their full potential, and parents are the most important of these support groups within the community. Parents, having a vested interest in the middle school, want to make the school's program as quality-oriented as possible and are eager to assist educators in this effort (Weller, 1993). Middle school parents are greatly concerned about the overall program of the school as reflected in their child's class schedule. Parental concerns about the positive social and psychological development of their children now supplement their concerns about cognitive development. Teachers at the middle school, therefore, play a more expanded role in their interactions with parents than do teachers at the elementary level whose interactions with parents focus on the cognitive skills of their children in reading, writing, and arithmetic. Standardized test scores take on more meaning to both parents and community members alike as skill levels increase in difficulty and their results become a source of media attention.

However, principals and teachers alone do not make up the middle school. Support personnel such as secretaries, cafeteria workers, and custodians are an important part of the middle school and are community members as well. Support personnel, like teachers, have their own informal networks within the community and are credible sources of information, good or bad, right or wrong, about the school. The impressions community members and parents receive about the school from these sources greatly impact their own impressions about the quality of the teaching staff, the administration, and the school curriculum. Bagin et al. (1994) note the importance of providing teachers and support personnel with training in promoting positive school-community relations as the best and most reliable way to create and sustain strong, supportive relationships with community members.

Today's image of public education is low and tensions are increasing between the public and educators over the public's demands for higher quality outcomes with the frustrations of educators mounting as they try to meet these demands with fewer tax dollars. Many think public education is wasting its fiscal resources through new school reform and restructuring methods while others are disgusted with high crime, vandalism, and dropout rates in the schools. The 1996 Gallup Poll of public opinion reveals that educators are doing a less than adequate job. Berliner (1993) notes, however, that public schools are not treated fairly in the reporting of data by the media and others who have made unsubstantiated indictments against the public schools which have eroded public confidence in the schools. Among those popular "myths," as Berliner calls them, are that education is excessively expensive and wasteful, that students are lazy and unproductive, and that America has fallen in world economic stature and productivity due to the inadequate education of its youth. Unfortunately, these misconceptions permeate the public thinking and the general perception exists that our schools are not providing the expected outcomes. What the public *perceives* about education becomes their *reality* of education. In education, the power of perception is a serious concern and negative perceptions are a power adverse to education. The challenge to middle school principals is to change these negative perceptions through programs which involve community members and through communication which is both factual and truthful.

BUILDING A SUCCESSFUL SCHOOL-COMMUNITY RELATIONS PROGRAM

The Role of the Principal

The principal is solely responsible for developing good school-community relations, and the kind of community support and the degree of confidence the community has in the school depends on the quality of the school's public relations program (Bagin et al., 1994). Principals must build a PR program with the following considerations in mind:

(1) Community support and confidence comes from citizen involvement in the school's affairs. Involvement increases the probability that parents and others will take a positive interest in the school and work cooperatively with school personnel toward achieving the school's goals. The importance of seeking the support of community members is made clear by the fact that by the year 2000 there will be one voter over age 65 for every parent having a child in school (Carroll and Carroll, 1994). From a fiscal standpoint, schools depend on bond referendum and property tax dollars to build new schools and operate their budgets. The fact that people over age 60 vote at higher rates than do 18-to-35-year-olds has severe implications for educators who do not target this age group for support. Relying on parents for the majority of support for the school and to spread goodwill about the school to the community is no longer a reality.

(2) An informed public is a trusting, supportive, and empathetic public. When the community hears about the successes of the school (what's right with public education), the many challenges and problems confronting educators, and the efforts under way to solve these problems and foster quality education outcomes, the public becomes more understanding of these matters and is more willing to support the school's efforts to meet these challenges.

(3) Principals cannot be effective in their public relations efforts without the full support and cooperation of their staff. The quest for quality must be a total school effort and all teachers and staff members must realize their important roles in building good school-community relations and

then work diligently toward that end. Bagin et al. (1994) relate that sometimes educators are their own worst enemies. Internal conflict among educators is newsworthy and when teachers and administrators criticize each other for the school's shortcomings, the image of the school and the profession suffers. Lack of educator agreement on what is best for students and how best to provide a quality education further erodes public confidence in the schools.

(4) The issue of quality is not a factor of quantity. Schools have many tasks to perform and expectations to fulfill. In recent years, schools have been asked to take on more social and health care related responsibilities and operate less as an educational institution and more as a social agency. Priorities for the school must be established regarding the school's role within the community. This is achieved through community consensus which can only come through informed community involvement.

(5) Public support and opinion must be aggressively sought. People need to be asked to help educators make schools a source of community pride. Many community members are eager to help but have little idea how they can best serve. When principals survey their constituents about the strengths and weaknesses of the schools, they can also solicit their assistance in areas community members feel they can make the greatest contributions.

(6) The principals must actively seek the support of local businesses and in- dustry to assist the school in providing quality educational programs. Both business people and educators want similar outcomes: graduates who are well-educated and have the necessary skills to enter the work- force and make positive contributions to society.

(7) The principal must adopt a solid, business-oriented marketing approach for building an effective school-community relations program. Customer-oriented marketing, according to Carroll and Carroll (1994), is gaining wide support with schools reaping many benefits from this systematic approach to improve school-community relations. Customer-oriented marketing includes collecting data, objectively ana- lyzing the data, planning and implementing the PR program, coordinat- ing the program for effectiveness, and evaluating the results of the program's goals and objectives. Marketing programs which focus on the needs of students and demonstrate the benefits of tax dollars in achieving this end, as well as those educational benefits which enhance society in general, have popular appeal, and are successful.

Marketing is a customer-oriented process geared toward selling a product. Convincing customers that the product is of high quality, is worthy of their investment, and will live up to their expectations takes time, effort, and dedication. Half-hearted marketing measures result in failure and further tarnish the image of the school (Bagin et al., 1994).

Power of Public Opinion

Public opinion is a reflection of a general widespread public attitude or belief which can be negative or positive, right or wrong. The opinion or belief reflects a composite of individual perceptions and when these individual perceptions are merged, they can reflect intense or moderate feelings. When the public issue is important to the community, public opinion triggers action. The power behind public opinion, therefore, is the collective action of the public at the ballot box over issues requiring civic trust and support. Public education is one of these issues.

Negative public opinion has its roots in criticism which often comes from misinformation or from community groups who have a specific vendetta against the school. Criticism is a good measure of the degree of public dissatisfaction and can be considered as both harmful and beneficial to the school. Kindred, Bagin, and Gallagher (1990) note that the harmful effects of criticism occur when unjust or unwarranted action is taken based on misinformation or for personal gain. Positive results occur when action is taken based on the input of interested community members concerning inadequate aspects of the school which need attention. Often, educators are too involved in their own programs or mission to be objective about the outcomes and frankness is needed to return us to reality. Four types of critics exist and each plays a part in shaping public opinion about education (Kindred et al., 1990):

(1) Hostile critics. These critics have displaced anger; instead of taking their anger out on the real cause, they target the schools. They are highly emotional, are personal in their complaints, demand immediate action, feel they have been wronged personally, are "name droppers" and threaten the use of status power, and have their own sense of right and wrong—they are right and everyone else is wrong.

(2) Uninformed critics. These are those critics who are indifferent or uninterested in school programs, rarely visit the schools, repeat criticisms rather than create them, pay attention to critics of those issues which are related to their own particular interests, and often are receptive to facts and explanations that seem logical.

(3) Professional critics. These critics are either self-appointed with special interests or are professional "experts" hired to investigate a particular area of the school's program. They are often knowledgeable on the issue they criticize, generally have a broad support base, seek attention and recognition, and may or may not be friendly toward the schools.

(4) Enlightened critics. These critics are friends of the school who have a positive association with education through personal experiences, are well-read and knowledgeable about the school and educational affairs,

and criticize on particular topics through fact-finding inquiry methods. They expect prompt, factual responses.

In general, the community is made up of these kinds of critics as well as ardent supporters of the schools. Conflict of interest between educators and the community is frequently the cause of criticism and discontent with education. The most inherent conflict is that of shared ownership between educators and the public. The community, the customer of the schools, has certain expectations from the cost paid for the school's product. When voting for bond referendums and increased property taxes, they expect a quality educational program which yields a graduate with the necessary skills to enter the job market and the self-discipline and knowledge needed to be a responsible citizen. Educators share these goals, but in doing so must meet a wide diversity of student needs and abilities; are asked to assume more social agency-related responsibilities; and must work within the guidelines of federal, state, and local statues, usually with austere budgets. Often, the community objects to new educational programs or instructional methods which educators deem relevant to learning. This is an added source of conflict. This conflict, as with other sources, is often a result of either misinformation or a lack of information (Dolan, 1996).

Middle school principals in particular are confronted with a variety of demands from parents and community members alike. The mission of the middle school differs from that of the junior high school, and the variety of programs and courses within the school's curriculum deemed essential to meet the developmental needs of transescents are often viewed as excessive or wasteful. Many question the need for teaching more than the basics and lack an understanding of the mission of the true middle school and its research base, while others see teacher planning time and independent study as wasting taxpayers' money. They often turn to poor student achievement test results to substantiate their assertions. Principals have the obligation to point out that such programs are necessary and to seek the support of the community in assuming a greater responsibility for shared ownership of the schools.

Joint ownership of the school means shared responsibility for the school's outcomes. Conflict comes when the community ceases to take on more ownership responsibility than paying taxes and supporting bond issues for new school construction. Educators need their support in setting priorities for the community's schools and assisting them in meeting the other demands placed on educators outside of teaching the school's curriculum. The result of community dissatisfaction is negative public opinion about the schools and withdrawal of community fiscal support. To change negative public opinion and develop sustained community support, the principal must take the initiative in developing a comprehensive school marketing program.

BUILDING A MARKETING PROGRAM

Data Collection

Marketing programs begin with the collection of data. In middle schools adopting the quality management principles of Deming (1986), data serves as the basis of all decision-making and problem-solving activity. Data is the beginning point of the quest for continuous progress and the basis for planned operations. In school-community relations, data is collected to ascertain the needs and expectations of citizens regarding public education, the demographic background of the school's constituency, the identification of those who are influential in the school's community, the immediate and long-term problems facing the school, and the identification of those who are friendly and unfriendly toward the school. This information can be obtained through formal research methods such as market questionnaires and personal interviews or through a combination of formal techniques supplemented by informal data gathering methods such as parent conferences, conversations with school staff and community members, and information gathered at social functions.

Population data or demographics supply the following important information: educational background, age, occupation, first language preference, race, and nationality. This information is important for home-school programs and to prepare printed material for distribution. Age is an important factor in that the younger the adult population, the more interested they tend to be in school affairs and the more demanding they are about quality educational programs (Bagin et al., 1994).

Preferred communication channels and social affiliations are also important information to know. Newspaper, radio, and television are the predominant modes of communicating and yet each person has a preference, a source they turn to most often for information. Clubs and other social affiliations also serve as information sources. Language preference and nationality are important considerations for ethnic groups who use English as a second language or are literate only in their native tongue. Printed material in these languages promotes better school-community communications and shows caring on the part of school personnel. Cultural pluralism is a fact of life in today's school and community. Attention to ethnic needs and concerns is a major issue which must be addressed in middle schools.

Community and group leaders, those who are most influential in the school's community, are key people to identify and work with. These people shape attitude and opinion toward education among their followers. Knowing their background provides important information for working with these influentials and for accessing their opinions about the school and gaining their support. Kindred et al. (1990) notes that "every neighborhood contains a number of men and women who are consulted by neighbors and friends whenever the questions come up about the school and its relations with pupils and parents. Their opinions and judgments are important determinants of grassroots public opinions" (p. 13).

Assessing the internal public's (school personnel) attitudes toward the school is just as important as assessing opinions of the external public. Teachers and staff personnel have opinions as community members and as professionals. They have insights which most external communities do not have and can offer valuable suggestions on how to strengthen the educational programs of the school. Moreover, it is this internal public who comes into contact most often with parents and other community members. The climate of the school reflects the attitude of those who work in the schools and climate is a factor used to judge the quality of the school itself. Having a spirit of goodwill, acting in a professional manner, and making external public members feel welcome and wanted is a vital part of the school's overall PR program.

Many studies have been conducted identifying power agents and power structures within the community. Dolan (1996) notes the importance of principals' identifying the power agents (key community influentials) and seeking their advice and inclinations about the school and matters affecting education. "Salvation by lunch," assessing the inclinations on school policy and proposed changes over lunch, has been a much used and beneficial business strategy. Usually, principals can identify these leaders through observations of group interactions and those names appearing most often in the local news media. Another way to identify these power agents is through a reputational approach (Hunter, 1953). In such an approach, the power agents identified will be those people who, in the eyes of others, have a reputation in the community for being "powerful." Hunter used this technique by first compiling a list of influential people in four areas: business, government, social status, and civic and community affairs. In compiling such a list, the names can come from those most frequently seen in the local news media; conversations with others; observations of interactions at school, community, civic, and social affairs; etc. Hunter then submitted these names to a panel of fourteen people who acted as "judges" to select the forty reputational leaders from the list. Depending on the size of the community, the number of names selected will vary as will the number of people on the panel of judges. The panel of judges votes on the people viewed as most powerful in the community, and the votes are tallied. The power agents will be those people receiving the greatest number of votes.

These power agents will include business and industrial leaders, bank presidents, prominent lawyers, government officials, newspaper publishers, and those with "old money" or whose family has long-standing ties to the community. These leaders can be characterized as formal or informal and they will vary in degree of power. Principals who identify and enlist the cooperation of these power agents will find their efforts to implement change less resisted and they are more likely to be successful.

Opinion research instruments and methods vary in kind and principals have a variety of data collection techniques from which to choose. For a complete discussion of research methods, the reader is referred to *Educational Research* (5th ed.) by Borg and Gall (1989). Each method has its own strengths and weaknesses, and data collection methods should be selected with these respective strengths and weaknesses clearly in mind.

Formal data gathering methods include the following:

(1) Mailed questionnaires
(2) Personal and telephone interviews

Informal data gathering methods include the following:

(1) Forums, advisory committees, panels, and parent conferences
(2) Newspapers, radio, television, and informal conversations in social situations
(3) Telephone calls from parents and concerned citizens about specific areas of concern

Planning the School-Community Relations Program

Data from opinion surveys serve as the foundation for planning the school's PR program. Ubben and Hughes (1992) state that any effective PR program begins and ends with the staff of the school. Consequently, planning the school's PR program should be a joint effort involving the principal, teachers, and staff personnel. Survey data from both internal and external sources serve as the basis for developing the school's five year improvement plan. Practically, some survey results may not appear valid, but these are public perceptions and must be addressed. Ubben and Hughes (1992) point out that external evaluations often reveal "blind spots" which the school's staff would not have noticed because their priorities were elsewhere. Therefore, all survey data must be examined objectively by the entire staff. The PR plan is developed in the following way:

(1) Survey results are analyzed and placed in priority order. These priorities become the goals for the PR program.

(2) Priorities are then arranged in broad categories, such as instruction, curriculum, school climate, etc.

(3) Individuals or groups are assigned responsibility to achieve each program goal. The improvement that will result from each goal's attainment is specified, how and when the improvement will be measured is realistically determined, possible obstacles to achieving the goal are listed as well as possible solutions to these obstacles, and the baseline data from the survey results which were used to identify this goal are listed (see Figure 10.1). This information is determined for each goal as part of the five-year plan.

(4) Specific action steps are specified for each program goal, the contact person responsible for the action step is listed, resources for implementing the action step are determined and the implementation date is specified (see Figure 10.2).

(5) Each year each program goal is evaluated by the individual or team responsible for that goal (see Figure 10.3).

(6) Results of the year's improvement effort are then analyzed and reported to the community.

Formal surveys should be conducted every two years with these results serving as the basis for an on-going update of the five-year PR plan. Equally important, these formal opinion surveys serve as the community's evaluation of the PR program.

Informal evaluation feedback from parent conferences and the like should be noted and filed. This data serves as a yearly and on-going progress report on the school's PR efforts. Each teacher and staff member is responsible for providing to the principal an information update twice a year with information being shared with the community and parents through the newspaper, PTO meetings, and open forums or town meetings where community participation is invited.

After the school's initial five-year PR plan is implemented, the principal should organize a school-community relations committee. This committee, composed of teachers, staff members, and the principal, coordinates the school's overall PR efforts and notes any external and internal problems. Weller (1993) maintains that the use of this quality circle technique is most helpful in building positive school-community relations when the quality

SCHOOL-COMMUNITY RELATIONS PROGRAM
FIVE-YEAR IMPROVEMENT PLAN

School_____	Date_____

PR Goal Area (circle one):

Instruction   Curriculum   School Climate   Other_____

PROGRAM GOAL (Specific, Measurable, Action-Oriented, Realistic, Time/Resource Constrained)

Individual or Group Responsible for Goal

EXPECTED IMPROVEMENT IN SCHOOL-COMMUNITY RELATIONS WHEN GOAL IS ACHIEVED
_____
_____
_____

HOW AND WHEN DIFFERENCE WILL BE MEASURED
_____
_____
_____

POSSIBLE OBSTACLES   POSSIBLE SOLUTIONS

_____   _____
_____   _____
_____   _____
_____   _____
_____   _____

BASELINE DATA FROM SURVEY RESULTS (attach additional sheets if necessary).
_____
_____

FIGURE 10.1. School-community relations five-year improvement plan.

320

PROGRAM GOAL:

SPECIFIC ACTION STEPS FOR ACHIEVING PROGRAM GOAL	CONTACT PERSON (resp. for activity)	RESOURCES NEEDED	IMPLEMENTATION DATE (month/year)
1.			
2.			
3.			
4.			
5.			
6.			
7.			
8.			
9.			
10.			

Principal's Signature

FIGURE 10.2. Action steps for implementing each PR goal.

SCHOOL-COMMUNITY RELATIONS PROGRAM
GOAL EVALUATION

PR GOAL AREA:

_____
SCHOOL/GRADE LEVEL

_____
DATE

PROGRAM GOAL:

_____

_____

SPECIFIC ACTION STEPS TAKEN TOWARD REACHING GOALS
(List materials purchased, workshops held, etc.)
1.
2. _____
3. _____
4. _____
5. _____
6. _____
7. _____
8. _____

DATA

Original Baseline Data   New Data

_____   _____

_____   _____

_____   _____

_____   _____

Should Goal Remain In Five-Year Improvement Plan? _____ Yes _____ No

FIGURE 10.3. PR goal evaluation.

circle or committee functions as a fact-finding and problem-solving group. Quality circles identify problems, carefully analyze the problems, recommend solutions, and propose ways to implement the solutions.

Staff Development in PR

What and how things are said convey to the public an image of the school. This message must come across to all school personnel and can best be accomplished through a comprehensive staff development program.

Principals are the PR leaders of the school and set the standard of behavior through modeling, behavior which will be emulated by the staff. Since perceptions determine attitudes, the exterior of the school is the beginning point for principals. School grounds should be well-manicured and clean, with ample parking space provided for visitors. First impressions do count. Next, office personnel, the first contact the external public has with school personnel, also convey an image of the school. Professional, courteous behavior is essential for the office staff. Telephone communication is frequently the extent to which many community members come in contact with the school and it is essential that professional and courteous telephone etiquette be continuously observed. School office personnel reflect the attitude of the principal and teachers toward the external publics and they are viewed as a direct extension of the principal. Finally, the interior of the school must remain neat and clean. Schools operate on austere budgets, but there is no excuse for clutter or poorly cleaned halls and classrooms.

The staff development program should motivate staff members to improve their PR skills and provide ways to strengthen good school-community relations. PR programs should be conducted for all new personnel entering the school with sessions being conducted for areas needing improvement as occasions arise.

Building and sustaining good school-community relations is a continuous effort that takes two-way communication skills. Bagin et al. (1994) and Kowalski (1996) stress the importance of a two-pronged staff development program, one for the school's internal public and another for its external public. The idea of having good two-way communication is central to the staff development program.

INTERNAL PUBLICS

Staff development for the school's internal publics, teachers, office staff, support personnel (including substitute teachers), and students, should focus on the importance of sharing information and opinions, joint problem solving, and respecting the rights and opinions of others. Pawlas (1995) relates that when internal publics feel comfortable in expressing their opinions and are treated professionally, their willingness to cooperate with one another increases, they feel free to make suggestions, and they feel personally responsible for creating a positive PR climate within the school. Staff development for internal publics should include the following information:

(1) Good teaching and effective classroom instruction earn the respect and confidence of students, parents, and community members alike. There is no substitute for quality education.

(2) Teachers must be caring and treat students with respect and kindness. Students are a school's best PR for parents.

(3) Teachers must initiate and maintain contact with parents. They must treat parents in a professional and courteous manner and encourage their support and participation in school activities. Above all, they must make parents feel welcome.

(4) Teachers and staff must be good listeners. Teaching good listening skills is an essential part of the staff development program.

(5) Good written and oral communications to parents and students are essential. Correct grammar and speech and written communications which are positive in nature and are personally written promote good PR. Teachers need to avoid educational jargon in their writing, use common words which are easily understood, and avoid complaining about school policies, colleagues, and administrators.

(6) Teachers should praise and reward students for good work and on special occasions. Students' attitudes toward teachers and their school greatly influence parent and public perception. Positive progress reports with specific examples should be sent to parents and shared with students. Rewarding good conduct and effort and praising achievement should be daily occurrences. Celebrating birthdays and special events in students' lives will contribute to good PR and the positive self-esteem of the students.

(7) Parent conferences which are productive, professional, and caring are essential. Pawlas (1995) relates that parent conferences have three essential components: "*to get* information, *to give* information, and *to find* solutions to academic or behavior problems" (p. 165). Good oral communication and listening skills are needed for these meetings to be effective. Two-way communication is essential if teachers are to be of maximum help to parents and parents to teachers. Parent conferences should establish and serve to sustain a good working relationship between parents and teachers in order to meet the needs of the students. More about parent conferences will be discussed under the topic of external publics.

Students are a very important segment of the school's internal publics. Ubben and Hughes (1992) relate that in effective middle schools, the principal solicits students' opinions about the school's program and works to maintain good relationships with students. "Tell it to the principal" sessions are held regularly with eight to ten students where they express their interests and concerns to the principal. Solutions are proposed which should become school improvement goals. Some principals involve students on teacher committees along with community members and parents. At the middle school, a student council can provide an open forum for students to share grievances and suggest new ideas and interests to the principal. Some principals hold office hours reserved for students who can sign up for an appointment and talk confidentially about personal problems or conflicts with teachers. Town meetings with students to obtain their thoughts, criticisms, and ideas are effective and allow students to have input in the operation of the school. Finally, student opinion surveys allow for direct feedback from students and assure confidentiality of response.

Student input is helpful only when it is used and not filed away or dismissed as invalid due to the students' age, or to the fact that they are expressing dissatisfaction with a teacher or program. When student ideas are incorporated into the school's operations, students feel that their opinions are valid and that the principal is sincere in making students a part of the school improvement effort.

Good external school-community relations programs are built on good internal PR. When staff members learn and practice good PR skills among themselves, their behaviors automatically carry over to members of the community. The behavior of the school's staff and the principal communicate to the public the image of the school. What the public thinks and says about the school is a function of communication. Therefore, what and how the internal public communicates to the community and parents reflect their feelings about the school, students, and themselves. When these feelings are positive, the image they project to the external public is positive as well.

EXTERNAL PUBLICS

Before any marketing campaign can be successful a marketing agency has to have "something" of worth and appeal to sell. For schools, the educational program is the marketing target. Pawlas (1995) argues that the community and parents "entrust schools with their most valued assets: their children and their money" (p. 71). Consequently, they are concerned about the quality of the education their children receive for the amount of dollars invested. As customers of public education they have the right to receive kind, courteous service with a product of the highest quality that either meets or exceeds their expectations (Deming, 1993). When customers are satisfied, they brag about their purchase and promote the product to others with pride in ownership. Conversely, dissatisfied customers are discontented with the product, refuse product loyalty, and make negative remarks about their purchase. Deming states that education is no different from industry in this respect and product loyalty comes only through quality educational services. But even if a product is of high quality, it can always improve and, indeed, has to improve to meet the ever changing demands of the customer.

Equally important is product visibility. Quality products which are not widely known receive little customer attention and, therefore, support. Schools who have high quality programs but who fail to market their quality products lack the support and public confidence they deserve. On the other hand, schools producing less than satisfactory products need customer input to adjust their outcome in order to increase public confidence. In each of these circumstances, a sound and aggressive external marketing program is the initial step.

As with internal publics, good human relations skills and communication are the essence of a successful PR program for external marketing. An informed public is a supportive public. Nothing can supplant open and honest communication with the community and parents. Here, both principals and teachers need to work together to target what the public wants to know and provide answers to these questions. Community surveys and informal assessments of community interest areas are the best data sources. Frequently, questions arise about student achievement test scores in relation to neighboring districts and states, discipline and violence problems, drug use, preparedness for college and the work force, the quality of teachers, and the adequacy of the curriculum and technology. Answers to these questions must be addressed cordially. Principals and teachers cannot overcome all of the school's problems alone, especially when many of these problems are rooted in the socioeconomic sphere of society. Open appeals for assistance from the school will be met with positive community response and support when school administrators are open and honest about their problems (West, 1985).

Support for the schools comes from goal communication and community involvement. The effective principal will target external groups for support in providing the quality education expected from both community members and parents in the following ways:

(1) Support should be sought from community and parent leaders who have power and influence and who provide direction for community growth. Business and industrial executives, lawyers, doctors, bank presidents,

and clergy are some of the typical influentials within the community. Pawlas (1995) notes the importance of targeting people in high-contact positions who are not leaders or power agents but who associate with numerous people daily. Barbers, store cashiers, bank tellers, and real estate agents can disseminate positive messages about the schools and shape public opinion. Bagin et al. (1994) labels these citizens "key communicators" and they are valuable disseminators of positive information about the school and for passing along negative impressions or concerns to the principal. These "gatekeepers" of information can quell rumors and help gain and sustain confidence in the schools. Identifying the power agents and gatekeepers, seeking their support, and keeping them informed about the school is the principal's responsibility.

The role of the middle school principal in the PR program with community and parent leaders is one of assertive leadership. The principal should take every opportunity to seek the support of community groups and organizations and the local news media. With local community groups, the principal is the ambassador for the middle school and should belong to service and civic organizations to represent the school. The principal should seize the opportunity to speak at local functions to emphasize the positive aspects of public education and the merits of the school and to seek the public's support in strengthening the school's programs. Lunch and morning coffees with parents and civic leaders are ways the principal can make individual contact with these leaders to share the successes of the school.

Working with the media and having a good relationship with their representatives is crucial to the overall success of the PR program. Keeping the media informed of school events and extending to them personal invitations to social and academic functions are important. Making them feel welcome in school and a part of the school-community partnership will reap dividends when school events need coverage and when negative events occur which need sensitive and discreet reporting. Being honest and factual when reporting information to the media builds trust and support for the school. The media can be a powerful friend and ally or it can be a powerful negative factor for the school-community PR program.

(2) Business leaders have high interest in the schools and have much to offer in terms of financial assistance, business expertise, and the promotion of the positive aspects of the school's programs. Partnerships with businesses allow schools to profit financially and gain the human resources of the business community. This is especially true in the area of advanced technology where business people often have the expertise to

train teachers on the use and application of technology in the classroom. Business executives are interested in a well-educated work force and are usually eager to assist schools in promoting quality education. The adopt-a-school concept has been popular and has helped many schools create stronger academic and technical programs.

Business leaders also learn much about the school's problems through their involvement. Once these business leaders are introduced to the complexities and the various demands placed on the public schools, they have a greater appreciation for the difficulties facing educators and for the positive strides they have made (Ubben and Hughes, 1992). Many business leaders have established scholarships and awards, donated technology, sponsored cultural events, and donated employee time to schools for inservice programs. The creative use of business-education partnerships is endless and principals have an exceptional resource in this private sector when they seek and develop their support.

(3) Many community groups and organizations need space for meetings and other activities. Principals can promote goodwill between the school and the community by making its facilities available to individuals, groups, and organizations after school hours and during the summer. This cooperative spirit reaps many rewards for the school. Kindred et al. (1990) relate that community use of school facilities prior to bond referendums positively correlates with successful election results. Allowing community members and groups to use such school facilities as the cafeteria for banquets; the gym for dances, athletics, and recreational programs; and the library (or instructional materials center) for research, leisure reading, or checking out materials shows non-parents and senior citizens that their tax dollars are not just used for the benefit of students.

Adult education classes can also be held in the school and can be conducted by teachers and other community members. Kindred et al. (1990) note the appeal for such a program to senior citizens who want to enhance their knowledge in formal, cultural, and practical ways. School dropouts often seek remedial work in reading and mathematics while some want to prepare for the GED examination. Politically, this impacts the school. It is easy to understand this impact when one considers that people over age 60 have the highest voting rates (and will outnumber those with school age children by the year 2000) and that the median age of America's population by the year 2000 will be 45 years old and less than 25 percent of the population will have children in school (Carroll and Carroll, 1994).

(4) Parents play a vital role in school-community relations, and a *partnership* relationship between educators and parents is essential for the overall success of the PR program. With parents, developing a strong two-way communication process is essential in meeting the educational and PR goals of the school. Educators must create an atmosphere that makes parents feel welcome in the school and assures them that their concerns are valid and needed. The principal can promote such a partnership in the following ways:

- Encourage teachers to contact parents regularly about the positive and negative behaviors of their children.
- Encourage teachers to listen carefully to parents to gain additional information about their students from how parents think and act and what values and attitudes they hold. Parent behaviors greatly influence the child and provide key information concerning student behavior.
- Encourage parents to visit classrooms, eat lunch with their children, and attend intramural activities.
- Encourage teachers to share reasonable expectations about their students with parents, carefully explaining their limitations while stressing their strengths. Often, parents expect more from the child than the child is capable of giving.
- Encourage teachers to inform parents that transescents are developmentally different and that the maturation process is a difficult time in the child's life.
- Encourage teachers to explain test scores, how scores are derived and what they really mean. Most parents are unaware of how tests are used and interpreted.
- Encourage teachers to have parents work with children at home on areas needing improvement. Helping with homework, class projects, and behavior is part of the school-parent partnership idea.
- Encourage parents to participate in school activities as volunteer judges or referees for intramurals and academic competition and to share their special skills and knowledge in mini-courses and as guest lecturers.

The principal can also promote parent involvement by appointing parents to school committees such as the school's PR committee and curriculum committee. The principal can form a parent-citizen advisee committee which meets on a regular basis to keep the principal informed of parent and community concerns and areas needing improvement. Having former students meet with the principal is a way to foster good community and parent relations by allowing these students to assess the middle school program in preparing them for high school work and the responsibilities of adolescent youth. Some principals invite parents to visit classrooms, have lunch, and attend open forums with teachers and the principal after school. Other principals hold office hours during the evenings and advertise these hours in parent letters and the newspaper for working parents to call or visit to express their concerns or keep up to date on school events. Some principals randomly call parents to discuss their child's progress and solicit their involvement. Most parents appreciate and respond to personal invitations for involvement in school activities and such invitations enhance the school-parent partnership.

Parent-teacher conferences, some maintain, are at the heart of good school-community relations. Negative impressions about teachers and the school's programs can arise from poorly conducted conferences. These negative impressions are then communicated to other community members through the various information networks (clubs and organizations) to which parents have access. These negatives can be kept in check if teachers are tactful, professional, courteous, and well-prepared for conferences. Principals need to help teachers prepare by outlining the steps which will ensure a positive conference:

- Send personal invitation letters to parents to attend the conference well in advance of the scheduled conference appointment.
- Schedule conferences to accommodate single working parents and have child care and transportation available to those parents needing assistance.
- Schedule adequate time for the conference. Rushed conferences accomplish little and frequently leave parents and teachers frustrated over lack of adequate closure on important concerns.
- Be prepared to talk about each child personally and have the student's file on hand with copies of the student's work, tests and test scores, and records of behavior.
- Set the climate of the conference with a professional and courteous greeting and make parents feel at ease. Conferences should begin with an emphasis on the positive aspects about the child followed by a discussion of those areas needing improvement. A prepared list of topics keeps the conference moving and ensures that each topic needing discussion will be covered.
- Make notes of specific concerns from parents which need further discussion and arrange time to discuss these concerns further at a later date.
- Develop a brief student improvement plan with the parents by the end of the conference which focuses on no more than three areas in which the child needs to improve. Delineate the teacher's and the parent's responsibilities and mutually determine ways to change student behavior in school and at home. Parents should be advised

to review the conference content with their children, go over those areas needing improvement, and carefully explain to the child the cooperative effort between the teacher and the parent. Periodic telephone calls should originate from the teacher and should provide a status report on the child's progress. Plans for improvement can be modified based on this progress.

- Keep the principal informed of the results of each conference and provide copies of student improvement plans. Have a post-conference evaluation instrument available for parents at the end of the conference (see Figure 10.4). Information provided can help teachers and principals conduct more effective parent-teacher conferences in the future.

Parents many times feel uncomfortable about parent-teacher conferences and principals can help ease this anxiety by providing a "tips for parents" list prior to the conference. This list helps facilitate a meaningful and productive conference and allows parents time to gather important information for the conference. Pawlas (1995) suggests the following items be included on a tips for parents list:

- Decide exactly what information is to be obtained from the teacher(s).
- Decide what specific information the teacher(s) needs to know about your child.
- Relate how the child feels about school and how you as a parent feel about the education your child is receiving.
- Relate specific social and/or academic problems or concerns your child is having at school and what school experiences are most satisfying and rewarding to the child.
- Obtain information about the grading policy at the school during the conference.
- Ask the teacher about the specific strengths and weaknesses of your child.
- Ask the teacher what you can do for your child at home as a parent.

(5) Written communications to parents from the school are vital in promoting good school-parent relationships. Each piece of information received by parents provides an image of the school and shapes parental attitude toward the school. The purpose of written communication is to keep parents informed about the school and their children. Newsletters, bulletins, and open letters should be informative and printed on quality paper with copies made available for interested citizens and the news media. Free of grammatical errors, these printed materials should keep parents and the community informed about the school's academic and

How Did the Conference Go?

We would like your opinion as a parent on the conference you attended concerning your child. This will help us not only in following up with other information you may need but in making future conferences better for all parents.

Did you feel welcome at the school? Why or why not?

Did the teacher listen to you and see your input as valuable?

Were you able to ask and get answers to the questions you intended to ask when you came to the conference? If not, what other questions do you have?

Was enough time allowed for the conference?

Was the teacher prepared for the conference with copies of your child's records and work samples?

Did the teacher plan some type of follow-up with you on concerns that may need further discussion?

Did you develop a plan with the teacher to help your child do better?

If a plan was developed, please list the items for which each person is responsible.

Teacher responsibilities:

Parent responsibilities:

Student responsibilities:

What would have made this conference better?

FIGURE 10.4. Post-conference evaluation instrument.

co-curricular programs; awards and recognitions received by teachers, principals, and students; fiscal matters; special school events; important community, social, cultural, and educational events; and information concerning new educational practices, programs, and research findings.

A handbook for students and parents can help greatly in conveying the image and philosophy of the school. The handbook should be professionally presented; policies and procedures for both parents and students should be written in clear and concise language; and information should include such things as the school calendar, bus schedules, telephone numbers of school offices, student grade reporting dates, teacher-parent conference dates, and school make-up days. Any printed material or letters going out to parents or community members should be on quality paper and be clearly written in an acceptable format with correct grammar and spelling. One of the quickest ways to tarnish the image of a school is to have errors in written communication.

(6) Evaluation of the PR program is crucial. Evaluation should determine if the program achieved its goals; and the results should be used to improve, add, or delete existing PR activities and to provide greater visibility to the achievements of the school and the PR effort (Kindred et al., 1990). Both internal and external publics should evaluate the PR program with evaluation criteria matching the different goals and objectives of each program. Formal assessment procedures, such as questionnaires and interviews, can be used or data can be collected through informal assessment techniques. Bagin et al. (1994) suggest using a combination of both formal and informal assessment procedures. Records of parent and citizen comments should be noted throughout the year and both principals and teachers should keep logs recording their observations, concerns, and ways to improve the PR program as the year progresses.

Results from the evaluation of the program should be analyzed by the principal and teachers and should be provided to parents and the community. This information-giving process lets the parents and community know that the school considers good school-community relations a top priority and it provides a forum to relate the benefits of the program. However, it is also important to relate where the school's program needs to be improved. Being open and honest with the public and providing data to support the findings are major tenets of a strong and successful PR program. In publicizing areas needing improvement, principals should capitalize on the opportunity to call for greater support and assistance. Moreover, any weaknesses in the PR program will provide the beginning point for the next year's school-community efforts.

BUILDING A SUCCESSFUL HOME-SCHOOL PROGRAM

Parent involvement in the schools and with their children at home has a positive impact on student achievement and student attitude toward school (Jones, 1991). Contributing to increased student achievement and positive school attitude are school programs which provide information and assistance to help parents create a learning environment in the home, which have teachers assist with home educational activities, and which have frequent communication between teachers and parents about the student's progress (Ogden and Germinario, 1994). These authors add that school-parent partnerships are strengthened through school programs which teach parenting skills and activities to improve parent-child relationships and which teach parents to become teachers of their children at home. Jenkins and Jenkins (1995) relate that in schools applying the quality management principles of Deming (1986), high parent involvement includes structured programs designed to assist parents in working as learning partners with their children. This is a natural extension of the team approach to promoting continuous progress for student learning and is important for reinforcing the middle school tenet of having a close working relationship between the home and the school. The importance of having parents involved in the school and in the home, assisting teachers in making the middle school curriculum meaningful, and in making learning more satisfying and rewarding cannot be overemphasized.

Rationale for Parent Involvement

Despite the fact that research supports strong parent involvement in the school and that educators have long recognized the importance of parental involvement, evidence exists that during the middle school years parent participation declines and some schools do not encourage strong parental participation programs (Carnegie Council, 1989). Some middle schools try to increase parent involvement in the schools and are unsuccessful. Clark and Clark (1994) and Pawlas (1995) suggest that lack of parent participation results from a variety of reasons:

- There is a lack of consistent, aggressive parent recruitment practices by principals and teachers. If parent programs do exist, many educators feel their obligation to solicit parent involvement is fulfilled by simply apprising parents of the existence of these programs.
- Some parents' school experiences were personally unrewarding or unpleasant. Being involved in the school provides memories of

failure or of unfriendly teachers and they resist involvement with educators despite their child's presence in the school.

- Schools are perceived as unfriendly places. When parents perceive they are not welcome at school or in the classroom or have been treated in a discourteous way, they feel their presence and involvement is not wanted and that requests for participation are insincere.
- Minority parents speaking English as a second language often feel uncomfortable in school situations and avoid public meetings which cause them embarrassment. Principals, Pawlas (1995) maintains, can help to overcome this embarrassment through use of an interpreter and by presenting printed material in languages of preference.
- Some parents may have had unpleasant experiences with certain teachers or feel that their children have been prevented from participating in certain school activities. These negative feelings and perceptions need the personal attention of the principal who must work with the parents and teachers involved to clear up misconceptions and misunderstandings.
- Some parents, especially single parents, have work schedules which do not permit participation in programs and others lack transportation and/or child care arrangements. Principals need to arrange program meeting times to accommodate these parents and provide transportation and child care facilities at the school for these parents.

Active and meaningful involvement for parents in the education of their children is the goal of any home-school program. Parents who are actively involved in the school have a better relationship with their children and use more positive forms of reinforcement (Becker, 1986). Becker (1986) also found parents who are involved in school programs improve their self-image and self-confidence and enroll in self-improvement programs at higher rates. These same parents develop a more positive attitude toward school, solicit greater community support for the school, and become active in more community programs. Parents who are active in school and home programs rate teachers' interpersonal skills higher and have a greater appreciation for classroom problems. This close parent-teacher relationship fosters better student conduct in the classroom (Lintos, 1992).

Positive effects are made on students as a result of parent involvement in the school and home. Lintos (1992) and the Child Developmental Studies Center (1994) identified the positive effects of parent home-school involvement:

- increased student achievement and self-concept

- improved student behavior and motivation
- improved student attendance and lower dropout rates
- improved help at home from parents who are more skilled and knowledgeable in the learning process and positive reinforcement techniques
- improved classroom behavior

Benefits to teachers of strong home-school programs include the following:

- reduced stress and feelings of isolation and fewer conflicts with parents
- improved support for the goals of the school and higher completion rates of homework and other school assignments

The Role of the Principal

Middle school principals play an important leadership role in initiating good home-school programs and parent-teacher relationships. Strong middle school principals take advantage of the strengths of others with whom they work (teachers and parents) and elicit their assistance in promoting the goals of middle school education. These effective principals broaden the interpretation of the middle school philosophy to include empowered parents who are willing to make a strong commitment to shared responsibility for their children's education. These principals jointly explore with teachers and parents opportunities for parent-home involvement which support the goals of middle school education.

Principals in quality-oriented middle schools stimulate parent involvement by developing a culture of collaboration between school personnel and parents. Such collaboration leads to collegial problem solving and the sharing of ideas which enhance the teacher-parent partnership. Collegial relationships break down barriers to communication, promote open and honest discussion, and build trust between parents and the school. However, principals must allow those involved full responsibility and empowerment to accomplish the task. Collaborative efforts must also be personally meaningful to the participants and all members must approach their work as if each individual alone is responsible for the success of the task.

One model for parent involvement programs in middle schools is Epstein's five-element model (1987) which consists of the following components:

- family obligations to students—health, safety, and a positive home environment

- school obligations to parents—communicating with parents about student progress and fostering parent involvement programs
- parent involvement at school—volunteer work and support for extracurricular activities and clubs
- parent involvement in helping their child learn at home—helping with homework and school projects, and teaching their children values and skills that will benefit them in the classroom
- parent involvement in school governance—decision-making groups and parent-teacher activities

Programs for Parent Support

Helping parents become effective learning partners is part of the child-centered middle school philosophy. Programs designed to strengthen the home learning environment vary with the most effective programs based on the needs of the parents and the children. Many parents, however, lack the knowledge and skills to maximize the benefits of this important role. Consequently, structured programs addressing topics such as general parenting skills, the nature and development of the middle school learner, school policies and practices, the middle school philosophy, tutoring and study skills, and peer relationships and pressures help parents help teachers in the education and healthy development of their child.

A strong home-school partnership begins with programs which inform parents of the important role they play in their children's education and provides them with the specific information they need to help the school teach the curriculum in the home. Gathering specific information on the skills and knowledge parents need precedes formal program planning. This data can be collected through mailed questionnaires or through informal means such as in conversations, meetings, or conferences with parents.

Programs, which can be designed around a series of workshops or seminars, should be arranged to accommodate varying work schedules of parents and should focus on the following topics:

(1) Parenting skills. Providing parents with information about meeting basic family obligations, healthy lifestyles, a positive home atmosphere, and positive reinforcement techniques for sound socio-emotional development is essential. Many parents lack an understanding of the emotional and social conflicts within their children during the transescent growth years and need information about the physical, social, emotional, and cognitive development characteristics of the transescent. Understanding the influence of peers and peer groups is also important for parental assistance.

(2) Communication and study skills. Sessions can include the nature of the

teaching and learning process, study and memory skills, the importance of good communication skills and open and honest conversations between child and parents, and conflict management skills. The importance of hard work, completing work on time, and taking pride in doing one's best are attitudes which parents can reinforce at home.

(3) Home shared activities. Sessions which stress to parents the importance of reading with their children, playing games, sharing hobbies, and discussing world and local events can help parents build sound parent-child relationships. Discussing school events, problems, and successes are also ways parents can build close relationships with their children. The importance of having a regular schedule for homework, family meals, and bedtime should be stressed.

(4) Student projects and work areas. Information on how parents can assist their children with school projects and learning activities and how they can provide a special homework area where students can consistently work undisturbed is important.

(5) Parent-support groups. Groups can be run by parents on special topics of interest to them. They can be coordinated by the school which may also provide experts to address different interest areas.

(6) Adult refresher classes. Classes designed to assist parents in becoming more competent in helping their children in reading, mathematics, and writing are important. Often parents are not acquainted with the new techniques in these skill areas and need assistance on new approaches to teaching. Refresher sessions on writing research papers and book reviews, for example, help parents become more effective home teachers.

(7) Homework hotline and parent-student study sessions. Many principals have certain evenings during the week set aside where teachers are available to answer student or parent homework questions on the telephone. Others provide space in the school cafeteria or library where teacher volunteers circulate among parents and their children who work together on homework or project assignments.

(8) Newsletters developed by the school. Newsletters help keep parents informed of the latest research on child development and learning as well as upcoming programs. Other topics may include additional ways parents can support the work of teachers at home, enrich the lives of their children, and help their children become well-adjusted adolescents.

COMMUNITY OR YOUTH SERVICE PROGRAMS

Getting transescents involved in the community and the school is an important part of the middle school concept. The Carnegie Council on Adolescent Development (1989) recommends that every middle school include a supervised and structured youth service program as part of its curriculum. Youth or community service programs take time and effort, but their benefits seem to override the amount of time and coordination necessary for these structured programs.

Research reports relate the following benefits to students in community and school programs:

- Students become better problem solvers and team members in improving their schools and communities.
- Students build increased self-esteem and feel valued and needed as a member of the community.
- Students increase their sense of social and personal responsibility.
- Students develop better working relationships with and attitudes toward adults.
- Students improve their understanding of the relationship between what is learned in school and how it applies to the real world (Clark and Clark, 1994).

Youth service programs also contribute to reduced involvement in at-risk behaviors of transescents. Benson and Roehlkepartain (1991) report that in a study of over 40,000 youth engaged in service or helping programs, there was less involvement in drug use, there was less school absenteeism and a lower dropout rate, there were fewer cases of depression, and there were fewer cases of vandalism and theft. The positive results of youth service involvement were higher self-esteem and the development of new social and leadership skills. Personal interaction with adults and the resulting bond from a helping relationship promote a sense of duty and responsibility more so than do demands and impersonal relationships with school authorities.

The types of community service programs found in middle schools vary; however, there are some common elements found among successful active learning programs. Benson and Roehlkepartain (1991), McPherson (1991), and Schine, Bianco, and Seltz (1991) found the following elements in successful service programs:

(1) Strong, assertive leadership by the middle school principal to gain the support of service agencies to assist students in reaping the personal and educational benefits of community service
(2) Teachers who are willing to serve as advisors and who strongly believe in the mutual benefits of community service for the student and the service agency

(3) Structured programs which clearly define the learning goals, the role, and the responsibilities of the student (Students should be involved in setting the learning goals and defining their roles and responsibilities with the teacher and service program advisor.)

(4) Clear expectations of what the service agency expects from the school, the teacher-advisor, and the student

(5) Student evaluation criteria and procedures which are written and agreed upon by the student, teacher and service advisor

(6) Periodic summative evaluation sessions among the student, teacher, and service advisor (Parents are advised of their children's progress and work through the teacher-advisor when problems occur.)

(7) A clear connection between the activities in which the student is engaged and the curriculum of the school

The logistics of service program participation such as transportation and time requirements must be mutually arranged. For this reason, many youth service programs take place after the school day ends. Principals play an important role in providing recognition for both the student and the service agency in these cooperative efforts. Recognizing service agencies for their support through the local media, at awards ceremonies, and through school publications promotes good public relations and helps ensure future agency participation.

LEADERSHIP FOR COMMUNITY AND HOME INVOLVEMENT: CASE STUDIES

Quality-oriented middle schools have programs which involve parents and the community in educating the whole student and in supplementing education in the classroom. Good communications skills are essential for the principal to be effective in this area, as well as the desire to pursue a strong, effective community-home involvement program. Many principals see the need and value for such a program, but unless they are personally dedicated to its development and personally committed to making it a leadership priority, the program will become ineffective, become a burdensome activity to principal and teachers, or, given low priority status, will soon disappear from the leadership agenda.

Trickum Middle School principal Mary Anne Charron has a strong community and home information network in Lilburn, Georgia. She and her leadership team encourage teachers and teacher aides to correlate the classroom curriculum with community historical events through field trips, guest speakers, and volunteers. Part of the teacher-developed school mission is to teach students their roles and responsibilities in their own community and in the world community. One of their clubs, "Clean and Beautiful," is dedicated to improving school grounds and the school's interior, and working with community agencies on projects designed to enhance the community in which they live.

Field trips to local parks and museums are used to supplement the classroom curriculum. Guest speakers from local and state government, the health fields, the law and order fields, and the business community conduct orientation sessions and lectures on a variety of topics grades six through eight. Community volunteers assist teachers in classrooms, as do parents, as aides, tutors, and officials and scorers with the intramural program.

Close working relationships are maintained with the local media with newsletters and calendars of current events going to newspapers and radio stations. Open invitations are extended to the media and community officials to attend meetings and special events sponsored by the school. Charron notes the important role of the teacher in making use of the community and its members in instructional activities and encourages teachers to talk about local events as a part of their regular classroom instruction. Some teachers use the local newspaper as part of their regular instructional materials and make extensive use of community members as guest speakers. To Charron, the school and the community must work together if students are to receive a holistic education and "gain a true understanding of their duties and responsibilities in community citizenship." If teachers don't see the importance of making the community part of their curriculum, she adds, students in these classrooms are deprived of the enrichment that other students enjoy.

At Trickum Middle School, the principal and staff believe that keeping the community informed of the school's academic accomplishments and goals is important to creating true community trust and support. Student and teacher accomplishments are topics of local media coverage and Charron and her leadership team participate in local community events and speak at local civic meetings about the accomplishments of their students and teachers. Charron believes an informed community is a supporting and trusting community, and sustaining a working, friendly partnership, beneficial to all, is her goal.

Parent involvement is high at Trickum Middle School due to the philosophy of the teachers and administrators. They believe that parent support is essential if the goals of middle school education are to be achieved. A partnership, based on mutual trust and cooperation, is essential if students are to achieve their potential and classroom learning is to have its intended impact. Charron believes that keeping parents well-informed about their children and the school's mission and program is all-important in having good home support and parent involvement. Parents must know what the school offers students and parents before they can be motivated to become involved. Charron is quick to note the "power of personality" in interacting with parents and stresses the importance of teachers, staff, and administrators making parents always feel welcome, important, and a member of the school's instructional team. This philosophy is enacted through friendly, consistent actions which do more than anything else to create a cooperative partnership, she adds.

Parents at Trickum receive a comprehensive orientation package of materials at the beginning of each school year which includes parent, student, and teacher handbooks; brochures outlining the various programs at the school; a copy of the first newsletter and school calendar; and a parent-teacher organization handbook announcing the year's program and calling for parent support by taking an active role in the various school and parent-teacher programs. Charron notes that parents of fifth grade students receive information packets as well to get them acquainted with Trickum Middle School and provide information about what their children will need and can expect in grade six. Formal parent-teacher organization meetings are held three times a year with formal programs designed by parents to address their specific interests. One such meeting had two modules with ten separate interest sessions featuring guest speakers. Parents could choose to attend the two sessions of highest interest or they could sit in classrooms and select sessions of interest over the school's closed circuit television.

Important for parents to know, Charron says, are the goals of the school for each academic year. She notes that monies from all school fundraising projects go directly to support the achievement of these academic goals. For school year 1996–1997, for example, the two school goals were developed by the teacher and parent Local School Improvement Committee and consisted of two of the eight county-wide goals. The two goals were to raise standardized test scores and teach students good work habits, study skills, and research skills. Specific objectives on what the school hoped to accomplish were clearly presented and specific requests for parent support were accompanied by helpful tips parents could use at home to assist in goal achievement. Figure 10.5 presents tips for parents for improving students' study habits.

Special programs are provided for parents of at-risk students with the identified school goals for 1996–1997 focusing on the direct academic improvement of these students through the Success School, discussed in Chapter 8, which provides a comprehensive program for parents with specific materials and seminars on how they can assist the school in making classroom learning personally rewarding and successful. Parents work closely with teachers to plan home learning experiences which reinforce

TIPS FOR PARENTS
IMPROVING YOUR CHILD'S STUDY HABITS

1. Encourage your child to talk with you about school and what he or she is learning. Listen and share what you know about the subject. This helps to generate enthusiasm and interest.

2. Provide a proper home study setting free from distractions which includes a place to work, good light and adequate materials.

3. Ask to see your child's homework assignments frequently.

4. With your child, plan a regular time for study each day. We recommend an hour a day. Consider family schedule, extra curricular activities of your child, as well as your child's best time for studying when deciding on study time.

5. Help your child understand that studying is more than just reading or doing homework. Share techniques you know for learning new material.

6. Help your child with organizational skills such as time planning and organizing notebooks and materials. Share ideas that help you.

7. Treat school as your child's job. Encourage regular attendance and punctuality. Habits are being set now which will follow the child into adulthood.

8. Be sensitive to your child's health needs. Proper sleeping, eating and exercising help your child to be more alert when studying.

9. Encourage your child to do his or her homework. Support and encouragement from parents are important but you should not do homework for him or her.

10. Make expectations realistic in terms of your child's abilities. Be sensitive to frustrations regarding schoolwork.

11. Try to be positive if your child brings home poor work or tests. Approach it from the standpoint of how you can help him or her to do better.

12. Notify the school counselor or teacher when family situations arise that may worry your child and keep him or her from concentrating at school. Teachers need to be aware of emotional concerns of students which may affect their day-to-day performance in class.

FIGURE 10.5. Handout for parents on improving study skills.

classroom instruction and they participate in seminars which they request on topics of their interest and which are taught by teachers and local consultants. This highly individualized program allows students to receive "personalized" classroom instruction and allows parents to learn more about such topics as parenting skills, study skills and habits, and communication and conflict resolution skills.

Creekland Middle School in Lawrenceville, Georgia has an excellent community-home relations program which is enthusiastically supported by principal Joan Akin. Akin agrees with Mary Anne Charron and the research literature that a successful program depends on the dedicated support and sustained commitment on the part of the principal. To Akin, community support is essential to quality schooling. Trusting communities, she says, support their schools through local bond referendums and increased property taxes, and they support school projects by participating as sponsors or purchasers.

Akin believes in the importance of fostering good media relations and keeps the local newspaper and radio informed of school events. She personally extends an open invitation to media and community officials to attend school functions and have lunch with teachers and students. Active in local civic organizations and community activities, Akin speaks at local meetings about the accomplishments of her students and teachers. She also believes the school should serve the community and opens the gym to community sponsored teams, church groups, Boy and Girl Scout meetings, and other community organizations needing school space. The community has an open invitation to use the walking trail surrounding the school and the track and playing fields for outdoor events.

Creekland Middle School has a strong, supportive business partnership with Jackson Electric Membership Corporation and Kroger Food Stores. Each year, members of the business partnership meet with the principal and teacher and parent representatives to plan ways to support the school, the business partners, and the community. Each year a different set of goals are developed with programs designed to benefit the community, the school, and their sponsors. The Teacher Mini Grant is one product of this joint effort. This grant is used to sponsor teachers who design new and different instructional programs to benefit students. Individual teachers or teacher teams apply for a $500 grant (total yearly grant funds available are $3,000) to purchase materials and equipment, train staff, and provide honoraria. Funds are awarded by the planning committee based on structured guidelines which call for a written evaluation regarding the successful accomplishments of each proposal.

Akin encourages her teachers to utilize the resources of the community for field trips and guest speakers. A speakers bureau, developed through the

Junior Achievement Program, provides a list of community members and business people volunteering their services to the school. The youth services program at Creekland participates in a variety of community sponsored projects and is active in raising donations for the under-privileged and handicapped. Activities such as the Adopt-a-Highway Program, volunteering at local nursing homes, and coordinating food and clothing drives for the needy during the holidays cause students to feel good about themselves, increase their knowledge of the community, and help them realize that the school, as part of the total community, has a responsibility in helping make the community a caring and friendly place to live. Students, with teacher assistance, run the school store where school supplies can be purchased. The profits go to assist special education students involved in guided learning experiences. One such project is having special education students buy food and clothing for the needy. Here, students learn how to shop, interact with salespeople, and make change.

Parent involvement at Creekland is high in both school programs and the classroom. Akin attributes this to the "welcoming and friendly atmosphere created by teachers, staff, and administrators." At Creekland, Akin says, parents are treated as "our friends, partners in providing their children love, support, and understanding as they go through the middle school years." In fact, Akin relates, "parents are VIPs and we let them know it."

Parents are used as classroom aides, tutors, and guest speakers. Parents volunteer to assist in the intramural program, in club activities, and on field trips. The PTA at Creekland is a strong, teacher-focused organization. The PTA leadership realizes the importance of teachers having updated equipment and instructional materials and the organization supports supplementary school funding through fundraising activities. The PTA opens membership to grandparents, has a total enrollment of over 80 percent of its parents, with more than 600 volunteers working in grades six through eight.

Parent workshops are PTA sponsored and are held three times a year. Topics vary depending upon parent interest, but most focus on how parents can better help their children in school and with problems associated with the transescent years. PTA meetings have guest speakers on topics such as drug abuse, gangs, tests and testing, and other topics of parent interest. Making PTA meetings practical, information-giving experiences on topics of high interest helps sustain and attract new members. Akin believes that "the more parents know about the characteristics and problems of preadolescence, the better prepared they are to help the school and their child." Subcommittees of the PTA are responsible for coordinating programs and activities for each grade level. Parents volunteer through these various committees which then coordinate parent participation with the teachers and administrators.

Providing parents with information about the school's academic programs and activities available for their children helps attract parent support and keeps their interest. A comprehensive orientation packet is provided to parents at the beginning of each school year which includes the first edition of the school newsletter, printed four times a year; the school calendar; parent, student, and teacher handbooks; crisis information; school rules and regulations; and tips on how parents can help students with schoolwork and deal with student problems. Parents are also encouraged to eat lunch with their children, "shadow" their children around school, and attend parent-teacher conferences. Conferences begin at 6:00 A.M. and are also scheduled after school until 6:00 P.M. to accommodate parent schedules. Teachers having early and/or late parent appointments are given compensation time.

Each school year begins with a parent orientation session conducted by each teacher team, and separate twenty-minute appointments are arranged where parents provide these teachers with personal information about their children. This helps to personalize team instruction and make parents aware of the highly caring, student-focused program at Creekland. At this time, the Home Information Handbook is explained to parents. This handbook is designed to make students more responsible for their own learning and keep parents informed of their children's daily and weekly assignments. Homework, project, and test grades are written in each child's handbook by the teacher, weekly, so parents have an on-going record of their children's progress. Students write daily and weekly class assignments in their books. Parents indicate that they have seen their child's handbook by initialing the appropriate page in the handbook and they can call for a teacher conference should progress decline or they wish to discuss problems affecting their children's work.

REFERENCES

Bagin, D., D. Gallagher, and L. Kindred. 1994. *The School and Community Relations.* Fifth edition. Boston: Allyn & Bacon.

Becker, R. 1986. "Parents and Schools," *ERIC Digest, ERIC Clearinghouse on Elementary and Early Childhood Education.* Urbana, IL.

Benson, P. and E. Roehlkepartain. 1991. "Kids Who Care: Meeting the Challenge of Youth Service Improvement," *Search Institute Source*, VII(3):1–4.

Berliner, D. C. 1993. "Education Myths: Eleven Current Ones That Serve to Undermine Confidence in Public Education," *Journal of Educational Public Relations*, 15(2):4–11.

Borg, W. R. and M. D. Gall. 1989. *Educational Research: An Introduction.* Fifth edition. White Plains, NY: Longman.

Carnegie Council on Adolescent Development. 1989. *Turning Points: Preparing Youth for the 21st Century.* Washington, DC: Carnegie Corporation of New York.

Carroll, S. and D. Carroll. 1994. *How Smart Schools Get and Keep Community Support.* Bloomington, IN: National Education Service.

Child Developmental Studies Center. 1994. *At Home in Our Schools: A Guide to School-wide Activities That Build Community*. Oakland, CA: Child Development Project.

Clark, S. N. and D. C. Clark. 1994. *Restructuring the Middle School: Implications for School Leaders*. Albany, NY: State University of New York Press.

Deming, W. E. 1986. *Out of the Crisis*. Cambridge, MA: MIT University Press.

Deming, W. E. 1993. *The New Economics for Industry, Government, Education*. Cambridge, MA: MIT Center for Advanced Engineering Study.

Dolan, G. K. 1996. *Communication: A Practical Guide to School and Community Relations*. Belmont, CA: Wadsworth Publishing Company.

Epstein, J. L. 1987. "What Principals Should Know about Parent Involvement," *Principal*, 66(3):6–9.

Farmer, R. F., M. W. Gould, R. L. Herring, F. J. Linn, and M. A. Theobald. 1995. *The Middle School Principal*. Thousand Oaks, CA: Corwin Press, Inc.

Hunter, F. 1953. *Community Power Structure: A Study of Decision Makers*. Chapel Hill, University of North Carolina Press.

Jenkins, K. D. and D. M. Jenkins. 1995. "Total Quality Education: Refining the Middle School Concept," *Middle School Journal*, 27(2):3–11.

Jones, L. T. 1991. *Strategies for Involving Parents in Their Children's Education*, Fastback No. 315, Bloomington, IN: Phi Delta Kappan Educational Foundation.

Kindred, L. W., D. Bagin, and D. R. Gallagher. 1990. *The School and Community Relations*. Fourth edition. Englewood Cliffs, NJ: Prentice Hall.

Kindred, L. W., R. J. Wolotkiewicz, J. M. Michelson, and L. E. Coplein. 1981. *The Middle School Curriculum: A Practitioner's Handbook*. Second edition. Boston: Allyn & Bacon.

Kowalski, T. J. 1996. *Public Relations in Educational Organizations: Practice in an Age of Information and Reform*. Englewood Cliffs, NJ: Merrill.

Lintos, L. B. 1992. *At-Risk Families and Schools Becoming Partners*. Eugene, OR: ERIC Clearinghouse on Educational Management.

McPherson, K. 1991. "Project Service Leadership: School Service Programs in Washington State," *Phi Delta Kappan*, 72(10):750–753.

Norris, J. S. 1984. *Public Relations*. Englewood Cliffs, NJ: Prentice Hall.

Ogden, E. H. and V. Germinario. 1994. *The Nation's Best Schools: Blueprints for Excellence, Volume 1, Elementary and Middle Schools*. Lancaster, PA: Technomic Publishing Company, Inc.

Pawlas, G. E. 1995. *The Administrator's Guide to School Community Relations*. Princeton Junction, NJ: Eye on Education.

Schine, J. C., D. Bianco, and J. Seltz. 1991. "Service Learning for Urban Youth," *Middle School Journal*, 23(5):40–43.

Ubben, G. C. and L. W. Hughes. 1992. *The Principal: Creative Leadership for Effective Schools*. Second edition. Needham Heights, MA: Allyn & Bacon.

Weller, L. D. 1993. *Total Quality Management: A Conceptual Overview and Applications for Education*. Athens, GA: College of Education, The University of Georgia.

West, P. T. 1985. *Educational Public Relations*. Beverly Hills, CA: Sage.

Wilcox, D., P. Ault. and W. Agee. 1992. *Public Relations: Strategies and Tactics*. Third edition. New York: Harper Collins.

CHAPTER 11

The Role of the Principal in Homogeneous and Heterogeneous Grouping Practices

Middle school principals are often asked whether there should be homogeneous or heterogeneous grouping in the middle school. Effective principals know the answer is both. Early research argued for homogeneous grouping to meet the needs of individual students while more current research questions ability grouping practices, especially among minority and low income students. In middle schools, some form of ability grouping seems to be a common practice, especially in the core courses of mathematics, reading, and English. Homogeneous grouping may place labels on students and lead to erroneous assumptions about their abilities. Heterogeneous grouping reduces the negative influence of cliques, forces the formation of new friends, and greatly promotes social development. Temporary grouping of students, which replaces total tracking structures, provides numerous opportunities for students to receive special instruction or enrichment without the danger of being labeled or stigmatized.

Found within this chapter will be examples of the ways principals can provide different grouping practices in middle schools and examples of temporary grouping practices within interdisciplinary teams and flexible block schedules. Examples of activities used for intra-class and inter-class grouping will also be presented, as well as the most common learning and teaching styles for student groupings. An example of a teacher staff development program on learning and teaching styles will also be offered. Case studies of grouping practices will conclude this chapter.

This chapter will focus on the following questions:

- What does the research say, both positive and negative, about homogeneous and heterogeneous grouping?
- Why are both types of groupings desirable for middle school

347

students and what are the major advantages of these groups to the developing adolescent?

- How can the principal best facilitate the advantages of group instruction and what are the roles and responsibilities of the principal and the teacher in these grouping practices?
- What are the teaching styles and diagnostic instruments necessary to facilitate the positive aspects of intra-class and inter-class groupings?

ORGANIZING FOR INSTRUCTION

Ability Grouping

Middle school learners are concerned with finding out who they are, identifying their own inner feelings, and understanding how they relate to others. They make comparisons between themselves and their peers and notice the differences more than the similarities. The individual physical, cognitive, social, and emotional changes they go through vary and, at times overlap. The way transescents are grouped for instruction during their daily activities and throughout their middle school years can impact self-concept and cognitive, social, and emotional development.

Each individual is different, unique in abilities, interests, needs, learning styles, personality, and background. As students continue to develop, these differences increase. Some differences can be measured more easily than others, such as diverse achievement levels as measured on standardized achievement tests. The tendency on the part of educators is to use these "easy" measures to classify students according to ability.

For more than two decades, middle school educators have relied on achievement test scores to group students by ability level, placing faster or higher achieving learners in one group and slower or lower achieving learners in another. This grouping practice is known as tracking. When tracking is used as the primary means to group students for instruction, students are "labeled." They know what the labels are and what they mean and students then behave or achieve according to these labels. Brophy and Good (1986) point out that it is not only the socioeconomic characteristics of students that determine achievement, but the explicit behavior of the teacher toward the students' perceived achievement levels in that teacher's classroom.

Achievement tests, along with I.Q. scores, previous grades, and teacher opinion provide one measure of predicting ability and one way for organizing students within the middle school. However, serious problems can arise when permanently grouping students on achievement test scores alone or even in combination with other measures since disparity can exist in student achievement across disciplines: "This method of grouping is usually not effective. No common denominator can be found for long-term grouping across disciplines or even within disciplines" (Ubben and Hughes, 1992, p. 215). Ubben and Hughes note that the achievement range of an age group of students is equal to approximately two-thirds of their chronological age. The achievement range, then, for a group of twelve-year-olds is eight years. The fastest achievers will achieve four years above chronological age while the slowest achievers will achieve approximately four years below.

Permanent grouping of students on a single measure does not take into account intangible variables such as student interest and motivation which can impact achievement within a discipline. Grouping by ability or homogeneity on I.Q., achievement tests, or other measures of skills and knowledge does not apply across the board since a low achiever identified by one grouping criteria for a given discipline may excel beyond that of a high achiever in another discipline. Ubben and Hughes (1992) note: "Homogeneous grouping as a broad-based or permanent grouping design simply does not work, and the homogeneity is a figment of the imagination of the staff" (p. 216). What many principals and teachers fail to realize when they argue that ability grouping evidences student gains is that an overlap in abilities exists from group to group and that ability grouping overlooks the individual student (Ubben and Hughes, 1992).

More middle schools than not practice ability grouping of some type. A common practice is to group students according to three breaks in achievement level: high, medium, and low ability. The rationale is that teachers will be able to use individual time more effectively with uniform ability groups since the range of student abilities is narrowed within each group.

GROUP SIZE

While the quality of instruction and the needs of students are major concerns, economics often dictate class size. The budget restrictions placed on principals limit the total number of teachers and aides that can be employed. Therefore, the most economical staffing ratio must be used by the principal for economic efficiency, and this may range from 10 to over 30 students for one teacher. Aides, even if they are parent or community member volunteers, must have special training in order to provide for maximum instructional effectiveness, and this also requires additional resources that may or may not be available.

Research on the most effective class size for instruction is conflicting. Studies conducted over a period of 50 years on the effects of class size were reviewed by Carson and Badarack (1989) who reported that "studies on the achievement effects of substantial reductions in class size indicate that smaller classes do have more positive effects than larger ones, but the effects are small to moderate. . . ." (p. 9). It must be kept in mind that teaching is a highly complex function and the quality of teaching and the instructional strategies and materials used vary from one classroom to another. Class size may also negatively affect teacher behavior and morale and may contribute to the effects of class size on student learning. Nonetheless, over time, small classes may have positive effects on student learning and they certainly contribute to improved teacher morale.

Other research on class size states that classes of between twenty to forty students made little difference in student achievement while benefits became more significant as class sizes fell *below* twenty students. With reduced class size, teachers have greater opportunities to individualize instruction, have greater student participation, and vary their instructional methods more often (Glass and Smith, 1978). Ubben and Hughes (1992) report research which states that classes of fifteen or less students to one teacher, particularly those of a five student to one teacher ratio, show greater academic achievement. A small student ratio allows teachers to use a tutorial style of instruction and to work individually with each student for concentrated time periods. Ubben and Hughes state that small groups also have positive impacts on low achieving and at-risk students. When class size is reduced from thirty or more students to a 25:1 ratio or below, significant student behavioral changes are evidenced. Teachers vary their instruction to meet different student learning styles and there are more opportunities to individualize instruction. The larger the class, the more tempting it is to teach to the class average achievement level and use lecture or other types of whole-class instructional strategies.

The temptation on the part of teachers to form subgroups of five or six students in a class of thirty or more students in order to reduce the range of student variability should also be resisted. Henson (1993) points out that the results of ability grouping are largely insignificant even though ability grouping tends to improve student learning and student motivation. What is needed in schools, argues The Educational Research Service (1978) are practical guidelines for flexible class size that will allow decision makers to vary class size to meet the needs of students, teachers, and the curriculum. This early identification of the need for principals to provide a schedule which allows teachers time and facilities to regroup students for instruction was largely ignored.

Homogeneous Grouping

Today, and during the past five decades, a paradox exists among many educators, parents, and the public about public education. Many want to use integration and other means to eliminate differences children receive in schools, but hold the line on eliminating differences in classrooms. Others, however, believe that heterogeneous grouping, placing students with diverse abilities and backgrounds into the same class, creates too difficult a task for a teacher to meet individual student needs and abilities. They argue that the diversity in range and readiness among students is too wide. Consequently, they point to homogeneous grouping, grouping students by ability, as a way to narrow this range and allow for a better match between student and curriculum (George, 1995).

To some, ability grouping is logical and an effective way to meet the wide range of student abilities, motivation, and readiness in classrooms. After all, schools mirror society and diversity in the real world is a given, and part of the school's job is to ready students for entrance into a society of competition where merit is based on achievement. Grouping students according to ability and correlating the curriculum and level of instruction to these abilities seems rational; and with such grouping it seems that teachers should be more effective, students should learn more, and their motivation and self-esteem should naturally increase.

Over 500 research studies during the past 50 years have focused on both the positive and negative affects of tracking, however, and, according to Slavin (1990a), have found little value in ability grouping. Its popularity centers on the ease with which students can be grouped for course scheduling when working with limited space and time, it raises the teacher-student ratio and stretches tight fiscal resources, it seems natural to group students by ability or some standard criteria, and it is easier to teach large numbers of students with similar abilities.

Critics say homogeneous grouping denies students access to an equal education and is based on psychological assumptions which are not true. Others question its value from a social perspective and note its negative impact on student attitudes and behaviors. Dentzer and Wheelock (1990) state that ability placement is neither fair nor accurate and that grouping impacts the perceived ability of students and may thwart effort and motivation. George and Rubin (1992) caution that ability grouping may lead to racial and socioeconomic segregation in classrooms. The use of single and narrow criteria, like achievement or I.Q. scores, strengthens the probability of classroom segregation. Teacher and counselor recommendations, as well as student and parental input, are needed to replace single or arbitrary placement criteria.

Other critics, like George (1995), argue that ability grouping in elementary school, even if done in intra-class groups to separate learners in reading, have negative effects later on. For example, when young learners are grouped by ability consistently, differences in learning will increase rapidly and will tend to separate high achievers from low achievers by years instead of months. Also, once children are placed in a certain group, they tend to be "locked into" those groups as they progress through the grades, and they form friendships and social networks that influence individual motivation and performance as schooling progresses. Labels often denote ability and work to the detriment of those not in classes labeled "honors" or "accelerated." Placement in ability groups is often rigid with little provisions made for moving from one group to another. For those who can achieve beyond lower track expectations and abilities, but who are forced to remain in this group, sustained motivation to excel and achieve is weakened. This is especially true in middle schools when students can and do excel in different areas because of their uniqueness but are ability grouped for the entire day or year. Stevenson and Lee (1990) note that Asian children succeed in academic achievement because their parents and teachers constantly stress effort, diligence, and enthusiasm for learning, and downplay innate ability. Bondura (1992) is critical of our lack of emphasis on stressing effort, promoting enthusiasm for learning, and having our students think of ability as an acquired skill attainable through learning and mastering competencies. Bondura relates that students who view ability in this way do better in learning than do others because they believe in themselves and have a stronger sense of self-efficacy. Low-achieving students in many schools receive little encouragement to excel, to get enthusiastic about learning, or to stretch their achievement levels.

Often, content rigor and depth of instruction are unequal between ability groups. Low achievers are too frequently taught without varied instructional strategies and materials and are provided a learning atmosphere often characterized by quiet and mundane seatwork with teachers who are less than enthusiastic about teaching and more concerned about classroom management (George, 1995). Oakes (1988) relates that in low-ability groups, teaching is more fragmented, worksheets and recitation are emphasized, and problem-solving skills and higher-order thinking skills are de-emphasized. Some teachers have little or no training in teaching in well-balanced heterogeneous classrooms while others lack training in teaching culturally diverse students. Darling-Hammond (1988) relates that in some schools, teaching assignments are a political process with the least experienced and skilled teachers assigned to teach low achieving students. When inexperienced teachers receive a heavy teaching assignment of low-achieving students, a pattern of lower achievement results for these students (George, 1995). In general, the quality of teaching is lower, course content and expectations are different between high and low ability groups, and instruction is slower paced. Moreover, ability grouping limits the diverse social interactions which should be taking place among students. Unless a program of intramurals or an advisor/advisee program exists in the middle school, the opportunity to make new friends and develop interpersonal skills with students from a wide variety of backgrounds is greatly reduced. Ability grouping contributes to a poor attitude toward school and education in general in low-achieving youth, especially when a negative, anti-school crowd forms among these students who demean the value of education. Schoolwork is viewed as having little importance and the students view themselves as having little self-worth.

The climate and the curriculum within schools have been criticized as having negative effects on students in low-achieving classes. Oakes and Lipton (1992) note that inclusive environments in schools need to exist in which all students are allowed to share in school decision-making processes. When students are allowed to make decisions about the academic program and have the opportunity to choose courses considered "beyond" their capabilities, low achievers feel part of the school and encouraged to excel and exert effort. Differences in abilities in difficult courses can be handled through flexible time requirements and grading. Creative writing or Algebra I could, for example, be extended another grading period for low achievers with a pass/fail option. Satisfactory completion could then result in a letter grade for the course.

Little evidence exists that teachers individualize instruction in homogeneous groups or provide different learning materials for students within these groups. Within any grouping of students based on test scores alone, there will be individual differences among these students which were not measured on these tests. These variables, such as motivation, good work habits, and effort, can impact more heavily on student achievement than a score at a certain level on an achievement test. When teachers fail to individualize their instruction to tap these resources or to increase student understanding, a self-fulfilling prophecy occurs.

The negative impact of ability grouping on achievement for minority and/or at-risk middle school youth is also documented. Ability grouping has negative effects on self-concept and motivation to learn. Fleming (1990) found that by nature, middle school students are self-conscious about themselves and that at-risk students are even more self-conscious. Consequently, when these students experience failure in the classroom and are then grouped with low-achieving peers who also fail and may hold education in low esteem, the situation is compounded.

Classroom or school groupings also affect the self-perception of at-risk students. Being labeled impacts their behavior both in and outside of school. Low-ability students isolate themselves from other students who are high achievers outside of class and, with little or no positive interaction with these high achievers, tend to perpetuate the behavior of stereotypical low-achieving students (Segro, 1995). Providing educational equity is a concern of principals and teachers alike; and, as Oakes (1988) points out, the evidence suggests that placing at-risk students in low-ability groups promotes a cycle of restricted opportunities and growing achievement differences between low and high-ability groups. In addition, Oakes notes that low ability students learn more, remember longer, and have more positive attitudes toward school when placed in high ability classes rather than in remedial classes.

Some schools have led themselves into a defacto racial and social segregation system while intending to integrate the school. George and Alexander (1993) maintain that there are three schools operating within many middle schools. First is the honors or advanced placement students who come from high income, mostly white families, and usually make up the majority of students in the school's gifted and talented programs. Second is the group of middle ability or regular students whose educational program lacks any special qualities and who are accepted as regular students. Third is the lower track or low ability group of students whose population is increasing and who mostly come from poor and minority cultures.

In addition to its impact on achievement, research has indicated that homogeneous grouping also has a negative impact on self-concept. The prophecy that children become what they say they are or what they think they are has direct implications for highly impressionable, emotional, and peer-oriented middle school youth. Both teachers and peers have a great deal of influence on middle school youth and impressions conveyed by these respected others impact these students' attitudes toward their own abilities and appearances and represent a major factor in future success or failure. Ubben and Hughes (1992), addressing this self-fulfilling prophecy and administrators who organize their schools by ability groups, state: "The placement of a child in a group on the basis of perceived ability can seem to prove itself correct by adjustments in productivity on the part of the child that in fact take place as a result of the placement, thus fulfilling the prophecy" (p. 217).

The practice of ability grouping for some teachers translates into a mission to treat all students within each group alike whether they are in high or low ability groups. It is important to remember that all students are not exactly alike, especially at the middle grades level, and that instructional methods involving independent study, individualized instruction, and cooperative learning are central to helping students achieve regardless of their group label.

The evidence, while somewhat mixed, strongly suggests that ability grouping is not beneficial for students in general. At the same time, recommendations go against teaching to the average student in heterogeneous classes. Instead there should be high academic standards for all students; varying teaching strategies and materials; and support, encouragement, and rewards for effort and hard work (Slavin, 1995). From an equality point of view, Slavin argues that "ability grouping by its nature works against democratic and egalitarian norms, often creates racial or ethnic divisions, risks making terrible and long-lasting mistakes, and condemns many children to low-quality instruction and low-quality futures" (p. 21).

Despite these arguments, many middle schools still practice some form of homogeneous grouping; and many practice ability grouping in more than the commonly accepted areas of mathematics and reading. In the 1980s, homogeneous grouping by middle school administrators was practiced in the majority of schools surveyed by Lounsbury and Clark (1990). They found that 89 percent of middle schools used some form of ability grouping and they agreed with Braddock (1990) that tracking for students increases in grades five through eight, and the proportion of students who are grouped by ability increases from grades five through nine. Students are more likely to be grouped in mathematics, reading, and English. While most students are ability grouped in only a few subjects, some students are tracked for the entire day. They conclude that the negative effects of tracking on students at this developmental stage may be long lasting and that grouping by ability will have to be greatly reduced if these schools are to promote the true middle school concept.

Heterogeneous Grouping

Heterogeneous groups have been defined as "groups of students with diverse and varied achievement levels, interests/experience levels, and socioeconomic or ethnic backgrounds" (Forte and Schurr, 1993, p. 161). One purpose of heterogeneous grouping is to include a wide range of students with varying abilities, interests, and backgrounds in learning so that each student can benefit from the social interactions with and contributions from others while receiving instruction from the same teacher. In whole-class instruction, students make unique contributions to the group and are, in turn, exposed to experiences valuable to their own development. Rewards are many, but working with others of different intellectual abilities and skills, learning to respect others for their own strengths and talents, and sharing insights and experiences are some of the most valuable for students in their educational growth and social maturation (Kindred, Wolotkiewicz, Michelson, and Coplein, 1981).

The middle school philosophy embraces the heterogeneous grouping concept, and proponents of the middle school strongly argue its benefits. Many middle school principals and teachers, however, are still divided in their beliefs about the efficacy of heterogeneous grouping. This debate causes disparity in grouping practices in middle schools with each side, those for and those against heterogeneous grouping, strongly believing in and advancing their perspective. Unfortunately, as George (1993) points out, "The real losers in these debates may be the students" (p. 17).

As mentioned before, identification and placement of students into ability groups is usually accomplished through achievement test scores or I.Q. scores. Cooper (1995) relates that middle school principals and teachers find ability grouping by test results a natural and easy way to organize for instruction. Test score phobia has caused many educators to lock into the "exclusive" mode of instructional thinking rather than embrace the "inclusive" thinking approach to teaching and learning. Inclusive thinking, Cooper maintains, is found in heterogeneous classrooms which challenge all students to achieve; encourage effort; reward hard work; and use a wide variety of teaching strategies to accommodate different learning styles, teach problem solving and higher order thinking skills, and tap student talents and skills for learner achievement.

Others, like Feldhusen (1995), call for principals and teachers to take a more global approach to assessing student abilities and rethink what I.Q. and achievement test scores really mean. Some of these tests have questionable validity and reliability coefficients while others may be culturally biased. Sometimes political pressure is applied to principals from parents and/or school board members to place students in certain groups (George, 1993). Test scores do not measure hard work or good work habits and they do not take into account personality styles nor the element of creativity which varies widely in definition and is found in successful people (Feldhusen, 1995).

When ability grouping is practiced, it is predetermined that differences in ability exist and that there are adequate measures to identify these differences. In this case, exclusive thinking has dominated. Consequently, learners are expected to learn at different rates which impacts both teacher and student expectations of success (Cooper, 1995). When ability grouping is based on achievement scores or I.Q., student abilities, talents, needs, and learning styles become secondary. Feldhusen (1995) stresses the need for principals and teachers to consider Gardner's (1983) multiple intelligences theory (see Chapter 1) and Jung's (1971) personality types (see Chapter 4) as a basis for assessing students. These theories can be used to group students in classes, with students included who range from gifted and talented to low achievers. Middle schools attempting to meet the diverse and unique needs of their students will globally assess students' different talents and abilities and provide appropriate instruction.

Teachers are the key to overall student success and principals have the responsibility of providing teachers with the knowledge and skills to transform classrooms into instructional laboratories where students can continuously improve and develop based on their individual strengths (Mason and Burns, 1995). Classrooms must also foster opportunities for student creativity and provide personal satisfaction in learning. Cooper (1995) advocates teachers being trained in and implementing in their classrooms an array of skills which challenge creativity, promote interest and learning, and are applicable to all students:

- Teachers should use cooperative learning strategies which promote teamwork.
- Teachers should teach research skills and how to base conclusions on data.
- Teachers should become facilitators of information, helping students to find information to solve problems and develop creative outputs.
- Teachers should use group work to teach the value of cooperation, respect for the knowledge and talents of others, and personal responsibility.
- Teachers should explore novel ideas and new ways for students to solve problems both in teams and individually through independent study and group projects.

Parent Support

Parents today are more mindful than in years past of the economic and social implications of an excellent education for their children. The middle class strata is shrinking and the differences between the "haves" and the "have nots" are widening. The opportunity for a good job and a secure future for their children is becoming less realistic and parents can no longer pass down promises of security or sizeable inheritances to guarantee a respectable middle class life style (Newman, 1993). Education, now more than ever before, has become essential to the future success and security of their children. Parents also feel that "schooling is a zero sum game, that there is not enough success to go around. Fear of the future has translated into a struggle to garner the best the school has to offer for one's child, at virtually all costs" (George and Grebing, 1995). These uncertainties have now impacted the middle school and there is a demand for programs that allow students to excel and which cater to students' unique talents and abilities. Parents of gifted and talented students are vocal about strong programs for their children while those advocates of lower achievers want a quality education for all students which allows all to succeed without the elitism fostered through ability grouping.

Parent support for heterogeneous grouping is absolutely essential in order for it to succeed in the middle school. Wheelock (1995) points out that parents of "special needs" children are sensitive to grouping practices and the perceived negative effects of heterogeneous grouping, and they tend to view this grouping practice as a threat to their children's education. The role of the principal is vital in educating parents about the research on mainstreaming and the fact that students have more to gain from learning together than from learning apart in differently labeled programs.

Some middle schools adopting heterogenous grouping find parent resistance high, especially when some special needs programs have to be eliminated. Wheelock (1995) recounts the story of one middle school principal facing parent dissatisfaction over the loss of the gifted and talented program. The principal gathered these parents together and asked *them* to choose the thirty students out of the fifty-five qualified students for the gifted class. A decision could not be reached even after much debate. After a great amount of internal dissention, the parents' conclusion was to have a gifted program for all students in the middle school. Another principal facing strong parent dissatisfaction conducted a series of parent seminars in which parents were taught the principles of the middle school philosophy and then taught portions of core subjects by teachers. Parent learning was then assessed on student assessment instruments. Through this experience, parents developed a greater appreciation for the quality of instruction and content found in heterogeneously grouped classrooms. One middle school principal pilot tested heterogeneous grouping in the sixth grade with experienced and highly motivated teachers. By applying a challenging curriculum, setting high expectations for student success, and providing learning experiences that stressed teamwork and problem solving, these teachers overcame the grouping concerns of parents through student performance and excitement about learning (Wheelock, 1995).

The Principal's Role

Effective middle school principals promote the middle school credo of success for all students and continuous personal development through team teaching and flexible scheduling configurations. George and Grebing (1995) believe that teacher teams and block scheduling can satisfy the demands of those parents of gifted and talented students, of those advocating the strengths of heterogeneous grouping, and of those who support the middle school philosophy of providing educational quality and success for all students. Fipp, Barry, Hargrave, and Countryman (1996) note, however, principals seems to be a particular barrier in promoting heterogeneous grouping. Problems with providing pull-out time for gifted and talented and other programs can be overcome by adding another period to the daily schedule—an eighth period to a seven-period day. Principals can move teachers toward interdisciplinary team teaching, the use of a topical or thematic curriculum, and alternative student assessment procedures. Fipp et al. (1996) note the advantages of qualitative assessment inventories which allow students and parents to see individual growth and progress more clearly while de-emphasizing academic comparisons with other students.

Block scheduling, in conjunction with teacher teaming, allows teachers to concentrate on academics and recognize effort and individual achievement. George and Grebing (1995) relate that teams of teachers, with adequate blocks of time in which *they* can schedule their own instructional activities, can provide individual instruction and reward all students for their effort, hard work, and personal achievements. Interdisciplinary teams with block schedules can work more closely with parents since they can schedule weekly conference time within their time blocks. Teacher teams can have regular weekly student recognition time when all students are honored for their achievements and parents are honored for their support. Finally, teacher teams can have common planning times where they can discuss the needs and achievements of individual students and tailor their instruction to ensure each student's continuous improvement.

A study by Slavin (1986) provides the following guidelines for schools when grouping children and preadolescents:

- With the exception of grouping students for mathematics and reading (which is important for achievement), students should be heterogeneously grouped.
- Any grouping of students must be continuously evaluated and flexible reassignment procedures must exist which cause minimum disturbance and loss of transition for the student.
- Teachers must vary their instructional techniques and materials to meet the readiness levels of the students in grouped classes.
- Group numbers should remain small enough to allow teachers to individualize instruction for each student.

Implementing Heterogeneous Grouping

Any change in a standard, commonly held school practice or policy will create turmoil and dissatisfaction among teachers, parents and community members. Changes of any magnitude in the instructional program are political in nature and need the support and cooperation of teachers and parents. Middle school principals undertaking an effort to eradicate ability grouping or creating a culture of detracking in the school should seek a broad base of support and carefully plan for the transformation. Making a change in grouping practices or detracking the school unilaterally will result in almost certain failure. Team effort is a must. While there are many change models a principal can follow in moving away from ability grouping, the quality change model of Weller (1993) is practical in scope, and simple in nature, and accounts for the political atmosphere surrounding school change.

The quality change model is adapted from Deming's theory (1986) of quality management found in his Fourteen Points for quality transformation. Principals proposing a change from ability grouping to heterogeneous grouping can apply the quality change model (see Figure 11.1) which consists of the following steps:

(1) Be firmly convinced in your own mind that heterogeneous grouping is the best way to achieve quality education for students. Your convictions will be sorely tested throughout the change process and they must withstand strong and consistent efforts from others to change your mind.

(2) Gather as much research-based data as possible, and become knowledgeable of the advantages and disadvantages of heterogeneous grouping. Knowledge is power.

(3) Know the "power agents" or influentials among your parents, community members, and teachers. (See Chapter 10 for methods of identifying these power agents.) Sound them out informally and listen to their reactions and concerns more than trying to "sell them" on your idea. Their concerns should be addressed with facts and reason, not emotion, and their concerns should become a basis for further research to find answers for future questions from others.

(4) Inform the faculty that you are investigating ways to reorganize student assignment to classes and the reasons for your research efforts. Apprise them of the way you plan to gather information and ask for their total involvement and help in gathering information. Provide research-based information on the positive and negative aspects of heterogeneous grouping. Remember, be open and honest in presenting the literature. Those who resist your efforts will find literature to support their views, so do not give them the first impression that you are trying to "stack the deck" in your favor.

(5) Seek assistance from the power agents in the community, your parents, and your teachers to speak about the benefits of heterogeneous grouping. Sometimes peer influence does more to convince others than does

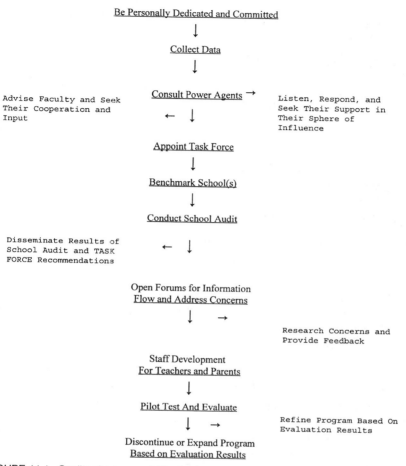

FIGURE 11.1. Quality change model for implementing heterogeneous grouping in middle schools.

the literature which often presents an impersonal tone and provides results difficult for some to understand. Research is nationally based and many feel that these findings are not relevant to their school or community.

(6) Establish a task force to investigate the pros and cons of implementing heterogeneous grouping. Care must be taken to involve community members, parents, and teachers who both favor heterogeneous grouping and those who want to retain ability grouping practices. Equal representation is a must if the opposition is to feel fully represented and

their views and concerns are to be equally addressed. Principals should ensure that power agents are among task force members and should have names submitted by all three groups (community members, parents, and teachers) for consideration for membership.

(7) Benchmark local middle schools which have heterogeneous grouping in place. Benchmarking is a quality vehicle for change which allows members of organizations seeking to implement a change to personally inspect the results of the change in an organization in which that change has already taken place. Allowing task force members to visit the school(s) and talk to the administrators, teachers, and other staff members provides the membership the opportunity to address their concerns with their counterparts and get honest answers to pressing questions. In fact, nothing has more credibility to a teacher or parent or community member than another peer. Moreover, the problems *they* had in implementing the change and are currently experiencing can prove valuable for the transformation process within your own school.

(8) Conduct a school audit which focuses on the needs of your students, the existing grouping practices and the criteria used to assign group members, and the methods currently being used to organize instruction in classrooms. This information can then be compared with national studies. George (1995) notes the importance of gathering and comparing local data with national data to convince educators and others that local change is needed. Many tend to believe that national data applies to everyone but themselves. Parents, teachers, students, and community members are key sources of information which can be gathered by questionnaires, formal interviews, and informal discussions. Questions should address the following concerns:

- Do current grouping practices achieve the desired student achievement results?
- Do grouping patterns have clear group distinctions, for example, high-, average-, and low-achieving groups?
- What measures are used to group students?
- Do teachers currently regroup students in their classes for instruction?
- How does the current grouping practice impact students' self-perceptions?
- Is there a relationship between group placement and class/school discipline problems and cases of vandalism and suspension?
- Do teachers find value in and support for current grouping practices?
- Which group of teachers and parents supports tracking and why?

- Do teachers currently individualize instruction within their classrooms and use a variety of instructional materials?
- Do parents of all socioeconomic levels and ethnicity approve of the current grouping practice and why?
- Which parental socioeconomic level(s) and race(s) most support the current grouping practices and why?

(9) Responses to the survey will now serve as fact-based information to confirm or refute the need for a change in the school's organization. If local results indicate that tracking practices are at a minimum and instructional procedures are yielding positive effects, little if any change may be needed. Should, however, these findings indicate racial isolation, locked-in placements, a lack of individualized instruction, behavior problems relating to group placement, or other negative outcomes, then these findings will become the most convincing reasons for organizational change and there will be data to support it. Transformation of the school's organization will progress slowly and the information provided to teachers, parents, and the community will need both process and incubation time.

(10) Several meetings or open forums should be held with the principal and task force members to discuss the results of the survey with national data as supportive information. Meetings should be confined to objective discussion of the data even though emotions will run high. Comments should be recorded and serve as a basis for further research or reflection for planning the reorganization.

(11) Decisions on how reorganization will take place should be made known to all through the local media and other sources, and pilot testing of the heterogeneous grouping plan should start with the lowest grade level in the school, usually sixth grade. Conventional wisdom states that those most resistant to change are those in higher grade levels.

(12) Conducting staff development for teachers and orientation sessions for parents prior to pilot testing is essential. Teachers must learn how to effectively teach a diverse range of students, how to regroup for instruction, how to use different teaching styles and materials, how to use alternative assessment procedures, and how to use other inclusion techniques. Parents will need information on how teachers are being prepared for heterogeneous grouping as well as periodic updates on the progress of the program. Their support and assistance in the home is vital to project success and their concerns should be both welcome and addressed.

(13) Evaluation of the pilot program should be both formative and summative in scope. Periodic feedback from teachers, parents, and students through interviews, questionnaires, and conversations should be docu-

mented throughout the year. Teachers should keep weekly progress reports documenting their own impressions as well as those of students and parents. Formative evaluation results can then be compared to summative results, such as teacher-made tests or achievement tests at the end of the year. Options vary, but usually a decision will be made either to refine the program and pilot test another year or expand the program to the next grade level the following year. It is important to remember that an informed public is a supportive public and the difficulties and successes of the pilot-testing process should be frequently shared.

The possibility of being unsuccessful in promoting heterogeneous grouping does exist. Experience suggests, however, that even in failure valuable lessons are learned from the process and a new sensitivity will exist among teachers, parents, and community members about the negative effects of ability grouping. In some cases, enough elapsed time will occur to revitalize an interest in detracking. Often a second attempt is successful since the number of supporters will have increased in number and commitment.

Retention

Retention, a form of ability grouping, is an issue of concern for many educators, parents and community members. The debate over its positive and negative effects continues with the research providing mixed information. Some argue that a student is retained in order for that student to attain a level of mastery in the curriculum deemed appropriate for the student's grade level. It is postulated that the necessary knowledge and skills will be attained through retention and the student can then move on to the next grade level for mastery. Little if any thought is given to bringing the curriculum to the child and providing appropriate levels of instruction. "Flunking" students is viewed as the solution to the child's inability to progress to the satisfaction of the teacher based on the mean performance of others. Retention often leads to frustration, embarrassment, and a defeatist attitude which results in school dropout.

Middle school educators need to be cognizant of the historical roots of the middle school and junior high school. The junior high school was founded, in part, to decrease the high number of school dropouts. At that time, many students dropped out of school after grade five and only one in ten students graduated from high school. While reasons for this high dropout rate are many, one reason was the high rate of student failure due to a lack of attention to individual student learning needs (Clark and Clark, 1994). The newly formed middle school, grounded in research, focused on the uniqueness of the individual student, a commitment to individual success, and the healthy development of the student in the social, emotional, physical, and intellectual maturation process. Central to the middle school philosophy is the acknowledgment of the wide variation of differences in student maturation levels throughout the transescent years and the need to adapt the curriculum to these differences. When teachers and principals fail to recognize the causes of individual student differences, erroneous beliefs about student progress occur. Often, teachers take the position that it is the student's responsibility to learn and that a lack of learning indicates laziness, poor study skills and work habits, or a lack of motivation. Developmental research on preadolescent growth and behavior finds these beliefs unfounded and points to the variability in developmental patterns and growth rates.

There are many negative effects of retention which include not only dropping out of school, but prolonged poor self-esteem and increased discipline problems. The impact of school dropout on society is costly. Possessing little if any job skills, these former students become or remain unemployed and they burden society with the need to support them. School dropouts and unemployment also lead to crime and incarceration which also require social expenditures. Carlson (1996) notes a 139 percent increase in prisoners from 1980 to 1990, an expenditure on average of $22,500 a year per prisoner, and the fact that 82 percent of the 1,115,111 prisoners in 1990 were high school dropouts. Benson and Roehlkepartain (1991) relate that successful experiences for students in middle schools, especially for at-risk students, promote a positive self-image and contribute to a decrease in school dropouts, violence, vandalism, depression, and drug usage.

Retention may be caused by a lack of readiness to learn certain concepts and skills but retention does not help to overcome this weakness. Johnson and Marble (1986) relate that retainees show less growth in subject achievement than when they are promoted and state that there is a lack of reliable evidence that retention is more beneficial than promotion, especially with students having serious academic problems. Promoting students or having them repeat only the courses or portions of the courses they failed is a viable alternative to grade retention. Failing a course has less stigma attached to it than failing a grade level.

Alternative student assessment practices are gaining popularity because of the grade retention-promotion controversy. Some middle schools are using standardized achievement tests to identify students' strengths and weaknesses in various subject matter areas in conjunction with teacher observations, checklists, or logs recording student progress in social and emotional development, work habits, motivation, and creative efforts. Performance tests and written work such as tests, essays, poems and other developmental data are also gathered and used for student evaluation.

These multiple student assessment instruments provide teachers a means to easily and quickly diagnose problem areas. Working closely with parents, teachers can then develop strategies to work individually with students to provide the special attention and assistance they need. George and Alexander (1993) note some of the important areas to assess for middle school student development: social relationships; effort, work and study habits, and motivation; creativity in a broad range of talent and skill areas; the student's ability and achievement compared to others; attitude toward school and schoolwork; and citizenship skills. When teachers closely follow individual progress and provide the necessary assistance to students in problem areas, the goals of the true middle school become reality.

Cooperative Learning

Cooperative learning, with its varied approaches, is active learning which promotes student motivation and decreases classroom discipline problems (Berryman, 1993). Slavin (1991a) and Braddock and McPartland (1993) note the benefits of cooperative learning as being increased academic achievement, development of more positive attitudes toward school and members of other racial groups, increased appreciation for the talents of others, and its use as a viable alternative to school tracking. Conrad and Hedin (1991) note that cooperative learning provides for peer tutoring which enhances social skills, self-esteem, and academic achievement. As part of the school's social curriculum, the ability to work in groups, to work as a team member, to learn responsibility and codependence, and to learn good social and citizenship skills are central to the middle school concept. Cooperative learning activities provide for these outcomes.

Cooperative learning provides benefits for every middle school student. Students learn to set goals, make decisions, and solve problems. It promotes communication among students and enhances articulation, the defending of ideas, and the expression of different points of view. Students learn to appreciate individual talents and to tap the strengths of others (Messick and Reynolds, 1992). Used as an instructional strategy, cooperative learning, not to be confused with cooperative effort, makes a group of students responsible for the success of a project through individual work and effort; the use of good intercommunication skills; and the sharing of ideas. Ideally, cooperative learning activities should allow for the use of preferred learning styles or multiple intelligences, the application of a variety of instructional materials, and the transfer of prior learning to the cooperative learning project. Cooperative effort merely means each student is responsible for doing a certain portion of the project with little interaction taking place among the students. In the case of cooperative effort, students are primarily graded on their own efforts and work with no agreement on common group goals or accountability for group progress. Slavin (1991a) notes that two factors are necessary for cooperative learning to achieve its full and multi-faceted benefits. First, the group must set common goals to be achieved on a student-determined or teacher-directed project and second, individual students must be held accountable for their own efforts and work as well as the group as a whole. When these two essential elements exist, positive outcomes will include improved academic achievement, enhanced self-esteem, improved intergroup communication skills, enhanced attitude toward school, and increased ability to work as a team member.

COOPERATIVE LEARNING METHODS

Work by Slavin (1990b) identified several effective cooperative learning models:

- Student team learning—students work together, are responsible for one another's learning, and *learn* together, not just *do* something as a team.
- Student teams-achievement divisions (STAD)—a four-member learning team with mixed achievement levels, sex, and race which ensures learning among members after a teacher-presented lesson. Individual tests are scored and teams are awarded prizes for performance. STAD is very effective for middle school students and for teaching skills and concepts in all subjects.
- Teams-games-tournament (TGT)—uses the same basic team formation as STAD but replaces weekly tests with tournaments in which teams compete with other teams. Teams are composed of students with similar achievement records and students are rotated on teams based on performance to ensure fair team competition. Low achievers compete with other low achievers and have the same opportunity to succeed as other ability-grouped teams. TGT is also effective in middle schools and can be used for all subjects.
- Jigsaw—students work in six-member teams, learning objectives are divided into sections, and each team member is responsible for learning a single section. Team members are then matched by section assignment with others, discussion among like-section members takes place with students then returning to their original team to "teach" others about their section assignments.

According to Salvin (1991b), cooperative learning promotes achievement, communication and social skills, self-esteem, and good work habits—all factors, which when absent, contribute to school dropout. Moreover, its use in a heterogeneous classroom is an effective interclass grouping method which can group high achievers with high achievers depending on the teacher's instructional objectives. For those concerned with the negative effects of cooperative learning for gifted students, Slavin found no evidence to support the claim that cooperative learning holds back high-achieving students.

What Type of Heterogeneous Grouping Should Be Used?

Principals implementing any type of grouping pattern must first take legal constraints into consideration. Grouping patterns which discriminate against students, especially grouping based on standardized tests, may be illegal according to the Office of Civil Rights (OCR) if racial identification or bias in grouping exists. "Public labeling, and potential stigmatizing, of students by ability is prohibited" (George, 1993, p. 23). The burden of proof rests with school officials to prove that their grouping practices have merit and do not intentionally discriminate. George relates certain criteria for legally acceptable grouping patterns within schools. He notes that few ability grouping practices in today's middle schools would meet the "burden of proof" standards. These criteria include the following:

- uses nondiscriminatory standards for group member placement and identification
- evaluates group assignment practices regularly for their effectiveness and desired results (When results do not meet expectations, practices are altered.)
- notifies parents of the potential outcomes based on the placement of their children
- reassigns students to groups regularly so that groups are not permanent on either a daily or yearly basis
- allows students to move between groups without penalty or extra work
- relates instruction objectives to the grouping practices being used

Only when these constraints are taken into consideration can grouping patterns be selected for school organization. Principals have the responsibility to advise their teachers and parents of these guidelines and then work within these parameters.

Practically, middle school principals are faced with a dilemma in detracking a school. State and federal regulations require some grouping for some "special needs" students and their identification by narrow criteria is a must. From a local political standpoint, board of education and parent pressure exists for some form of grouping for some students, especially the gifted and talented. The best procedure to follow is to first live within the guidelines of federal and state regulations. Local regulation cannot conflict with superior law. Second, and from a local political perspective, disengage in grouping where resistance is least. Third, work to eliminate the lower-tracked groups, if more than one level exists, by combining them into one group. And finally, eliminate grouping in subjects other than reading, mathematics, and English.

Detracking plans vary in approach; however, Marsh and Raywid (1994) support the importance of the commitment to equal access as a successful approach to develop heterogeneous grouping. Any plan to detrack should have at its core practices which promote and sustain heterogeneous groups in classrooms. This includes teachers and parents who believe in and are committed to the merits of heterogeneous grouping, interdisciplinary teacher teams and thematic instructional units, flexible block scheduling, cooperative learning practices, and manageable class sizes. The single exception to subject heterogeneous grouping, throughout the literature, is in the areas of reading, mathematics, and English. Slavin (1990b) argues that grouping students in these areas is important due to the inherent sequence in learning in these areas.

THE JOPLIN PLAN

The Joplin Plan, named for the Missouri city where the plan was first implemented, groups students in reading and mathematics without regard for grade level placement. This narrows the range of ability levels and allows for large group instruction without arranging groups in a single class based on high, average, and low achievement. More teacher-directed instruction can exist and individual instruction can take place based on students' progress within the narrower range of abilities. George and Alexander (1993) discuss the variations of the Joplin Plan. One variation is "multi-age grouping" in which students become a member of one of several interdisciplinary teaching teams for their three-year middle school stay. Each teacher team has a content area teacher and a reading teacher with student teams consisting of sixth, seventh, and eighth grade students. Teams are heterogeneous in age, race, sex, achievement, and background. Students who are grouped together for three years have a greater sense of community, improved peer relationships more positive home-school relations, and reduced discipline problems both inside and outside the classroom.

Another multi-age group plan varies from the above example in that eighth grade students are grouped separately for mathematics and language arts while sixth and seventh grade students are grouped together for these subjects. Another variation allows for parent and student choice in grouping patterns. Options include self-contained classrooms for seventh grade or a two- or four-teacher team configuration. Sixth grade and seventh grade are taught with interdisciplinary teams, and eighth grade is taught strictly with either two- or four-teacher teams (George and Alexander, 1993).

SPLIT-LEVEL GROUPING PLAN

Split-level grouping represents a compromise between ability grouping and heterogeneous grouping. Teachers are in grade-level teams with students placed in one of five ability levels: low, low average, average, high average, and high. Each student group is subdivided into two groups, at five levels, for a total of ten groups. Teachers are assigned to each of these small student ability groups with no more than two ability levels in one class at any one time. Teachers can be assigned students from all five levels. Students remain with their peer group based on ability, but never spend the entire day with one ability group. Electives, exploratory courses, and physical education are heterogeneously grouped. A variation of the split-level plan is to group low achievers with average or high achievers for certain subjects such as social studies while keeping similar ability students grouped together for science, reading, math, and English. George (1992) relates that with the split-level plan, ability grouping is most likely to exist in subjects that are hierarchical in content, such as mathematics and reading.

These approaches to detracking are the result of innovative thinking and pilot testing. There are no limitations on innovative thought. Creativity is not limited to a select few but is fostered by need and dissatisfaction with current practice. As long as the goals of the true middle school are in focus, educators will continue to seek ways to provide success for all transescents as they develop in their own unique ways.

HOMOGENEOUS AND HETEROGENEOUS GROUPING PRACTICES: CASE STUDIES

The question of homogeneous versus heterogeneous grouping for middle school instruction presents a dilemma for some principals and teachers. Feelings on this issue often run deep, regardless of what the literature states, among teachers and parents. Often, the perspective taken by parents and teachers depends on personal philosophy, past experience, and/or intuition. Parents of low and middle achievers often support heterogeneous grouping, arguing the benefits their children receive from peers labeled "high achievers." Some parents of low achievers feel special programs specifically designed for their children, taught by teachers who care about raising low achiever performance, are best and support this kind of homogeneous grouping. On the other hand, the same argument is espoused by many parents of gifted and talented students.

In quality-oriented, effective middle schools, most of these principals practice heterogeneous grouping in grades six through eight. These principals are well acquainted with the research literature on grouping practices and realize that certain students can benefit more from homogeneous grouping, especially those students needing special kinds of instruction in certain skill and knowledge areas, than can others. The result is that these principals practice both types of student grouping through temporary grouping, pull-out programs, or in-class instruction with special teachers or regular teacher teams.

At Gilmer Middle School, Wesley Clampitt believes in the merits of heterogeneous grouping and balances teacher teams in grades six through eight with an even distribution of students. Students are assigned to each grade based on achievement test scores, sex, ethnicity, and disciplinary problems. Teacher teams at each grade level then make student assignments based on these student characteristics to ensure a normal curve distribution exists by teacher team, by grade level. "In effect," says Clampitt, "allowing teachers to assign students within teams provides a sense of ownership, and vested interest in the practice which triggers greater commitment on the part of teachers to succeed with their students."

For gifted and talented students in grades six through eight in mathematics and language arts, students are taught by certified gifted teachers during the same time block that regular students receive instruction in these areas. Clampitt realizes his position is unique in that several teachers on each grade level team are certified for gifted and talented instruction. Clampitt relates that if this were not the case, he would use teacher aids to facilitate instruction while teachers instructed these gifted students within the regular classroom setting. "Pull-out programs are least desirable for stigma reasons and loss of continuity," he states.

For science and social studies students, and exploratory courses, gifted and talented students receive accelerated instruction within teacher teams during the regular time block of classroom instruction. These students use contract grading, are assigned special projects, and meet regularly with teachers who coordinate this accelerated program. Clampitt relates that "this type of instruction satisfies some students who do not want to be characterized among their peers as being a nerd." Many students and parents like contract grading. Students have input into their projects and how their grades will be determined. Parents like it because it keeps them informed of what their child is doing. The same holds true for special projects which require parent consent. These projects can be group or individual work and require indepth investigation into an area of interest a student wishes to pursue. Parents have to consent to having their child enroll in this program and have the option of discontinuing program participation for their child should they wish to do so.

In the fine arts, for example, talented students are given special instruction and projects which challenge their ability. Music and art are examples where in-class instruction is individualized to meet the wide range of talents among students. This is primarily a function, however, of small class size. Clampitt feels that heterogeneous grouping is the best overall practice, "but exceptions have to be made for those students with special needs and talents or the educators would not be doing the job of providing the best possible education for each and every student," he says. But the secret to success in any in-class instruction for special students "lies with the willingness and dedication of teachers who believe special instruction is not only necessary but must be provided to these students regardless of the existing circumstances," relates Clampitt.

Trickum Middle school also practices heterogeneous grouping in grades six through eight with students being assigned by grade level teacher teams based on achievement test scores, sex, ethnicity, socioeconomic background, and discipline problems. This assignment by the administrative team ensures each teacher team a wide range of students and allows teachers to break up cliques and assign students based on individual needs to teachers within teams who can best address those needs.

Gifted and talented instruction is in mathematics for all students and is conducted on a pull-out basis when their peers are taught mathematics in a regular classroom setting. Language arts is being considered as a gifted and talented area but the current rationale is that regular classroom instruction may be equally beneficial. Reading and language arts skills are somewhat different from those of mathematics where sequence mastery is all important and where teachers do not apply mathematics to other content areas on a regular basis, as they do reading and language arts. With all teacher teams working on reading and language arts and challenging accelerated students in these subject areas, a separate program may be difficult to justify according to Mary Anne Charron, principal of Trickum Middle School.

At Trickum, at-risk students are receiving instruction in the Success School as discussed in Chapter 8. This program is for eighth grade students who are below grade level in language arts and mathematics and who need indepth, concentrated instruction to enter ninth grade with their peers. If students reach grade level mastery prior to ninth grade, they are infused into a regular eighth grade team for traditional instruction.

"The importance of teachers within teams being willing to plan for and then implement instruction specifically designed to meet different needs of students at different levels cannot be over emphasized," Charron relates. Teachers are the key to learning "and dedicated, caring teachers provide quality instruction and do make the difference," states Charron.

Principals at other quality middle schools, such as Joan Akin at Creekland and Wayne Watts at Edwards, also practice heterogeneous grouping with some homogeneous group instruction. Both principals assign students to grade level teacher teams based on student achievement scores, sex, ethnicity, socioeconomic status, and discipline problems. At Creekland, gifted and talented students are taught through pull-out programs by certified teachers in grades six through eight in mathematics, language arts, science, and social studies. Students are allowed to enroll in one gifted and talented subject per year. A Success School exists for seventh and eighth grade at-risk students performing at or below two grade levels. In these self-contained classrooms, with one teacher team each, students are taught reading, language arts, and mathematics with social studies and science supplementing basic skills instruction. At Edwards Middle School, gifted students in language arts are taught by one of three certified teachers in grades six through eight during the regularly scheduled language arts time for their respective grade levels. Accelerated students in other subjects are taught by regular teacher team members who individualize instruction within the content area and regularly scheduled time block. Exploratory teachers also individualize their instruction based on the talents of each student.

Special education students at both schools are taught in self-contained classrooms, pull-out resource classes, and mainstream classrooms. Parent permission is required for each type of program and, in each case, an Individualized Education Plan is developed for each student. Movement between placements is possible based on student needs.

At West Jackson Middle School, heterogeneous grouping is also practiced and gifted and talented students are taught within regular classes by teacher team members in mathematics and language arts. Students are identified as gifted and talented by I.Q. scores, teacher recommendations, and prior academic performance. Certified gifted and talented teachers are interdisciplinary team members in grades six through eight and lead the instruction of these students. Walker Davis, principal of the school, has strong beliefs in the area of grouping practices. Walker states that "middle school students need individual attention based on their individual needs, abilities, and talents, and gifted and talented students can be served best by teaching these students within the regular classroom by certified gifted teachers." Davis is not against special classes or pull-out programs "since the research literature is inconclusive on exactly what is the most effective way to serve these students," he says. To Davis, the principal has to make a decision on how best to serve gifted and talented students and then "follow through" on this belief. He is quick to add, however, "that any principal that makes such as decision independent of the faculty and the research literature walks on thin ice."

The gifted and talented students do a lot of independent study and group projects in language arts where students are encouraged to select topics of personal interest and explore these interests with direct teacher assistance. Walker says that having interdisciplinary teacher teams adds to the strength of the gifted program. Each team member can serve as an "expert" to these students in a variety of ways. With teacher teams, scheduling is not a problem and with daily planning periods being the same, teachers can not only plan together to meet the needs of the gifted student, but discuss among themselves the best way to assist these students. If Davis had the resources, he would have gifted teachers certified in science and social studies as well. "In the real world, principals have lofty goals and dreams. This is good and it is a characteristic of a good leader—vision is what some say. However, I have only so much money in my instructional budget and I have to work within that limitation. Math and language arts are the most important subjects for standardized tests and the public judges our quality by test scores. My money simply has to go to those areas," concludes Walker.

REFERENCES

Benson, P. and E. Roehlkepartain. 1991. "Kids Who Care: Meeting the Challenge of Youth Service Involvement." *Search Institute Source*, VII(3):1–4.

Berryman, S. E. 1993. "Learning for the Workplace," in *Review of Research in Education, Vol. 19*. L. Darling-Hammond, ed. Washington, DC: American Educational Research Association, pp. 343–401.

Bondura, A. 1992. "Perceived Self-Efficacy in Cognitive Development and Functioning." Paper presented at the annual meeting of the American Educational Research Association, San Francisco, April, 1992.

Braddock, J. H. 1990. "Tracking in the Middle Grades: National Patterns of Grouping for Instruction," *Phi Delta Kappan*, 71(6):445–449.

Braddock, J. H. and J. M. McPartland. 1993. "Education of Early Adolescents," in *Review of Research in Education, Vol. 19*. L. Darling-Hammond, ed. Washington, DC: American Educational Research Association, pp. 135–170.

Brophy, J. E. and T. Good. 1986. "Teacher Behavior and Student Achievement," in *Handbook of Research on Teaching*. Third edition. M. Wittrock, ed. New York: Macmillan.

Carlson, R. V. 1996. *Reforming and Reform: Perspectives on Organization, Leadership, and School Change*. White Plains, NY: Longman.

Carson, M. D. and G. Badarack. 1989. *How Changing Class Size Affects Classrooms and Students*. Riverside, CA: University of California at Riverside, California Educational Research Cooperative.

Clark, S. H. and D. C. Clark. 1994. *Restructuring the Middle School: Implications for School Leaders*. Albany, NY: State University of New York Press.

Conrad, D. and D. Hedin. 1991. "School-Based Community Service: What Do We Know from Research and Theory?" *Phi Delta Kappan,* 72(10):743–749.

Cooper, C. R. 1995. "Integrating Gifted Education into the Total School Curriculum," *The School Administrator,* 52:9, 12–15.

Darling-Hammond, L. 1988. "Teacher Quality and Educational Equity," *The College Board Review,* No. 148, pp. 17–23.

Deming, W. E. 1986. *Out of the Crisis.* Cambridge, MA: MIT University Press.

Dentzer, E. and A. Wheelock. 1990. *Locked In/Locked Out: Tracking and Placement in Boston Public Schools.* Boston: Massachusetts Advocacy Center. *Administrator,* 52:10–11.

The Educational Research Service. 1978. *Class Size: A Summary of Research.* Arlington, VA: Educational Research Service.

Feldhusen, J. F. 1995. "A Call for Overhaul: Gifted Education Overlooks Talent," *The School Administrator,* 52:10–11.

Fipp, M., C. Barry, C. Hargrave, and C. Countryman. 1996. "With Equity and Excellence for All: Moving Toward Heterogeneous Grouping at Muirlands Middle School," *Middle School Journal,* 27:15–23.

Fleming, W. E. 1990. "The Program for Disadvantaged Youth: Reform Efforts in the Middle Grades," *Educational Horizons,* 68:82–87.

Forte, I. and S. Schurr. 1993. *The Definitive Middle School Guide: A Handbook for Success.* Nashville, TN: Incentive Publications, Inc.

Gardner, H. 1983. *Frames of Mind: The Theory of Multiple Intelligences.* Tenth Anniversary Edition. New York: Basic Books.

George, P. S. 1992. *How to Untrack Your School.* Alexander, VA: Association for Supervision and Curriculum Development.

George, P. S. 1993. "Tracking and Ability Grouping in the Middle School: Ten Tentative Truths," *Middle School Journal,* 24:17–24.

George, P. S. 1995. "Is It Possible to Live with Tracking and Ability Grouping?" in *Beyond Tracking: Finding Success in Inclusive Schools.* H. Pool and J. A. Page, eds. Bloomington, IN: Phi Delta Kappa.

George, P. S. and W. M. Alexander. 1993. *The Exemplary Middle School.* Second edition. Fort Worth, TX: Harcourt Brace Jovanovich College Publishers.

George, P. S. and W. Grebing. 1995. "Talent Development and Grouping in the Middle Grades: Challenging the Brightest without Sacrificing the Rest," *Middle School Journal,* 26:12–17.

George, P. S. and K. Rubin. 1992. *Tracking and Ability Grouping in Florida: A Status Study.* Sanibel, FL: Florida Educational Research Council.

Glass, G. V. and M. L. Smith. 1978. "Meta-Analysis of Research in the Relationships of Class Size and Achievement," in *The Class Size and Instruction Project.* Leonard S. Chaen, Principal Investigator. San Francisco, CA: Far West Laboratory for Educational Research and Development.

Henson, K. T. 1993. *Methods and Strategies for Teaching in the Secondary and Middle Schools.* Second edition. White Plains, NY: Longman.

Johnson, J. H. and G. C. Marble. 1986. *What Research Says to the Middle Level Practitioner.* Columbus, OH: National Middle School Association.

Jung, C. 1971. "Psychological Types" (H. G. Baynes, Trans. Revised by R. F. C. Hull), in

The Collected Works of C. G. Jung, Vol. 6. Princeton, NJ: Princeton University Press. (Original work published in 1921.)

Kindred, L. W., R. J. Wolotkiewicz, J. M. Michelson, and L. E. Coplein. 1981. *The Middle School Curriculum: A Practitioner's Handbook.* Second edition. Boston: Allyn & Bacon.

Lounsbury, J. H. and D. C. Clark. 1990. *Inside Grade Eight: From Apathy to Excitement.* Reston, VA: National Association of Secondary School Principals.

Marsh, R .S. and M. A. Raywid. 1994. "Make Detracking Work," *Phi Delta Kappan,* 76:314–317.

Mason, D. A. and R. B. Burns. 1995. "Teachers' Views of Combination Classes," *The Journal of Educational Research,* 89:36–45.

Messick, R. G. and K. E. Reynolds. 1992. *Middle Level Curriculum in Action.* White Plains, NY: Longman.

Newman, K. 1993. *Declining Fortunes: The Withering of the American Dream.* New York: Basic Books.

Oakes, J. 1988. "Tracking: Can Schools Take a Different Route?" *NEA Today,* January, p. 3.

Oakes, J. and M. Lipton. 1992. "Detracking Schools: Early Lessons from the Field," *Phi Delta Kappan,* 73(6):448–454.

Segro, G. 1995. "Meeting the Needs of All Students: Making Ability Grouping Work," *National Association of Secondary School Principals Bulletin,* 79:18–26.

Slavin, R. E. 1986. *Ability Grouping and Student Achievement in Elementary Schools: A Best Evidence Synthesis.* Baltimore, MD: Center for Research on Elementary and Middle Schools, Johns Hopkins University.

Slavin, R. E. 1990a. *Cooperative Learning: Theory, Research, and Practice.* Englewood Cliffs, NJ: Prentice-Hall.

Slavin, R. E. 1990b. "Research on Cooperative Learning: Consensus and Controversy." *Educational Leadership,* 47:52–55.

Slavin, R. E. 1991a. "Are Cooperative Learning and 'Untracking' Harmful to the Gifted?" *Educational Leadership,* 48(6):68–71.

Slavin, R. E. 1991b. "Research on Cooperative Learning: Consensus and Controversy," *Educational Leadership,* 46:4–13.

Slavin, R. E. 1995. "Detracking and Its Detractors: Flawed Evidence, Flawed Values," *Phi Delta Kappan,* 77:20–21.

Stevenson, H. W. and S. Y. Lee. 1990. *Context of Achievement: A Study of American, Chinese, and Japanese Children.* Chicago: University of Chicago Press.

Ubben, G. C. and L. W. Hughes. 1992. *The Principal: Creative Leadership for Effective Schools.* Second edition. Needham Heights, MA: Allyn & Bacon.

Weller, L. D. 1993. *Total Quality Management: A Conceptual Overview and Applications for Education.* Athens, Georgia: College of Education, The University of Georgia.

Wheelock, A. 1995. "Winning Over Gifted Parents: Handled Thoughtfully, a Move to Heterogeneous Grouping Can Benefit All Students," *The School Administrator,* 52:16–20.

CHAPTER 12

Continuous Improvement and Action Research: The Quality Methods, Tools, and Techniques for School Improvement

Continuous improvement is a key factor in providing quality educational programs and instructional outcomes. Principals in effective middle schools know the value of research and data-based decision making and apply the basic principles of the scientific method to evaluate and improve the instructional and service programs of their schools. These high achieving principals make continuous improvement a goal for themselves, their staff, and their students.

This chapter will provide specific examples of the continuous improvement process; the use and application of continuous improvement quantitative research tools, charts and graphs; and the basic principles and research designs used in action research for school and classroom improvement. Central to this chapter will be a series of case studies which will provide examples of the use of the continuous improvement process and action research.

The following questions will be addressed in this chapter:

- What is the continuous improvement process and why is it essential in promoting effective middle schools?
- What is the Plan, Do, Check, Act (PDCA) cycle and what are the tools and techniques used to make quality decisions and evaluate PDCA activities?
- How can the PDCA cycle be applied to improve the decision making process and instructional program?
- How can the PDCA cycle and continuous improvement tools and techniques be taught to and applied by students?
- How can the continuous improvement process be used with teachers teams to make instructional improvements in the school and classroom?

- What is action research and how is it applied to the PDCA cycle?
- How can action research designs be used to pilot test new programs or practices, and how can the PDCA cycle tools and techniques be used to evaluate the outcomes of these activities?
- Why is action research more meaningful and important to teachers and principals than general research findings printed in professional journals?

QUALITY IN EDUCATION

According to Aristotle, "We are what we repeatedly do. Excellence, then, is not an act, but a habit." To change our habits requires a strength for self-transformation and an acceptance of newer and better ways to achieve desired outcomes. We need to work smarter, not harder, at achieving our goals. To many, the quality theory of W. Edwards Deming (1986, 1993) provides a way to transform and work more effectively and efficiently at achieving our goals. The habits we must attain for excellence lie in working for continuous improvement, and transformation is possible through constancy of purpose. These quality principles become central to achieving and sustaining quality outputs.

Quality is not a one time thing, but an all time thing—a continuous quest to provide quality products and services to the customer. When customers are satisfied with what they receive, indeed, when they get more than what they paid for, they remain loyal, are proud and boastful, and tout the product's excellence. This is, perhaps, the best advertisement, the most reliable test of quality and excellence any product or service can have for education or business outputs (Weller, 1993).

The quality movement, in which Total Quality Management (TQM) is central, originated in the business sphere and enjoys abundant success with testimonials from corporations such as IBM, Xerox, Cadillac, Ford, Motorola, and Federal Express, as well as many others. The leaders in these corporations replaced the traditional scientific management principles of Frederick W. Taylor (1911) with those of Deming (1986, 1993). Taylorism largely ignored the existence of psychological and sociological variables in the workplace and emphasized efficient production through tightly structured work procedures dominated by management. Workers were there to work as extensions of the machines they operated and managers saw to it that their work was done efficiently in the prescribed manner or they were quickly replaced. TQM holds that people want to do their best, take pride in their work, and want to be actively involved in the workplace. It is management's job to help them do so by improving the system in which they work.

Schools and school systems have adopted the principles of TQM with success as well. Weller and Hartley (1994), Weller (1996), Johnson (1993), Schmoker and Wilson (1993), and Murgatroyd and Morgan (1993) document both school and school systems' success in applying the TQM principles and reaping its intended rewards of promoting academic achievement and self-esteem for students and increasing teacher morale and self-concept. Several reasons are attributed to TQM's success in both the business and school setting, but general agreement focuses on its systematic, structured management principles which maximize the use of human potential, provide for ongoing cooperation and communication between management and labor, stress the need for constancy of purpose, and emphasize the idea of continuous improvement. The quality management principles are generic in that they allow for the inclusion of many positive developments in education, such as team teaching and decision making, continuous progress, and site-based management. Moreover, by combining the quality principles and the quality improvement tools with action research methods, educators have the means to transform their schools into schools which provide effective learning outcomes.

Middle school principals can apply the quality principles and tools of Deming (1986) to methods of action research methods to achieve quality outcomes. In high achieving middle schools, the value placed on research and making improvement decisions based on data is high. Continuous improvement is a daily goal for principals, teachers, students, and staff members whose mission is to produce quality in everything they do. The combination of a quality-oriented state of mind along with the application of the quality principles and action research makes for high achieving middle schools (Weller, 1996).

Quality Tools and Action Research

Quality tools and action research can be applied at the school level as well as in individual classrooms. Weller and Hartley (1994) note that applying the quality principles and tools makes decision making more effective for principals and teacher teams because it forces problem identification and decision making into the realm of research and data and away from the standard practice of relying on intuition and experience.

PLAN, DO, CHECK, ACT CYCLE

The infrastructure of continuous improvement is, like the Fourteen Points of Deming's theory (1986), a structured, systematic approach to improvement. Research-centered, the Plan, Do, Check, Act (PDCA) cycle forms the data-based model for school and classroom improvement. The PDCA cycle is not new to education. This cycle is exactly what good classroom instruction calls for and what effective teachers do daily. That is, they plan their lessons, they teach (do) their lessons, they evaluate the impact of the teaching (check), and they decide whether or not to reteach the lesson or go forward to the next lesson based on the effectiveness of their teaching (act). Whether they reteach or move forward, they begin the PDCA cycle again by "planning" for instruction.

In the vernacular of quality, the PDCA cycle encompasses the following:

(1) *Plan.* Identifying opportunities to improve or problems to solve. One plans how to study and analyze the problem or area needing improvement and then decides what can be done to improve the situation or solve the problem. Feigenbaum (1983) views the quality planning process as part of the traditional problem solving models which emphasize team effort to identify problems and where plans are then made for improvements with criteria clearly stated to evaluate the results. In quality planning, two or three plans may be designed at once and, rank ordered, may be used if the first or second plan yields ineffective results.

Quality planning focuses on ways to improve or to solve problems. Quality planning should begin with these questions (Weller, 1993):
- Where are we?
- Where do we want to be?
- What is keeping us from getting there?
- How will we know when we get there?

Next, a series of more specific questions is asked to delineate the planning effort. These questions include the following (Weller, 1993):
- What data currently exist that need to be analyzed to get a clear and accurate picture of where we are? These data provide a picture of the current situation and serve as an index, a kind of pretest, to judge the results or effects of the plan.
- What data need to be collected during and at the conclusion of the improvement plan? Formative and summative evaluations allow for adjustments or modifications in the improvement process and an end-of-process assessment, respectively.
- How is the data to be analyzed? Selecting the right assessment tools is important for obtaining reliable and accurate evaluation results.

The results of the improvement process will be incomplete and will yield fragmented answers and partial solutions if these preliminary questions are not fully addressed.

(2) *Do.* Implement the plan as formulated. Do not alter the plan unless formative evaluation results indicate the need for midcourse adjustments.

In quality operations, pilot testing of new ideas or solutions to problems is highly recommended.

(3) *Check.* Evaluate the effects of the improvement plan as it unfolds by applying the quality tools deemed appropriate to measure the effectiveness of the change.

(4) *Act.* Adopt the program. If the improvement yields the desired outcomes, implement the improvement. If the results are unsatisfactory, implement a contingency plan by returning to the Do and Check phases of the cycle and then complete the cycle with the Act phase. Figure 12.1 presents the Plan, Do, Check, Act cycle of continuous improvement.

After improvements are made, problems may occur. Careful monitoring allows for detection of such problems and the PDCA cycle is used to solve them. Consequently, continuous improvement is promoted. Weller and Hartley (1994) note that teachers and teacher teams are more willing to apply the PDCA cycle to solve school, grade level, and classroom problems when principals first model the improvement cycle themselves and then provide training for teachers in how to apply the PDCA cycle.

The Plan, Do, Check, Act cycle can also be used to resolve staff problem(s) within the school. The author was involved as a consultant in one situation which involved a poorly motivated custodial staff which had a high rate of turnover and work which was consistently inadequate. Having fired custodians in the past, the principal no longer deemed this action a viable solution since the quality of the work did not improve and motivation was virtually non-existent. Applying the PDCA cycle and a few of the quality tools, the problem was solved in the following way.

Step One: Each custodian was interviewed to get an assessment of the internal problems preventing quality work performance. The results included

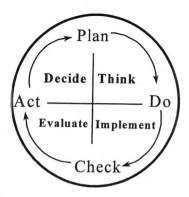

FIGURE 12.1. The Plan, Do, Check, Act cycle of continuous improvement.

the following: General discontentment with work assignments, inadequate supply of cleaning materials, equipment which was broken and outdated, and lack of supervision. When the principal left for the day, the supervising custodian was rarely on campus to provide help or direction and much time was spent playing cards, telling jokes, or watching TV.

Step Two: The custodians were required to attend a series of several weekly meetings during the first few hours of their shift. The initial meetings focused on the importance of pride in one's work, the need for and value of teamwork, and the importance of trust and open and honest communication. Next, a practical version of Maslow's (1970) hierarchy of needs was discussed to stress the importance of satisfying individual needs before quality outcomes could be expected. As these informal sessions progressed, custodians became more trusting of the consultant, more trusting of each other, and they began to express their feelings freely. Team structured activities were used to develop a bond between custodians and to emphasize the importance of working cooperatively and communicating openly and honestly. Maslow's hierarchy and group work allowed custodians to explore their individual work values and practice one of Deming's (1986) tenets: Those closest to the problem should be allowed to solve the problem. The PDCA cycle was then presented and discussed as a way to solve problems, implement new programs, and continuously improve. Custodians were now ready to apply two of the quality improvement tools of Deming.

Step Three: The quality tools of brainstorming and force field analysis (discussed later) were used to get at the root cause(s) of the lack of quality performance, poor morale, and the high turnover rate. Results of brainstorming yielded some general findings: The job is not personally challenging, there is no choice in job assignment, there is a lack of adequate cleaning supplies and modern equipment, and there is a lack of assistance in setting cleaning priorities as well as in overall supervision. Personal reasons for poor job performance were also discussed: Some preferred to clean, wax, and buff large areas rather than clean small areas; some preferred to work in pairs while some preferred to work independently; some preferred to work in different parts of the building (especially women who felt more secure in well-lighted areas with telephone access); and some wanted to order their own supplies, while all custodians wanted new equipment. Force field analysis was used to construct a plan for change in custodial operations.

Instead of talking about driving and restraining forces, which is characteristic of the force field model, the discussion focused on the force fields of the current situation and the ideal situation in the workplace. Current situational factors were listed under the current heading with proposed solutions to each offset by the ideal solution. An improvement plan was then devel-

Problem Statement: Causes of Poor Quality Work

Current Situation →→→→→→→→→→→→→→→→→→→→→→→→→→→→→→→ Ideal Situation

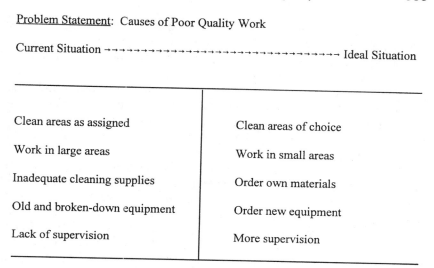

Clean areas as assigned	Clean areas of choice
Work in large areas	Work in small areas
Inadequate cleaning supplies	Order own materials
Old and broken-down equipment	Order new equipment
Lack of supervision	More supervision

FIGURE 12.2. Force field analysis exercise.

oped as a result of the force field analysis exercise. Figure 12.2 presents the abbreviated results of the force field analysis.

Step Four: The head custodian understood the application of the PDCA cycle and took the initiative to use brainstorming and force field analysis as the *plan* part of the PDCA cycle. The *do* part, it was suggested, would be a plan to present to the principal which would allow each custodian to have input regarding their job assignments (empowering custodians to make decisions), by work area; allow each custodian to order their own supplies (through the supervisor); and list all new equipment needed to perform their work. The plan was presented to the principal and was accepted. A four-week pilot period became the *check* part of the cycle with teacher, parent, staff, and administrator observations serving to evaluate the results of the plan. After four weeks and much positive feedback, the plan was adopted, the *act* phase of the cycle. As a result, morale increased, turnover was no longer a problem, and work assignments were completed in half the time allotted. This freed some custodians for work in other schools which became cost effective for the school system.

Action Research

According to McMillan (1996), "Action research is a specific type of applied research. Its purpose is to solve a specific classroom or school problem, improve practice, or make a decision at a single local site" (p. 12). Principals and teachers conduct action research in quality middle schools to seek solutions to problems needing immediate attention and to improve the school's instructional program. Action research is like experimental research but with two noticeable and important exceptions: First, action research lacks random sampling and second, it lacks tight control within groups which controls for variance within independent variables (Anderson and Burns, 1989). These constraints, however, pose no real problem to the action researcher whose primary objective is to solve immediate local problems with no intent of generalizing the findings to a different population. In essence, action research findings are situation-specific.

Three different types of action research exist: independent research, collaborative research, and school wide research (Calhoun, 1994). Independent research, where the teacher or principal becomes the lone investigator, has recently been called for in the literature on school reform, but has not yet fully materialized (Schmoker and Wilson, 1993). Weller (1993) suggests this is due to an overall lack of training and emphasis on teachers and administrators as researchers and a general lack of knowledge about action research skills and their application to improve schooling and classroom instruction. Such research is a powerful tool for school improvement because it provides results that have practical significance to specific problems and quantifies experimental-type results through data-based analysis techniques.

Collaborative research is when two or more teacher-researchers jointly investigate a mutual problem or when teachers and administrators team together to solve problems impacting the educational process. Schoolwide research is the investigation of problems which are generic to the school's population but do not impact on individual classrooms, grade levels, or departments.

Principals and Teachers as Researchers

The idea that principals and teachers are merely consumers of research is incompatible with the current definitions of teacher empowerment and teachers-as-instructional-leaders (Weller, 1996). The role of the principal in quality middle schools has shifted to that of a facilitative leader and cooperative problem solver. Lunenburg and Ornstein (1996) note the recent emphasis on empowered teachers to identify and solve classroom and school problems both independently and as teams. They also note that the principal's primary contribution in school-based research is in providing the necessary time, resources, and training for teachers to adequately fulfill these new roles.

Principals in these quality middle schools provide teachers with the necessary training in action research methods and make the direct connection between action research, the quality principles of Deming, and the PDCA cycle of continuous improvement. Moreover, while teacher staff-development programs progress, principals themselves apply action research methods to administrative problems and share their results with teachers. Modeling research behavior, and at the same time providing evidence of successful application of action research, stimulate teacher motivation and interest and present proof that immediate and practical problems can be solved at the school level.

The basic approach to solving problems with action research does not differ in scope from that of the PDCA cycle for continuous improvement. In fact, they share the same basic characteristics of scientific inquiry. Action research consists of six steps:

(1) Identify and define a problem or an area needing improvement. The problem should be clearly stated and described as it currently exists.

(2) Gather as much fact-based data as possible about the problem and present the data objectively and accurately. This is done through observation and a review of the related research.

(3) Develop a hypothesis about the problem. This can be a statement of the problem or an informal guess about what the correct solution to the problem will be. Two or more hypotheses can be developed per problem depending on its complexity.

(4) Develop a research design to test the hypothesis. A research design is a "roadmap" which specifically provides ways to gather data and generate information from or about the problem being studied which will answer the question(s) posed by the hypotheses.

(5) Select and specify the appropriate data collection and data analysis techniques for the research design. These measures will provide an analysis of the data collected from the research project.

(6) Make a decision based on the results of the research findings (Weller, 1993).

An example of a classroom action research project is presented using the six steps of action research discussed above. The example is a sixth grade teacher who is dissatisfied with low student test scores in mathematics.

(1) *Problem identification:* A sixth grade teacher is dissatisfied with low student performance in mathematics on classroom tests. The textbook and workbook series seem too advanced for the average and low ability students, but not for high achieving students. An alternative mathematics series seems more applicable for the entire cognitive range of students in class. The alternative series is highly thought of by colleagues and, in fact, the teacher occasionally supplements classroom instruction

with exercises and examples from the alternative series when more difficult concepts have to be taught. The teacher noticed when using the alternative series that students seemed to grasp the concepts more easily and had higher test grades. Since the teacher does not have time to personally develop supplementary materials for a year-long course, the question becomes the following: "Will the alternative mathematics series promote greater student mastery across all cognitive levels of students than does the currently used mathematics series?"

(2) *Gather data:* The teacher gathers copies of past tests and homework and keeps a log of student comments and specific problems they have with the current mathematics series and any comments or problems students have with the alternative series. Parent comments also serve as data and should be recorded.

(3) *Develop a hypothesis:* The following statement is the hypothesis for the study: "There will be a more positive difference in student test performance for all students using the alternative mathematics series than for students using the current mathematics series." This is an educated guess about the answer to the teacher's question which predicts what the teacher expects the results to be at the conclusion of the study. Proving the hypothesis correct can be done only through data, not intuition, and this data will provide fact-based information on whether or not to adopt a new mathematics series.

(4) *Develop a research design:* Classic research designs are found in Campbell and Stanley's *Experimental and Quasi-Experimental Designs for Research* (1963) which is a useful text for the researcher when conducting action research. The volume discusses the various types of research designs and precautions for controlling for the intervention of extraneous variables which could otherwise provide serious problems in the research experiment.

For this experiment, the single split-half group, pre-post-test design is most appropriate given the inability to randomly select and assign students to a classroom by dividing students into experimental and control groups. In this experiment, the number of high, average, and low achieving students is equally divided into two groups within the same class, with one group being taught with the current series and the other group being taught with the alternative series. Pre- and post-tests are given each group from each unit from each series before and after the instructional units are taught. By keeping teaching methods and homework consistent, the teacher can compare pre- and post-test results at the end of the units to see if any change in student performance took place over the time allowed for investigation. Time is mostly an arbitrary variable, but for a research project a period of four to five weeks to a year is suggested. In this example, at least five or more weeks should be allowed for assessment purposes.

(5) *Data collection and analysis:* Data are pre- and post-test results. Some teachers may want to include homework which can be included as long as it is quantifiable (has objective evaluative criteria and is given to both student groups). Teacher observations and student reactions should be noted in a log to supplement the results of pre- and post-testing and homework. Data can be analyzed through a variety of statistical techniques which include descriptive statistics (mean, frequency count, median and mode) and inferential statistics (t-tests, chi-square, analysis of variance, etc.) When comparing student means of test score averages between two groups, a t-test or chi-square test can be used. Here, either test of significance would be appropriate to use in this example. Formulas are presented in any standard, introductory statistics textbook and are easy to compute by hand or calculator. Campbell and Stanley (1963) provide a list of suggested statistical techniques to be applied in each of the research designs discussed in their work. Also helpful to action researchers is Walter Borg's book *Applying Educational Research: A Practical Guide for Teachers* (2nd ed.) (1987).

(6) *Decide what to do:* Results from the action research experiment provide data-based information for teacher decision making. Assuming the alternative series produced greater student learning across all cognitive levels, as originally guessed by the teacher, adopting the alternative series may be the most appropriate decision, especially if supporting data such as homework, teacher-made tests, documented observations, and parent feedback reinforce pre- and post-test results.

When possible, action research projects should be conducted by more than one teacher. In the above example, results from two or more similar sixth grade classes would provide a more convincing argument for teachers making textbook decisions and for teachers who conference with parents about student achievement and the appropriateness of the instructional material used in teaching their children.

Deming's System of Profound Knowledge

In quality-oriented middle schools, quality improvement tools are used to solve problems, make decisions, improve classroom instruction, and improve the management process within the school itself. Quality improvement tools, when combined with action research and the PDCA cycle provide sound data-based decisions for school reform. Data-based decision making is the heart of the improvement process for middle schools of excellence. Principals in these schools use data to improve, not blame, and believe that Deming (1993) is correct when he states that 90 percent of the problems in any organization are created by the management system while only 10 percent of the organization's problems lie with the work force. Therefore, the emphasis is on improving the system so employees can work at optimal performance to attain the goals of the organization.

In making quality improvements, a conceptual understanding of Deming's system of profound knowledge (1986, 1993) is essential since the component parts must work together to optimize organizational output. Profound knowledge serves as the foundation for Deming's Fourteen Points of Quality Management and the application of the quality improvement tools. The four component parts of profound knowledge are briefly summarized and are as follows:

(1) Appreciation for a system is understanding the competition between components of a social system which destroys the system. A system is a network of people and the activities they must perform together to achieve common, clearly stated goals. Deming (1993) relates that schools are social systems which are made up of students, teachers, administrators, and parents, with each group interacting to pursue the goals relative to their own group and themselves. When these groups work in harmony, the goals of the school are maximized. When these groups work at cross purposes, the school flounders in uncertainty and indecision, and the goals are unattainable.

(2) Knowledge about variation is important to quality attainment and has specific implications for statistics which are central to the PDCA cycle. Variation will always exist between people, their performance, and the product. There will always be a performance mean (average) and a mean product which comes from the worker. Management's goal is to reduce variation in the system, by providing a stable system and understanding the special and common causes of variation. Bringing the system into a state of stability through statistical control means the process is predictable in terms of performance and product output.

(3) Theory of knowledge allows one to develop a rational plan and make rational predictions. When a knowledge of statistics and a knowledge of subject matter are combined, management can apply statistical findings to problem areas and reduce variation within the system.

(4) Knowledge of psychology helps us understand people, their interactions, and their motives. Understanding motivation, both intrinsic and extrinsic, is essential for management. Employees have an innate need for self-esteem, respect, and appreciation. If management's system denies employees any one of these three needs, intrinsic motivation is

drastically decreased. Extrinsic motivation places us under the influences of external forces, such as salary, and makes intrinsic motivation subordinate to these outside forces. Outside forces often neutralize intrinsic motivation which equals a lack of motivation on the part of the employees which equals trouble in the system, trouble in the process, and trouble in the product (Weller, 1993).

Of the four areas of profound knowledge, knowledge of variation is central to improving work productivity, reducing waste, and improving the outputs of the organization through fact-based decision making. Variation, or variance in measurement terms, is that which exists between present performance and desired performance. Finding the cause of variation and reducing the variance between present performance and desired performance is the primary purpose of the quality improvement tools. Practically speaking, human variation or human error will always exist and achieving zero variance is almost impossible. However, the quality tools will do much to eradicate a large portion of process variance which falls outside of human error.

SPECIFIC QUALITY TOOLS TO REDUCE VARIANCE IN THE SCHOOL

The improvement tools are used to plan, solve problems, generate new ideas, reach consensus, better understand the customer, and produce quality outcomes. These quality improvement tools are a significant part of daily life in quality-producing middle schools and are used by principals, teachers, teacher teams, and students. The improvement tools presented below are selected for their most common and practical use in school improvement reform. The tools listed also represent samples of many of the quality improvement tools used to develop project plans, to generate innovative ideas and programs, to evaluate ideas and analyze project accomplishments, and to determine root causes of problems in quality-oriented middle schools. The reader may want to consult Peter Mears' *Quality Improvement Tools and Techniques* (1995) for a comprehensive list of improvement tools and references to other relevant sources.

Tools to Generate Innovative Ideas

The following tools are primarily used to help generate new ideas and solve problems. These tools include brainstorming, benchmarking, and affinity diagramming and are best used in large group sessions of peers or with teacher teams. In each example, there are certain procedures or ground rules to follow in order to maximize quality outcomes.

BRAINSTORMING

Brainstorming is excellent for generating many new ideas from team members or peer groups about problems and opportunities for improvement. The power of collective thinking builds on individual ideas and yields creative ideas and viable solutions to complex problems in a short period of time.
Procedure to be followed:

- Review the problem or topic under discussion so the entire team understands what is to be accomplished. Use why, what, and how questions to get started. Why are we here? What do we want to do? How do we do it? Focus on improvement since solution connotes a definite answer and can restrict broad thinking among group members.
- All members must participate—the objective is volume, the more ideas the greater the chances of viable solutions to the problem. Unconventional ideas often solve the hardest problems.
- No one is allowed to criticize or evaluate the idea of another. This stops creative flow.
- Generate ideas until no one has any more to contribute—this exercise could last from 15 minutes to one hour. (Sometimes written answers are allowed to encourage total participation in groups where some members feel too inhibited to speak out. This practice depends on the make-up of the group.)
- Write down the creative ideas on a flip chart or blackboard for all to see.
- When all new ideas are exhausted, have the group "piggyback" on each of the ideas presented by discussing each idea thoroughly. Keep building on ideas if the group feels progress is being made.
- Identify two or three ideas that are the most viable ways to solve the problem or attain the target goal of the exercise. Rank order each idea for the planning phase of the PDCA cycle.

BRAINWRITING

Brainwriting is a nonverbal form of brainstorming and is used when ideas are needed on controversial or emotionally charged topics. The exercise also allows those who are less likely to speak out in a group to participate, especially when a team is dominated by a few vocal or opinionated members.
Procedure to be followed:

- The question or problem is clearly stated and then written on a flip chart and on several sheets of paper. Team members are seated at tables and given paper, pencils, and a sheet of paper with the problem or task written as it appears on the flip chart.

- Members are asked to write down five or more ideas about the task at hand and each member's response sheet is placed into a container. Sheets of paper are then drawn from the container by each team member, read silently, and new ideas are then added to the existing ideas with no criticism or evaluation made on paper responses.
- This process goes on for three or four rounds or until all ideas or comments have been made.
- Sheets of paper are then collected by the facilitator and responses are copied on a flip chart or blackboard.
- Members select the top two or three ideas for the quality improvement planning process.
- Rank order each idea for the planning phase of the PDCA cycle. During this step, if heated disagreement exists, the facilitator can initiate the process again and limit responses to the issue at hand.

BENCHMARKING

Benchmarking is an exercise in comparative analysis and is used to identify best practices of those organizations which have received recognition for excellence in a particular area. Benchmarking is a systematic way to generate new ideas and to integrate quality processes into an organization from existing practices.

Two types of benchmarking prevail:

- *Internal* benchmarking is the examination of quality departments, quality classrooms, and quality programs which exist within one's own school.
- *External* benchmarking is the examination of other schools or school systems to see how quality outputs are attained.

Procedures for external benchmarking:

- Select members for the benchmarking team. Team members should consist of those having the most expertise about, interest in, or stake in the problem or area being benchmarked.
- Identify quality schools or programs through reputation and/or the literature.
- Identify exactly what is to be benchmarked by the visiting team and what data will be collected.
- Identify exactly how the data is to be collected and by whom. This is

important since confusion over these matters can negate the value of benchmarking.

- Identify what is specifically causing the gap between your program and the quality program being benchmarked.
- Identify how best to achieve quality outcomes in your school through the brainstorming technique and other quality tools. Several plans may be developed for improvement, so rank order the plans.
- Identify the plan most likely to bring the desired quality outcomes and begin the planning process.

Internal benchmarking procedures are similar to those used for external benchmarking; however, internal staff are benchmarking their peers which negates concerns of scheduling time away from school, transportation, and the like. Internal benchmarking is less formal and less structured than external benchmarking, but certain procedures must be followed to achieve maximum benefit from this quality improvement method.

Procedures for internal benchmarking:

- Select those internal members to be benchmarked for their quality programs and practices and then select those needing to benchmark their quality-producing peers.
- Identify specifically what is to be benchmarked and how the data will be collected. This formal structure keeps the process objective in scope and reduces the temptation to become complacent through familiarity.
- Have those being benchmarked in turn benchmark those doing the benchmarking.
- Identify the gaps between the two programs or practices through the data collection and observation process.
- Develop a plan to achieve quality outcomes with assistance from benchmarked personnel.
- Implement the plan with continuous assistance from the benchmarked peers as the improvement process unfolds. The advantage to internal benchmarking is continuous, on-site assistance.

THE AFFINITY DIAGRAM

The affinity diagram organizes a plethora of ideas into natural relationships and promotes a high level of creative thinking among team members. The affinity diagram is so named because within it, ideas which have a special attraction or kinship for each other are grouped accordingly. Some use affinity diagrams as a supplementary planning tool. However, affinity diagrams are best used when problems are difficult to understand, when problems appear to be too large to be handled, and when the situation is in or near chaos. The affinity diagram also helps to generate new ideas, to define a problem, and to build consensus among those team members studying the problem.

Procedure to be followed:

- Organize the members into small groups—three to five members per group.
- Under the direction of a facilitator, the team identifies the problem to be solved or the issue to be addressed. The problem is clearly defined and stated and written on a flip chart or blackboard. (If the affinity diagram is to be used right after brainstorming, brainstorming ideas should be placed on sticky notes or flip chart and the process of refining each idea should then take place.)
- Working in groups and silently, each individual writes an idea (answer) to the problem on a single sticky note and places it on the blackboard or flip chart in a random fashion.
- When all ideas are posted randomly, each team member, in turn, begins to arrange the ideas in some logical order, for example, side-by-side. The grouped notes now have an "affinity" for each other. This process is done silently by each group member until all ideas are grouped to general satisfaction. Usually three independent tries for each person at grouping the ideas are sufficient. It's permissible to have "loner" ideas and if these ideas seem to fit into a new group, group them together. No idea is ever discarded.
- Now have each group discuss the ideas as they are grouped. Each group then comes up with a heading for the grouping of the ideas appearing on the flip chart or blackboard. Headings are written on sticky notes which capture the major ideas having an affinity for each other. Each group posts their headings silently and then arranges existing ideas under each heading. This process is completed three times. Ideas which are "loners" are placed under a new heading or combined with existing ideas.
- When the groups complete their silent tasks of arranging ideas under headings, open discussion now takes place to develop general agreement. These headings and ideas now serve as the beginning for the planning phase of the project.

Figure 12.3 presents an example of an affinity diagram identifying obstacles to implementing authentic assessment methods in a middle school. The example shows affinity ideas placed side-by-side with no heading as yet developed by the groups.

Figure 12.4 presents the same example with identified headings.

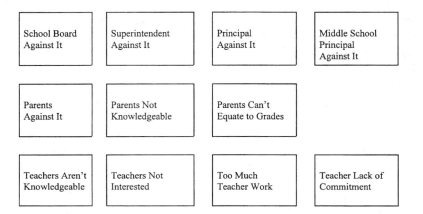

FIGURE 12.3. Affinity diagram showing side-by-side grouping of ideas identifying obstacles for implementing authentic assessment in a middle school.

PLANNING TOOLS

Planning tools are used to frame the investigation and experimentation process that leads to the ultimate improvement of products and services. Energies spent in planning reduce waste in time, effort, and materials in developing quality outcomes. In essence, using quality planning tools ensures that quality is built into the product from day one.

Used effectively, the quality planning tools identify the underlying barriers to improvement and provide the improvement plans to achieve quality outcomes. By identifying the root causes thwarting quality outputs, repetition of the same problems is halted, and improvement efforts become more effective and efficient. If the root causes of the problem are not identified,

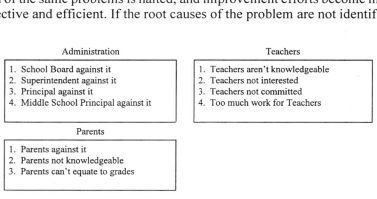

FIGURE 12.4. Completed affinity diagram identifying the obstacles for implementing authentic assessment in middle school.

no process will fix the problem. Planning tools function as a way to identify root causes of problems, problems which are both seen and heard daily, and the more dangerous ones—forced hidden problems—which are known to exist but few people want to actually confront (Weller, 1993). It is these forced hidden problems which are the biggest danger to advancing quality improvements.

Nested within the planning stage of the Plan, Do, Check, Act (PDCA) cycle, discussed earlier, are several planning tools which provide for continuous improvement. Using these planning tools in the initial stage of the PDCA cycle is the first step in making quality improvements. When principals and teachers use these quality planning tools to solve daily problems, the principle of continuous improvement becomes actualized (Weller, 1993).

Force Field Analysis

This planning tool provides an analytical approach to identify barriers or resistors to change. Force field analysis identifies the driving forces that support change and the restraining forces which prevent change. The theory behind Kurt Lewin's force field analysis model (1938) is that for change to occur, the driving forces must be stronger than the restraining forces. Equal force strength yields a no change climate. Restraining forces keep factors from improving or changing while driving forces strive toward improvement or change. In this analysis technique, it is important to look for existing strengths within the organization and then classify these strengths as the driving forces in the model. Restraining forces are those which keep the driving forces from prevailing. The idea is to alter conditions in such a way as to allow the driving forces for change to do so free from, or in spite of, their restraining forces. By increasing the driving forces or eliminating or decreasing the restraining forces, or both, plans can be made to bring about successful change. See Figure 12.5 for an example of force field analysis for introducing interdisciplinary team teaching.

Procedure to be followed:

- Divide the members into small groups, clearly state the problem to the group, and then write the problem on a flip chart or blackboard. Don't fall into the trap of what can or cannot be done. Focus only on the problem to be solved!
- Brainstorm with the group the driving or positive forces and place them on a flip chart to the left of a vertical line drawn down the middle of the paper with arrows pointing to the center line, or current status.
- Brainstorm the restraining or negative forces and place them to the

Driving Forces (Positive)	Restraining Forces (Negative)
Drivers →→→→→→→→→→→→→→→→→Current Status ←←←←←←←←←←←←←←←←←Restrainers	
(1.) Students are taught the knowledge that is of most worth	(1.) Changes the entire curriculum
(2.) Students instructed from different teaching styles	(2.) Teachers apprehension about team work
(3.) Students get more individualized instruction	(3.) No rewards for change
(4.) Students see more relationships across subject areas	(4.) Thematic units have to be developed
	(5.) No funds available for developing new materials
	(6.) Teachers must revise teaching techniques

FIGURE 12.5. Force field analysis example for implementing interdisciplinary team teaching.

right side of the center line with arrows pointing toward the center line.

- List all forces on the flip chart or, if done silently, have each group write their forces on sticky notes and place them on the flip chart.
- Have each group present the rationale as to why their presented forces are important. The forces can be deleted or fused together under a single heading. Group consensus must be achieved.
- Have the group prioritize each of the positive and negative forces based on an agreed upon ranking procedure. For example, in Figure 12.5, there are six restraining forces and four driving forces. The group may decide that changing the entire curriculum is the most important restraining force and, using the rank order method, assign it number one. Likewise, driving forces are rank ordered according to their benefit and assigned a number. In the example, ranked number one is "Students are taught the knowledge that is of most worth" in all curricular areas.
- After ranking all forces, the group makes recommendations on how each of the driving and restraining forces can be accommodated to effect the change. Recommendations from group members also include how each one can personally achieve the desired changes

and what others can do to achieve change. Each recommendation for change should directly correlate with one or more of the driving and restraining forces listed. For example, one recommendation might read: Principal pays for a series of staff development sessions for teachers on interdisciplinary team teaching. This would accommodate restrainers 1, 2, 4, and 6, and drivers 1 through 4.

- These recommendations then serve as ways to plan for the implementation of interdisciplinary team teaching. They have been developed by the teachers themselves and will meet their needs as they go through the change process. Here, two important things happen: First, teachers have direct input into what they need and will have a positive attitude about the training process and second, through the force field analysis process, the plan part of the PDCA cycle has been completed. In this example, the do stage becomes staff development with the rest of the cycle stages following in sequence. A practical note: In practice, implement this kind of team teaching on a pilot basis first with the pilot team completing the Do, Check, Act stages of the PDCA cycle.

Gantt Chart

Developed by Henry Gantt, the Gantt chart is a planning tool that was a forerunner of the Program Evaluation and Review Technique (PERT) and the Critical Path Method (CPM). The Gantt chart is useful in planning for the implementation of new programs and for developing long-range plans (Mears, 1995). The Gantt chart lists tasks in sequential order, dates designated for the start and finish of project activities, and persons responsible for each task, and deadlines. Gantt charts allow for the monitoring of the progress of the project by delineating the exact timing of when activities begin, who is responsible for the activity, the ordering and allocation of resources, and the evaluation of the activities.

The Gantt chart can be used independently for planning a project or it can be used after force field analysis, affinity diagraming, or brainstorming. Figure 12.6 presents an abbreviated example of a Gantt chart for benchmarking a school of quality. Gantt charts can be as detailed as planners choose to make them or they can be as simple as the example in Figure 12.6.

Procedure to be followed:

- After using the methods of brainstorming, force field analysis, or the affinity diagram, place the tasks that need to be accomplished in sequential order on a flip chart or blackboard. Some tasks may occur simultaneously.

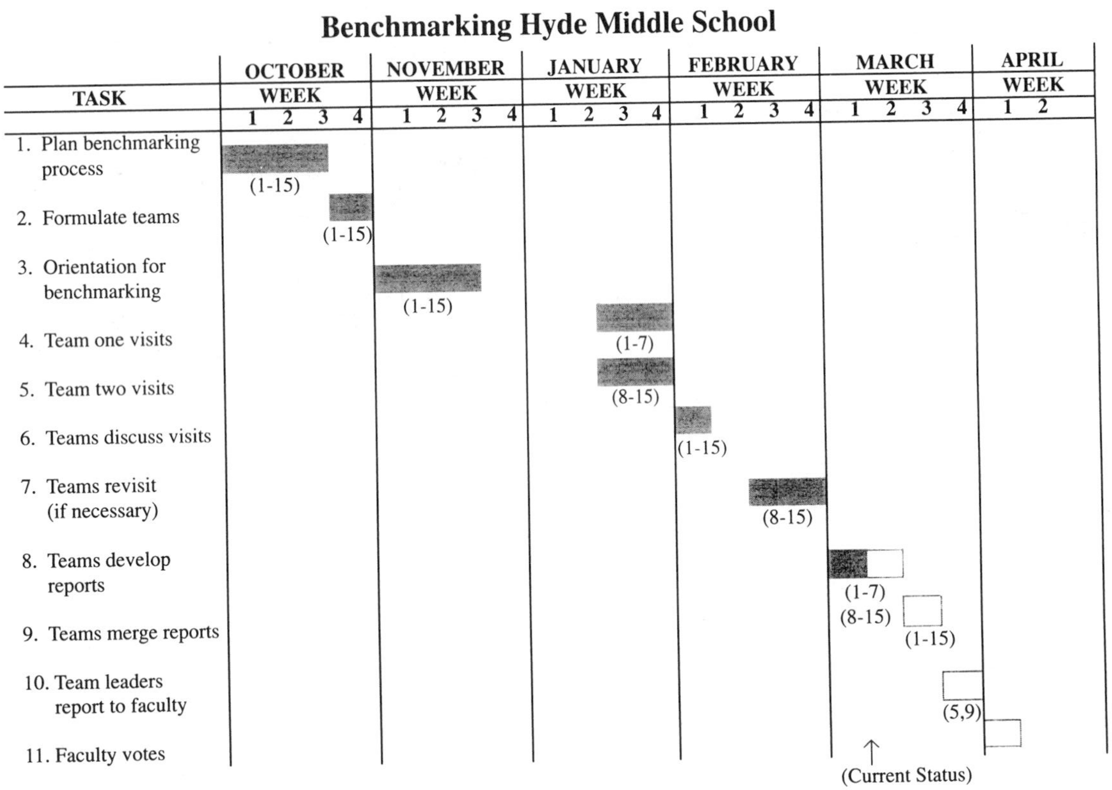

398

Benchmarking Hyde Middle School

TASK	OCTOBER WEEK				NOVEMBER WEEK				JANUARY WEEK				FEBRUARY WEEK				MARCH WEEK				APRIL WEEK	
	1	2	3	4	1	2	3	4	1	2	3	4	1	2	3	4	1	2	3	4	1	2
1. Plan benchmarking process		(1-15)																				
2. Formulate teams				(1-15)																		
3. Orientation for benchmarking						(1-15)																
4. Team one visits										(1-7)												
5. Team two visits											(8-15)											
6. Teams discuss visits													(1-15)									
7. Teams revisit (if necessary)															(8-15)							
8. Teams develop reports																	(1-7)					
9. Teams merge reports																		(8-15)				
10. Team leaders report to faculty																			(1-15)			
11. Faculty votes																				(5,9)		

← (Current Status)

FIGURE 12.6. Gantt chart example for benchmarking a school of quality.

- On a flip chart, draw horizontal lines denoting time modules under the project title and mark them in the appropriate time scales, usually in months, weeks, and days.
- Draw a vertical line down the left side of the chart and write each project task on the left side of the chart in the order they are to be completed. Time needed to accomplish each project is indicated by a bar outline corresponding to each task and placed under the starting and ending time allocated for each task.
- Code the person(s) responsible for each task. Usually a number is used for each person and is placed in parenthesis under each outline bar (see Figure 12.6).
- As events are completed, shade in the bars. Place an arrow at the current status of project tasks.
- Post the chart and give each team member a copy.

Meetings should be held frequently and used to provide project updates and identify specific problems needing attention. Sometimes replanning and reprioritizing tasks are necessary and these should be decided upon through group consensus.

Tree Diagram

Tree diagrams identify project goals and objectives and actions to solve problems or implement solutions. Tree diagraming helps one to think in a logical progression (much like the Gantt chart) and, more specifically, to move one's thinking from broad goals to specific objectives. Tree diagrams can include names of people or codes identifying people responsible for task completion. The diagram is ideal for completing large, complex projects needing graphic communication. With adjustments, the tree diagram can become part of a Gantt chart by coding completed projects. Tree diagrams may be used in the initial project planning stage where key issues need to be identified. Figure 12.7 provides an example of a tree diagram to plan for implementing interdisciplinary team teaching.

Procedure to be followed:

- Use small group of three to five members.
- On a flip chart or blackboard, write goal to be attained or problem to be solved on the left side of the chart.
- Use brainstorming or an affinity diagram exercise to determine how the goal can be accomplished. The facilitator then asks the question: "How can this best be achieved?" Group members now write their

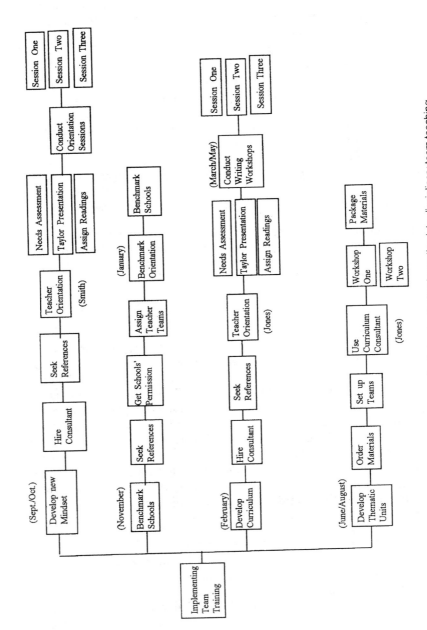

FIGURE 12.7. Tree diagram example of planning for implementing interdisciplinary team teaching.

ideas on sticky notes and place them to the right of the goal or problem on the flip chart. The first responses to the question will most likely be general in nature. The idea is to get as specific as possible.

- Again, ask the question "How can this best be achieved?" for each of the ideas completed in the first round. Group responses are again placed to the right of the problem but on a second tier.
- Have small groups now examine each idea and check its merit by asking the question: "Can we accomplish the goal by doing this?" If the answer is no, discard the idea.
- Each small group now goes to a separate room, elects a facilitator, and has one hour to develop a specific way to solve the problem and denote those responsible to achieve each task. This is done by taking the ideas generated from the total group and, with sticky notes, arranging the steps in the process needed to solve the problem in sequential order. During this exercise, group members discuss their rationales for placing the steps in the order they deem appropriate and may "branch" certain steps that have certain relationships.
- All group facilitators present their respective group ideas to the total group with each proposed problem solving process being discussed by the total group. Members from the total group can now rearrange the steps in the process recommended by each group facilitator by rearranging the order of sticky notes. Total group time for rearranging the process for each small group should take no more than fifteen minutes.
- The total group must then agree on a sequential process to solve the problem complete with names of people responsible for completing each task and the time required for each task to be completed.

After this planning phase is completed, the do part of the PDCA cycle can now begin. Periodic meetings should be scheduled to check on the progress of the improvement plan and to address any changes which may be needed in the plan itself. A Gantt chart should be developed for the total project and for each of the large tasks within the improvement process. This helps those responsible for task completion to keep current with the improvement project's progress.

Ishakawa Diagram

Kaoru Ishakawa developed this diagram to get at root causes of specific problems and for planning quality improvements. Also known as a cause-and-effect diagram or "fishbone" diagram, the Ishakawa diagram can be used with the affinity diagram and brainstorming to look at root causes of problems in different ways. The diagram sorts ideas into different and useful categories and stimulates broad thinking about possible causes of problems. It is also useful when "group thinking" starts to dominate the planning process and/or problem-solving sessions (Weller, 1995).

The diagram somewhat resembles the skeleton of a fish and consists of a "spine" with a fish's head or the effect which contains the problem or activity under discussion and is always pointing to the right. Ribs come out from the spine with a box at the end of each rib containing the major causal categories. The most common categories are people, procedures, materials, equipment, and environment. These categories can change based on the nature of the problem. Frequently, teachers and students feel more comfortable with headings of who, what, why, where, and how. Using these categories is a good beginning exercise to get people comfortable with the fishbone technique. More appropriate categories usually replace the who, what, why, where, and how categories as the exercise progresses. Figure 12.8 presents a fishbone diagram with the essential structure for completing a cause-and-effect exercise.

Procedure to be followed:

- State the problem to be solved as a group activity. The problem must be clearly stated and written on a flip chart or blackboard and all must agree to the effect or problem to be solved.
- Brainstorm the major categories of causes of the problem with the group. Standard category headings can be replaced by situation specific headings. Don't get bogged down in terminology at this point. The facilitator must exercise judgment here.
- Draw a fishbone diagram on a flip chart and fill in the category headings with arrow lines leading from the category heading box to the spine of the fish.

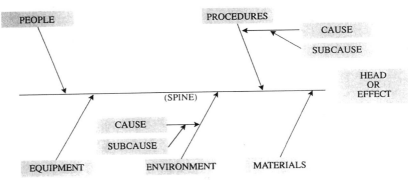

FIGURE 12.8. Example of the basic structure of a fishbone diagram.

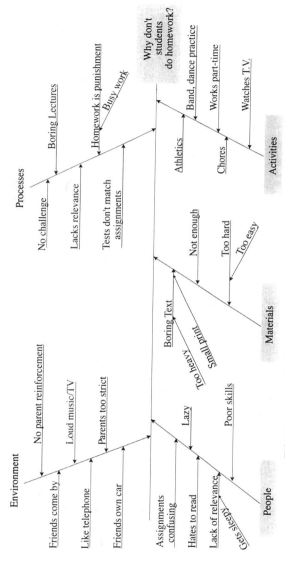

FIGURE 12.9. Fishbone diagram example of why students don't do homework.

- Brainstorm all possible causes of the problem by asking "Why does this happen?"
- At this point, the facilitator writes all causes on separate flip chart paper and any subcauses identified by the group. Subcauses are branches of the main cause in each category. This exercise continues until the group exhausts its ideas. If an affinity diagram was developed as a group exercise, use the sticky notes as causes, group them, and then determine category headings. Using the headings as main causes, arrange the ideas on the fishbone as subcauses and sub-subcauses. In both processes, sub-subcauses may need to be identified.
- Usually, one category will fall short of causes and subcauses and the facilitator will have to probe for responses. Practically speaking, this is usually an area where hidden, nonspoken causes and subcauses exist and some group members feel threatened in voicing an open opinion. Often, this is the area causing most of the problem and it is important to get member input in this area. Written responses greatly facilitate the completion of this exercise.

Sometimes, the fishbone diagram can be more effectively used by stating the desired result at the head of the diagram than stating the problem or activity. If this is done, use brainstorming to identify ways to achieve the desired result as a question. One example would be "How can we best implement an advisor/advisee program?". Whether one uses the effect or the result as the fish's head, it is a good idea to have an independent, unbiased reviewer examine the fishbone for additional ideas after the exercise is completed. Often, someone who has first-hand knowledge and experience in the area is of the most help. Figure 12.9 presents an example of a fishbone diagram on causes why students do not do their homework. This exercise was developed by eighth grade middle school students and a teacher in Calhoun City (Georgia) school system.

DATA COLLECTION AND ANALYSIS TOOLS

Data collection and analysis tools answer the basic question "How well are we doing?" by measuring project outcomes. Data provide indicators of progress and monitor the quality improvement process from start to finish. Both process and product measures are important in producing quality products and services with process measures telling how well/poorly things are going and product measures assessing the degree of quality in the product or outcomes. Both kinds of measures are essential for assessing quality improvements. When planning how to collect data, think how the data will be used and analyzed since this affects the kind of data you will want to collect as well as how the data will be collected (Weller, 1993).

Operational Definitions

To collect the most appropriate data to be analyzed, one must be able to state precisely the expected result from the improvement or intervention process used to improve the current situation. The problem or improvement goal must first be fully understood and then well defined. Well-defined terms and data analysis and collection procedures eliminate ambiguity from words or procedures that can be interpreted differently by different people. This is best done in question form. For example, a teacher might ask: "How can I increase student appreciation of Walt Whitman's poems?". The outcome to be measured is appreciation for Whitman's poetry in general, and students' demonstrating an appreciation for Whitman's use of words and symbolism in particular. The actual assessment method used must then precisely fit the criteria being assessed. In this example, the affective domain is the learning domain being tested. The goal is to have all students show an appreciation for Whitman's work and appreciate his word choice and symbolism. The test then must reflect students' gains in appreciation and be designed specifically for this purpose. Test results, if the test is valid and reliable, will demonstrate the number of students demonstrating appreciation.

Deming (1986) notes the importance of operational definitions for quality improvement in Chapter 9 of *Out of the Crisis*. Operational addresses the question: "Do we all agree what we need to do?" and definition addresses the question: "Do we all agree what every word means?". Without clear understanding on these matters, the quality improvement efforts will not yield valid and reliable data for making quality improvements.

Procedure to be followed:

- Define each term within the problem or area needing improvement.
- Ask what exactly is to be measured.
- Ask how the activity is to be measured.
- List the data collection procedures.
- List the criteria to be assessed.
- Define each measurement variable in the process or problem.
- Make sure all people involved in the quality improvement process fully understand the exact meaning of each term or activity associated with the process.

- Make sure all members involved in the improvement process know exactly what they are to do and what the end goal of the improvement process is.

Histograms

A histogram is a form of bar graph which depicts distributions of data regarding the number of times or frequency of occurrence of the data investigated. Histograms are used to assess variation in a given process or activity quickly and easily. Histograms are often used in conjunction with control charts which identify common or special causes of variation within a system. However, histograms are best used for analyzing group variation in order to detect changes taking place over time. Individual values are not seen in a histogram, but the graph does indicate if the data is distributed in a normal or bell curve approximation.

Procedure to be followed:

- Collect data on the variable(s) which are to be improved both prior to and after the improvement. Data is collected by observation, interviews, records, test scores and the like and are then transferred into numerical values or an agreed upon code for graphing.
- Draw X and Y axes on graph paper with the X axis representing the variable investigated and the Y axis the frequency of occurrence. This measure provides an index of variation or change within the existing process. Results can be presented to the group for discussion and for comparative data after the improvement process. When using a histogram for comparison purposes, data need to be collected and graphed prior to implementation of the improvement process.
- Implement the improvement activity, collect the necessary data, and then chart the data on graph paper using X and Y axes. Now compare the preintervention data with the postintervention data.
- Before drawing any conclusions, make sure the process undergoing change was stable when data were compiled for the preintervention histogram. That is, any change in the process could mask the change caused by the improvement process and the postintervention histogram would not provide an accurate assessment.
- Analyze the meaning of the shape of the histogram. Shapes provide meaning to the data and allow one to investigate further particular areas needing improvement.

Interpreting a histogram focuses on the statistical concept of central tendency which indicates where the center of the distribution tends to be lo-

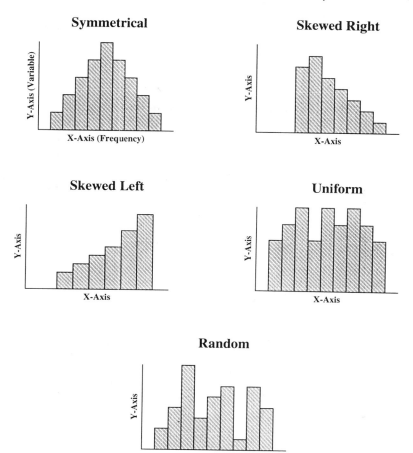

FIGURE 12.10. Examples of histograms.

cated. Shapes of histograms also reveal the current status of a program or activity. Figure 12.10 presents several examples of histograms.

A symmetrical shaped histogram, or bell-shaped curve, or normal curve, indicates a system under control. The mean (average score), median (midpoint), and mode (most frequent score) are equal and account for 99.73 percent of the area under the curve (plus and minus three standard deviations). Figure 12.11 presents an example of a totally heterogeneous class of students with mean, median, and mode of the distribution being equal.

Skewed distributions, as seen in Figure 12.10, are either negatively or positively skewed depending on the direction of the tail relative to the bulk

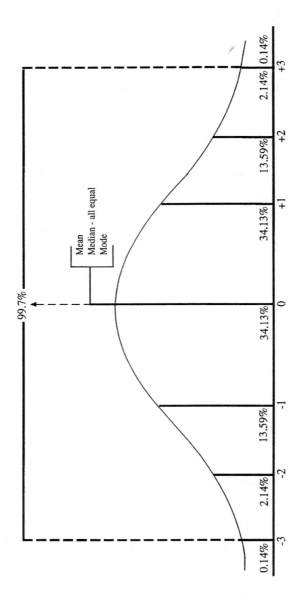

FIGURE 12.11. Example of normal curve with standard deviations and percent of score dispersion.

408

of the distribution of scores. For example, if the tail is to the right of the bulk of scores, the graph is skewed positively. Uniform or random distributions indicate a system is out of control or that there were not enough data sets for a clear image of the results of the intervention to emerge. Usually, thirty or more data sets are suggested for a reliable "snapshot" of the investigated process. One exception to the number of observations necessary for providing meaning to histograms is to use the median, rather than the mean, to describe the central tendency of a low number of data sets. For a more indepth discussion of measures of central tendency, their calculations, and when a researcher should choose one of these measures over others as a more reliable interpretation of data, the reader is referred to any introductory textbook on basic statistics for the behavioral sciences.

An example of graphing students pre- and post-test is presented in Figure 12.12 using histograms to depict student test results. A seventh grade teacher was interested in seeing if cooperative learning increased student achievement for a particular learning goal more than the traditional approach to teach the instructional goal. In this experiment, the same teacher taught two identically matched classes of students, during successive class periods, with the experimental class being taught the goal with cooperative learning methods and the control class being taught by the conventional teaching methods. As seen in Figure 12.12, students in Class B, the experimental group, performed better on the post-test than did Class A, the control group students. Here, because all variables in the experiment were evenly matched, the teacher can confidently change the instructional technique to cooperative learning methods when teaching the instructional goal.

Pareto Chart

A Pareto chart is based on the work of Vilfredo Pareto, an Italian economist. A Pareto chart is a bar chart or histogram which is used for analyzing data by groups to detect unnoticed patterns or to determine the most significant problem(s) or cause(s) of problems. Pareto charts can also be used to show cause and effect by comparing one Pareto chart denoting causes with the other chart denoting effects. However, cause and effect diagrams precede Pareto chart use in many cases (Weller, 1993).

Pareto analysis operates under the assumption that a large percentage of the results of a given variable are attributed to a small percentage of causes. Hunt (1992) states that Pareto charts help identify the "vital few" in contrast with the "trivial many" problems that exist. Moreover, Weller (1993) maintains that this chart's importance for school administrators lies in its ability to depict the how, what, when, where, and why of suspected problems. The Pareto chart is based on the 80/20 rule, that approximately 20 percent of the error in a

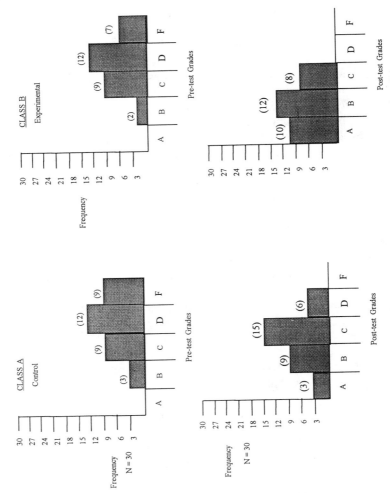

FIGURE 12.12. Pre-test and post-test scores for cooperative learning experiment.

410

system produces 80 percent of the problems. By focusing on the 20 percent of the errors that causes the greatest number of problems, the improvement task is more manageable, more efficient, and becomes easier to correct.
Procedure to be followed:

- In a large group, identify the errors in a process causing problems and collect the type of data needed over a specified time period. Data can be frequency count, percent, cost, etc.
- Specify who will collect what kind of data when, where, and how. Have a date when all data collection is to be completed.
- When data gathering is completed, develop a Pareto chart by drawing a horizontal line (*X* axis) and placing the bars representing the problem areas above the axis. Draw a vertical line (*Y* axis) to the left and place the frequency of the problem areas to the left of the line (*Y* axis).
- Construct the height of the bars based on the frequency of occurrence with the tallest bar to the left and then the rest of the bars to the right in descending order of occurrence.
- Frequency counts on the *Y* axis are determined by the data collected and are arranged in descending order on the left. Corresponding to the right of each frequency number is the percent that number represents. Bar heights are drawn to the number and percent representing the frequency and percent of occurrence.
- With a line, connect the plotted data on the left, from the tallest bar graph, to the data point of the *Y* axis on the right representing 100 percent. The line forms a curve shape and begins with 0 percent at the base of the Y axis on the right and goes to 100 percent, the total number of occurrences.
- All problem causes are now represented by the frequency and percent of each individually.

An example of a Pareto chart is presented in Figure 12.13 which depicts the results of a sixth grade teacher team who investigated why there was an overall lack of student enthusiasm and involvement in unit lessons. Results are presented on student and parent data both before and after unit lessons revisions were made.

The list of causes for the lack of student enthusiasm and involvement in unit lessons was developed by a team teacher through a cause-and-effect diagram. However, the teachers wanted to verify these causes with actual data collected from students and through teacher-made observations, logs, and checklists. Teachers also wanted to verify their data through student and parent interviews. A simple checklist was developed by the team which identified the possible causes for student apathy which were then placed on the left side of a sheet of paper. On the right of each category, adequate

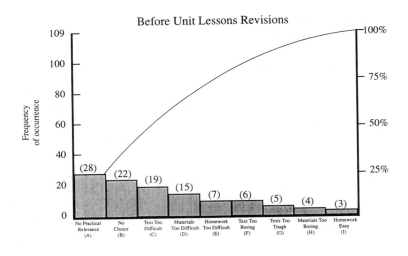

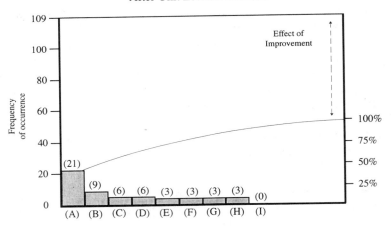

FIGURE 12.13. Pareto charts comparing teacher, student, and parent data on pre- and post-unit lesson revisions.

space was provided to check the frequency of occurrence of each cause. Data were collected over a four-week time period through two units of instruction. Figure 12.14 presents this checklist.

After the data were collected by each teacher team member, the data were summarized and placed into a grand checklist for whole-team analysis.

Student Apathy Toward Unit Lessons
10/1/96 - 11/1/96

COURSE	Mr. Brown - Science Frequency of Occurrence	
1.	Textbook too difficult	✓✓✓✓✓✓✓✓✓✓✓✓✓✓ (19)
2.	Supplementary materials too difficult	✓✓✓✓✓✓✓✓✓✓ (15)
3.	Tests too difficult	✓✓✓✓ (5)
4.	Homework too difficult	✓✓✓✓✓ (7)
5.	Textbook too boring	✓✓✓✓✓ (6)
6.	Supplementary materials too boring	✓✓✓ (4)
7.	Homework too easy	✓✓✓ (3)
8.	Students have no choice in topics	✓✓✓✓✓✓✓✓✓✓✓✓ (22)
9.	Assignments have no practical relevance	✓✓✓✓✓✓✓✓✓✓✓✓✓✓✓✓✓✓ (28)

FIGURE 12.14. Checklist of causes of student apathy toward unit lessons.

413

Student Apathy Toward Unit Lessons
10/1/96 - 3/31/97
Sixth Grade Team

	Course	Number of Occurrences	Cumulative Occurrences	Cumulative Percent(%)
1.	Assignments have no practical relevance	28	28	25
2.	Students have no choice in topics	22	50	45
3.	Textbook too difficult	19	69	62
4.	Supplementary materials too difficult	15	84	75
5.	Homework too difficult	7	91	82
6.	Textbook too boring	6	97	88
7.	Tests too difficult	5	102	93
8.	Supplementary materials too boring	4	106	97
9.	Homework too easy	3	109	100

FIGURE 12.15. Cumulative frequency chart for courses for student apathy.

Checklist data reveal that "material assignment has no practical relevance" and "students have no choice in what they study" as the two most frequent responses. "Textbook's too difficult" and "supplementary class materials too difficult" are ranked third and fourth, respectively. Other causes, while important, rank somewhat lower in causes of student apathy.

Next, a cumulative frequency chart like the one presented in Figure 12.15 was developed. This chart lists the total number of occurrences, cumulative frequency of occurrences, and their corresponding cumulative percent. To simplify, the data used in this example reflect only that which are found in Figure 12.14. A grand checklist of four or five teacher team member responses would contain higher frequency counts, but in this example it is assumed that total team rankings for causes of student apathy is the same as Mr. Brown's.

With this information, a Pareto chart can be drawn by using the identified causes of the problem and their frequency and percent of occurrence (see Figure 12.13). This provides a comprehensive picture of the major causes of student apathy toward unit lessons, originally derived at through a fishbone diagram, and now substantiated and ranked through teacher observation and student and parent interviews and comments. Teachers now have the necessary information to revise their unit lessons. After revisions are made, the same check process should be repeated with the next cohort of students to see if the necessary adjustments lead to decreased student apathy and then act accordingly. In essence, this teacher team is following the Plan, Do, Check, Act cycle of continuous improvement.

As seen in Figure 12.13, improvements made in unit lessons increased student interest. After unit lessons were revised, twenty-one students indicated lessons lacked relevance, while nine indicated they had no choice in what was learned in the lessons. Six students each thought the textbooks were too difficult and supplementary materials were too difficult. To continue to improve, teachers need to continue to monitor potential problems in the classroom and take steps to address these problems with the quality improvement tools.

Run Chart

A run chart is sometimes referred to as a line graph or trend graph and displays the frequency of occurrence over time and is one of the easiest tools to construct and use. The run chart is an effective visual aid which, when either plotting current data or comparing pre- and post-data, can indicate the amount of progress made by the change variable. Run charts are the first step in developing control charts which are used to discover how much variability in a process is due to random variation and how much is due to individual actions to determine whether the process is in statistical control. Put another way, control charts assess which variables are common or "normal" causes of variation and which variables are special causes of variation. Special causes of variation are the real targets for quality improvement since they are attributed to non-random events. [The reader is referred to Peter Mears' *Quality Improvement Tools and Techniques* (1995) for the statistical calculation procedures for the upper and lower control limits for constructing control charts since time and book space do not allow for the explanation of this very powerful but somewhat time-consuming quality improvement tool.] Run charts are powerful improvement tools in themselves and allow one to visually focus on truly vital changes in the process and identify meaningful trends or shifts in the average performance or occurrence variables.

Procedure to be followed:

- On graph paper, draw a horizontal (*X*) axis and label it either with the time or sequence under study. Flip charts can be used for large group work with approximate graph-line measurements.
- Draw a vertical (*Y*) axis and label it with the frequency or percent of the variable being studied.
- Draw a straight line from the point on the vertical or *Y* axis to the end of the horizontal or *X* axis indicating the average of the data being measured or investigated.
- Collect the data being investigated and plot it on horizontal and

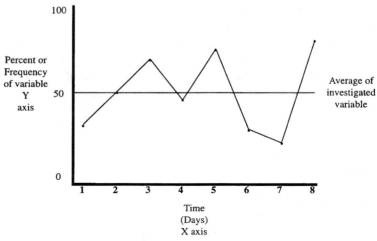

FIGURE 12.16. Run chart.

vertical coordinates. Look for patterns or trends compared to the average.

- Data displayed can be historical and used for pre- and post-intervention comparison of the effects of a catalyst or data can be displayed to analyze the effects-only of the change process. No more than two or three variables should be plotted on one run chart for effect. While some run charts plot four or more variables, these data points can become hard to read even when color coded. Figure 12.16 is an example of a run chart.

Run charts can be used to investigate a variety of variables and reveal insights to variation not provided by a histogram or a Pareto chart. These charts are often developed prior to a run chart to analyze data. A rule of thumb is that twenty or more data points need to be collected and plotted to suggest a trend or pattern in the investigated variable. Another rule of thumb is that when nine or more data points in a row fall or "run" on one side of the average, it indicates a statistically unusual event and that the average has changed (Weller, 1993). The assumption is that there will be an equal number of points falling above and below the line. A trend is too many points on either side of the average line with the word "run" describing several points in a row on either side of the average line. Again, statistical methods can determine whether or not a trend or pattern is statistically random and the reader is referred to Peter Mears' work. However, mere observation of data points on a run chart provides a good indication of the variability of the investigated variable(s).

USING THE QUALITY TOOLS FOR CONTINUOUS IMPROVEMENT: CASE STUDIES

In a Georgia suburban middle school, the principal was getting concerned about the number of discipline referrals made to the office by teachers. It seemed that more students were sent to the office this year than in previous years. The office secretary was instructed to keep a record and use a checklist for one grading period of the number of students sent to the office and the reason for the referral. At the end of the six week grading period, the principal placed the data in chart form as presented in Figure 12.17.

Averaging the school's infractions, the principal found that Mondays and Fridays had the highest rate of student referrals to the office for disciplinary action with an average of 10.50 and 7.41 referrals, respectively. Lateness to school and lateness to class were the two major causes of discipline referrals with fighting and disrespectfulness to teachers needing disciplinary action. Each area needing the principal's attention was graphed on a run chart by week for the six week grading period. An average was computed for each week. An example of the graph is presented in Figure 12.18.

Next, the principal presented the data to the faculty for discussion and problem solving. The principal pointed out that teachers had the primary task of handling discipline problems and that only major infractions of school rules should be referred to the office. Lateness was not considered to be a major policy infraction, but fighting and showing disrespect for teachers fell into that category. The principal stressed the importance of taking preventive measures and asked the faculty to come up with some solutions to the problem.

Teachers were then divided into small groups of five or six and asked to brainstorm the reasons and solutions for the four major discipline problems. Each group used the affinity diagram and cause-and-effect diagram to arrive at root causes and possible solutions to the problems. Some groups used force field analysis to help solidify their thinking. At the end of the exercise, which took three, two-hour faculty meetings, the following solutions to the problems were proposed and then implemented.

First, teachers surveyed their students regarding the causes for the problems. Next, teachers kept a log documenting disrespectful comments from students and acts leading to other infractions of school rules. Second, teachers personally called parents of students having discipline problems, arranged a conference, discussed the problem, and sought parental assistance in solving the problem. Third, teachers examined the days of the week when infractions occurred most frequently and decided to make Mondays and Fridays days when fun and exciting learning activities would be scheduled. Student interest questionnaires were distributed asking students the types of learning activities they enjoyed most and what interested them most about

Cause	Week 1					Week 2					Week 3				
	M	Tu	W	Th	F	M	Tu	W	Th	F	M	Tu	W	Th	F
Late to School	20	8	5	7	10	17	5	8	7	9	15	8	4	7	11
Late to Class	17	3	4	8	11	19	8	4	3	10	17	5	9	4	10
Fighting	7	0	1	1	4	6	2	3	1	7	4	3	0	0	5
Disrespectful	6	0	0	1	3	2	2	1	0	3	5	0	1	1	2

Cause	Week 4					Week 5					Week 6				
	M	Tu	W	Th	F	M	Tu	W	Th	F	M	Tu	W	Th	F
Late to School	18	5	9	2	10	21	7	15	8	16	16	8	4	6	11
Late to Class	12	6	5	4	11	15	4	9	7	11	11	8	2	3	12
Fighting	4	1	1	0	3	5	0	3	0	3	2	1	0	0	4
Disrespectful	4	2	3	1	5	4	1	1	0	3	7	1	0	2	4

FIGURE 12.17. Data collection of student discipline referrals.

the upcoming units of study. Fourth, since fights mostly erupted in parts of the building in which few classrooms were located, teachers volunteered to monitor these areas on a rotating basis. Fifth, it was decided that for teachers to gain respect, they had to give respect to their students. Teachers formed informal discussion groups on how to show more respect toward students. For first-year teachers, infractions were the highest. Informal discussion

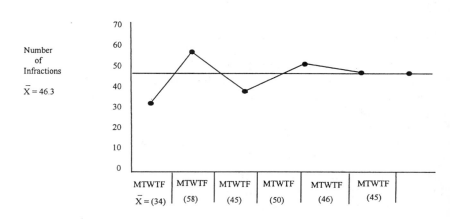

FIGURE 12.18. Run chart of student discipline referrals.

groups with veteran teachers provided practical suggestions on how to handle difficult students and how to avoid possible conflicts with students.

During the last six week grading period, data were again collected and all problem categories were reduced by 60 percent with infractions for teacher disrespect being reduced by over 90 percent. Faculty morale increased as a result of the principal allowing the teachers to develop their own solutions to these problems and a support network for new teachers was established as a result of this activity.

At a rural Georgia middle school, the principal and seventh grade teacher teams were disturbed about the poor reading scores on the Iowa Test of Basic Skills (ITBS) for their seventh grade students. Each teacher team knew that reading was taught across the content area and the reading teacher provided remedial instruction and helped team members infuse reading in their specific content areas. However, the seventh grade reading scores were 10 percentile points below the state average for these middle school students.

Brainstorming with the seventh grade teachers about the causes of the low reading scores, the principal helped the teachers develop a cause-and-effect diagram to identify the root causes of the problem. While many of the identified causes were plausible, one cause seemed more apparent than the others and a plan was developed to address the reading problem. The projected cause was the lack of teachers' individually diagnosing student subtest scores on the reading portion of the ITBS. Reading scores for each seventh grade were always grouped together, reporting total scores only, with subtest scores ignored for reporting purposes. Over the summer, seventh grade reading and language arts teachers examined each sixth grade student's subtest scores on the ITBS for entering seventh grade students. Notes were made on each student's file concerning their strengths and weakness on the subtests. In the fall, these notes were given to all teacher team members and a list of supplementary instructional materials to assist students in regular classroom instruction was presented to the principal for purchase. The reading teacher provided inservice to content teachers regarding the use of these additional instructional aids and worked independently with new teachers throughout the year.

At the end of seventh grade, each student's reading score was at or above grade level with an overall increase of 15 percentile points for all seventh grade students. This success caused sixth and eighth grade teacher teams to adopt similar measures for their students and sparked interest in several elementary schools. Through the use of the quality tools, the desire on the part of teachers and principals to "fix the problem," and the principal's support, both moral and financial, were facilitated quality outcomes.

In another Georgia suburban middle school, a teacher team of sixth grade teachers was dissatisfied with their student's mathematic scores on the ITBS. This team brainstormed the possible causes, used a fishbone diagram to identify the major causes, and focused on the lack of adequate skills as a major cause of poor student performance. They decided to benchmark two middle schools with high mathematics scores on the ITBS to observe their teaching methods and review their curriculum. It was determined that these schools made extensive use of computers for remedial and basic skills work and for enrichment and reinforcement.

Over the summer, teachers assessed entering sixth grade students' fifth grade test scores and noted the subtest results of each student. Requests were made to the principal for more classroom computers and for specific software packages. With extra funds from the central office, these instructional materials were purchased with each teacher team receiving four new computers and additional time scheduled in the school's computer laboratory. A mathematics consultant was also hired to help sixth grade team members teach mathematics skills in the content area. Throughout the school year, teachers worked individually with students needing remedial work and supplemented their instruction with daily work on the computer. Parents were asked to assist teachers by making sure their children had adequate time at home to complete both homework and group projects. At the end of the year, post-test data scores revealed that all students were at or above grade level in mathematics and their average score on the ITBS increased overall by 5 percentile points.

Examples of Students Using Quality Tools

The following selected examples are taken from the Calhoun City (Georgia) School System where middle school teachers and students regularly use the quality tools in classrooms to solve problems, make decisions, and learn academic content skills and knowledge. Weller and Hartley (1994), Schmoker and Wilson (1993), Murgatroyd and Morgan (1993), and others maintain that the full benefits of quality education are maximized when teachers and students apply the quality management principles and tools to classroom and real-life situations. It is in the classroom that the quest for continuous improvement and constancy of purpose must be instilled and practiced if the pursuit of quality is to become standard practice.

AFFINITY DIAGRAM

The affinity diagram was used to help teacher teams decide what students were most interested in learning in a sixth grade unit on space exploration.

Types of Spacecraft	How Launches Occur
satellites rockets shuttles Apollo Challenger	rocket fuel Training Places Kennedy Space Center space camp
Where Space Flights Go other planets the moon orbit earth	NASA astronaut selection careers
Things on a Mission clothes food payload	

FIGURE 12.19. Affinity diagram for unit topics on space exploration.

After using the brainstorming technique, students developed an affinity diagram and decided, by category, the areas of most interest regarding space exploration. Topics were fused into the unit and served as group projects and independent study topics. Figure 12.19 presents the results of the affinity diagram.

BRAINSTORMING

In a seventh grade social studies class, the teacher team members wanted to know what students perceived to be the major social problems impacting their lives. Topics were fused into current and future units and served as topics for group work and independent study. The teacher also asked students to survey their parents, relatives, and neighbors to see if their responses differed from students. These topics were peer and group pressure, drugs, teenage pregnancy, AIDS, drive-by shootings, rape, pollution, war, sex abuse, latchkey kids, violence, and starving children in other nations. Survey research methods were taught as part of mathematics instruction. The language arts teacher used the topics for essays, poems, and short stories. The science teacher tied the pollution and drugs topics into the unit on geology and minerals and studied local water samples, soil erosion, and other impacts of pollution.

FISHBONE DIAGRAM

The fishbone or cause-and-effect diagram was used by eighth grade students in a language arts class as a study tool to organize information for a poem. The example presented in Figure 12.20 is "Jabberwocky," a poem by Lewis Carroll. Students first brainstormed the important characteristics of a poem in general and then the specific topics within "Jabberwocky" itself.

Students then used the fishbone to identify the major categories or influences which impacted the "effect" of the poem "Jabberwocky." These were characters, author, vocabulary, tone, and plot. The causes and subcauses were then listed under each category with each one serving as a basis for class discussion as to its relevance to the poem. This exercise served three purposes: First it allowed students to apply the quality improvement tools to an actual learning situation; second, it provided a study guide for students; and third, it served as a class review of the poem for a test.

THE FIVE WHY'S

The five why's is an exercise which is often combined with brainstorming or it can be used independently to get at root causes of problems. The exercise is more specific in nature than brainstorming and it promotes the use of higher level thinking skills among students. Moreover, the five why's allow students to get to the core of the problem without getting sidetracked on irrelevant issues. The teacher must keep the class focused on the why and keep the class moving at a steady pace until the root cause(s) of the why is identified. The procedure is to first identify a problem then ask why. This continues each time until the ultimate cause or root of the problem is determined. There could be more than five whys in an exercise depending on the nature of the problem. An example of the use of the five why's is presented below. Here, a teacher attempts to determine why a student did poorly on a test.

Q. Why did you not do well on the test?
A. I didn't study.
Q. Why didn't you study?
A. I didn't have a book.
Q. Why didn't you have your book?
A. I forgot to take it home.
Q. Why did you forget to take it home?
A. I didn't write down the assignment.
Q. Why didn't you write down the assignment?
A. I was talking and didn't hear the assignment.
Q. What are you going to do now?
A. Pay attention to you in class.

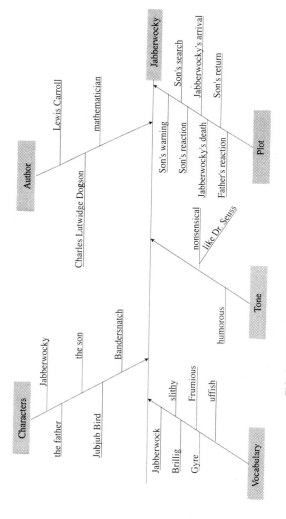

FIGURE 12.20. Fishbone diagram of the poem "Jabberwocky."

Change from Teacher-Centered to
Student-Centered Classroom

Current	⟶	Ideal
Driving Forces (+)	**Restraining Forces (-)**	
Study subjects of interest More hands-on learning Students will be more enthusiastic Students can talk to and work with friends Set own time limits, standards, and grades Responsible for own learning	Students will waste time Everyone won't do their share Students will forget to do their work Students don't know as much as teacher	

FIGURE 12.21. Force field analysis of teacher-centered versus student-centered class-room.

FORCE FIELD ANALYSIS

Force field analysis is used to discover essential forces which drive and prevent change. Figure 12.21 presents an example of a seventh grade class responding to a question regarding the advantages and disadvantages of changing to a student-centered classroom. The question was one asked of all middle school students early in the school system's planning stage to adopt Deming's (1986) quality theory as a means of school reform and restructuring. Responses from students in certain aspects of instruction were deemed vital for decision-making purposes.

PARETO CHART

A Pareto chart is a bar chart or histogram which displays collected data and is based on the 80/20 principle which states that 80 percent of a problem comes from approximately 20 percent of the causes. Pareto charts help to identify the most critical problems or those over which one has influence to change. Pareto charts allow for creative thinking, they identify major problems, they organize data for effective visual presentation, and pre- and post-Pareto charts can indicate the degree of change in a process attributed

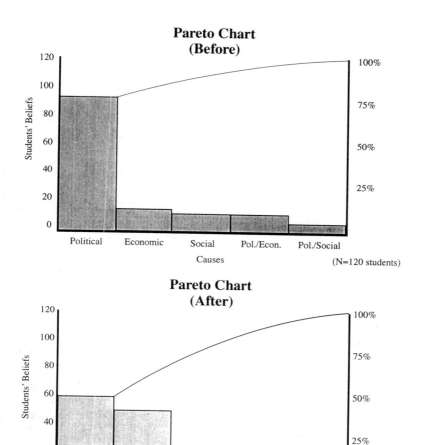

FIGURE 12.22. Pareto charts of the various causes of the American Revolution.

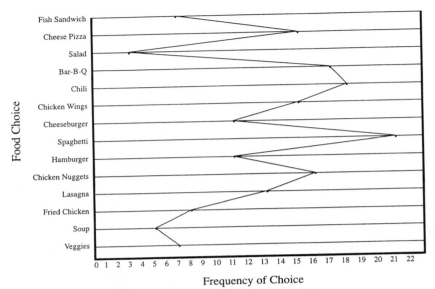

FIGURE 12.23. Run chart of student buffet preferences.

to a specific catalyst. Figure 12.22 presents the results of an eighth grade social studies class after studying the causes of the American Revolution. During instruction, the teacher challenged students to think of different reasons why the American colonies wanted freedom from British rule. Discussion resulted from supplementary readings on the various historical interpretations of the causes of the War.

Figure 12.22 shows the students' responses to what they felt were the causes of the American Revolution before reading the historical interpretations of the causes of the War and then after reading the interpretations. Political reasons for the cause of the war, the most popular belief, was no longer the most dominant belief held by the class when economic and social interpretations were read and discussed.

RUN CHART

The school's cafeteria supervisor was thinking about introducing some new items to the school menu on a regular basis and decided to try these new foods, for one month, along with the traditional foods on the buffet menu. Teachers in the middle school were asked to survey their students to determine their preferences so food could be standardized and food waste minimized. Data were tabulated at the end of the time period and a run chart was constructed for the cafeteria supervisor. Figure 12.23 presents student data on a run chart for a class of 25 students.

REFERENCES

Anderson, L. W. and R. B. Burns. 1989. *Research in Classrooms: The Study of Teaching, Teachers, and Instruction.* Oxford, England: Pergamon Press.

Borg, W. R. 1987. *Applying Educational Research: A Practical Guide for Teachers.* Second edition. White Plains, NY: Longman.

Calhoun, E. M. 1994. *How to Use Research in the Self-Renewing School.* Alexandria VA: Association for Supervision and Curriculum Development.

Campbell, D. T. and J. C. Stanley. 1963. *Experimental and Quasi-Experimental Designs for Research.* Chicago: Rand McNally.

Deming, W. E. 1986. *Out of the Crisis.* Cambridge, MA: MIT University Press.

Deming, W. E. 1993. *The New Economics: For Industry, Government, and Education.* Cambridge, MA: MIT Center for Advanced Engineering Study.

Feigenbaum, A. V. 1983. *Total Quality Control Handbook.* New York: McGraw Hill.

Hunt, V. D. 1992. *Quality in America: How to Implement a Competitive Quality Program.* Homewood, IL: Technology Research Corporation.

Johnson, J. H. 1993. "Total Quality Management in Education," *Oregon School Study Council Bulletin,* 36(6). Eugene, OR: University of Oregon.

Lewin, K. 1938. *The Conceptual Representation and the Measurement of Psychology.* Durham, NC: Duke University Press.

Lunenburg, F. C. and A. C. Ornstein. 1996. *Educational Administration: Concepts and Practices.* Second edition. Belmont, CA: Wadsworth Publishing.

Maslow, A. H. 1970. *Motivation and Personality.* Second edition. New York: Harper and Row.

McMillan, J. H. 1996. *Educational Research: Fundamentals for the Consumer.* Second edition. New York: Harper Collins.

Mears, P. 1995. *Quality Improvement Tools and Techniques.* New York: McGraw Hill.

Murgatroyd, S. and C. Morgan. 1993. *Total Quality Management and the School.* Briston, PA: Open University Press.

Schmoker, M. J. and R. B. Wilson. 1993. *Total Quality Management Education: Profiles of Schools That Demonstrate the Power of Deming's Management Principles.* Bloomington, IN: Phi Delta Kappa.

Taylor, F. W. 1911. *Principles of Scientific Management.* New York: Harper.

Weller, L. D. 1993. *Total Quality Management: A Conceptual Overview and Applications for Education.* Athens, GA: College of Education, The University of Georgia.

Weller, L. D. 1995. "Quality Teams: Problems, Causes, Solutions," *The TQM Magazine,* 7(3):45–49.

Weller, L. D. 1996. "The Next Generation of School Reform," *Quality Progress,* 29(10):65–74.

Weller, L. D. and S. H. Hartley. 1994. "Total Quality Management and School Restructuring: Georgia's Approach to Educational Reform," *Quality Assurance in Education,* 2(2):18–25.

This *State of the School Report* was mentioned in Chapter 2 which deals with leadership as a necessary component for effective, quality-oriented middle schools. It is included here for two reasons: as an innovative example of leadership in action and as a template for those middle school principals who may wish to make such a report an annual part of their leadership efforts. Of particular interest is Dr. Watts' even-handed use of both psychological and philosophical motivators and firm guidance. The report has been edited in the interests of space considerations and to eliminate references of specific names.

Dr. Wayne Watts
EDWARDS MIDDLE SCHOOL
(Conyers, Georgia)
State of the School Report
August 1996

OVERVIEW

This is our first State of the School Report. Complied from data, personal observation, and discussions with parents, teachers, and central office administrators, these observations are offered so that we can responsibly educate the young people in our charge.

Edwards Middle School (EMS) is an above-average achieving school, with student achievement levels clustering around the 65th percentile for a number of years. Recently, we have been challenged to improve our student achievement levels as measured by standardized achievement tests. A Strategic Plan was developed to meet our goals; however, before this can happen effectively, our entire faculty must be together in our focus and our approach. We depend on each other for our success, so it behooves us to be as cooperative and supportive of each other as possible, both professionally and personally.

Education is sometimes a world of isolation because adults spend the entire workday away from the company of other adults. Middle schools are designed to counter this isolation somewhat by fostering collaborative planning. This is supported financially by allowing for double the amount of planning time allotted to high school teachers. All of these organizational strategies and practices are designed to enhance the individual teacher's ability to meet our ultimate, *raison d'être*—to lead students through a process that results in increased achievement and preparation for the next step.

Test scores are our game, regardless of your opinion of them. Certainly, schools and their programs are more than test score results. But in our "bottom line" society, we simply must perform well on tests. Performance on test scores that is less than our students' potential or less than our comparison group levels indicates that something is not happening that should be happening. This means that we must make some changes in order to be on track.

My definition of successful teaching is very simple. Teaching success equals student achievement. A student's success is the result of successful teaching. Using test scores as an indicator, there is evidence based on data that the middle school concept is not working effectively at Edwards Middle School. My assessment is that we have become extremely comfortable with our reputation and are a bit slow to recognize the things that have changed around us.

The question is—will we be proactive in our efforts or reactive? By being proactive, we are in control of our own destiny. Being reactive means playing catch-up to someone else's priorities. Efforts in the past to apprise this faculty of current trends and expectations have sometimes been met with disbelief, denial, and even hostility. What will we do? My fear is that many of the things that have to be done are now out of our realm of influence. Some of the gentle proddings that I've offered in the past two years haven't gotten the desired results, so now it's time to take action to maintain control of our own destiny.

I've taken a hard look at our entire program—every component of our offerings, our practices, our attention to our responsibilities. In my view, we must start from our sources of authority and have a clear understanding of everyone's role in our business. [Refer to handout on the process of education tracing the division of duties and responsibilities.]

THE ROLE OF THE TEACHER IN THE ORGANIZATION OF EDUCATION

Where does the classroom teacher fit into the overall scheme of education in the United States? What is the position that classroom teachers occupy? Are teachers by themselves when it comes to meeting the needs of students? Where do all of those rules and regulations come from anyway? And why are they needed? All of these questions can be answered simply by knowing the official role of each office and person in the organization. Perhaps starting at the beginning is the best place to learn.

Because the Constitution of the United States does not mention education specifically, education has been the responsibility of each state. Each state establishes its organizational structure to meet needs through legislation. This includes a state board of education to oversee the process and a chief executive officer. Also, a state establishes a support structure to develop curriculum, oversee funding from the legislature, monitor teacher credentials, provide for teacher benefits, establish standards for school facilities, determine maximum class size, and so on. The bulk of funding for education comes from state tax coffers.

The state, in turn, charters what are called Local Units of Administration (LUAs) or Local Boards of Education (BOEs) to deliver the state guidelines to their chartered areas. The BOE is a locally elected, state-sponsored body of public officials who are charged with enforcing and supporting state policies, regulations, and procedures for their designated geographic area. Local BOEs hire a superintendent and establish a local support system staff to operate the local system. The BOE defines local school attendance areas and builds and maintains schools to educate students, establishes class sizes within state law, approves the school calendar, operates transportation systems and lunch programs, and reflects the wishes of the community in graduation requirements or other curricular considerations. Only by acting as a group can the BOE make decisions. All hiring decisions are made by the BOE based on the recommendation of the superintendent. All employees work for the system and can be transferred, reassigned, or placed in any work environment for which they are qualified according to the needs of the system.

The superintendent of schools is the executive officer of the board and is recognized as a state official. The superintendent is responsible for the day-to-day operations of the system and is charged with enforcing state and local policies and procedures. Superintendents cannot hire personnel, but can recommend hiring decisions to the BOE.

The principal of each school is charged with enforcing local and state policies and regulations on the local school level. He or she answers to the superintendent. Recommendations for hiring in a local school go from the principal to the superintendent to the BOE for ratification. The principal oversees the day-to-day and long-range operation of the school within the guidelines and policies for the state and the local system and is responsible for their enforcement.

The classroom teacher, then, is the direct on-line representative of the local BOE and state BOE in the delivery of instruction to students. Teachers report to the school principal in terms of evaluation and accountability. Teachers are responsible to see that the locally developed curriculum is delivered to the students in such a manner that they can learn, be successful, and demonstrate acceptable competencies in specified areas and appropriate increases in achievement levels.

Local decisions regarding instructional change are often made with teacher input because of the teacher's expertise in working with students. This model is usually drawn top-down, with the classroom teacher at the bottom, but this is not really the case when it comes to the influence that the individual teacher has in the entire process. Teachers now have more opportunity to give input than ever before, so this model now would look like a cycle, with all components of the cycle interacting in each of their defined areas to ensure a quality education for the children of the state.

The federal government has a role in public education through the basic rights of all students. Because all citizens have certain protections under the law, the federal government can be involved through civil rights or due process issues. This often means that special education services and/or discipline issues can invoke federal guidelines.

Because the state and the LBOE have a charge to keep, certain procedures and activities are required to establish accountability, such as staff development and continuing upgrades in certification. Also, things like record keeping and duties, as well as expectations in conduct, behavior, and performance, are regularly mandated to assure community expectations and the attainment of the goals of the system. Knowing each role helps to clearly see where appropriate decisions are made, who has the responsibility to make them, and where accountability is measured.

Situational Leadership

One of the most intriguing things I've studied about being a leader is what is referred to as *situational leadership*. Ted Engstrom, in his book *The Making of a Christian Leader,* defines situational leadership as a style that "depends on the task of the organization, the phase of life of the organization, and the needs of the moment." Some people and situations are best managed by a "do this, now do this" approach. Others have more success and productivity if the leader asks for their ideas and then gets out of the way while they do the job. Circumstances can require a different leadership style from the leader in different situations, hence, situational leadership. My approach will be toward the situational realities I find today regarding our school. The rest of my report will come from my assessment of what should be done. In some cases, I'll be saying what we will be doing. In others, I'll be opening up ideas for discussion at a future time.

The first thing I'll assess is our professional staff, speaking in general terms, of course. Many of our staff members are already doing those things I'll be directing and requiring of each. For those individual problems that I address globally, I'll be doing follow-up discussions with individual staff members as deemed appropriate.

All for One, One for All

Remember—we rely on each other to be successful. If one component is not working, then there is a cumulative effect on the entire enterprise.

Let's take a generic example. Suppose that you are the assistant principal. You have just received a discipline referral for a student where the teacher says that this is the 10th consecutive time the student has failed to turn in the assignment. You call the parent to assign the student to detention for failure to complete work, and the parent is surprised. Now, many times the teacher has made an attempt to contact the parent and has not been able to get in touch, but this is not the norm when we've been involved. Scenarios where the teacher has made contact don't usually end up in the office. We have to persuade the parent that we contact that the teacher is not deliberately out to get the child, which is their first assumption. Usually, a conference is then scheduled, and we are expected by the staff to defend the teacher in such a situation.

These situations take up a tremendous amount of administrative time, which impacts the operations of the school. This time could better be spent in the classroom, which is a common concern that teachers raise. Here are a few more examples of time-consuming situations:

- Teacher turns in a class set of novels with three books missing, and can't account for who still has them.
- Colleague is consistently late to work or to team meetings.

- Announcement on the intercom: "Will the person who borrowed VCR # 7 please return it to the Media Center?"

These scenarios show how easily problems can mushroom out of control. Do you see the cumulative effects that they have on the workplace and how they impact everyone? Do you see how your resources are redirected away from where they are needed to combat critical and essential instructional problems?

FACULTY

Administration: My Personal Value System

Theorists have devised a two-part model of the way leaders view their followers. The model is based on whether you are a Theory X person or a Theory Y person. A Theory X person believes that people are innately lazy and unreliable. Theory Y adherents believe that people can be self-directed and are able to accomplish things if given the proper motivation. The interesting thing about situational leadership is that you can treat everyone the same way, yet be perceived as either type, depending on who is doing an evaluation of your performance.

I believe that teachers are capable of doing anything. The school setting has some of the most highly educated people in one work location in our society. I have read with fascination about schools that have no principal, but are run by executive committees. These schools intrigue me because they match my values of competence, dedication, and ability that I hold for teachers. Yet I also am very aware that no war was ever won, no team has ever come out on top, nor has any successful company has ever "made it" by committee. A strong leader is required in any successful organization that includes people. This blend of committee advice and leadership is the preferred organizational strategy from all theorists and practitioners of leadership training.

Very idealistically, I entered administration because I believed that I could make a difference by working through the system. Many of my colleagues were the type that always had a gripe or could always tell someone how it should be done, but when it came down to working for positive change, they didn't want to get involved. On the other hand, other administrations were very control-oriented and seemed to assume that we teachers were just one or two notches above the amoeba on the intelligence scale and treated us like this, which is definitely a Theory X approach.

One of the first things that I encountered as an assistant principal (AP) was an "us vs. them" mentality. I was astounded to experience the reaction from some staff that I was an administrator and therefore believed that teachers were inferior. It was thought that I was a Theory X person simply because I was an administrator. It took me about a year to learn my task as an AP, which was to be supportive of staff and to be an extension of my boss.

The difference between AP and principal is like the difference between being the batboy and Bobby Cox. The span of view increases exponentially, and so does the span of responsibility. Some changes have taken place because of my priorities. Some of these have not been noticed by the faculty; some have. Some have been welcomed; some have met with opposition.

I have progressively gained an increasing view of our enterprise. The big picture is more clearly defined now for me, since I've had to deal with areas outside of my first field of training. I've had to temper my idealism in some ways to deal with unanticipated realities, but overall, I still am somewhat idealistic. I still believe the following, which I consider to be a Theory Y viewpoint:

- People are basically good at heart.
- People don't mess up intentionally.
- Differences in philosophies create most disagreement and internal tension.
- Given enough information, folks will make the right decisions for the circumstances.
- Everyone who is impacted should have an opportunity to give input.
- If the news is bad, you don't need to hear it through the grapevine.
- Everyone has something to contribute.
- All the standards I expect of teachers I expect of myself.

One of my essential goals is to help everyone see the big picture. Likewise, I want to see your views as we make these important decisions. So I plan to continue to ask for your input and opinions on our projects and to incorporate these into any final decision that would be made. With all of my emphasis on collaboration, I had not anticipated the reality that some people don't want to change. I also have had new experiences with people who don't seem to share my value system, who write uninformed assumptions in the newspaper, or who assume that we are intentionally trying to brainwash our students because of some hidden social agenda.

I believe in success, achievement, and accomplishment, whether it's in our students or in our faculty. My biggest mistakes have been made on the side of following my beliefs and principles. What has happened many times is that, because I believe that educators are responsible and professional, I have felt that directing and requiring certain practices would be inappropriate. I did not want to be an administrator who was a control freak. In reality, and for whatever reason, things haven't run so smoothly in certain areas. As your principal, I now have to step in and give more direction regarding certain things. I still hold to my belief, though, that well-informed people make appropriate decisions. I will be issuing more directives to assure that we are meeting our expectations and responsibilities.

When we hired our new APs, a representative committee of teachers was asked for input in the selection. They were charged with recommending candidates, and I've been pleased with their recommendations. With your administrative team, you get varied experience, expertise, and a consistent philosophy. We are continually learning and reflect often in our weekly team meetings about how to manage given situations better, how to provide assistance to specific situations in a better way, how to break unpleasant news to the staff, how to relieve certain excessive expectations, and so on.

I hope every day that I will be the leader that EMS needs. Note that this is not the same as the leader that you want. This State of the School Report is part of this leadership. I have asked for guidance as I crafted these words, to be fair, to inform you, and to challenge you to be colleagues, rather than subordinates or mavericks.

Teachers

We have a capable and individually talented staff of teachers. Our past success is directly because of the abilities of our teaching faculty. We have been leaders instructionally for many years. We get along with each other very well personally and are quick to help in times of crisis. Teachers have great opportunities here to be a part of decisions, which is evidenced by teachers having input in the hiring process of their colleagues. Last year, our faculty collectively held 53 advanced degrees from over 40 different colleges or universities. We have a wide representation of experiences from many different parts of the continent.

Guidance

Our counseling staff is continually striving to serve our students according to their individual needs. Last year, the guidance plan was completely revised in order to be ready for the needs we'd observed. Changes in our orientation programs are one visible example of these revisions, and they have been positive. Other changes may be behind the scenes, but they are also very productive and positive. With the assistance of our adjunct staff, we've tackled many new things and meet the needs of our kids in ways that were not possible previously. They are constantly seeking to improve their service.

Media and Technology

We have media specialists and technology support staff who provide excellent support and are well informed of trends and expectations. They do a superb job of balancing resources and supporting teachers, as well as leading classes for students. I'd like to see teachers coming to our Media Specialists more often to include them in their collaborative planning for the coming year.

Regarding technology, our hardware, software, and support are the envy of most schools in the southeast and, from my experiences, even the nation. There is much available to us, and with the beginning of a new effort this year we expect great strides in our student achievement levels. Every teacher is expected to utilize the technology support to its fullest potential. We've added the position of Technology Specialist this year to continue to help teachers in applying technology to your instructional bag of tricks. Part of staff development will include instruction in Technology Benchmark Competencies for teachers, which we all will do. This is because we must now utilize the investment that the taxpayers have made for us in the integration of technology into our schools' instructional programs.

Secretarial Support Staff

Our secretaries are second to none in competence, professionalism, and loyalty to our school. Each of them brings expertise to us and is quick to share knowledge and assistance in any way. Their tasks, no matter how varied or overwhelming, are carried out with tact and professionalism. I hope that all of us will continue to recognize this excellence.

Teacher Assistants

Possibly one of the strongest groups we have here is our TA staff. They are willing on a moment's notice to help anybody in any way, and they do it cheerfully and effectively. During the past few years, they have shouldered the load more and more with class coverages, and so forth. Their primary purpose is to be with students. This work with students is to be in small-group settings or one-on-one. This year, we will return to this format. Teachers—do not expect aide coverage for you to handle your errands or to let your personal business be managed. Should class coverage for these reasons be needed, you will need to arrange for it yourself with a colleague and/or expect to take personal leave.

Maintenance

Again, we have an excellent staff. We have a countywide reputation about how supportive and cooperative our staff is, and the *Atlanta Journal/Constitution* noted the cleanliness of our facility when they visited us last year. With our new facility, they will have a harder and an easier job: easier, in that it's easier to maintain new carpet, fresh walls, and new facilities; harder, in that keeping the facility "new" will be a challenge. With all of our new classrooms, we were only able to afford one-half of an increase in maintenance positions. That means they've got to do more with less because the overall area of service for each one will increase. We've all got to help to manage these things for them and for us. This is our facility, and we must keep it up. I'm going to call on teachers this year to designate students to monitor the cafeteria each lunch period so that their workload is more reasonable. Some of the classes left the cafeteria in a mess each day and there's no reason for this.

Cafeteria

The cafeteria has an excellent staff, very loyal, dedicated, and supportive of our whole school program. We would have to go a long way to find a staff that fits our school any better.

ACADEMICS

Characteristics of High-Achieving Middle Schools

In high-achieving middle schools,

- The focus is on student achievement.
- School improvement is continuous.
- Interdisciplinary teaching is practiced: blocks of time are devoted to instruction; students are grouped and regrouped for instruction; and multi- and interdisciplinary lessons are planned and presented.
- There is no choice between being child-centered and achievement-centered. Both exist and are mutually supportive.
- Staff members understand their obligation to monitor student achievement and adjust their teaching based on these data.

We are a team of professionals with one basic charge: to see that our students progress satisfactorily. We consider our core classes as critical, but we also believe that our additional offerings are essential components in a complete education. Our academic programs have traditionally been successful. The community still considers EMS to be sound academically. But in some areas, we are slipping, based on the data you've seen and on public perception. Where we miss the boat sometimes is in the manner in which we organize for instruction. Observation of classes reveals, in many cases, there is very little difference from the old lecture method of instruction. Our past success has been directly correlated to the talents and abilities of individual teachers, yet after hearing the test score data, we know that it will take a combined effort from all of us to meet our challenges. Has our past success been because of the teacher being a random variable? Will our future results be because of the same reason? If you keep doing the same things, should you expect to get different results? I think you can see from my earlier comments that I hold our faculty and programs in high regard. Yet—if we are as competent and talented as I believe—why are our students not achieving to their potential?

Except in some notable cases, interdisciplinary planning does not exist. Many teachers seem to be doing their own thing and not working together toward meeting instructional goals. If we are a true middle school, then we should not be functioning as a high school! If we believe that middle school is the way to go, then we must practice middle school organizational and instructional strategies. Are you a teacher that wants the teacher perks that come with the middle school organizational setting, but not the instructional responsibilities? As a teacher, you must understand that the ultimate goal of any school is to produce a well-rounded, functioning person. Many measures are used in evaluating this, the most basic of which is: Has the child progressed one year academically after spending a year with us? Can you see the value in using the expertise of your colleagues in realizing your own responsibilities? Are we using sound and varied instructional methods? Are we doing the things that we have learned from brain research, or are we doing what we've always done?

(1) What would be the strongest areas of our school last year? What would be the weakest?

(2) How are we using the team structure to improve student achievement?

(3) If a team structure is the way to go, why are we not achieving at our expected levels?

(4) When was the last time you talked about student achievement at your team meeting?

(5) When did you analyze your students' test scores to see where their strengths and weaknesses were, and what plans have you made to address those weaknesses?

Testing

Testing simply must be given a priority by everyone in the school. This is the only indicator that is taken into account by most people, and it is the standard by which we are judged. Every staff member is directly impacted by our results, and our school's reputation is built upon our academic success record.

Each teacher will emphasize testing as they plan for instruction. Objectives that are on the ITBS will be emphasized in our teaching and will be reflected on the long-range plans that you will submit to me. Instruction will be offered on everything that is assessed on the ITBS before the ITBS is administered in March. Those parts of our curriculum that are not assessed on the ITBS can, for the most part, be addressed after the ITBS is administered. This alignment of our curriculum with what is tested is essential to giving our students their best shot at doing well. Even with excellent preparation academically, students must be given the opportunity to practice test procedures. We will do this by using testing preparation materials like many of you did last year. We will meet by disciplines soon to determine the materials for our use and will purchase accordingly. I attribute much of our success last year in Language Arts to the use of these preparation materials.

From my classroom experience, let me relate an experience I had that is a form of curriculum alignment. Those of us who have coached or sponsored any competitive activity know that you never really get too worried about annual evaluations. That's because when you are in the public eye, every game or competition is an evaluation. In my field, the annual Spring Concert Festival competition was one of those benchmark-setting experiences. There are two parts of a concert festival competition—the prepared section and the sight-reading section. The prepared section is just that—you are graded on your work and preparation. Some people practice on three pieces for six months to get them flawless, but to combat this, the sight-reading section was implemented to assure that the teaching of music was taking place.

In preparing for the concert festival with my first high school band (believing that sight-reading was a necessary evil and that we would do OK), I spent the bulk of my time working on the prepared section. But when it came to the sight-reading, my kids were lost, not because they could not read music, but because they did not know how to operate in an intense environment. Now their work had been judged unacceptable.

To avoid this happening again, I began to think about the sight-reading competition. What were the skills that we would need to be successful? The kids needed to be able to read and interpret the musical notation—but I realized that we had no game plan at sight-reading. A procedure for this competition was soon devised. Our procedure now established, we worked on it, not intensely for two weeks before the festival, but every day in class. Part of the daily warm-up routine included scales, exercises, and a sight-reading selection. The kids got to hate it, but it was only 5 minutes at the beginning of each class, so they tolerated it. The next year at the festival, we did very well in the prepared section. We felt good moving into the sight-reading room. When we started, I could see some nervousness on the part of the kids, but we once again went over our procedures. I held up my baton and began. We started well! They kept in tempo! They didn't get lost at the repeat signs where everyone gets lost. Best of all, we all stopped together at the same time. We had done it!

It came time for ratings to be announced, and I'm proud to say that we earned a superior rating in both the prepared and the sight-reading sections of concert festival. But one thing sticks out—one of my students afterwards came up and said. "Thanks for making us do that sight-reading." They could do it all along. I did not "teach them the test." I did teach them about the test, how to manage the challenge, and the content they needed to be prepared.

Our game now is test scores. We value our kids' performance and know that we have done our best to prepare them. We have prepared ourselves. We will do the same for our kids when we give them a procedure—a game plan to follow. It will work, and we will be successful.

After an analysis of last year's test scores, weaknesses have been identified that must be addressed. Conveniently, these weaknesses tend to be representative of the core academic disciplines, so that means that each of the four classes can have a major emphasis this year. We will begin each class with a sponge activity that addresses an area of weakness, and we will do this every day. If you are not sure what a sponge activity is, ask a teammate or an administrator. As I address each academic area, I will be naming the topic for our sponge activity. I expect these sponge activities to begin by the second week. In the first week your sponge activity should consist of teaching your classroom procedures and practices.

Language Arts

Most of us realized, soon after we began whole language, that misapplication of these practices have resulted in some of our students being less prepared than they should be. Rightfully so, we began as individuals to revisit some effective practices from the past to insure that our students had an understanding of basic grammar, which is an area we've seen as low recently. Savvy teachers realize that strategies from all philosophies work in many situations, and no one system of instruction works 100% of the time for 100% of the students. We should continue to blend those effective traditional practices with newer, equally effective practices in order to meet the needs of our students. Areas we must continue to emphasize are spelling, grammar, parts of speech, and so on—the benchmarks for our students.

Our eighth grade Language Arts scores improved by 8 percentiles last year over the previous year. Our sixth grade scores were also pretty good. *Both can be better.*

Sponge activity: Spelling. Every day.

Mathematics

We have strong teachers with much experience and great insight into student motivation. Past efforts have been commendable—we have met the quality performance standard in previous years on the statewide test. Yet, with notable exceptions, on last year's ITBS our students scored below the 50th percentile in math computation. This is not quality performance, nor is it acceptable! Our Strategic Plan addresses the steps we will follow. Also, as earlier stated, we should practice essential skills every day as a warm-up activity. We should never fall below the quality level of student performance, and that quality level should extend into other assessments as well.

Sponge activity: Math computation. Every day.

Social Sciences

Each grade level should continue to focus on its specific curriculum and plan and organize activities that support it. Collaborative planning is essential in the social sciences. Your participation on a large scale in the Social Sciences Fair is excellent. Every teacher of the Social Sciences will participate in this activity this year. Eighth grade teachers—will we continue Savannah? I hope so. Seventh grade teachers—where is your Latin American Festival? This will be revived. Sixth grade—what can you do to celebrate or enact some sort of event for your kids that would be interdisciplinary? I expect the Social Sciences teachers to take the lead in these interdisciplinary activities.

Sponge activity: Maps, diagrams, and reference materials. Every day.

Try this opening activity on the very first day of school to assist with reading maps, charts, and coordinates. Assign your classroom rows with letters horizontally, and numbers vertically. Make cards that say C1, E5, etc., and write each student's name on one card. Then, give the students their cards and have them find their seats. They'll have to use coordinates immediately to do the assignment. This will give practical application to an essential skill. You can read more about excellent, simple strategies like this one in *The First Days of School* by Harry and Rosemary Wong.

Sciences

Our biggest needs here are with instructional methods. We simply do not do enough hands-on activities with our students. You can read all day about sunspots and look at pictures, but nothing beats setting up the telescope and projecting the sun so you can have the students actually see them for themselves. Lab experiences must be offered more frequently. The science fairs planned for this year should really help to get the kids into more application. Secondly, our materials are in great need of organizing and purging. The amount of money we are allotted for our programs is never enough to replace lost or mismanaged materials. Part of the problem may be that anyone can get into the room at any time; while this is a wonderful convenience, it also creates this kind of problem where nobody knows what happened to our materials or how. Science teachers will be charged this year with getting our science equipment organized, and a check-out system will be established to provide accountability for all of our resources.

Sponge activity: Diagrams, charts, and reference materials. Every day.

Exploratory Offerings

We have exceptional offerings in these areas for students. Exploratory classes are the first introduction to life skills for many of our students. Those academic skills only practiced in class are now called on by the exploratory teacher to be put into direct application. Therefore, exploratory classes are critical to support the overall program of instruction and are indeed academic exercises. We need to recall that exploratory courses exist because we believe that students should be well rounded and prepared for the next level of schooling. Exploratory classes should also stress achievement and should assist students in seeing those real-world applications to the skills taught in other classes.

Need: Exploratory teachers will be working this year to identify those parts of their curriculum that are directly correlated to the ITBS test. When these lessons are taught, exploratory teachers should stress these skills as being on the ITBS. These crossover skills should be emphasized regularly. I expect exploratory teachers to be well versed in the ITBS in general and specifically in its relation to your curriculum.

In exploratory classes, your sponge activities will be determined by your course content for your procedures. Just remember that the ITBS is your responsibility, too.

Physical Education and Health

Expanded facilities mean more opportunity for our students in physical development. With this luxury, we should now begin to offer more individual class activities and fewer large-group activities. Much of our instructional time in PE is lost because of procedural requirements. Our PE department has wanted for several years to schedule units of instruction in various activities and hasn't had the facilities. We do now.

Regarding Health—I am quite satisfied with our offerings. New facilities mean that these classes will not be nomadic!

Needs:

- Schedule a variety of units of instruction based on student input.
- Refine procedures to minimize lost instructional time and enhance supervision.
- More small group, less large group classes.
- In Health, identify the science ITBS objectives that correspond to the curriculum and stress these each time you teach them.

As with exploratory teachers, I expect PE teachers to be well versed in the ITBS in general and specifically aware of its relation to your curriculum.

Special Education

Again, we have committed, talented, and dedicated teachers who are well trained and well suited emotionally to work with these demanding groups of students. Our special education faculty is to be commended for being flexible, willing to try new approaches, and willing to say when something doesn't work after they've tried it. These teachers spend hours before and after school dealing with individual kids in planning, SST, IEP meetings, and staffings.

Something else to consider—because special education students are assigned regularly to "regular education" classes, *this makes every teacher who works with these students a special education teacher, too,* even though you may not have had any formal training in the instruction of special education students. We all are bound by IEPs, laws, special programs, or special considerations. In order to do this, we have to rely on the expertise of our colleagues as we work with these students.

Now, this leads me into the next hot topic—modifications. Many folks see modifications as a lowering of standards. "It's not fair," some say, to expect less of others because that lowers the level of accomplishment for the entire group. Let me put things in a different light. When you think about it, in some circumstances, it's not fair to treat everyone the same way!

Let me give you an example. How many of you have had to make a choice between going to a soccer game for one child or a chorus program for another? Sure, you do everything you can to meet both kids' set of needs, but you have to make adjustments. These adjustments are modifications—you give the child what is needed to the best of your ability under the circumstances.

Modifications are not an option. Time after time, this subject creates tension and dissent. Competent and talented people may have honest disagreement on the standards for students and what a student may be able to do. Also, time and time again, the courts have repeatedly upheld the denial of services to a special education student as a civil rights violation, and teachers have been held personally responsible for monetary damages. Not only have teachers been held liable, principals, superintendents, and local boards have been held personally liable for punitive damages.

At EMS, the special education teacher will be the person who will make the call on what modifications are appropriate. This decision will be made with extensive, collaborative input from the regular education teacher; nevertheless, the final say on modifications must be with the special education teacher. As the people in our building who have the most expertise in these areas, we will call on their wisdom, and we will abide by what they recommend. This way, we will all minimize the risk of dissension or litigation over modifications.

Discipline

You know how you approach students—how you organize for class, how you respond to them, how you interact with them, and how organized you are make up many of the factors that impact how your year will go. Are you well organized? Do you know the material? Have you assigned seats for optimal performance? Do you have consistent procedures for dealing with problems, or do you let six or seven little things build up until you lose it with a kid and then send him/her to the office? How do you start from the first minute that will assist you in building success? Again—see Harry Wong's book.

Last year, we had 1707 office discipline referrals from teachers. Of those referrals, many resulted in detention, suspension, or Saturday School. This included everything from failure to complete assignments to bus misbehavior to fighting to drugs and theft. This averaged 6.5 assignments per day. Figuring about two hours as the average amount of time it takes to investigate an individual incident, schedule a parent conference, and resolve the situation, that means that 13 hours of the available 16 hours for two assistant principals are taken up dealing with discipline. With the other responsibilities that the APs have, it's incredible that anything else gets done—like calling for subs, class observations, and so on. Added to this time are documenting and maintaining records, writing letters of notification, and preparing for disciplinary hearings—anyone can see that a tremendous amount of time is spent managing our discipline system. Many of the students involved are repeat offenders, and the most severe of these are eventually removed from the school after sufficient due process has been established and followed.

The figures that you just heard do not include the times where investigations of reports found insufficient evidence to take action. The average number of referrals for the school per teacher was 25.9. Most common infraction: Rule 8.1, failure to follow instructions (39% of the referrals schoolwide). Twenty-five of 67 teachers had more referrals than the EMS average. This means that a minority of the faculty submitted a majority of the discipline referrals. We simply had too many random, sporadic, manageable problems referred to the office last year that could have been managed in a proactive manner by the teacher.

Most of the faculty here are very capable of handling discipline. Just like with the kids, 80% of our time is spent with 20% of the people with problems. We have many teachers who send as few as one to two referrals a year to the office. Don't read in that I consider too many referrals as bad—it just means that we need to look at procedures and practices to see if patterns exist. Does the teacher have adequate procedures and routines in place to govern and manage classes? Then we'll try to account for the patterns. Everyone, even the most seasoned teacher, can expect to have a few problems each year or a rough year now and then.

We will be sharing with each of you on an individual basis your percentage of discipline referrals for the previous year, and we will be giving guided suggestions and directives to teachers who seem always to have the same kinds of problems. While you may have some classes that are tough to handle—this happens, regardless of our experience or our best preparations—teachers are expected to manage their classes so that discipline problems are minimized. Excessive office referrals will indicate to me that the teacher may be having a problem with their organization and communication skills or may have not been in contact with parents enough or in the most effective manner. As trained adults, we are expected to be able to understand students of this grade level, anticipate the problems, plan for the problems, and manage the problems. There are at least five teams of teachers I have observed doing just these things over the years—they could conduct staff development in this.

Our discipline procedures are sound. Our rules express high expectations, are fair, and are administered consistently. You will be supported by the administration regarding discipline every time you follow our procedures as posted in the handbook. We find that, frequently, teachers with continuing problems with discipline have organizational problems that contribute to their situation, or they have not communicated with parents.

One final note—when you send a referral to the office, you are surrendering your control over the situation. The decision becomes completely the responsibility of the administration from that moment, and you are then out of the loop on resolving the situation. Do not write referrals that suggest solutions, or you'll get a little reminder from the administration about procedures.

Every now and then, you have to look inward to find your solutions and take charge of your situation. If discipline problems regularly happen, what are you doing personally to manage them?

STUDENT ATTENDANCE

Our student attendance last year was 94%. For the first time since I've been here, teacher attendance was better than student attendance. While that is really worth celebrating, we've got to do some things to improve on our student attendance, and the most effective person in the encouragement of student attendance is the teacher. Do your students know that they should be here? How do you encourage them? Do you have a welcoming, yet challenging learning environment? Do you tell them to be here every day so that they won't miss something wonderful? This is a school problem that the administration will be addressing, but each of us must emphasize and encourage our students to be here.

SCHOOL CLIMATE

I believe that school climate is a frame of mind. Whether you are an optimist or a pessimist makes a difference. "Morale" is another one of those nebulous things that likes to creep up into discussions like this. Your expression of your frame of mind can have an effect on your colleagues. It can also temper your morale, especially if you consider yourself to be a victim of circumstances. Usually, when I've heard people say there was a "morale problem," it's come right after folks have been required to do something that they didn't want to do or didn't like hearing. You make your own school climate.

CUSTOMER SERVICE AND PUBLIC PERCEPTION

Do you value your public perception? Do you care about what they say about you at the soccer field? Do you want to be famous in the community for being a fair teacher with high expectations who gets results, or infamous as a "screamer" who nobody wants teaching their child? The choice is obvious.

Let me again encourage you to consider your role as a service provider for our enterprise. As a service provider, you have an expectation of customer service to meet. This should be your goal: to have everyone think highly of you and respect you after every interaction, even when you told them an answer they didn't want to hear. This means a professional appearance, a businesslike approach, organization toward meeting your goals, and communication with your customers when they have a question or a concern.

Consider that you are an entrepreneur in your classroom. What are you doing from a customer service standpoint to ensure student success and parental support for you? From my standpoint as the principal, I'm very cognizant of public perception and customer service. In my customer service role, I'm sometimes called on to address the absence of customer service from one of our staff members. So far, it's been basically easy to stand by the teacher in these situations, and yes, for the most part, people have a higher degree of respect for the school after they have interacted with us because these issues are dealt with in a professional, businesslike manner. A high public perception and a good record in customer service go a long way toward avoiding or resolving difficulties, and I intend to see that our perceptions are exemplary.

STAFF DEVELOPMENT

We have two types of staff development here—formal and informal. Our informal staff development is when you ask each other, "How did you do that?" or "Can you help me with this?". This informal staff development, however, is not efficient in dealing with system or schoolwide objectives. That's what our formal staff development program is for.

For too long, staff development has been a pain for folks. Some folks say that staff development is a burden or that it is irrelevant, or they make other negative comments about their experiences. Yet continual learning is essential to stay current in any field. Staff development is not required simply so you can have a convenient route to being recertified; it is intended to be for your assistance in meeting system and school goals, the refinement of your skills and duties, and your continual improvement as a professional. Multiple attempts have been made to make staff development more and more relevant and helpful to you with your needs, but an essential element is lacking. Teachers, if they are professional and truly desirous of doing a better job, should continually seek experiences and assistance in those areas they consider weak or that they wish to develop further. Until this year, our schoolwide staff development program has rarely reflected this, despite our attempts to identify areas for teachers through surveys and various group decision-making strategies.

When we plan staff development, we consider teachers to be our class. So, we spend lots of time looking at the nature of our class in order to get results. Too many petty and insignificant activities have been offered in the name of staff development simply to have teachers be recertified. This will cease. I am a great proponent of staff development, and we worked hard to give the faculty everything you said you needed. The most well-received programs offered seemed to have been those that were more entertaining than informative, and when we had programs that had substance, or that required active participation, these programs were met with crossed arms, glazed looks, and polite silence. Negative comments regarding staff development indicate that you may not value continual learning. Don't get me wrong—you certainly may have had irrelevant or non-useful staff development experiences in the past, but we've got to know what you need in order to meet your needs. Teachers have even been encouraged to work on their own plans each year. So far, no one has done this, yet the negative feelings still persist.

With technology as a system emphasis, we must strive to be current in those skills associated with technology. Our staff development program will reflect this, but what we must do here is use staff development to help us be better.

- How many of you are completely confident in your ability to design and present sponge activities in the areas I've required of you?
- What are you now going to need to be able to do this?
- How many need help with discipline?
- Have you asked to be able to get materials or attend a conference to get this help?

Your energy should be spent determining the staff development you may need to assist you in acquiring these skills. Where are you going to need help in your other teaching or procedural responsibilities? You make yourself a valuable part of the enterprise when you identify your areas of need and then do what it takes to get help. It is not a sign of weakness to say that you need assistance or that you want to get better in any area. This is a sign of professionalism.

Since the options teachers have had do not seem to help, at this point I'll be more directive in what I perceive to be areas of need. This year, if we see a teacher in need of assistance in an area, we will be giving them some direction in seeking staff development that will help them.

GUIDELINES

We have seen where we stand. We have reviewed those formal responsibilities that we each have. We have seen and hopefully agreed that we are all in this together. You have heard my assessments of our programs and practices. You've heard my take on our strengths and weaknesses. In my role as principal, I'm responsible to see that state and system guidelines are followed by everyone, including myself. If I do not assure that these are being done, I'm deficient in my responsibilities. I'm now giving you my guidance and expectations regarding procedural changes that address those areas where we need to improve.

Agendas

The agenda is a tool with great potential that is not being used to the optimum level. This was evidenced last year when we tried our first agenda blitz. With our eighth grade, it took us about 20 tries before we had someone who had their agenda in hand and in order. My impression: students do not place value on having their agendas. Therefore, we will be following these procedures with the agenda immediately. The agenda will be the hall pass for every student in every case unless he/she is being escorted by a staff member. No student will be in the hall without an agenda. For those of you worried about damage in the restroom, remind the students of the value of their books. If they lose or damage their agendas beyond use, each will have to purchase or provide another in order to have hall pass privileges. If students are seen in the hall without their agendas, they will be escorted back to the teacher who released them. We must make the agenda of value to the students.

Communication

Communication with parents must continue to improve. Many of the faculty do a terrific job of this, but others aren't as communicative. We had an exceptionally busy time after teachers had left this past year dealing with parents whose kids had been assigned low grades and did not know in advance. Again, this consumed a tremendous amount of time that was not necessary. Beginning this year, parents of students who will be assigned a D, an F, or will drop two or more letter grades must be notified before the end of the grading period. These communications will be made by completing a Deficiency Notice, which will be sent home two weeks before the end of the grading period. Should a child be assigned an F, in addition to the Deficiency Notice, teachers will make communication through voice-to-voice or face-to-face contact. Notes home or leaving messages on a machine will not be sufficient. You will attempt to contact parents at least three times. If you haven't gotten them after three attempts, this will be considered reasonable effort on your part. You will be required to document your attempts to contact parents and submit this documentation when you turn in your grades. No grade that fits the published criteria may be posted without your documentation of contact. Various scenarios include the following:

(1) Parent who claims no notification, but complains about grade, and teacher has documentation of attempts
(2) Parent who claims no notification, but complains about grade, and teacher has made contact with parent prior to grade being posted
(3) Parent who calls, claims no notification, and student got an F

PROFESSIONAL EXPECTATIONS

Certain expectations exist on the state and system level that are nonnegotiable. Following are my expectations for each of you and for myself as well. The administration will see that these expectations are enforced because that's our responsibility. While they are certainly open to debate among the faculty, they are not subject to revision.

Dress

I will expect each of you to dress appropriately for your activity. Your image as a professional is marred if you are not presentable. In my view, that means that we will not wear jeans or sweats when students are here, unless you are engaged in a field day activity or are taking a field trip where jeans are appropriate. The practice of dressing down on Friday will not be a part of this year. Spirit days may certainly be observed, but jeans or sweats are not appropriate.

Supervision

Each of us will work with our colleagues to insure that we will have an orderly school. I expect the following:

(1) Every staff member will stop students in the hall with no agenda and ask them for their pass. If they have no agenda, escort them to the office.
(2) Every teacher will stand in their doorway with every class change.
(3) Everyone will be in their rooms at all times when you have students. Leaving your class is completely unacceptable, endangers you for liability, and sends a message to your students that time on task is not of value. Use your emergency button if you need to call for someone.
(4) Every teacher who has planning at the end of the day will have either bus duty or front drive duty at some time during the year. Schedules will be posted for those assigned. You are to be there by 3:17 P.M. each day.

Lesson Plans

Lesson plans will now be due by 8:00 on the first day of each week. They will be turned in to my box, and you will check your name off the sheet when you have turned them in. If you're late, you'll need to see me. Two tardies with lesson plans result in a letter to your file. Continuing problems will result in documentation of deficiency on the Duties and Responsibilities Instrument. I want to see these things on your lesson plans: ITBS objectives, warm-up (sponge) activity, Rockdale County curriculum or benchmarks to be covered, class activities, assessment, and plans for team time.

Resources and Materials

Too much of our resources is going for replacement of items. We have had in place for two years the requirement that teachers establish a check-out system for items such as classroom novels, calculators, and so on. Each year, we get back incomplete sets. When you check out a resource, you become personally responsible for it—just like the students. Please protect our resources.

Tardies/Leaving during the Day

This year, we will improve in the area of not being tardy to work or professional appointments. Our workday begins at 7:45. Everyone is expected to be in their work area or at their duty station by this time. Likewise, for team meetings, grade level meetings, and faculty meetings, you are expected to be on time. We will give reasonable beginning times to allow you to take care of creature comforts, but tardiness is unacceptable.

We will curtail the frequency of leaving the building during the day for personal reasons. Certainly, situations will arise that will require you to leave briefly, and we'll continue to work with you as those situations arise. Also, leaving early—before 3:45—is unacceptable unless you have a meeting that is school-related or a class.

Team Meetings

Team meetings will be held the first and second day of each week for one hour each. Detailed notes of your meetings must be kept on file in the team leader's room. During these meetings, teams will discuss their individual plans for the week. Students having discipline or academic success problems will be discussed, problems noted, and corrective actions planned and documented. Weekly follow-through on these plans will be a part of the common planning meetings.

Interdisciplinary Planning

At least once every 9 weeks, teams will plan and present interdisciplinary or multidisciplinary units. These will be collaboratively developed. Grade levels are strongly encouraged to work together for these units around common themes.

FINAL THOUGHTS

In summary, EMS is a good school, with tremendous potential, excellent community support, talented and dedicated teachers, and capable students. We have within our means the ability to meet the expectations placed before us. Compared to other similar schools, though, we are behind in our student achievement. We have an excellent plan to address these needs, and it will take every one of us working together to achieve our goals. They can be and will be met.

As teachers, we can inspire, or we can exasperate. We can build up, or we can tear down. We can support, or we can deny support. We can encourage, or we can discourage. I believe that there is not one among us who went to school to prepare to do the latter of each of these options. We must simply take control of our circumstances. For most of us, these expectations won't be that difficult. I appeal to each of you now to be colleagues, of one accord, with common purpose, and let's go about our tasks.

L. David Weller is a professor in the Department of Educational Leadership at The University of Georgia. He has been a high school teacher, a middle school principal, a Marketing Representative for Xerox Corporation, and Department Head of Middle School Education at The University of Georgia. He serves as a consultant to public and private schools and universities in the areas of organizational development and Total Quality Management. He has also been a visiting lecturer at several British universities teaching in the areas of leadership theory and Total Quality Management.